Postmodern Theory

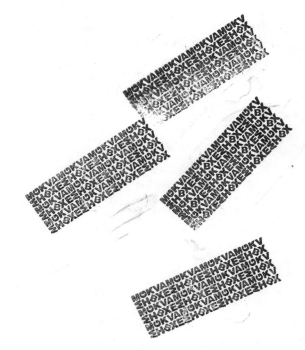

CRITICAL PERSPECTIVES

A Guilford Series edited by
DOUGLAS KELLNER
University of Texas, Austin

Postmodern Theory: Critical Interrogations
Steven Best and Douglas Kellner

A Theory of Human Need
Len Doyal and Ian Gough

Postmodern Theory

Critical Interrogations

Steven Best
Douglas Kellner

THE GUILFORD PRESS
New York

Published by The Guilford Press
A Division of Guilford Publications, Inc.
72 Spring Street, New York, N.Y. 10012

This book is printed on acid-free paper

Last digit is print number: 9 8 7 6

Library of Congress Cataloging-in-Publication Data

Best, Steven.
    Postmodern theory: critical interrogations/Steven Best and
Douglas Kellner.
        p.   cm. — (Critical perspectives)
    Includes bibliographical references and index.
    ISBN 0–89862–412–6. — ISBN 0–89862–418–5 (pbk.)
    1. Criticism.   2. Postmodernism (Literature)   I. Kellner,
Douglas, 1943–   II. Title.   III. Series: Critical perspectives
(New York, N.Y.)
PN98.P67B4   1991   91–2634
801′.95′09045—dc20   CIP

Contents

Preface and
Acknowledgements

'Tis all in peeces, all cohaerence gone (John Donne).

There is nowhere anything lasting, neither outside me, nor within me, but only incessant change. I nowhere know of any being, not even my own. There is no being. I *myself* know nothing and am nothing. There are only *images*: they are the only thing which exists, and they know of themselves in the manner of images . . . I myself am only one of these images (J. G. Fichte).

It is not difficult to see that ours is a birth-time and a period of transition to a new era . . . The frivolity and boredom which unsettle the established order, the vague foreboding of something unknown, these are the heralds of approaching change (G. W. F. Hegel).

State and Church, law and customs, were now torn asunder; enjoyment was separated from labour, means from ends, effort from reward. Eternally chained to only one single little fragment of the whole, Man himself grew to be only a fragment; with the monotonous noise of the wheel he drives everlastingly in his ears (Friedrich Schiller).

There is no firm ground under the feet of society. Nothing any longer is steadfast . . . Hence the chaos seen in certain democracies, their constant flux and instability. There we get an existence subject to sudden squalls, disjointed, halting, and exhausting (Emile Durkheim).

Dramatic changes in society and culture are often experienced as an intense crisis for those attached to established ways of life and modes of thought. The breaking up of once stable social orders and patterns of thought frequently evoke a widespread sense of social incoherence, fragmentation, chaos and disorder. The response is often despair and pessimism, panic and hyperbolic discourse, and desperate searches for solutions to the apparent crisis.

The quotes from Donne, Fichte, Hegel, Schiller and Durkheim cited above signify that the transition from traditional to modern society was experienced as a crisis which required new perspectives and solutions to the perceived social and political problems. From this vantage point, theoretical discourses can be read as responses to historical crises, to unsettling economic and technological developments, and to social and intellectual turbulence produced by the disintegration of previously stable or familiar modes of thinking and living. New theories and ideas articulate novel social experiences and the proliferation of emergent discourses therefore suggests that important transformations are taking place in society and culture.

During the 1960s, sociopolitical movements, new intellectual currents ignited the cultural revolutions of the West against the stifling conformity of the previous generation of the 'affluent society' produced a sense that a widespread rebellion was occurring against the old and oppressive modern society. Sixties radicalism put in question modernist structures and practices, culture, and modes of thought. While the radical political movements of the era eventually dispersed and failed and even through the revolution that many thought would follow the tumultuous events of 1968, a series of socioeconomic and cultural transformations in the 1970s and 1980s suggested that a break with the previous society had indeed taken place. An explosion of media, computers and new technologies, a restructuring of capitalism, political shifts and upheavals, novel cultural forms and new experiences of space and time produced a sense that dramatic developments have occurred throughout culture and society. The contemporary postmodern controversies can therefore be explained in part by an ongoing and intense series of crises concerned with the breaking up of the 'modern' modes of social organization and the advent of a new, as yet barely charted, 'postmodern' terrain. From this vantage point, the writings of Michel Foucault, Gilles Deleuze and Felix Guattari, Jean Baudrillard, Jean-François Lyotard, Fredric Jameson, Ernesto Laclau, Chantal Mouffe, and others articulate new perspectives that map the allegedly novel postmodern sociocultural conditions and develop new modes of theorizing, writing, subjectivity, and politics. In this book we shall sort out and appraise the contributions and limitations of these perspectives which present themselves as the newest avant-garde in theory and politics, more radical than radical, and newer than new: the hyperradical and hypernew.

While the writers we consider develop quite diverse projects, they can be seen as representatives of 'postmodern theory' to the extent that they criticize and break with the dominant goals and assumptions informing modern theories of society, history, politics, and the individual, while embracing a variety of new principles and emphases. While the term 'postmodern theory' may seem problematical, since postmodern critiques are directed against the notion of 'theory' itself – which implies a systematically developed conceptual structure anchored in the real – the writers we classify under the postmodern rubric nonetheless develop theoretical positions on diverse topics. We approach these positions through 'critical interrogations' that assess their usefulness for developing critical theories of society and radical politics for the present age, as well as pointing to their deficiencies. The specific projects of critical theory and radical politics that we have in mind will build on our earlier works (see our Bibliography) and will be developed in the course of our inquiries.

For discussion of the ideas in this book and criticism of various drafts of the manuscript we are grateful to an anonymous Macmillan reader, to Stephen Bronner, Harry Cleaver, Chuck Epp, Beldon Fields, Roger Gathmann, Larry Grossberg, Ali Hossaini, Pierre Lamarche, Mary Beth Mader, Susan McDowell, Linda Nicholson, Elie Noujain, Renan Rápalo, Bill Schroeder, Charles Stivale, Dennis Weiss, Emrys Westacott, and members of study groups and seminars on postmodern theory at the University of Texas during the spring and fall semesters of 1989 when the book was conceived and the first draft was written. For technical assistance with computer imbroglios, we owe thanks to Keith Hay-Roe. For copy-editing help thanks to Janet Byrnes, Tom Denton, and members of the fall 1990 seminar on Poststructuralism and Feminism at the University of Texas. For helpful support in the production of the book we are grateful to our editors Steven Kennedy and Dilys Jones, as well as to Keith Povey for coping with our editing. We are especially indebted, however, to Robert Antonio who read and criticized the entire manuscript, discussed the project with us, and provided support and friendship.

We would like to dedicate this book to the next generation of radical intellectuals and activists who we hope will use the insights of postmodern theory and other critical discourses to develop new

theories and politics to meet the challenges of the current decade
and next century.

STEVEN BEST
DOUGLAS KELLNER

Chapter 1

In Search of the Postmodern

For the past two decades, the postmodern debates dominated the cultural and intellectual scene in many fields throughout the world. In aesthetic and cultural theory, polemics emerged over whether modernism in the arts was or was not dead and what sort of postmodern art was succeeding it. In philosophy, debates erupted concerning whether or not the tradition of modern philosophy had ended, and many began celebrating a new postmodern philosophy associated with Nietzsche, Heidegger, Derrida, Rorty, Lyotard, and others. Eventually, the postmodern assault produced new social and political theories, as well as theoretical attempts to define the multifaceted aspects of the postmodern phenomenon itself.[1]

Advocates of the postmodern turn aggressively criticized traditional culture, theory, and politics, while defenders of the modern tradition responded either by ignoring the new challenger, by attacking it in return, or by attempting to come to terms with and appropriate the new discourses and positions. Critics of the postmodern turn argued that it was either a passing fad (Fo 1986/7; Guattari 1986), a specious invention of intellectuals in search of a new discourse and source of cultural capital (Britton 1988), or yet another conservative ideology attempting to devalue emancipatory modern theories and values (Habermas 1981 and 1987a). But the emerging postmodern discourses and problematics raise issues which resist easy dismissal or facile incorporation into already established paradigms.

1

In view of the wide range of postmodern disputes, we propose to explicate and sort out the differences between the most significant articulations of postmodern theory, and to identify their central positions, insights, and limitations. Yet, as we shall see, there is no unified postmodern theory, or even a coherent set of positions. Rather, one is struck by the diversities between theories often lumped together as 'postmodern' and the plurality – often conflictual – of postmodern positions. One is also struck by the inadequate and undertheorized notion of the 'postmodern' in the theories which adopt, or are identified in, such terms. To clarify some of the key words within the family of concepts of the postmodern, it is useful to distinguish between the discourses of the modern and the postmodern (see Featherstone 1988).

To begin, we might distinguish between 'modernity' conceptualized as the modern age and 'postmodernity' as an epochal term for describing the period which allegedly follows modernity. There are many discourses of modernity, as there would later be of postmodernity, and the term refers to a variety of economic, political, social, and cultural transformations. Modernity, as theorized by Marx, Weber, and others, is a historical periodizing term which refers to the epoch that follows the 'Middle Ages' or feudalism. For some, modernity is opposed to traditional societies and is characterized by innovation, novelty, and dynamism (Berman 1982). The theoretical discourses of modernity from Descartes through the Enlightenment and its progeny championed reason as the source of progress in knowledge and society, as well as the privileged locus of truth and the foundation of systematic knowledge. Reason was deemed competent to discover adequate theoretical and practical norms upon which systems of thought and action could be built and society could be restructured. This Enlightenment project is also operative in the American, French, and other democratic revolutions which attempted to overturn the feudal world and to produce a just and egalitarian social order that would embody reason and social progress (Toulmin 1990).

Aesthetic modernity emerged in the new avant-garde modernist movements and bohemian subcultures, which rebelled against the alienating aspects of industrialization and rationalization, while seeking to transform culture and to find creative self-realization in art. Modernity entered everyday life through the dissemination of modern art, the products of consumer society, new technologies, and new modes of transportation and communication. The dynamics by which modernity produced a new industrial and colonial world can be described as 'modernization' – a term denoting those processes of individualization, secularization, industrialization, cultural differentiation, commodification, urbanization, bureaucratization, and rationalization which together have constituted the modern world.

Yet the construction of modernity produced untold suffering and misery for its victims, ranging from the peasantry, proletariat, and artisans oppressed by capitalist industrialization to the exclusion of women from the public sphere, to the genocide of imperialist colonialization. Modernity also produced a set of disciplinary institutions, practices, and discourses which legitimate its modes of domination and control (see our discussion of Foucault in Chapter 2). The 'dialectic of Enlightenment' (Horkheimer and Adorno 1972) thus described a process whereby reason turned into its opposite and modernity's promises of liberation masked forms of oppression and domination. Yet defenders of modernity (Habermas 1981, 1987a, and 1987b) claim that it has 'unfulfilled potential' and the resources to overcome its limitations and destructive effects.

Postmodern theorists, however, claim that in the contemporary high tech media society, emergent processes of change and transformation are producing a new postmodern society and its advocates claim that the era of postmodernity constitutes a novel stage of history and novel sociocultural formation which requires new concepts and theories. Theorists of postmodernity (Baudrillard, Lyotard, Harvey, etc.) claim that technologies such as computers and media, new forms of knowledge, and changes in the socioeconomic system are producing a postmodern social formation. Baudrillard and Lyotard interpret these developments in terms of novel types of information, knowledge, and technologies, while neo-Marxist theorists like Jameson and Harvey interpret the postmodern in terms of development of a higher stage of capitalism marked by a greater degree of capital penetration and homogenization across the globe. These processes are also producing increased cultural fragmentation, changes in the experience of space and time, and new modes of experience, subjectivity, and culture. These conditions provide the socioeconomic and cultural basis for postmodern theory and their analysis provides the perspectives from which postmodern theory can claim to be on the cutting edge of contemporary developments.

In addition to the distinction between modernity and postmodernity in the field of social theory, the discourse of the postmodern plays an important role in the field of aesthetics and cultural theory. Here the debate revolves around distinctions between modernism and postmodernism in the arts.[2] Within this discourse, 'modernism' could be used to describe the art movements of the modern age (impressionism, *l'art pour l'art*, expressionism, surrealism, and other avant-garde movements), while 'postmodernism' can describe those diverse aesthetic forms and practices which come after and break with modernism. These forms include the architecture of Robert Venturi and Philip Johnson, the musical experiments of John Cage, the art of Warhol and Rauschenberg, the novels of Pynchon and Ballard, and films like *Blade Runner* or *Blue Velvet*. Debates centre on whether there is or is not a sharp conceptual distinction between modernism and postmodernism and the relative merits and limitations of these movements.

The discourses of the postmodern also appear in the field of theory and focus on the critique of modern theory and arguments for a postmodern rupture in theory. Modern theory – ranging from the philosophical project of Descartes, through the Enlightenment, to the social theory of Comte, Marx, Weber and others[3] – is criticized for its search for a foundation of knowledge, for its universalizing and totalizing claims, for its hubris to supply apodictic truth, and for its allegedly fallacious rationalism. Defenders of modern theory, by contrast, attack postmodern relativism, irrationalism, and nihilism.

More specifically, postmodern theory provides a critique of representation and the modern belief that theory mirrors reality, taking instead 'perspectivist' and 'relativist' positions that theories at best provide partial perspectives on their objects, and that all cognitive representations of the world are historically and linguistically mediated. Some postmodern theory accordingly rejects the totalizing macroperspectives on society and history favoured by modern theory in favour of microtheory and micropolitics (Lyotard 1984a). Postmodern theory also rejects modern assumptions of social coherence and notions of causality in favour of multiplicity, plurality, fragmentation, and indeterminacy. In addition, postmodern theory abandons the rational and unified subject postulated by much modern theory in favour of a socially and linguistically decentred and fragmented subject.

Thus, to avoid conceptual confusion, in this book we shall use the term 'postmodernity' to describe the supposed epoch that follows modernity, and 'postmodernism' to describe movements and artifacts in the cultural field that can be distinguished from modernist movements, texts, and practices. We shall also distinguish between 'modern theory' and 'postmodern theory', as well as between 'modern politics' which is characterized by party, parliamentary, or trade union politics in opposition to 'postmodern politics' associated with locally based micropolitics that challenge a broad array of discourses and institutionalized forms of power.

To help clarify and illuminate the confusing and variegated discourse of the postmodern, we shall first provide an archaeology of the term, specifying its history, early usages, and conflicting meanings (1.1). Next, we situate the development of contemporary postmodern theory in the context of post-1960s France where the concept of a new postmodern condition became an important theme by the late 1970s (1.2). And in 1.3 we sketch the problematic of our interrogations of postmodern theory and the perspectives that will guide our inquiries throughout this book.

1.1 Archaeology of the Postmodern

Our archaeology of postmodern discourse explores the history of the term in its uneven development within diverse theoretical fields. We begin by searching for sediments and layers of postmodern discourses as they have accumulated historically. We thereby use the term archaeology in a broad and metaphorical sense rather than in Foucault's technical sense of an analysis that articulates the rules which constitute and govern a given discourse (see 2.2). In undertaking such an inquiry, one discerns that there are anticipations of and precursors to ideas and terminology which gain currency at a later date. For example, an English painter, John Watkins Chapman, spoke of 'postmodern painting' around 1870 to designate painting that was allegedly more modern and avant-garde than French impressionist painting (Higgins 1978: p. 7). The term appeared in 1917 in a book by Rudolf Pannwitz,

Die Krisis der europäischen Kultur, to describe the nihilism and collapse of values in contemporary European culture (cited in Welsch 1988: pp. 12–13). Following Nietzsche, Pannwitz described the development of new 'postmodern men' who would incarnate militarist, nationalistic, and elite values – a phenomenon soon to emerge with fascism which also called for a break with modern Western civilization.

After World War II, the notion of a 'postmodern' break with the modern age appeared in a one-volume summation by D. C. Somervell of the first six volumes of British historian Arnold Toynbee's *A Study of History* (1947), and thereafter Toynbee himself adopted the term, taking up the notion of the postmodern age in Volumes VIII and IX of his *A Study of History* (1963a and 1963b; both orig. 1954). Somervell and Toynbee suggested the concept of a 'post-Modern' age, beginning in 1875, to delineate a fourth stage of Western history after the Dark Ages (675–1075), the Middle Ages (1075–1475), and the Modern (1475–1875) (Somervell 1947: p. 39). On this account, Western civilization had entered a new transitional period beginning around 1875 which Toynbee termed the 'post-Modern age'. This period constituted a dramatic mutation and rupture from the previous modern age and was characterized by wars, social turmoil and revolution. Toynbee described the age as one of anarchy and total relativism. He characterized the previous modern period as a middle-class bourgeois era marked by social stability, rationalism, and progress – a typical bourgeois middle-class conception of an era marked by cycles of crisis, war, and revolution. The postmodern age, by contrast, is a 'Time of Troubles' marked by the collapse of rationalism and the ethos of the Enlightenment.

Toynbee, however, did not develop a systematic theory of the new postmodern era and his universalistic philosophy of history with its notion of historical cycles of the rise and decline of civilizations, his philosophical idealism, and the religious overtones of his analysis would be totally foreign to those who took up the concept of postmodernity in the contemporary scene. Toynbee's scenario is reminiscent in some ways of Nietzsche's *Will to Power* and Spengler's *Decline of the West* with their diagnosis of social and cultural nihilism in the present age. All projected a historical process of regression combined with different projects of cultural renewal. All saw the modern age rapidly approaching its end and interpreted this as a catastrophe for established traditional values, institutions, and forms of life.

Several historical–sociological notions of a new postmodern age appeared in the 1950s in the United States within a variety of disciplines. In his introduction to a popular anthology on *Mass Culture*, cultural historian Bernard Rosenberg used the term postmodern to describe the new conditions of life in mass society (Rosenberg and White 1957: pp. 4–5). Rosenberg claimed that certain fundamental changes were taking place in society and culture:

> As Toynbee's Great West Wind blows all over the world, which quickly gets urbanized and industrialized, as the birth rate declines and the population soars, a certain sameness develops everywhere. Clement Greenberg can meaningfully speak of a universal mass culture (surely something new under the sun) which unites a resident of Johannesburg with his neighbors in San Juan, Hong Kong, Moscow, Paris, Bogota, Sydney and New York. African aborigines, such as those recently described by Richard Wright, leap out of their primitive past – straight into the movie house where, it is feared, they may be mesmerized like the rest of us. First besieged with commodities, postmodern man himself becomes an interchangeable part in the whole cultural process. When he is momentarily freed from his own *kitsch*, the Soviet citizen seems to be as titillated as his American counterpart by Tin Pan Alley's products. In our time, the basis for an international sodality of man at his lowest level, as some would say, appears to have been formed (1957: p. 4).

Rosenberg describes the ambiguity of the new postmodern world, its promising and threatening features, and concludes: 'In short, the postmodern world offers man everything or nothing. Any rational consideration of the probabilities leads to a fear that he will be overtaken by the social furies that already beset him' (1957: p. 5). The same year, economist Peter Drucker published *The Landmarks of Tomorrow* subtitled 'A Report on the New Post-Modern World' (1957). For Drucker, postmodern society was roughly equivalent to what would later be called 'postindustrial society' and Drucker indeed came to identify himself with this tendency. In his 1957 book, however, he argued that: 'At some unmarked point during the last twenty years we imperceptibly moved out of the Modern Age and into a new, as yet nameless, era' (Drucker 1957: p. ix). He describes a philosophical shift from the modern Cartesian world-view to a 'new universe of pattern, purpose, and process'; to new technologies and power to dominate nature with their resulting responsibilities and dangers; and to transformations wrought by the extension of education and knowledge. In the optimistic mode of theorists of the 'postindustrial society', Drucker believed that the postmodern world would see the end of poverty and ignorance, the decline of the nation state, the end of ideology, and a worldwide process of modernization.

A more negative notion of a new postmodern age emerges in C. Wright Mills' *The Sociological Imagination* (1959). Mills claims that: 'We are at the ending of what is called The Modern Age. Just as Antiquity was followed by several centuries of Oriental ascendancy, which Westerners provincially call The Dark Ages, so now The Modern Age is being succeeded by a post-modern period' (1959: pp. 165–6). Mills believed that 'our basic definitions of society and of self are being overtaken by new realities' and that it is necessary to conceptualize the changes taking place in order to 'grasp the outline of the new epoch we suppose ourselves to be entering' (1959: p. 166). In conceptualizing transformations of the present situation, he claimed that many previous expectations and images, and standard categories of thought and of feeling, are no longer of use. In particular, he believed that Marxism and liberalism are no longer convincing because both take up the Enlightenment belief in the inner connection between reason and freedom, which holds that increased rationality would produce increased freedom. By contrast, Mills claims that in the present this can no longer be assumed.

In an analysis close to that of the Frankfurt School, Mills points to some of the ways that increased societal rationalization is diminishing freedom and he paints the spectre of a society of 'cheerful robots' who might well desire, or happily submit to, increased servitude. Mills, however, like Toynbee and the other theorists cited, is very much a modernist, given to sweeping sociological generalization, totalizing surveys of sociology and history, and a belief in the power of the sociological imagination to illuminate social reality and to change society. Consequently, the early uses of the term postmodern in social and cultural theory had not made the conceptual shifts (described in the next section), which would come to characterize the postmodern turn in theory.

In his 1961 essay, 'The Revolution in Western Thought', Huston Smith (1982), however, found that postmodern conceptual shifts had greatly affected contemporary science, philosophy, theology, and the arts. For Smith, the twentieth century has brought a mutation in Western thought that inaugurates the 'post-modern mind'. He describes the transformation from the modern world-view that reality is ordered according to laws that the human intelligence can grasp, to the postmodern world-view that reality is unordered and ultimately unknowable. He suggests that post-modern scepticism and uncertainty is only a transition to yet another intellectual perspective, one that hopefully will be characterized by a more holistic and spiritual outlook.

A more systematic and detailed notion of the postmodern age than is found in the works mentioned so far is present in British historian Geoffrey Barraclough's *An Introduction to Contemporary History* (1964). Barraclough opens his explorations of the nature of contemporary history by claiming that the world in which we live today is 'different, in almost all its basic preconditions, from the world in which Bismarck lived and died' (1964: p. 9). He claims that analysis of the underlying structural changes between the 'old world' and the 'new world' requires 'a new framework and new terms of reference' (ibid.). Against theories which emphasize continuity in history, Barraclough argues: 'What we should look out for as significant are the differences rather than the similar-ities, the elements of discontinuity rather than the elements of continuity. In short, contemporary history should be considered as a distinct period of time, with characteristics of its own which mark it off from the preceding period, in much the same way as what we call 'medieval history' is marked off ... from modern history' (1964: p. 12). After discussing some of the contours of the new era, Barraclough rejects some previous attempts to characterize the current historical situation and then proposes the term post-modern to describe the period which follows modern history (1964: p. 23). He describes the new age as being constituted by revolutionary developments in science and technology, by a new imperialism meeting resistance in Third World revolutionary movements, by the transition from individualism to mass society, and by a new outlook on the world and new forms of culture.

While the term postmodern was occasionally used in the 1940s and 1950s to describe new forms of architecture or poetry, it was not widely used in the field of cultural theory to describe artifacts that opposed and/or came after modernism until the 1960s and

1970s. During this period, many cultural and social theorists began discussing radical breaks with the culture of modernism and the emergence of new postmodern artistic forms. Irving Howe (1970; orig. 1959) and Harry Levin (1966; orig. 1960) were generally negative toward the new postmodern culture, which they interpreted in terms of the decline of Enlightenment rationalism, anti-intellectualism, and loss of the modernist hope that culture could advance social change. For Susan Sontag (1972), Leslie Fiedler (1971), and Ihab Hassan (1971), by contrast, postmodern culture is a positive development which opposes the oppressive aspects of modernism and modernity. Expressing her dissatisfaction with modernist fiction and modes of interpretation, Sontag's influential essays from the mid-1960s celebrated the emergence of a 'new sensibility' (a term first used by Howe) in culture and the arts which challenges the rationalist need for content, meaning, and order. The new sensibility, by contrast, immerses itself in the pleasures of form and style, privileging an 'erotics' of art over a hermeneutics of meaning.

The 1960s were the period of pop art, film culture, happenings, multi-media light shows and rock concerts, and other new cultural forms. For Sontag, Fiedler, and others, these developments transcended the limitations of previous forms like poetry or the novel. Artists in many fields began mixing media and incorporating *kitsch* and popular culture into their aesthetic. Consequently, the new sensibility was more pluralistic and less serious and moralistic than modernism.

Even more than Sontag, Fiedler applauded the breakdown of the high–low art distinction and the appearance of pop art and mass cultural forms. In his essay 'The New Mutants' (1971: pp 379–400; orig. 1964), Fiedler described the emergent culture as a 'post-' culture that rejected traditional values of Protestantism, Victorianism, rationalism, and humanism. While in this essay he decries postmodern art and the new youth culture of nihilistic 'post-modernists', he later celebrated postmodernism and saw positive value in the breakdown of literary and cultural tradition. He proclaimed the death of the avant-garde and modern novel and the emergence of new postmodern artforms that effected a 'closing of the gap' between artist and audience, critic and layperson (Fiedler 1971: pp. 461–85; orig. 1970). Embracing mass culture and decrying modernist elitism, Fiedler called for a new postmodern criticism that abandons formalism, realism, and highbrow pretentiousness, in favour of analysis of the subjective response of the reader within a psychological, social, and historical context.

But the most prolific celebration and popularization of literary postmodernism was carried through by Hassan, who published a series of discussions of postmodern literature and thought (1971, 1979, 1987) – although he has recently tried to distance himself from the term on the grounds that it is inadequate and that we are beyond even postmodernism (Hassan 1987: pp. xi–xvii). In a body of work which is itself often postmodern in its non-linear, playful, assemblage-like style that constructs a pastiche text comprised largely of quotations and name-dropping, Hassan characterizes postmodernism as a 'decisive historical mutation' from industrial capitalism and Western categories and values. He reads post-modern literature as symptomatic of the changes occurring throughout Western socity. The new 'anti-literature' or 'literature of silence' is characterized by a 'revulsion against the Western self' (Hassan 1987: p. 5) and Western civilization in general.

Postmodern forms in literature, poetry, painting, and architecture continued developing in the 1970s and 1980s and were accompanied by a proliferation of postmodern discourses in the arts. In architecture, there were strong reactions against the purity and formalism of the high modern style. The utopian dreams of architects like Le Corbusier to engineer a better world through architecture were belied in sterile skyscrapers and condemned urban housing projects. Charles Jencks' influential book, *The Language of Modern Architecture* (1977), celebrated a new postmodern style based on eclecticism and populism, and helped to disseminate the concept of the postmodern.

Against modernist values of seriousness, purity, and individuality, postmodern art exhibits a new insouciance, a new playfulness, and a new eclecticism. The elements of sociopolitical critique characteristic of the historical avant-garde (Burger 1984) and desire for radically new art forms are replaced by pastiche, quotation and play with past forms, irony, cynicism, commercialism, and in some cases downright nihilism. While the political avant-garde of the modernist movement celebrated negation and dissidence, and called for a revolution of art and life, most postmodernist art often took delight in the world as it is and happily coexisted in a pluralism of aesthetic styles and games.

Other theorists and artists, however, such as Jenny Holzer, Barbara Kruger, and Hans Haacke sought an oppositional current in postmodern art and produced interesting new forms of political art that challenge and subvert prevailing ideologies and codes of representation (see Foster 1983; Conner 1989; Hutcheon 1989).

While Sontag, Fiedler, Hassan, and others valorize postmodern culture as a refreshing break with stale conventions and practices in the arts and life, cultural theorist George Steiner (1971), by contrast, attacked the new 'post-culture' which he claims has rejected and destroyed the foundational assumptions and values of Western society. For Steiner this involves: a loss of geographical and sociological centrality, where the Western world, and the United States in particular, could claim moral superiority and rights over 'uncivilized' peoples; an incredulous attitude toward progress as the trajectory and goal of history, accompanied by a dark pessimism toward the future and a decline of utopian values; and a scepticism toward the modernist belief in a direct correlation between liberal–humanist principles and moral conduct, a position made questionable in this century by the savagery of world wars and the harmonious coexistence of high culture and concentration camps. Thus, for Steiner post-(Enlightenment/humanist/modern) culture no longer blindly and unproblematically trusts in science, art, and reason as beneficent, humanizing forces, and, consequently, there has been a loss of ethical absolutes and certainties. As a cultural conservative, he attacks the political struggles of the 1960s, the countercultural movements, and radicalism within the academy. Steiner bemoans the loss of community, identity, and classical humanism, while deploring the rise of mass culture for eroding standards of classical literacy. He acknowledges, however, that society cannot turn back and must therefore move as best it can into the brave new world of science and technology.

A similar sense that an old era is coming to an end and a new historical situation and choices now confront us is found in *The Active Society* by sociologist Amitai Etzioni (1968) who advances the notion of a postmodern society which he interprets more positively than Steiner. For Etzioni, World War II was a turning point in history; he argued that the postwar introduction of new modes of communication, information, and energy inaugurated a postmodern period. He hypothesized that relentless technological development would itself either destroy all previous values, or would make possible the use of technology to better human life and to solve all social problems. Etzioni championed an 'active society' in which normative values would guide technological developments and human beings would utilize and control technology for the benefit of humanity. This activist normative ideal was one of the few positive visions of a postmodern future, although Etzioni was also aware of the dangers.

In the mid-1970s, more books appeared in the United States which used the term postmodern to designate a new era in history. Theologian Frederick Ferre's *Shaping the Future. Resources for the Post-Modern World* (1976) projected an alternative set of values and institutions for a postmodern consciousness and new future. His emphasis was primarily positive and took the form of quasi-religious prophecy and advocacy of religious values to guide the new age. In *The Cultural Contradictions of Capitalism* (1976), sociologist Daniel Bell also took up the theme that the modern era was coming to an end and that humanity now faced fundamental choices for the future: 'We are coming to a watershed in Western society: we are witnessing the end of the bourgeois idea – that view of human action and of social relations, particularly of economic exchange – which has molded the modern era for the last 200 years' (1976: p. 7). He interprets the postmodern age much like Toynbee: it represents for him the unleashing of instinct, impulse and will, though, like Steiner, he tends to identify it with the 1960s counterculture (1976: pp. 51f.). For Bell, the postmodern age exhibits an extension of the rebellious, anti-bourgeois, antinomic and hedonistic impulses which he sees as the legacies of the modernist movements in the arts and their bohemian subcultures. He claims that cultural modernism perpetuates hedonism, the lack of social identification and obedience, narcissism, and the withdrawal from status and achievement competition. The postmodern age is thus a product of the application of modernist revolts to everyday life, the extension and living out of a rebellious, hyperindividualist, hedonist lifestyle.

Bell sees contemporary postmodern culture as a radical assault on tradition which is fuelled by an aggressive narcissism that is in profound contradiction with the bureaucratic, technocratic, and organizational imperatives of the capitalist economy and democratic polity. This development, in Bell's view, portends the end of the bourgeois world-view with its rationality, sobriety, and moral and religious values (1976: pp. 53f.). In response to the corrosive force of postmodernism on traditional values, Bell calls for a revivification of religious values.

Yet as Habermas has argued (1981: p. 14),[4] Bell tends to blame culture for the ills of the economy and polity, as when he refers to 'cultural crises which beset bourgeois societies and which, in the longer run, devitalize a country, confuse the motivations of individuals, instil a sense of *carpe diem*, and undercut its civic will. The problems are less those of the adequacy of institutions than of the kinds of meanings that sustain a society' (1976: p. 28). Yet in other passages, Bell notes the extent to which the development of the consumer society itself with its emphasis on consumption, instant gratification, easy credit, and hedonism is responsible for the undermining of traditional values and culture and the production of what he calls the 'cultural contradictions of capitalism'. Thus while Mills' (1959) early critique of a postmodern society of cheerful robots derived from a progressive concern with diminution of the ability to shape, control, and change the conditions of society and one's life, Bell's critique derived from fear of the collapse of the bourgeois world-view and its value system.

Our archaeological inquiries have disclosed that there are two conflicting matrices of postmodern discourse in the period before it proliferated in the 1980s. One position – Drucker, Etzioni, Sontag, Hassan, Fiedler, Ferre, and others – gave the term a predominantly positive valence, while others produced negative discourses (e.g. Toynbee, Mills, Bell, Baudrillard). The positive perspective was itself divided into social and cultural wings. The affirmative social discourse (Drucker, Etzioni, Ferre, and theorists of the postindustrial society) reproduced 1950s optimism and the sense that technology and modernization were making possible the break with an obsolete past. These theories replicated the ideologies of the 'affluent society' (Galbraith), 'the end of ideology', and the 'Great American celebration' (Mills) that affirmed contemporary capitalist modernity in the 1950s and 1960s, believing that capitalism had overcome its crisis tendencies and was on the way to producing a 'great society'. The positive culturalist wing (Sontag, Fiedler, Hassan) complemented this celebration by affirming the liberating features of new postmodern cultural forms, pop culture, avant-gardism, and the new postmodern sensibility.

This positive culturalist discourse and the proliferation of postmodern cultural forms helped prepare the way for the reception of the discourse of the postmodern in the 1980s. In general, the cultural discourse had a much greater impact on later postmodern theory than the sociohistorical discourses, which were rarely noted or discussed. The cultural discourses also shared certain epistemological perspectives with later postmodern theoretical discourse which emphasized difference, otherness, pleasure, novelty, and attacked reason and hermeneutics. The affirmative social discourse of the postmodern, by contrast, continued the modern modes of thought (reason, totalizations, unification, and so on) which later postmodern theory would assault.

The negative discourses of the postmodern reflected a pessimistic take on the trajectories of modern societies. Toynbee, Mills, Bell, Steiner, and others saw Western societies and culture in decline, threatened by change and instability, as well as by the new developments of mass society and culture. The negative discourse of the postmodern thus posits a crisis for Western civilization at the end of the modern world. This pessimistic and apocalyptic discourse would be reproduced in postmodern theorists like Baudrillard. The negative cultural discourse of Howe, Steiner, Bell and others would also prepare the way for the neo-conservative attacks on contemporary culture in the 1980s.

Both the positive and negative theorists were responding to developments in contemporary capitalism – though rarely conceptualizing them as such – which was going through an expansionist cycle and producing new commodities, abundance, and a more affluent lifestyle. Its advertising, credit plans, media, and commodity spectacles were encouraging gratification, hedonism, and the adoption of new habits, cultural forms, and lifestyles which would later be termed postmodern. Some theorists were celebrating the new diversity and affluence, while others were criticizing the decay of traditional values or increased powers of social control. In a sense, then, the discourses of the postmodern are responses to socioeconomic developments which they sometimes name and sometimes obscure.

Thus, by the 1980s, the postmodern discourses were split into cultural conservatives decrying the new developments and avant-gardists celebrating them. Postmodern discourses were proliferating through different academic fields and by the 1980s debates erupted concerning breaks with modernity, modernism, and modern theory. More extreme advocates of the postmodern were calling for ruptures with modern discourses and the development of new theories, politics, modes of writing, and values. While the discussions of postmodern cultural forms were primarily initiated in North America, it was in France that Baudrillard and Lyotard were developing notions of a new postmodern era that were much more comprehensive and extreme than those produced earlier in Britain and the United States. The developments in postmodern theory in France constituted a rupture with the French rationalist tradition founded by Descartes and further developed in the French Enlightenment. New French Theory can be read as one of a series of revolts against Cartesian rationalism ranging from the Enlightenment attack on theoretical reason in favour of promoting rational social change, through Comte and Durkheim's revolt against philosophical rationalism in favour of social science, to Sartre and Merleau-Ponty's attempts to make philosophy serve the needs of concrete human existence. As we shall see in the next section, French structuralism, poststructuralism, and postmodern theory constituted a series of attacks on rationalist and Enlightenment theory. Yet these critiques built on another French counter-Enlightenment tradition rooted in the critiques of reason by de Sade, Bataille, Artaud, and others whom Habermas (1987a) terms 'the dark writers of the bourgeoisie'. A French 'dandy' and bohemian tradition stemming from Baudelaire, Rimbaud, and others also helped produce the aestheticized, ironic, and subversive ethos of French postmodern theory. In addition, the French reception of Nietzsche and Heidegger played a major role in turning French theory away from Hegel, Marx, phenomenology and existentialism and toward development of new theoretical formations that eventually produced postmodern theory.

1.2   The French Scene: From Structuralist to Postmodern Theory

While the discourses of the postmodern circulated throughout the world in the 1980s, the most significant developments of postmodern theory have taken place in France and it is upon French postmodern theory that we shall largely focus in this book. As we shall argue in this chapter, a series of socioeconomic, cultural, theoretical, and political events occurred in France which helped give rise to new postmodern theories.

French theories of a postmodern break in history were influenced by the rapid modernization process in France that followed World War II, exciting developments in philosophy and social theory during the 1950s and 1960s, and the dramatic sense of rupture produced by the turbulent events of 1968, in which a student and workers' rebellion brought the country to a standstill, appearing to resurrect French revolutionary traditions. While the political hopes of the day were soon dashed, the apocalyptic impulses of the time were translated into the postmodern theories of a fundamental rupture in history and inauguration of a new era.

Post-World War II modernization processes in France produced a sense of rapid change and a feeling that a new society was emerging. At the end of World War II, France was still largely agricultural and suffered from an antiquated economy and polity. John Ardagh (1982: p. 13) claims that between the early 1950s and mid-1970s 'France went through a spectacular renewal. A stagnant economy turned into one of the world's most dynamic and successful, as material modernization moved along at a hectic pace and an agriculture-based society became mainly an urban and industrial one. Prosperity soared, bringing with it changes in lifestyles, and throwing up some strange conflicts between rooted French habits and new modes . . . Long accused of living with their eyes fixed on the past, they now suddenly opened them to the fact of living in the modern world – and it both thrilled and scared them.'

New social theories emerged to articulate the sense of dynamic change experienced by many in postwar France, analyzing the new forms of mass culture, the consumer society, technology, and modernized urbanization. Throughout France, high-rise buildings, highways, drugstores, shopping centres, consumer goods, and mass culture created dramatic changes in everyday life. The new social configurations were theorized in terms imported from the United States as the 'postindustrial society' (Aron, Touraine) and through original theories that were subsequently highly influential throughout the Western world. Roland Barthes critically dissected the ways that mass culture naturalized and idealized the new social configuration through 'mythologies' which provided propaganda for the new consumer society; Guy Debord attacked the new culture of image, spectacle, and commodities for their stultifying and pacifying effects, claiming that the 'society of the spectacle' masked the continuing reality of alienation and oppression; Baudrillard analyzed the structures, codes, and practices of the consumer society; and Henri Lefebvre argued that the transformations of everyday life were providing new modes of domination by bureaucracies and consumer capitalism.

In addition, developments in literary and cultural criticism advanced new concepts of writing, theory, and discourse (for example, the 'structuralist revolution', the theories of the *Tel Quel* group, and the development of poststructuralist theory which we discuss below).

The rapid changes in the social and economic spheres were thus paralleled by equally dramatic changes in the world of theory. In postwar France, the intellectual scene had been dominated by Marxism, existentialism, and phenomenology, as well as by attempts to synthesize them (Poster 1975; Descombes 1980). By the 1960s, however, these theories were superseded by the linguistically-oriented discourses of structuralism and Lacanian psychoanalysis which advanced new concepts of language, theory, subjectivity, and society (Jameson 1972; Coward and Ellis 1977; Frank 1989).

Structuralists applied structural–linguistic concepts to the human sciences which they attempted to re-establish on a more rigorous basis. Lévi-Strauss, for instance, applied linguistic analysis to structural studies of mythology, kinship systems, and other anthropological phenomena, while Lacan developed a structural psychoanalysis and Althusser developed a structural Marxism. The structuralist revolution deployed holistic analyses that analyzed phenomena in terms of parts and wholes, defining a structure as the interrelation of parts within a common system. Structures were governed by unconscious codes or rules, as when language constituted meaning through a differential set of binary opposites, or when mythologies codified eating and sexual behaviour according to systems of rules and codes. In Barthes' words (1964: p. 213): 'The aim of all structuralist activity, in the fields of both thought and poetry, is to reconstitute an object, and, by this process, to make known the rules of functioning, or "functions", of this object. The structure is therefore effectively a *simulacrum* of the object which . . . brings out something that remained invisible, or, if you like, unintelligible in the natural object.'

Structural analysis focused on the underlying rules which organized phenomena into a social system, analyzing such things as totemic practices in terms of divisions between the sacred and profane in traditional societies, or cuisine in modern societies in terms of culinary rules. Structural analysis aimed at objectivity, coherence, rigour, and truth, and claimed scientific status for its theories, which would be purged of mere subjective valuations and experiences.

The structuralist revolution thus described social phenomena in terms of linguistic and social structures, rules, codes, and systems, while rejecting the humanism which had previously shaped the social and human sciences. Althusser, for example, advocated a theoretical anti-humanism and eliminated human practice and subjectivity from the explanatory scheme of his version of Marxism. The structuralist critique wished to eliminate the concept of the subject which had dominated the philosophical tradition stemming from Descartes through Sartre. The subject was dismissed, or radically decentred, as merely an effect of language, culture, or the unconscious, and denied causal or creative efficacy. Structuralism stressed the derivativeness of subjectivity and meaning in contrast to the primacy of symbolic systems, the unconscious, and social relations. On this model, meaning was not the creation of the transparent intentions of an autonomous subject; the subject itself was constituted by its relations within language, so that subjectivity was seen as a social and linguistic construct. The *parole*, or particular uses of language by individual subjects, was determined by *langue*, the system of language itself.

The new structuralist currents were in part products of a linguistic turn which had roots in the semiotic theory of Ferdinand de Saussure (1857–1913). Arguing that language can be analyzed in terms of its present laws of operation, without reference to its historical properties and evolution, Saussure interpreted the linguistic sign as comprised of two integrally related parts: an acoustic–visual component, the signifier, and a conceptual component, the signified. Language is a 'system of signs that expresses ideas', or signifieds, through differing signifiers that produce meaning. Saussure emphasized two properties of language that are of crucial importance for understanding contemporary theoretical developments. First, he saw that the linguistic sign was arbitrary, that there is no natural link between the signifier and the signified, only a contingent cultural designation. Second, he emphasized that the sign is differential, part of a system of meanings where words acquire significance only by reference to what they are not: 'In language, there are only differences *without positive terms*' (Saussure 1966: p. 120).

As linguist Emile Benveniste and Derrida argued, Saussure nonetheless believed that speech gives presence to the world, that the sign has a natural and immediate relation to its referent, and that the signifier stands in a unitary and stable relationship with the signified (Coward and Ellis 1977; Harland 1987). By contrast, later poststructuralists would emphasize, in a far more radical way than structuralists and semioticians, the arbitrary, differential, and non-referential character of the sign. Indeed poststructural and postmodern theorists would stress the arbitrary and conventional nature of everything social – language, culture, practice, subjectivity, and society itself.

1.2.1   The Poststructuralist Critique

Just as structuralists radically attacked phenomenology, existentialism, and humanism, so too did poststructuralists assault the premises and assumptions of structuralist thought. The poststructuralists attacked the scientific pretensions of structuralism which attempted to create a scientific basis for the study of culture and which strove for the standard modern goals of foundation, truth, objectivity, certainty, and system. Poststructuralists argued as well that structuralist theories did not fully break with humanism since they reproduced the humanist notion of an unchanging human nature. The poststructuralists, by contrast, criticized the claims of structuralists that the mind had an innate, universal structure and that myth and other symbolic forms strove to resolve the invariable contradictions between nature and culture. They favoured instead a thoroughly historical view which sees different forms of consciousness, identities, signification, and so on as historically produced and therefore varying in different historical periods. Thus, while sharing with structuralism a dismissal of the concept of the autonomous subject, poststructuralism stressed the dimensions of history, politics, and everyday life in the contemporary world which tended to be suppressed by the abstractions of the structuralist project.

The critiques of structuralism were articulated in a series of texts by Derrida, Foucault, Kristeva, Lyotard, and Barthes which produced an atmosphere of intense theoretical upheaval that helped to form postmodern theory. Unlike the structuralists who confined the play of language within closed structures of oppositions, the poststructuralists gave primacy to the signifier over the signified, and thereby signalled the dynamic productivity of language, the instability of meaning, and a break with conventional representational schemes of meaning. In traditional theories of meaning, signifiers come to rest in the signified of a conscious mind. For poststructuralists, by contrast, the signified is only a moment in a never-ending process of signification where meaning is produced not in a stable, referential relation between subject and object, but only within the infinite, intertextual play of signifiers. In Derrida's words (1973: p. 58): 'The meaning of meaning is infinite implication, the indefinite referral of signifier to signified . . . Its force is a certain pure and infinite equivocality which gives signified meaning no respite, no rest . . . it always signifies again and differs.' This production of signification that resists imposed structural constraints, Derrida terms 'dissemination', and we shall see the same sort of dynamic emphases in Deleuze and Guattari's concept of desire, Lyotard's theory of intensities, Baudrillard's concept of semiurgy, and Foucault's concept of power.

The new theories of language and discourse led to radical critiques of modern philosophy, attacking its root assumptions.[5] It was claimed that modern philosophy was undermined by its impossible dream of attaining a foundation for knowledge, an absolute bedrock of truth that could serve as the guarantee of philosophical systems (Rorty 1979). Derrida (1976) termed this foundationalist approach to language and knowledge a 'metaphysics of presence' that supposedly guaranteed the subject an unmediated access to reality. He argued that the binary oppositions governing Western philosophy and culture (subject/object, appearance/reality, speech/writing, and so on) work to construct a far-from-innocent hierarchy of values which attempt not only to guarantee truth, but also serve to exclude and devalue allegedly inferior terms or positions. This binary metaphysics thus works to positively position reality over appearance, speech over writing, men over women, or reason over nature, thus positioning negatively the supposedly inferior term.

Many later poststructuralists and postmodern theorists followed Derrida in concluding that a thoroughgoing deconstruction of modern philosophy and a radically new philosophical practice were needed. Precursors of the postmodern critique of philosophy were found in Nietzsche, Heidegger, Wittgenstein, James, and Dewey, and in writers like de Sade, Bataille, and Artaud (Foucault 1973b; Rorty 1979). In particular, Nietzsche's attack on Western philosophy, combined with Heidegger's critique of metaphysics, led many theorists to question the very framework and deep assumptions of philosophy and social theory (Derrida 1976; Vattimo 1985; Dews 1987; Frank 1989 and Ferry and Renault 1990).

Nietzsche took apart the fundamental categories of Western philosophy in a trenchant philosophical critique, which provided the theoretical premises of many poststructuralist and postmodern critiques. He attacked philosophical conceptions of the subject, representation, causality, truth, value, and system, replacing Western philosophy with a perspectivist orientation for which there are no facts, only interpretations, and no objective truths, only the constructs of various individuals or groups. Nietzsche scorned philosophical systems and called for new modes of philosophizing, writing and living. He insisted that all language was metaphorical and that the subject was only a product of language and thought. He attacked the pretensions of reason and defended the desires of the body and the life-enhancing superiority of art over theory.

Both Nietzsche and Heidegger also provided thoroughgoing critiques of modernity that influenced later postmodern theory. Nietzsche saw modernity as an advanced state of decadence in which 'higher types' are levelled by rationalism, liberalism, democracy, and socialism, and where instincts go into steep decline. Heidegger (1977) developed a critique of the modern, representational subject and analyses of the corrosive effects of technology and rationalization. For Heidegger, the triumph of humanism and the project of a rational domination of nature and human beings is the culmination of a process of the 'forgetting of Being' that began with Socrates and Plato. Heidegger undertook to destroy the history of Western metaphysics and called for a new mode of thinking and relating that rejected Western modes of thought in order to attain a more 'primordial' relation to Being. His radical rejection of modernity influenced some postmodern theory, as did his advocacy of premodern modes of thought and experience.

Building on the legacy of Nietzsche and Heidegger, poststructuralists stressed the importance of differences over unities and identities while championing the dissemination of meaning in opposition to its closure in totalizing, centred theories and systems. Indeed, later postmodern theory was often to carry through a collapse of the boundary between philosophy and literary theory (see Derrida 1981b; Rorty 1979 and 1989; and the critique in Habermas 1987b), or between philosophy, cultural critique, social theory, and other academic fields. This collapsing, or problematizing, of boundaries has led to more playful and diverse modes of writing, while subverting standard academic boundaries and practices.

The intellectual upheavals were soon accompanied by political upheavals which fostered a further questioning of conventional assumptions. The events of 1968 and turbulent politics of the period brought about a return to history and concrete politics. The dramatic French student strikes in May were followed by a general strike and the entire country was paralyzed. The upheaval signalled desires for a radical break with the institutions and politics of the past and dramatized the failure of liberal institutions to deal with the dissatisfaction of broad masses of citizens. The student radicals called for 'all power to the imagination' and a complete break from 'papa's' values and politics. De Gaulle promised new elections and manoeuvred many groups and individuals to return to business as usual; the Communist Party supported this move and attacked the 'student rabble-rousers', thus discrediting their own allegedly revolutionary ambitions and alienating many in the radicalized sectors.

The May 1968 upheaval contributed in significant ways to the later developments of postmodern theory. The student revolts politicized the nature of education in the university system and criticized the production of knowledge as a means of power and domination. They attacked the university system for its stultifying bureaucratic nature, its enforced conformity, and its specialized and compartmentalized knowledges that were irrelevant to real existence. But the students also analyzed the university as a microcosm of a repressive capitalist society and turned their attention to 'the full range of hidden mechanisms through which a society conveys its knowledge and ensures its survival under the mask of knowledge: newspapers, television, technical schools, and the *lycée* [high school]' (Foucault 1977: p. 225). It was through such struggles as waged by students and workers that Foucault and others began to theorize the intimate connection between power and knowledge and to see that power operates in micrological channels that saturate social and personal existence.

The force of circumstances made it difficult to avoid conceptualizing the constituent role of history in human experience and the exciting political struggles of the day politicized poststructuralist thinkers who feverishly attempted to combine theory and practice, writing and politics. In addition, more attention was paid to subjectivity, difference, and the marginal elements of culture and everyday life. While poststructuralists continued to reject the concept of the spontaneous, rational, autonomous subject developed by Enlightenment thinkers, there was intense debate over how the subject was formed and lived in everyday life, as well as the ubiquity and multiplicity of forms of power in society and everyday life. In particular, attention was focused on the production of the subject through language and systems of meaning and power. Both structuralists and poststructuralists abandon the subject, but, beginning with poststructuralism, a major theoretical concern has been to analyze how individuals are constituted as subjects and given unified identities or subject positions. Lacan, for example, argued that subjectivity emerged in the entrance of the individual into the 'symbolic' of language, while Althusser theorized the 'interpellation' of individuals in ideology, whereby they were called upon to identify with certain subject positions.

Many of the theorists we shall interrogate began to perceive the new social movements emerging in France, the United States, and elsewhere as the most radical political forces and subsequently began to bid adieu to the proletariat and Marxism, embracing micropolitics as the authentic terrain for political struggle. The May 1968 events led many to conclude that Marxism – particularly the version of the French Communist Party – was too dogmatic and narrow a framework to adequately theorize contemporary society and its diverse modes of power. Postmodern theorists were instead drawn to political movements such as feminism, ecology groups, and gay and lesbian formations. These emerged in response to the oppressive effects on social and personal life of capitalism, the state, and pernicious ideologies such as sexism, racism, and homophobia. The new social movements posed a strong challenge to traditional Marxist political conceptions based on the primacy of the labour movement by calling for a more democratic form of political struggle and participation which addresses the multiple sources of power and oppression that are irreducible to the exploitation of labour. In place of the hegemony of the proletariat, they proposed decentred political alliances. Hence, the new social movements anticipated postmodern principles of decentring and difference and presented important new avenues of politicizing social and cultural relations, in effect redefining the socialist project as that of radical democracy (Laclau and Mouffe 1985).

While the Althusserians were trying to rewrite Marxism as a science by drawing from a structuralist problematic, other French thinkers were gravitating toward Nietzsche as a radical alternative to phenomenology and to Marxism, while attempting to develop a more satisfactory theory of power. Marx's emphasis on the primacy of economic relations of power was replaced with a Nietzschean focus on multiple forms of power and domination. In the aftermath of the failure of 1960s movements and the disenchantment with Marxism another new intellectual movement emerged in the early 1970s: the new philosophers, such as André Glucksman and Henri Bernard-Lévy, who denounced Marxism as a discourse of terror and power. The poststructuralists, while remaining political radicals, tended to include Marxism as a target of attack in their critique of traditional philosophy and social theory which were all accused of resting on obsolete epistemological premises. They positioned their work as a new theoretical avant-garde and claimed as well to advance new political positions congruent with their theories. The poststructuralist critique permeated literary, philosophical, sociological, and political discourse in France and elsewhere during the late 1960s and the 1970s and had a decisive impact on postmodern theory.

1.2.2   The Postmodern Turn

Poststructuralism forms part of the matrix of postmodern theory, and while the theoretical breaks described as postmodern are directly related to poststructuralist critiques, we shall interpret poststructuralism as a subset of a broader range of theoretical, cultural, and social tendencies which constitute postmodern discourses. Thus, in our view, postmodern theory is a more inclusive phenomenon than poststructuralism which we interpret as a critique of modern theory and a production of new models of thought, writing, and subjectivity, some of which are later taken up by postmodern theory. Indeed, postmodern theory appropriates the poststructuralist critique of modern theory, radicalizes it, and extends it to new theoretical fields. And in the political arena, most poststructuralist and postmodernist theory takes up post-Marxist positions which claim that Marxism is an obsolete or oppressive discourse that is no longer relevant for the current era.

The discourse of the postmodern also encompasses a socio-historical theory of postmodernity and analysis of new postmodern cultural forms and experiences. The cultural analysis is influenced by poststructuralist discussions of modernism and the avant-garde by Barthes, Kristeva, Sollers, and others associated with the *Tel Quel* group, but the later postmodern socio-historical discourses develop more comprehensive perspectives on society, politics, and history. On the other hand, most of the individuals that we discuss in this book can be considered as either postmodern or poststructuralist theorists, but our focus will be on the ways in which they deal, in one way or another, with what we shall define as postmodern positions towards theory, society, history, politics, and culture.

Postmodern theory generally follows poststructuralist theory in the primacy given to discourse theory. Both structuralists and poststructuralists developed theories which analyzed culture and society in terms of sign systems and their codes and discourses. Discourse theory sees all social phenomena as structured semiotic-ally by codes and rules, and therefore amenable to linguistic analysis, utilizing the model of signification and signifying prac-tices. Discourse theorists argue that meaning is not simply given, but is socially constructed across a number of institutional sites and practices. Hence, discourse theorists emphasize the material and heterogeneous nature of discourse (see Pecheux 1982). For Foucault and others, an important concern of discourse theory is to analyze the institutional bases of discourse, the viewpoints and positions from which people speak, and the power relations these allow and presuppose. Discourse theory also interprets discourse as a site and object of struggle where different groups strive for hegemony and the production of meaning and ideology.

Discourse theory can be read as a variant of semiotics which develops the earlier project of analyzing society in terms of systems of signs and sign systems. Saussure had proposed develop-ing a semiotics of 'the life of signs in society' and Barthes, the early Baudrillard, and others followed through on this to analyze the semiotics of myth, culture, consumption, and other social activi-

ties. Eventually, however, discourse theory superseded and subsumed the previous semiological theories, and we shall see that
much postmodern theory follows discourse theory in assuming that
it is language, signs, images, codes, and signifying systems which
organize the psyche, society, and everyday life. Yet most postmodern theorists are not linguistic idealists or pan-textualists, who
reduce everything to discourse or textuality.[6] Foucault, for
instance, defines the apparatus that constitutes the social body as
'a thoroughly heterogeneous ensemble consisting of discourses,
institutions, architectural forms, regulatory decisions, laws,
administrative measures, scientific statements, philosophical,
moral and philanthropic propositions – in short, the said as much
as the unsaid' (1980a: p. 194). While some postmodern theory
comes close to positing a linguistic idealism, whereby discourse
constitutes all social phenomena, or is privileged over extra-discursive material conditions, there are also countervailing tendencies
toward analysis of the pragmatics of language use, materialist
analysis of discourses, institutions, and practices which avoid the
traps of linguistic idealism.

By the 1970s, French theorists were attacking modern theories
rooted in humanist assumptions and Enlightenment rationalist
discourses. Foucault (1973a, 1980a, 1982a and 1982b) proclaimed
the 'death of man' while advancing new conceptions of theory,
politics, and ethics. Baudrillard (1983a and 1983b) describes the
implications for a theory and politics of a postmodern society in
which 'radical semiurgy', the constantly accelerating proliferation
of signs, produces simulations that create new forms of society,
culture, experience, and subjectivity. Lyotard (1984a) describes a
'postmodern condition' that marks the end of the grand narratives
and hopes of modernity and the impossibility of continuing with
the totalizing social theories and revolutionary politics of the past.
Deleuze and Guattari (1983 and 1987) propose developing a
'schizoanalysis' and 'rhizomatics' which maps the repressive 'territorializations' of desire throughout society and everyday life while
seeking possible 'lines of escape'. And Laclau and Mouffe (1985)
develop radical democratic political theories based on poststructuralist epistemology and a critique of modern political
theory, including Marxism.

Postmodern theory, however, is not merely a French phenomenon but has attained international scope. This is fitting because, as

noted, German thinkers like Nietzsche and Heidegger already began the attack on traditional concepts and modes of philosophy. The American philosopher William James championed a radical pluralism and John Dewey attacked most of the presuppositions of traditional philosophy and social theory, while calling for their reconstruction. Furthermore, it was the English historians Toynbee and Barraclough and North American social theorists such as Drucker, Mills, Etzioni, and Bell who introduced the concept of a postmodern age in history and social theory, while North American cultural theorists introduced the term in the arts. It has indeed been in the English-speaking world that interest in all facets of the postmodern controversies has been most intense with conferences, journals, and publishing lists proliferating in these countries. In particular, the debates over postmodernity have been intense in the United States, England, Canada, and Australia.

Thus, a diversity of theoretical and political responses and strategies have emerged in the postmodern debates. They took on an international scope and resonance by the 1980s and have penetrated every academic field, challenging regnant orthodoxies and affirming new postmodern perspectives and positions. One even finds a postmodern turn in the field of science where 'postmodern science' refers to a break with Newtonian determinism, Cartesian dualism, and representational epistemology. Advocates of postmodern science embrace principles of chaos, indeterminacy, and hermeneutics, with some calling for a 're-enchantment of nature' (see Prigogine and Stengers 1984; Griffin 1988a and 1988b; and Best 1991a). Postmodern discourse has even penetrated mass culture with frequent articles on such disparate topics as the postmodern presidency, postmodern love, postmodern management, postmodern theology, the postmodern mind, and postmodern television shows like MTV or *Max Headroom*. During the 1980s and 1990s, lines are being drawn between those who aggressively promote the discourse of the postmodern, those who reject or ignore it, and those who strategically deploy postmodern positions with previous modern positions to develop new syntheses and theories. In this book, we shall enter into these debates and indicate what is at stake for critical theory and radical politics.[6]

1.3 Critical Theory and the Postmodern Challenge

Postmodern discourses thus denote new artistic, cultural, or theoretical perspectives which renounce modern discourses and practices. All of these 'post' terms function as sequential markers, designating that which follows and comes after the modern. The discourse of the postmodern thus involves periodizing terms which describe a set of key changes in history, society, culture, and thought. The confusion involved in the discourse of the postmodern results from its usage in different fields and disciplines and the fact that most theorists and commentators on postmodern discourse provide definitions and conceptualizations that are frequently at odds with each other and usually inadequately theorized. Moreover, some theorists and commentators use the term postmodern descriptively to describe new phenomena, while others use it prescriptively, urging the adoption of new theoretical, cultural, and political discourses and practices.

There is, in fact, an ambiguity inherent in the word 'post' which is played out in various postmodern discourses. On the one hand, 'post' describes a 'not' modern that can be read as an active term of negation which attempts to move beyond the modern era and its theoretical and cultural practices. Thus, postmodern discourses and practices are frequently characterized as anti-modern interventions which explicitly break with modern ideologies, styles, and practices that many postmodernists see as oppressive or exhausted. The prefix 'post', in this prescriptive sense, signifies an active rupture (*coupure*) with what preceded it. As we have noted, this rupture can be interpreted positively as a liberation from old constraining and oppressive conditions (Vattimo 1985) and as an affirmation of new developments, a moving into new terrains, a forging of new discourses and ideas (Foucault 1973b; Deleuze and Guattari 1983 and 1987; Lyotard 1984a). Or the new postmodernity can be interpreted negatively as a deplorable regression, as a loss of traditional values, certainties, and stabilities (Toynbee 1963a and 1963b; Bell 1976), or as a surrender of those still valuable elements of modernity (Habermas 1981 and 1987a).

On the other hand, the 'post' in postmodern also signifies a dependence on, a continuity with, that which it follows, leading some critics to conceptualize the postmodern as merely an intensification of the modern, as a hypermodernity (Merquior 1986; During 1987), a new 'face of modernity' (Calinescu 1987), or a 'postmodern' development within modernity (Welsch 1988). Yet many postmodern theorists deploy the term – as it was introduced by Toynbee – to characterize a dramatic rupture or break in Western history. The discourses of the postmodern therefore presuppose a sense of an ending, the advent of something new, and the demand that we must develop new categories, theories, and methods to explore and conceptualize this novum, this novel social and cultural situation. Thus, there is an intrinsic pathos of the new which characterizes the discourses of the postmodern and its celebrants tend to position themselves as theoretical and political avant-gardes (just as 'modern' theorists did in an earlier era).

We will therefore use the term 'postmodernist' to describe the avatars of the postmodern within the fields of philosophy, cultural theory, and social theory. A postmodernist describes and usually champions imputed breaks in knowledge, culture, and society, frequently attacking the modern while identifying with what they tout as new and 'radical' postmodern discourses and practices. A postmodernist thus calls for new categories, modes of thought and writing, and values and politics to overcome the deficiencies of modern discourses and practices. Some postmodern theorists, like Lyotard and Foucault, focus on developing alternative modes of knowledge and discourse, while others, like Baudrillard, Jameson, and Harvey emphasize the forms of economy, society, culture, and experience. Within social theory, a postmodernist claims that there are fundamental changes in society and history which require new theories and conceptions, and that modern theories are unable to illuminate these changes. Jameson, however, utilizes modern (primarily Marxist) theory to analyze postmodern cultural and social forms, while Habermas and many of his associates criticize what they consider to be the ideological nature of post-modern theory *tout court*. Laclau and Mouffe, by contrast, use postmodern critiques to go beyond Marxism and to reconstruct the project of radical democracy.

Thus not everyone we discuss in this book is a full-blown postmodernist. Foucault eschews all labelling procedures and never identified with postmodern theory or used the term in any substantive way; moreover, in his later work Foucault sometimes aligned his work with aspects of the Enlightenment tradition and specified both continuities and discontinuities between modernity and the era which followed it. Deleuze and Guattari do not explicitly adopt the discourse of the postmodern, but they do present new models of theory, practice, and subjectivity which they counterpose and offer as alternatives to modern models. Baudrillard was at first reluctant to embrace the term postmodern to describe his work, but he now uses it upon occasion to identify his own positions. Lyotard has expressed ambivalence toward the label and Guattari has attacked it, while Laclau and Mouffe remain wedded to many modern political values and Jameson continues to identify with Marxism.

In the following chapters, we attempt to provide comprehensive explications and critiques of postmodern theory, exploring a variety of postmodern positions and perspectives. Yet we exclude systematic discussion of such major poststructuralist theorists as Derrida, Kristeva, Barthes, or Lacan who are often linked to postmodern theory. While their work can be articulated with social and political theory – as Ryan (1982) and Spivak (1987) have shown – the main focus of most poststructuralist theory is on philosophy, cultural theory, or psychoanalysis, and poststructuralist theory does not provide an account of postmodernity or intervene in the postmodern debates. Our book, by contrast, will focus on the theories of history, society, culture, and politics by theorists who we believe contribute most to developing postmodern theory, even if they do not explicitly describe themselves as postmodernists.

Thus, we shall discuss the opposing positions concerning whether we are or are not in a new postmodern age or are still within modernity, and whether modern theory does or does not have the resources to deal with the problems of the present age. We will not, however, do a sociological analysis of postmodernity in this book, nor do we assume that there is a postmodern society, culture, and experience out there waiting to be described. Instead, this text will be primarily a theoretical work dealing with postmodern theories and is not another account of the 'postmodern condition'. Our task will be to assess the extent to which postmodern theories contribute to the project of developing a critical theory and radical politics for the present age. We shall assess the contributions and limitations of the theories under interrogation as to whether they do or do not contribute salient critiques of modernity and modern theory, useful postmodern theories, methods, modes of writing, and cultural criticism, and a new postmodern politics.

In each study of various postmodern theorists, we shall examine how they: (1) characterize and criticize modernity and its discourses; (2) postulate a break with modernity and modern theory; (3) produce alternative postmodern theories, positions, or perspectives; (4) create, or fail to create, a theory of postmodernity; and (5) provide, or fail to develop, a new postmodern politics adequate to the supposed postmodern situation. We shall compare and contrast the various critiques of modernity, the characterizations of the basic trends of postmodern culture or postmodernity, and the development of postmodern theories in Foucault, Deleuze and Guattari, Baudrillard, Lyotard, Jameson, Laclau and Mouffe. We examine some recent configurations of feminism and postmodernism, as well as the ways that the earlier generation of the Frankfurt School, especially Adorno, anticipated certain trends of postmodern theory. We also inquire into why Habermas and the current generation of critical theorists have for the most part rejected postmodern theory as a species of irrationalism.

We shall delineate our own theoretical perspectives as we proceed and will elaborate our theoretical and political positions in more detail in the conclusion. Our project therefore is to interpret and come to terms with postmodern theory as a challenge to modern theory and politics which contains both promising new perspectives and problematical aspects. We do not ourselves accept the postmodern postulate of a radical rupture or break in history which requires totally new theories and modes of thought. Yet we recognize important changes in vast domains of society and culture which require a reconstruction of social and cultural theory, and which sometimes warrant the term 'postmodern' in theory, the arts, society, and politics. Likewise, we accept some aspects of the postmodern critique of modernity and its theories, but are not ready either to throw out all the theories and methods of the past or to renounce modernity altogether. We shall neither be apologists and celebrants of the discourse of the postmodern, nor shall we be merely dismissive. Instead, we shall be open to its challenges and critiques, while sceptical of some of its exaggerations and rhetoric.

Notes

1. For previous discussions of postmodern theory, see the articles in *New German Critique* 33 (1984); *Minnesota Review* 23 (1984); *Journal of Communication Inquiry* 10/2 (Summer 1986); *Cultural Critique* 5 (1986–87); *Screen* 28/2 (1987); *Social Text* 18 (Winter 1987–88); *Theory, Culture and Society* (1988); *Polygraph* 2/3 (1989) and *Thesis Eleven* 23 (1989). See also our own previous writings on the topic listed in the bibliography and the essays in Turner 1990; and Dickens and Fontana 1991.

2. On the distinction between modernism and postmodernism in the arts and for surveys of different forms of postmodern culture, see Foster 1983; Trachtenberg 1985; Kearney 1988; Conner 1989; and Hutcheon 1989. It should be noted that there is an ongoing debate over what modernism is, whether postmodernism constitutes a decisive break with it, or a development within it. Nor is there agreement concerning what are the defining features of postmodernism as a mode of culture.

3. We are aware that some versions of modern social theory do not follow positivist correspondence theories of truth or interpret categories as 'covering devices' or 'pictures' of social reality, instead using categories as mere heuristic devices or ideal types to interpret a complex social reality. Yet much modern theory follows Enlightenment models of science, representation, and totality, and is thus vulnerable to the postmodern critique. Some modern theory, however, anticipated elements of the postmodern critique of modern theory, as well as some of the postmodern perspectives on society; see Antonio and Kellner 1991.

4. Habermas also projected the possibility of a postmodern social organization in *Legitimation Crisis* (1975: p. 17), writing: 'The interest behind the examination of crisis tendencies in late- and post-capitalist class societies is in exploring the possibilities of a "post-modern" society – that is, a historically new principle of organization and not a different name for the surprising vigor of an aged capitalism.' Yet Habermas has never really undertaken an inquiry into what might follow modernity and has generally treated postmodern theories as irrationalist ideologies – a point that we take up in Chapter 7.

5. On discourse theory, see Coward and Ellis 1977 and Macdonell 1986. Callinicos (1985: p. 86f.) distinguishes between a version of linguistic idealism he finds in poststructuralism which he terms textualism (that reduces everything to textuality, to discursive formations), contrasted to what he calls worldly poststructuralism that articulates the said and the unsaid, the discursive and the non-discursive. 'Textualism, however, denies us the possibility of ever escaping the discursive.' Most of the postmodern theory which we shall examine is worldly in this sense, but sometimes comes close to discursive reductionism, or textualism.

6. We are using 'critical theory' here in the general sense of critical social and cultural theory and not in the specific sense that refers to the critical theory of society developed by the Frankfurt School, whose project we discuss in Chapter 7.

Chapter 2

Foucault and the Critique of Modernity

> Is it not necessary to draw a line between those who believe that we can continue to situate our present discontinuities within the historical and transcendental tradition of the nineteenth century and those who are making a great effort to liberate themselves, once and for all, from this conceptual framework? (Foucault 1977: p. 120)

> What's going on just now? What's happening to us? What is this world, this period, this precise moment in which we are living? (Foucault 1982a: p. 216)

> [T]he impression of fulfillment and of end, the muffled feeling that carries and animates our thought, and perhaps lulls it to sleep with the facility of its promises . . . and makes us believe that something new is about to begin, something that we glimpse only as a thin line of light low on the horizon – that feeling and impression are perhaps not ill founded (Foucault 1973b: p. 384).

Foucault's critique of modernity and humanism, along with his proclamation of the 'death of man' and development of new perspectives on society, knowledge, discourse, and power, has made him a major source of postmodern thought. Foucault draws upon an anti-Enlightenment tradition that rejects the equation of reason, emancipation, and progress, arguing that an interface between modern forms of power and knowledge has served to create new forms of domination. In a series of historico-philosophical studies, he has attempted to develop and substantiate this theme from various perspectives: psychiatry, medicine, punishment and criminology, the emergence of the human sciences, the formation of various disciplinary apparatuses, and the constitution of the subject. Foucault's project has been to write a 'critique of our historical era' (1984: p. 42) which problematizes modern forms of knowledge, rationality, social institutions, and subjectivity that seem given and natural but in fact are contingent sociohistorical constructs of power and domination.

While Foucault has decisively influenced postmodern theory, he cannot be wholly assimilated to that rubric. He is a complex and eclectic thinker who draws from multiple sources and problematics while aligning himself with no single one. If there are privileged figures in his work, they are critics of reason and Western thought such as Nietzsche and Bataille. Nietzsche provided Foucault, and nearly all French poststructuralists, with the impetus and ideas to transcend Hegelian and Marxist philosophies. In addition to initiating a postmetaphysical, posthumanist mode of thought, Nietzsche taught Foucault that one could write a 'genealogical' history of unconventional topics such as reason, madness, and the subject which located their emergence within sites of domination. Nietzsche demonstrated that the will to truth and knowledge is indissociable from the will to power, and Foucault developed these claims in his critique of liberal humanism, the human sciences, and in his later work on ethics. While Foucault never wrote aphoristically in the style of Nietzsche, he did accept Nietzsche's claims that systematizing methods produce reductive social and historical analyses, and that knowledge is perspectival in nature, requiring multiple viewpoints to interpret a heterogeneous reality.

Foucault was also deeply influenced by Bataille's assault on Enlightenment reason and the reality principle of Western culture. Bataille (1985, 1988, 1989) championed the realm of heterogeneity, the ecstatic and explosive forces of religious fervour, sexuality, and intoxicated experience that subvert and transgress the instrumental rationality and normalcy of bourgeois culture. Against the rationalist outlook of political economy and philosophy, Bataille sought a transcendence of utilitarian production and needs, while celebrating a 'general economy' of consumption, waste, and expenditure as liberatory. Bataille's fervent attack on the sovereign philosophical subject and his embrace of transgressive experiences were influential for Foucault and other postmodern theorists. Throughout his writings, Foucault valorizes figures such as Hölderlin, Artaud, and others for subverting the hege-

mony of modern reason and its norms and he frequently empathized with the mad, criminals, aesthetes, and marginalized types of
all kinds.[1]

Recognizing the problems with attaching labels to Foucault's
work, we wish to examine the extent to which he develops certain
postmodern positions. We do not read Foucault as a postmodernist *tout court*, but rather as a theorist who combines
premodern, modern, and postmodern perspectives.[2] We see
Foucault as a profoundly conflicted thinker whose thought is torn
between oppositions such as totalizing/detotalizing impulses and
tensions between discursive/extra-discursive theorization, macro/
microperspectives, and a dialectic of domination/resistance.
We begin with a discussion of his critique of modernity (2.1).
This critique is developed in the form of new historiographical
approaches which he terms 'archaeology' and 'genealogy'. We
shall then explicate Foucault's postmodern perspectives on the
nature of modern power and his argument that the modern subject
is a construct of domination (2.2). After analyzing the political
implications of Foucault's genealogical method (2.3) and his later
studies of ethics and techniques of the self, we shall conclude with
some critical remarks on the tensions and lacunae in his work as a
whole (2.4).

2.1 Postmodern Perspectives and the Critique of Modernity

> I think that the central issue of philosophy and critical thought since the
> eighteenth century has always been, still is, and will, I hope, remain the
> question: *What* is this Reason that we use? What are its historical
> effects? What are its limits, and what are its dangers (Foucault 1984:
> p. 249).

> My objective . . . has been to create a history of the different modes by
> which, in our culture, human beings are made subjects (Foucault
> 1982a: p. 208).

Foucault was born in Poitiers, France, in 1926 and died in 1984.
He began his academic career as a philosopher, studying with Jean
Hyppolite at the Lycée Henri IV and Althusser at the Ecole
Normale Supérieure. Becoming intolerant of the abstractness of
this discipline and its naive truth claims, Foucault turned to
psychology and psychopathology as alternative forms of study and

observed psychiatric practice in French mental hospitals during the early 1950s (see Sheridan 1980). These studies led to his first two books on the theme of mental illness and began his lifelong preoccupation with the relationship between knowledge and power. For a time, he was a member of the Communist Party, but could not accept the straitjacket of orthodoxy and broke with them in 1951, holding ambiguous feelings about Marxism throughout his life. Foucault taught in French departments in Sweden, Poland, and Germany during the 1950s and returned to France in 1960 in order to complete his *doctorat d'état* in the history of science under Georges Canguilhem. After the May 1968 protests, Foucault became chairman of Department of Philosophy at Vincennes. In 1970, he was appointed to the (self-titled) chair of Professor of History of Systems of Thought at the Collège de France where he taught for the rest of his life.

Foucault's work provides an innovative and comprehensive critique of modernity. Whereas for many theorists modernity encompasses a large, undifferentiated historical epoch that dates from the Renaissance to the present moment, Foucault distinguishes between two post-Renaissance eras: the classical era (1660–1800) and the modern era (1800–1950) (Foucault 1989: p. 30). He sees the classical era as inaugurating a powerful mode of domination over human beings that culminates in the modern era. Foucault follows the Nietzschean position that dismisses the Enlightenment ideology of historical progress: 'Humanity does not gradually progress from combat to combat until it arrives at universal reciprocity, where the rule of law finally replaces warfare; humanity installs each of its violences in a system of rules and thus proceeds from domination to domination' (Foucault 1977: p. 151). Yet, ironically, Foucault believes that the modern era is a kind of progress – in the dissemination and refinement of techniques of domination. On this point, his initial position is similar to that of Adorno, who spoke of the continuity of disaster 'leading from the slingshot to the megaton bomb' (Adorno 1973: p. 320), and quite unlike that of Marx, Weber, or Habermas who attempt to identify both the emancipatory and repressive aspects of modernity.

Like Horkheimer and Adorno (1972), Foucault therefore believes that modern rationality is a coercive force, but where they focused on the colonization of nature, and the subsequent repression of social and psychic existence, Foucault concentrates on the domination of the individual through social institutions, discourses, and practices. Awakening in the classical world like a sleeping giant, reason finds chaos and disorder everywhere and embarks on a rational ordering of the social world. It attempts to classify and regulate all forms of experience through a systematic construction of knowledge and discourse, which Foucault understands as systems of language imbricated with social practice. He argues that various human experiences, such as madness or sexuality, become the objects of intense analysis and scrutiny. They are discursively (re)constituted within rationalist and scientific frames of reference, within the discourses of modern knowlege, and thereby made accessible for administration and control. Since the eighteenth century, there has been a discursive explosion whereby all human behaviour has come under the 'imperialism' of modern discourse and regimes of power/knowledge. The task of the Enlightenment, Foucault argues, was to multiply 'reason's political power' (1988d: p. 58) and disseminate it throughout the social field, eventually saturating the spaces of everyday life.

Foucault therefore adopts a stance of hostile opposition to modernity and this is one of the most salient postmodern features of his work. Postmodern theory in general rejects the modern equation of reason and freedom and attempts to problematize modern forms of rationality as reductive and oppressive. In his genealogical works of the 1970s, Foucault stigmatizes modern rationality, institutions, and forms of subjectivity as sources or constructs of domination. Where modern theories tend to see knowledge and truth to be neutral, objective, universal, or vehicles of progress and emancipation, Foucault analyzes them as integral components of power and domination. Postmodern theory rejects unifying or totalizing modes of theory as rationalist myths of the Enlightenment that are reductionist and obscure the differential and plural nature of the social field, while politically entailing the suppression of plurality, diversity, and individuality in favour of conformity and homogeneity.

In direct opposition to modern views, postmodernists valorize incommensurability, difference, and fragmentation as the antidotes to repressive modern modes of theory and rationality. For example, Foucault valorizes 'the amazing efficacy of discontinuous, particular and local criticism' as compared to the 'inhibiting effect of global, *totalitarian theories'* at both the theoretical and political level. While he acknowledges that global theories such as Marxism and psychoanalysis have provided 'useful tools for local research' (1980a: p. 81), he believes they are reductionistic and coercive in their practical implications and need to be superseded by a plurality of forms of knowledge and microanalyses. Consequently, Foucault attempts to detotalize history and society as unified wholes governed by a centre, essence, or telos, and to decentre the subject as a constituted rather than a constituting consciousness. He analyses history as a non-evolutionary, fragmented field of disconnected knowledges, while presenting society as a dispersed regularity of unevenly developing levels of discourses, and the modern subject as a humanist fiction integral to the operations of a carceral society that everywhere disciplines and trains its subjects for labour and conformity.

Perhaps the fundamental guiding motivation of Foucault's work is to 'respect . . . differences' (Foucault 1973b: p. xii). This imperative informs his historical approach, perspectives on society, and political positions and takes numerous forms: a historical methodology which attempts to grasp the specificity and discontinuity of discourses, a rethinking of power as diffused throughout multiple social sites, a redefinition of the 'general intellectual' as a 'specific intellectual', and a critique of global and totalizing modes of thought. Foucault analyzes modernity from various perspectives on modern discourses and institutions. On Nietzsche's understanding, perspectivism denies the existence of facts, and insists there are only interpretations of the world. Since the world has no single meaning, but rather countless meanings, a perspectivist seeks multiple interpretations of phenomena and insists there is 'no limit to the ways in which the world can be interpreted' (Nietzsche 1967: p. 326). Nietzsche's reflections on the origins of values, for instance, proceeded from psychological, physiological, historical, philosophical, and linguistic grounds. For Nietzsche, the more perspectives one can gain on the world or any of its phenomena, the richer and deeper will be one's interpretations and knowledge.[3]

Following Nietzsche, Foucault rejects the philosophical pretension to grasp systematically all of reality within one philosophical system or from one central vantage point. Foucault believes that 'Discourse . . . is so complex a reality that we not only can, but should, approach it at different levels with different methods' (1973b: p. xiv). Hence, no single theory or method of interpretation by itself can grasp the plurality of discourses, institutions, and modes of power that constitute modern society. Accordingly, while Foucault is strongly influenced by theoretical positions such as structuralism or Marxism, he rejects any single analytic framework and analyzes modernity from the perspectives of psychiatry, medicine, criminology and sexuality, all of which overlap in complex ways and provide different optics on modern society and the constitution of the modern subject.

2.1.1 Archaeology and Discontinuity

In his initial books, Foucault characterizes his position as an archaeology of knowledge. He employs the term archaeology to differentiate his historical approach, first, from hermeneutics, which seeks a deep truth underlying discourse or an elucidation of subjective meaning schemes. The surface-depth and causal models utilized by modern theory are overturned in favour of a postmodern description of discontinuous surfaces of discourse unconnected by causal linkages. The 'hermeneutics of suspicion' itself becomes suspect. Archaeology is also distinguished from 'the confused, under-structured, and ill-structured domain of the history of ideas' (Foucault 1975a: p. 195). Foucault rejects this idealist and humanist mode of writing which traces a continuous evolution of thought in terms of tradition or the conscious productions of subjects.

Against this approach, archaeology attempts to identify the conditions of possibility of knowledge, the determining rules of formation of discursive rationality that operate beneath the level of intention or thematic content. 'It is these rules of formation, which were never formulated in their own right, but are to be found only in widely differing theories, concepts, and objects of study, that I have tried to reveal, by isolating, as their specific locus, a level that I have called ... archaeological' (Foucault 1973b: p. xi). Unlike structuralism, to which his early analyses bear some resemblances (see Dreyfus and Rabinow 1982), these rules are not universal and immutable in character, or grounded in the structure of the mind, but are historically changing and specific to given discursive domains. Such rules constitute the 'historical *a priori*' of all knowledge, perception, and truth. They are 'the fundamental codes of a culture' which construct the '*episteme*', or configuration of knowledge, that determines the empirical orders and social practices of a particular historical era.

In *Madness and Civilization* (1973a; orig. 1961), for example, his first major work, Foucault attempts to write the 'archaeology of that silence' whereby madness is historically constituted as the other of reason. He returns to the discontinuity marked by the great confinement of 1656 where modern reason breaks off communication with the mad and attempts to 'guard against the subterranean danger of unreason' (1973a: p. 84) through discourses of exclusion and institutions of confinement. Classical and modern discourses construct oppositions between sane and insane, normal and abnormal that work to enforce norms of reason and truth. In his next book, *The Birth of the Clinic* (1975a; orig. 1963), subtitled 'An Archaeology of Medical Perception', Foucault analyzes the shift from a premodern speculatively-based medicine to a modern empirically-based medicine rooted in the rationality of the scientific gaze. Rejecting a history based on the 'consciousness of clinicians', he pursues a structural study of discourse that seeks to determine 'the conditions of possibility of medical experience in modern times' (Foucault 1975a: p. xix) and the historical conditions whereby a scientific discourse of the individual can first emerge.

Then, in *The Order of Things* (1973b; orig. 1966), subtitled 'An Archaeology of the Human Sciences', Foucault describes the emergence of the human sciences. He gives his most detailed analysis of the underlying rules, assumptions and ordering proce-dures of the Renaissance, classical, and modern eras, focusing on the shifts in the sciences of life, labour, and language. In this analysis, Foucault uncovers the birth of 'man' as a discursive construct. 'Man', the object of philosophy as the human sciences (psychology, sociology and literature), emerges when the classical field of representation dissolves and the human being for the first time becomes not only an aloof representing subject, but also the object of modern scientific investigation, a finite and historically determined being to be studied in its living, labouring, and speaking capacities.

Embedded in a new field of temporality and finitude, the status of the subject as master of knowledge becomes threatened, but its sovereignty is maintained in its reconstitution in transcendental form. Foucault describes how modern philosophy constructs 'Man' – both object and subject of knowledge – within a series of unstable 'doublets': the cogito/unthought doublet whereby Man is determined by external forces yet aware of this determination and able to free himself from it; the retreat-and-return-of-the-origin doublet whereby history precedes Man but he is the phenomeno-logical source from which history unfolds; and the transcendental/ empirical doublet whereby Man both constitutes and is constituted by the external world, finding secure foundations for knowledge through *a priori* categories (Kant) or through procedures of 'reduction' which allow consciousness to purify itself from the empirical world (Husserl). In each of these doublets, humanist thought attempts to recuperate the primacy and autonomy of the thinking subject and to master all that is other to it.

Foucault's initial critique of the human sciences is that they, like philosophy, are premised on an impossible attempt to reconcile irreconcilable poles of thought and posit a constituting subject. It is only in his genealogical works, as we shall see, that this critique assumes its full importance as Foucault becomes clear on the political implications of humanism as the epistemological basis of a disciplinary society. Having analyzed the birth of 'man', *The Order of Things* concludes by anticipating the 'death of man' as an epistemological subject in the emerging posthumanist, postmodern epistemic space where the subject is once and for all dethroned and interpreted as an effect of language, desire, and the uncon-scious. This development begins in the twentieth century with the appearance of the 'counter-sciences' (psychoanalysis, linguistics, and ethnology), and archaeology itself clearly belongs to this space. No longer a sovereign cogito or transcendental ground, the subject in this episteme becomes an epiphenomenon of prepersonal forces.

Finally, in *The Archaeology of Knowledge* (1972; orig. 1971), Foucault pursues a metatheoretical reflection on his project and methodology in order to clarify his ideas and criticize some of his past mistakes. Drawing from the work of French historians of science, Bachelard and Canguilhem, Foucault self-consciously announces that 'a new form of history is trying to develop its own theory' (1972: p. 5). From within this new conceptual space the modern themes of continuity, teleology, genesis, totality, and subject are no longer self-evident and are reconstructed or abandoned.

Unlike in modern historiography, discontinuity is no longer seen as a blight on the historical narrative and stigmatized in principle. Rather, Foucault adopts discontinuity as a positive working concept. He opposes his postmodern concept of a general history to the modern concept of a total history that he attributes to figures such as Hegel and Marx. Foucault summarizes the difference in this way: 'A total description draws all phenomena around a single centre – a principle, a meaning, a spirit, a world-view, an overall shape; a general history, on the contrary, would deploy the space of a dispersion' (1972: p. 10). The types of totality that Foucault rejects include massive vertical totalities such as history, civilization, and epoch; horizontal totalities such as society or period; and anthropological or humanist conceptions of a centred subject.

For Foucault, evolutionary history such as written by Hegel or Marx attains its narrative totalizations in an illegitimate way, through the construction of abstractions that obscure more than they reveal. Beneath these abstractions are complex interrelations, a shifting plurality of decentred, individualized series of discourses, unable to be reduced to a single law, model, unity, or vertical arrangement. His goal is to break up the vast unities 'and then see whether they can be legitimately reaffirmed; or whether other groupings should be made' (1972: p. 26). The potential result of such detotalizing moves is that 'an entire field is set free' – the field of discursive formations, complex systems of dispersions. Hence, as a postmodern historiography, archaeology 'does not have a unifying but a diversifying effect' (1972: p. 160), allowing the historian to discover the multiplicity of discourses in a field of knowledge.

Foucault's archaeological approach can be distinguished from theorists such as Baudrillard, Lyotard or Derrida in two significant ways. First, Foucault does not dissolve all forms of structure, coherence, and intelligibility into an endless flux of signification. Having cleared the ground, he attempts to grasp what forms of regularities, relations, continuities, and totalities really *do* exist. The task of archaeology is not just 'to attain a plurality of histories juxtaposed and independent of one another', but also 'to determine what form of relation may be legitimately described between ... different series [of things]' (1972: p. 10). Second, unlike Baudrillard's apocalyptic trumpeting of postmodernity as a complete break with industrial modernity, political economy, and referential reason, Foucault employs a cautious and qualified use of the discourse of discontinuity. While he appropriates this discourse to attack the traditional interpretation of history as the steady accumulation of knowledge or the gradual progress of truth or reason, and to show that sudden and abrupt changes occur in configurations of knowledge, he rejects the interpretation of his work as simply a 'philosophy of discontinuity' (Foucault 1988d: pp. 99–100). Instead, he claims that he sometimes exaggerated the degree of historical breaks 'for pedagogical purposes', that is, to counter the hegemony of the traditional theories of historical progress and continuity (see also Foucault 1980a: pp. 111–12).

For Foucault, discontinuity refers to the fact that in a transition from one historical era to another 'things are no longer perceived, described, expressed, characterized, classified, and known in the same way' (1973b: p. 217). In the shift from the Renaissance to the classical *episteme*, for example, 'thought ceases to move in the element of resemblance. Similitude is no longer the form of knowledge but the occasion of error' (1973b: p. 51) that is derided as the poetic fantasy of an age before Reason. But there is no rupture or break so radical as to spring forth *ex nihilo* and negate everything that has preceded it. Rupture is possible 'only on the basis of rules that are already in operation' (Foucault 1972: p. 17). Anticipating a similar position employed by Raymond Williams and Fredric Jameson (see Chapter 6), Foucault argues that rupture means not some absolute change, but a 'redistribution of the [prior] *episteme*' (1973b: p. 345), a reconfiguration of its elements, where, although there are new rules of a discursive formation redefining the boundaries and nature of knowledge and truth, there are significant continuities as well.

Hence, Foucault employs a dialectic of continuity and discontinuity; historical breaks always include some 'overlapping, interaction, and echoes' (1980b: p. 149) between the old and the new. In *The Order of Things* (1973b: pp. 361ff.), for example, he emphasizes the continuities between the modern and the emerging postmodern *episteme*, such as the continued importance of the problematic of representation in the space of the counter-sciences. Similarly, in his works on sexuality, he describes a continuity between medieval Christianity and modernity in terms of the constitution of the individual whose deep truth is its sexuality. Also in his later work, he seeks to identify 'that thread that may connect us with the Enlightenment' (1984: p. 42), a still existing historico-critical outlook.

The Archaeology of Knowledge was the last work Foucault explicitly identified as an archaeology and it marks the end of his focus on the unconscious rules of discourse and the historical shifts within each discursive field. This perspective has led theorists such as Habermas (1987a: p. 268) and Grumley (1989: p. 192) to wrongly argue that Foucault's archaeologies grant 'total autonomy' to discourse over social institutions and practices. This critique of the early Foucault as idealist is belied, most obviously, by the focus on institutional supports of discourse in *Madness and Civilization*, but one also finds a concern with policing, surveillance, and disciplinary apparatuses already in *The Birth of the Clinic*, and an emphasis on the 'materiality' of discourse (albeit vaguely defined) in *The Archaeology of Knowledge* (see also Foucault 1989: pp. 18–19).

Nevertheless, there is no doubt that Foucault's archaeologies privileged analysis of theory and knowledge over practices and institutions. While Foucault's limited focus had a legitimate philosophical justification, recasting traditional views of history and seeking an immanent clarification of the intelligibility of discourse in terms of linguistic rules unperceived by human actors, a more adequate analysis would ultimately have to focus more directly on practices and institutions to situate discourse within its full social and political context. Working through the influence of Nietzsche, this became Foucault's project and marks his turn to genealogy and an explicit concern with power relations and effects.

2.1.2 Nietzsche and Genealogy

In 1970 Foucault began to make the transition from archaeology to genealogy and thereby to a more adequate theorization of material institutions and forms of power. In his essay, 'The Discourse of Language', he speaks of employing a new genealogical analysis of 'the effective formation of discourse, whether within the limits of control, or outside them' (1972: p. 233). In a summary of a course he gave in the Collège de France (1970–71), he stated that his earlier archaeological studies should now be conducted 'in relation to the will to knowledge' (1977: p. 201) and the power effects this creates. In his 1971 essay 'Nietzsche, Genealogy, and History', he analyzes the central Nietzschean themes that will inform his new historical method, which appears in mature form in his next major book, *Discipline and Punish* (1979; orig. 1975).

While genealogy signals a new shift in focus, it is not a break in his work, but rather a widening of the scope of analysis. Like archaeology, Foucault characterizes genealogy as a new mode of historical writing, calling the genealogist 'the new historian' (1977: p. 160). Both methodologies attempt to re-examine the social field from a micrological standpoint that enables one to identify discursive discontinuity and dispersion instead of continuity and identity, and to grasp historical events in their real complexity. Both methodologies, therefore, attempt to undo great chains of historical continuity and their teleological destinations and to historicize what is thought to be immutable. Foucault seeks to destroy historical identities by pluralizing the field of discourse, to purge historical writing of humanist assumptions by decentring the subject, and to critically analyze modern reason through a history of the human sciences.

In the transition to his genealogical stage, however, Foucault places more emphasis on the material conditions of discourse, which he defines in terms of 'institutions, political events, economic practices and processes' (1972: p. 49), and on analyzing the relations between discursive and non-discursive domains. Consequently, he thematizes the operations of power, particularly as they target the body to produce knowledge and subjectivity. This transition is not then a break between the idealist archaeological Foucault and the materialist genealogical Foucault, but rather marks a more adequate thematization of social practices and power relations that were implicit in his work all along.

Archaeology and genealogy now combine in the form of theory/ practice where theory is immediately practical in character. As Foucault states (1980a: p. 85), ' "archaeology" would be the appropriate methodology of the analysis of local discursivities, and "genealogy" would be the tactics whereby on the basis of the descriptions of these local discursivities, the subjected knowledges which were thus released would be brought into play'. Where archaeology attempted to show that the subject is a fictitious construct, genealogy seeks to foreground the material context of subject construction, to draw out the political consequences of 'subjectification', and to help form resistances to subjectifying practices. Where archaeology criticized the human sciences as being grounded in humanist assumptions genealogy links these theories to the operations of power and tries to put historical knowledge to work in local struggles. And where archaeology theorized the birth of the human sciences in the context of the modern *episteme* and the figure 'Man', genealogy highlights the power and effects relations they produced.

In *Discipline and Punish*, for example, Foucault describes the historical formation of the soul, body, and subject within various disciplinary matrices of power that operate in institutions such as prisons, schools, hospitals, and workshops. Disciplinary techniques include timetables for constant imposition and regulation of activity, surveillance measures to monitor performance, examinations such as written reports and files to reward conformity and penalize resistance, and 'normalizing judgement' to impose and enforce moral values such as the work ethic. The life of the student, soldier and prisoner are equally regulated and monitored. The individual now is interpreted not only as a discursive construct, but as an effect of political technologies through which its very identity, desires, body, and 'soul' are shaped and constituted. 'Discipline "makes" individuals; it is the specific technique of a power that regards individuals both as objects and as instruments of its exercise' (Foucault 1979: p. 170). The ultimate goal and effect of discipline is 'normalization', the elimination of all social and psychological irregularities and the production of useful and docile subjects through a refashioning of minds and bodies.

Similarly, in *The History of Sexuality* (1980b; orig. 1976) Foucault attempts to write the history of the 'polymorphous techniques of power' that since the end of the sixteenth century have rigorously inscribed the body within discourses of sexuality governed by a scientific will to knowledge. Power operates not through repression of sex, but through the discursive production of sexuality and subjects who have a 'sexual nature'. 'The deployment of sexuality has its reason for being ... in proliferating, innovating, annexing, creating, and penetrating bodies in an increasingly detailed way, and in controlling populations in an increasingly comprehensive way' (Foucault 1980b: p. 107). The production of the sexual body allows it to be inscribed within a network of normalizing powers where a whole regime of knowledge-pleasure is defined and controlled.

In order to theorize the birth of modern disciplinary and normalizing practices, genealogy politicizes all facets of culture and everyday life. Following Nietzsche's genealogies of morality, asceticism, justice, and punishment, Foucault tries to write the histories of unknown, forgotten, excluded, and marginal discourses. He sees the discourses of madness, medicine, punishment and sexuality to have independent histories and institutional bases, irreducible to macrophenomena such as the modern state and economy. Hence, against 'the tyranny of globalizing discourses' (Foucault 1980a: p. 83), he calls for 'an insurrection of subjugated knowledges' (1980a: p. 81), of those 'disqualified' discourses that positivistic science and Marxism delegitimate because they are deemed marginal and/or non-formalizable. Genealogies are therefore 'anti-sciences', not because they seek to 'vindicate a lyrical right to ignorance or non-knowledge' and attack the concepts and methods of science *per se*, but rather because they contest 'the [coercive] effects of the centralizing powers which are linked to the institution and functioning of an organized scientific discourse' (1980a: p. 84).

2.2 Power/Knowledge/Subjectivity: Foucault's Postmodern Analytics

[W]e had to wait until the nineteenth century before we began to understand the nature of exploitation, and to this day, we have yet to fully comprehend the nature of power (Foucault 1977: p. 213).

Beginning in the early 1970s, Foucault attempts to rethink the nature of modern power in a non-totalizing, non-representational, and anti-humanist scheme. He rejects all modern theories that see power to be anchored in macrostructures or ruling classes and to be repressive in nature. He develops new postmodern perspectives that interpret power as dispersed, indeterminate, heteromorphous, subjectless and productive, constituting individuals' bodies and identities. He claims that the two dominant models for theorizing modern power, the juridical and economistic models, are flawed by outmoded and erroneous assumptions. The economistic model, as espoused by Marxists, is rejected as a reductionistic subordination of power to class domination and economic imperatives. The juridical model, his primary target, analyzes power in terms of law, legal and moral right, and political sovereignty. While the bourgeois revolution decapitated the king in the sociopolitical realm, Foucault argues that many concepts and assumptions of the sovereign–juridical model continue to inform modern thought (for example, in liberal theory and repression theories of power in general). He therefore attempts 'to cut off the head of the king' in the realm of theory with a genealogical guillotine.

Foucault marks a rupture in history that inaugurates a radically different mode of power than theorized on the juridical model, a power that is productive, not repressive, in nature, one which is 'bent on generating forces, making them grow, and ordering them, rather than one dedicated to impeding them, making them submit, or destroying them' (Foucault 1980b: p. 136). As evident from the dramatic historical shifts Foucault outlines in *Discipline and Punish*, from the gruesome torture of Damiens to the moral reform of prisoners, schoolchildren, and others, this power operates not through physical force or representation by law, but through the hegemony of norms, political technologies, and the shaping of the body and soul.

In *The History of Sexuality*, Foucault terms this new mode of power 'bio-power'. Its first modality, as we have already discussed, is a disciplinary power that involves 'an *anatomo-politics of the human body*' (1980b: p. 139). Most generally, Foucault defines disciplines as 'techniques for assuring the ordering of human multiplicities' (1979: p. 218). Initially developed in monasteries and in late-seventeenth-century plague towns that required methods of spatial separation and population surveillance, disciplinary techniques soon extended throughout society, thereby forming a gigantic 'carceral archipelago'.

The second modality of bio-power, emerging subsequent to disciplinary power, focuses on the 'species body', the social population in general. 'Governments perceived that they were not dealing simply with subjects, or even with a "people", but with a "population", with its specific phenomena and its peculiar variables: birth and death rates, life expectancy, fertility, state of health, frequency of illnesses, patterns of diet and habitation' (Foucault 1980b: p. 25). The ensuing supervision of the population represents 'the entry of life into history', into a densely constituted field of knowledge, power, and techniques. Hence, in the eighteenth century, sexuality became an object of discursive administration and regulation. The 'deployment of sexuality' produced perversions and sexual categorizations of various sorts in accordance with normalizing strategies of power.

Against modern theories that see knowledge as neutral and objective (positivism) or emancipatory (Marxism), Foucault emphasizes that knowledge is indissociable from regimes of power. His concept of 'power/knowledge' is symptomatic of the postmodern suspicion of reason and the emancipatory schemes advanced in its name. The circular relationship between power and knowledge is established in Foucault's genealogical critiques of the human sciences. Having emerged within the context of relations of power, through practices and technologies of exclusion, confinement, surveillance, and objectification, disciplines such as psychiatry, sociology, and criminology in turn contributed to the development, refinement, and proliferation of new techniques of power. Institutions such as the asylum, hospital, or prison functioned as laboratories for observation of individuals, experimentation with correctional techniques, and acquisition of knowledge for social control.

The modern individual became both an object and subject of knowledge, not 'repressed', but positively shaped and formed within the matrices of 'scientifico-disciplinary mechanisms', a moral/legal/psychological/medical/sexual being 'carefully fabricated . . . according to a whole technique of force and bodies' (Foucault 1979: p. 217). As Foucault understands it, the term 'subject' has a double meaning: one is both 'subject to someone else by control and dependence, and tied to . . [their] own identity by a conscience or self-knowledge' (1982a: p. 212). Hence, as Dews (1987) has noted, Foucault rejects the Enlightenment model which links consciousness, self-reflection, and freedom, and instead follows Nietzsche's claim in *The Genealogy of Morals* that self-knowledge, particularly in the form of moral consciousness, is a strategy and effect of power whereby one internalizes social control.

Against modern theories that posit a pregiven, unified subject or an unchanging human essence that precedes all social operations, Foucault calls for the destruction of the subject and sees this as a key political tactic. 'One has to dispense with the constituent subject, and to get rid of the subject itself, that's to say, to arrive at an analysis which can account for the constitution of the subject within a historical framework' (Foucault 1980a: p. 117). The notion of a constituent subject is a humanist mystification that occludes a critical examination of the various institutional sites where subjects are produced within power relations. Taking his cue from Nietzsche, Foucault's task is to awaken thought from its humanist slumbers and to destroy 'all concrete forms of the anthropological prejudice', a task which would allow us 'to renew contact ... with the project of a general critique of reason' (Foucault 1973b: p. 342). To accomplish this, the subject must be 'stripped of its creative role and analyzed as a complex and variable function of discourse' (Foucault 1977: p. 138). Hence, Foucault rejects the active subject and welcomes the emerging postmodern era as a positive event where the denuding of agency occurs and new forms of thought can emerge (Foucault 1973a: p. 386).

As we see, Foucault's account of power emphasizes the highly differentiated nature of modern society and the 'heteromorphous' power mechanisms that operate independent of conscious subjects. This postmodern theory attempts to grasp the plural nature of modernity itself, which Foucault believes modern social theory such as Marxism has failed to adequately understand. Modernity is characterized by the fact that 'never have there existed more centres of power ... more circular contacts and linkages ... more sites where the intensity of pleasures and the persistency of power catch hold, only to spread elsewhere' (Foucault 1980b: p. 49). Hence, Foucault defines power as 'a multiple and mobile field of force relations where far-reaching, but never completely stable effects of domination are produced' (1980b: p. 102). Modern power is a 'relational' power that is 'exercized from innumerable points,' is highly indeterminate in character, and is never something 'acquired, seized, or shared'. There is no source or centre of power to contest, nor are there any subjects holding it; power is a

purely structural activity for which subjects are anonymous con-
duits or by-products.

In opposition to modern totalizing analyses, Foucault undertakes a pluralized analysis of power and rationality as they are
inscribed in various discourses and institutional sites. Demarcating
his approach from the Frankfurt School and other modern
approaches, Foucault rejects a generalized description of 'rationalization'. Instead, he analyzes it as a process which occurs 'in
several fields, each grounded in a fundamental experience: madness, illness, death, crime, sexuality, etc.' (1988d: p. 59). Consequently, Foucault conducts an 'ascending' rather than 'descending'
analysis which sees power as circulating throughout a decentred
field of institutional networks and is only subsequently taken up by
larger structures such as class or the state. These macroforces 'are
only the terminal forms power takes' (Foucault 1980b: p. 92).
Moreover, this explains why Foucault calls his approach an
'analytics', rather than a 'theory' of power. The latter term implies
a systematic, unitary viewpoint which he seeks to destroy in favour
of a plural, fragmentary, differentiated, indeterminant, and historically and spatially specific mode of analysis.

We should therefore distinguish between a theory of postmodern power and a postmodern analytics of modern power.
While there are salient postmodern aspects to his analysis of
power, whereby he dissolves power into a plurality of microforces,
and while he anticipates a new postmodern era, Foucault never
theorizes those technologies and strategies that some theorists
identify as constituting a postmodern power. For theorists such
as Baudrillard (see Chapter 4), a postmodern power involves
electronic media and information technologies and semiotic systems that undermine the distinction between reality and unreality
and proliferates an abstract environment of images and manipulated signifiers. In fact, given Foucault's desire to theorize 'this
precise moment in which we are living', it is peculiar that he says
nothing about these new forms of power which have emerged in
this century as powerful social and cultural forces, and which are
only partially illuminated by the model of a disciplinary bio-power
in that they involve the circulation of information and abstract sign
systems. On Foucault's scheme, therefore, there have been no
significant developments in the mechanisms and operations and
power since the nineteenth century, an assumption that theorists

such as Baudrillard sharply contest by positing the existence of a new postmodern society and a 'disembodied' semiotic power.

While Foucault does not identify a postmodern form of power, we have seen that he does anticipate a new postmodern *episteme* and historical era, describing his strong impression that 'something new is about to begin, something that we glimpse only as a thin line of light low on the horizon' (1973b: p. 384). But this era is not specified beyond its conception as a posthumanist era and is therefore not explored more broadly in terms of new social, economic, technological, or cultural processes. Indeed, as we shall show below, the move of Foucault's later thought was to shift from an analysis of modernity toward an analysis of premodernity in order to further develop his genealogy of the modern subject.

Moreover, in later essays such as 'What is Enlightenment?' (Foucault 1984: pp. 32–50) we find that far from positing a radical rupture in history, he draws key continuities between our current era and the Enlightenment. In doing this, he modifies his earlier critique of rationality in important ways which force rethinking of charges that he is an unrepentent irrationalist or aestheticist (see, for example, Megill 1985; Wolin 1986). While still critical of Enlightenment reason, Foucault attempts to positively appropriate key aspects of the Enlightenment heritage – its acute historical sense of the present, its emphasis on rational autonomy over conformity and dogma, and its critical outlook. He now sees the uncritical acceptance of modern rationality and its complete rejection as equally hazardous: 'if it is extremely dangerous to say that Reason is the enemy that should be eliminated, it is just as dangerous to say that any critical questioning risks sending us into irrationality' (1984: p. 249). This qualification rescues Foucault from the aporia of repudiating reason from a rational standpoint. Critical thought must constantly live within a field of tension; its function is to accept and theorize 'this sort of revolving door of rationality that refers us to its necessity, to its indispensability, and at the same time to its intrinsic dangers' (Foucault 1984: p. 249).

Hence, Foucault modified his attitude toward the Enlightenment, modernity, and rationality. While his early critiques of modernity are sharply negative, in his later work he sometimes adopts a more positive attitude, seeing a critical impulse in the modern will-to-knowledge which should be preserved. This leads him, as we will show below, to qualify his position that subjectivity is nothing but a construct of domination. Such changes are symptomatic of a shift in French thought away from earlier denunciations of reason and subjectivity. As we shall see, Lyotard made a similar reappraisal of reason and appropriated certain Kantian positions in his work (5.3). For now, let us examine the political implications of Foucault's genealogical method and analytics of power, before examining the shifts in the later Foucault.

2.3   Domination and Resistance: Foucault's Political Fragments

> Free political action from all unitary and totalizing paranoia. Develop action, thought, and desires by proliferation, juxtaposition, and disjunction, and not by subdivision and pyramidal hierarchization (Foucault 1983: p. xiii).

> Maybe the target nowadays is not to discover what we are, but to refuse what we are (Foucault 1982a: p. 216).

The cumulative effect of Foucault's archaeologies and genealogies is perhaps enervating. For, in his description, power is diffused throughout the social field, constituting individual subjectivities and their knowledges and pleasures, colonizing the body itself, utilizing its forces while inducing obedience and conformity. Since the seventeenth century, individuals have been caught within a complex grid of disciplinary, normalizing, panoptic powers that survey, judge, measure, and correct their every move. There are no 'spaces of primal liberty' in society; power is everywhere. 'What I am attentive to is the fact that every human relation is to some degree a power relation. We move in a world of perpetual strategic relations' (Foucault 1988d: p. 168).

Despite this intense vision of oppression, it is a mistake to see Foucault as a fatalist with respect to social and political change for his work can be read another way. Indeed, Foucault's own interventions into political struggles and debates would make little sense if he felt that the deadlock of power was unbreakable. One might even speak of Foucault's optimism that issues from his belief in the contingency and vulnerability of power: 'There's an optimism that consists in saying that things couldn't be better. My optimism would consist rather in saying that so many things can be changed, fragile as they are, bound up more with circumstances than necessities, more arbitrary than self-evident, more a matter of complex, but temporary, historical circumstances than with inevitable anthropological constraints' (Foucault 1988d: p. 156). Ultimately, this attitude proceeds on the belief that 'Knowledge can transform us' (1988d: p. 4) – hence the importance of archaeology and genealogy as historical methods that expose the beginnings and development of current subjectifying discourses and practices.

Misinterpretations of Foucault turn on a conflation between power as omnipresent and as omnipotent. While power is every-where, it is indissociable from contestation and struggle: 'I am just saying: as soon as there is a power relation, there is a possibility of resistance. We can never be ensnared by power: we can always modify its grip in determinate conditions and according to a precise strategy' (Foucault 1988d: p. 123). The common argument that Foucault presents subjects as helpless and passive victims of power fails to observe his emphasis on the contingency and vulnerability of power and the places in his work where he describes actual resistances to it. In *Discipline and Punish*, for example, he briefly discusses 'popular illegalities' and strategies of indiscipline to counter the mechanisms of discipline and normal-ization (1979: pp. 273ff.). Similarly, in *The History of Sexuality*, he argues that while the discourses of 'perversity' multiplied the mechanisms of social control, they also produced a reverse dis-course where homosexuals appropriated them in order to demand their legitimacy as a group (1980b: p. 101).

Admittedly, such passages are rare and the overriding emphasis of Foucault's work is on the ways in which individuals are classified, excluded, objectified, individualized, disciplined, and normalized. Foucault himself became aware of this problem and shifted his emphasis from 'technologies of domination' to 'tech-nologies of the self', from the ways in which individuals are transformed by others to the ways in which they transform themselves (see 2.3.2 below). Throughout his work, Foucault's remarks on political tactics are highly vague and tentative, and nothing like a 'Foucauldian politics' – which would entail the very systematic theory that he rejects – ever emerges. Nevertheless, there are distinctly Foucauldian strategies that break from the assumptions of the Marxist revolutionary tradition and constitute a postmodern approach to politics.

2.3.1   *Post-Marxist/Postmodern Strategies: Politics of Genealogy*

Instead of the Marxist binary model of class struggle between antagonistic classes, Foucault calls for a plurality of autonomous struggles waged throughout the microlevels of society, in the prisons, asylums, hospitals, and schools. For a modern concept of macropolitics where clashing forces struggle for control over a centralized source of power rooted in the economy and state, Foucault substitutes a postmodern concept of micropolitics where numerous local groups contest diffuse and decentred forms of power spreading throughout society.

The 'general intellectual' who 'represents' (that is, speaks on behalf of) all oppressed groups is demoted to the 'specific intellectual' who assumes a modest advisory role within a particular group and form of struggle. Foucault rejects nearly the entire vocabulary of classical Marxism. The concepts of liberation or emancipation, for example, imply for Foucault an inherent human essence waiting to be freed from the shackles of a repressive power. The notion of ideology, moreover, assumes the possibility of a true consciousness and a form of truth constituted outside the field of power, as well as a power based on mental representations rather than physical discipline. Finally, Foucault finds the very idea of revolution to be erroneous insofar as it entails a large-scale social transformation radiating from a central point (the state or mode of production), rather than a detotalized proliferation of local struggles against a relational power that no one owns. '[T]here is no locus of great Refusal, no soul of revolt, source of all rebellions, or pure law of the revolutionary. Instead there is a plurality of resistances, each of them a special case' (Foucault 1980b: pp. 95–6).

If Foucault is right that modern power is irreducibly plural, that it proliferates and thrives at the local and capillary levels of society, and is only subsequently taken up by larger institutional structures, then it follows that a change only in the form of the state, mode of production, or class composition of society fails to address autonomous trajectories of power. Thus, the key assumption behind the micrological strategies of thinkers like Foucault, Deleuze and Guattari, and Lyotard, is that since power is decentred and plural, so in turn must be forms of political struggle. A Foucauldian postmodern politics, therefore, attempts to break with unifying and totalizing strategies, to cultivate multiple forms of resistance, to destroy the prisons of received identities and discourses of exclusion, and to encourage the proliferation of differences of all kinds.

The political task of genealogy, then, is to recover the autonomous discourses, knowledges, and voices suppressed through totalizing narratives. The subjugated voices of history speak to hidden forms of domination; to admit their speech is necessarily to revise one's conception of what and where power is. As Marx attempted to break the spell of commodity fetishism in capitalist society, or as the surrealist and Russian formalists practised 'defamiliarization' techniques to shatter the grip of ordinary sensibility, so genealogy problematizes the present as eternal and self-evident, exposing the operations of power and domination working behind neutral or beneficent facades. In Foucault's words (1974: p. 171): 'It seems to me that the real political task in a society such as ours is to criticize the working of institutions which appear to be both neutral and independent; to criticize them in such a manner that the political violence which has always exercized itself obscurely through them will be unmasked, so that one can fight them.'

Genealogies attempt to demonstrate how objectifying forms of reason (and their regimes of truth and knowledge) have been made, as historically contingent rather than eternally necessary forces. Consequently, 'they can be unmade, as long as we know how it was they were made' (Foucault 1988d: p. 37). Foucault's genealogy of sexuality was written with such purposes in mind. He attempted to problematize contemporary notions of sexual liberation by demonstrating that the concepts of sexual nature or sexuality originated in early Christian culture and in modernity became articulated with disciplinary and therapeutic techniques that work to imprison individuals in normalizing discourses and identities.

In our reading, a Foucauldian micropolitics includes two key components: a discourse politics and a bio-politics. In discourse politics, marginal groups attempt to contest the hegemonic discourses that position individuals within the straitjacket of normal identities to liberate the free play of differences. In any society, discourse is power because the rules determining discourse enforce norms of what is rational, sane, or true, and to speak from outside these rules is to risk marginalization and exclusion. All discourses are produced by power, but they are not wholly subservient to it and can be used as 'a point of resistance and a starting point for an opposing strategy' (Foucault 1980b: p. 101). Counter-discourses provide a lever of political resistance by encapsulating a popular memory of previous forms of oppression and struggle and a means of articulating needs and demands. In bio-struggle, by contrast, individuals attempt to break from the grip of disciplinary powers and to reinvent the body by creating new modes of desire and pleasure. Foucault believes that the development of new bodies and pleasures have the potential to subvert the construction of normalized subject identities and forms of consciousness. The political deployment of the body, however, could not take the form of a 'liberation of sexuality', as Reich or Marcuse call for, since sexuality is a normalizing construct of modernity. Hence, for Foucault, 'the rallying point for the counterattack against the deployment of sexuality ought not to be sex-desire, but bodies and pleasures' (1980b: p. 157).

There is some tension between these two strategies since discourse politics promotes a critical reflexivity and a popular counter-memory and bio-politics explores the trangressive potential of the body. The first perspective emphasizes the historical constitution of everything human and the second sometimes verges toward a naive naturalism. Ultimately, this reflects the tension that runs throughout Foucault's work between discursive and extra-discursive emphases. There is also tension between the emphases on the ubiquity of domination and the possibility of resistance insofar as the balance of description is tipped toward the side of a domination that shapes every aspect of mental and physical existence, while very few specifics about resistance are given and the efficacy of human agency, at least theoretically, is denied. Moreover, as Fraser notes (1989: p. 60), it is not clear how the 'bodies and pleasures' Foucault valorizes are not, like 'sexuality', also power effects or implicated in normalizing strategies. Foucault contradicts himself in claiming that everything is historically constituted within power relations and then privileging some realm of the body as a transcendental source of transgression. He thereby seems to reproduce the kind of essentialist anthropology for which he attacks humanism.

Nevertheless, discourse and bio-struggle are intended to facilitate the development of new forms of subjectivity and values (Foucault 1982a: p. 216). The precondition for the development of new subjectivities is the dissolution of the old ones, a move first anticipated in *The Order of Things*. While Foucault never provided any conception of human agency, he did, unlike Althusser and other structuralist or poststructuralist thinkers, gesture towards a positive reconstruction of subjectivity in a posthumanist problematic. This move occurs in his later works – the second and third volumes of his history of sexuality and various essays and interviews from the 1980s – and it moves into the forefront of Foucault's thought a concern with ethics and technologies of the self.

2.3.2   Ethics and Technologies of the Self

We have to create ourselves as a work of art (Foucault 1982b: p. 237).

[Genealogy] is seeking to give new impetus, as far and wide as possible, to the undefined work of freedom (Foucault 1984: p. 46).

In this section we describe the third major shift in Foucault's work, from the archaeological focus on systems of knowledge in the 1960s, to the genealogical focus on modalities of power in the 1970s, to the focus on technologies of the self, ethics, and freedom in the 1980s. There are both continuities and dramatic discontinuities if we compare the early and middle with the later Foucault. The continuities concern the extension of his archaeological and genealogical investigations to a new field of study that seeks the beginnings of the modern hermeneutic of desire – the search for the deep truth of one's being in one's 'sexuality' – in Greek, Roman, and Christian culture; the discontinuities arise in regard to his new focus on a self-constituting subject and his reconsideration of rationality and autonomy.

Throughout his career, Foucault has been concerned with the problematization of fundamental domains of experience in Western culture such as madness, illness, deviance, and sexuality. He has shown how subjectivity is constituted in a wide range of discourses and practices, within a field of power, knowledge, and truth. His project is to develop a multiperspectival critique of modernity and its institutions, discourses, practices, and forms of subjectivity. In his books, essays, and interviews from the 1980s, however, Foucault leaves the familiar terrain of modernity to study premodern Greek, Roman, and Christian cultures.

This temporal shift was prompted by the demands of the project initiated in *The History of Sexuality* (envisaged as a six-volume study of the genealogy of modern sexuality). The attempt to theorize how and when individuals first seek the truth of their being as subjects of desire through a hermeneutics of the self, led Foucault to analyze the beginnings of this process in early Christian cultures and the continuities and discontinuities between Christian and modern morality. In trying to locate the beginnings of the constitution of the self as a subject of desire, he traced the matrices of Christian morality to Greek and Roman culture. In the second and third volumes of his project, *The Use of Pleasure* (1986; orig. 1984) and *The Care of the Self* (1988a; orig. 1984), he analyzed the similarities and differences between Greek and Roman morality, and the continuities and discontinuities between Greco-Roman morality and Christian and modern morality. For Foucault, there are continuities throughout Western culture in terms of a problematization of desire as a powerful force that needs to be morally regulated; the discontinuities arise, as we shall see, in terms of the different modes of regulation.

The most dramatic transformations in the later Foucault, however, concern not the temporal changes in the fields of study, or the new expository writing style, but the focus of the new project and the revaluation of previous positions. As we have already seen, one important shift in Foucault's later work involves a revaluation of the Enlightenment in terms of its positive contributions to a critique of the present era and his identification of his own work with a trajectory of critical theory running from Kant to Nietzsche to the Frankfurt School. The second major difference involves a qualified turn to a problematic of the creative subject, which was previously rejected as a humanist fiction, along with the use of the vocabulary of freedom, liberty, and autonomy, previously eschewed by the theorist of the death of man. Foucault's concern is still a history of the organization of knowledge and subjectivity, but now the emphasis is on the knowledge relation a self has with itself.

These changes occur as Foucault shifts the focus from technologies of domination, where subjects are dominated and objectified by others through discourses and practices, to technologies of the self, where individuals create their own identities through ethics and forms of self-constitution. Explaining his motivations in an 'auto-critique', Foucault says: 'If one wants to analyze the genealogy of the subject in Western civilization, one has to take into account not only techniques of domination, but also techniques of the self. One has to show the interaction between these two types of self. When I was studying asylums, prison, and so on, I perhaps insisted too much on techniques of domination . . . I would like, in the years to come, to study power relations starting from techniques of the self' (Foucault and Sennet 1982c: p. 10).

Foucault defines technologies of the self as practices 'which permit individuals to effect by their own means or with the help of others a certain number of operations on their own bodies and souls, thoughts, conduct, and way of being, so as to transform themselves in order to attain a certain state of happiness, purity, wisdom, perfection, or immortality' (1988c: p. 18). Given this new emphasis, subjectivity is no longer characterized only as a reified construct of power; the deterministic view of the subject is rejected; impersonal, functionalist explanations give way to a study of how individuals can transform their own subjectivities through techniques of the self. Discipline, in the form of these techniques, is no longer viewed solely as an instrument of domination. Furthermore, issues concerning the freedom and autonomy of individuals emerge as central concerns.

These changes in Foucault's work were influenced by his study of Greek and Roman cultures where techniques of the self, as practiced by free males (slaves and women were excluded from the ethical field) provided models of the practice of freedom. In *The Use of Pleasure* and *The Care of the Self*, Foucault analyzes how Greek and Roman citizens problematized desire as an area of intense moral concern and defined key domains of experience (diet, family relations, and sexuality) as areas requiring moderation and self-control. For the Greeks, especially, ethics was immediately bound up with an 'aesthetics of existence' where it was admirable to turn one's life into a work of art through self-mastery and ethical stylization.

In *The Use of Pleasure*, Foucault debunks the common interpretation of Greek culture as wholly libertarian in its attitudes toward desire to show that the Greeks saw desire as a powerful and potentially destructive force in need of moderation and regulation.

The practice of austerity and self-formation through knowledge, therefore, begins not with the Christians, but in antiquity itself. In *The Care of the Self*, Foucault describes how the problematization of pleasure in Roman society takes basically the same form as in Greek society, with the difference that there is less emphasis on aesthetics of existence, a greater emphasis on marriage and heterosexuality, an increase in austerity in the form of a 'care of the self', and a greater tendency to situate ethics and self-knowledge within the discourse of truth. Thus, although Roman morality is more continuous with Greek morality than with Christianity, Christian culture constitutes a genuine rupture within Western societies and is far more continuous with modern culture than with Greco-Roman culture.

Unlike Christian morality, Greek and Roman morality aimed not at abstinence *per se*, but at moderation and self-control; it was not a question of banishing or stigmatizing desire and pleasure, but of their proper use. Where Romans saw desire as potentially evil in its effects, Christians saw it as evil by its very nature. In Christian culture, caring for the self took the form of renunciation and debasement of the self. Moreover, where in Greek and Roman culture moral problematizations were ultimately the responsibility of each individual who wished to give style, beauty, and grace to his existence, Christian culture employed universal ethical interdictions and rigid moral codification. Beginning in Christian cultures, the care for the self shifts from aesthetic or ethical grounds towards a hermeneutics of desire where individuals seek the deep truth of their being in their 'sexuality', a move that opens the way to modernity and its normalizing institutions. Thus, despite the fact that in secularized modern cultures science replaces religion as the locus of knowledge and value, there are fundamental continuities in terms of the hermeneutical search for the deep truth of the self and an essentialist view of the self which this project entails.

In Foucault's reading of Greco-Roman culture, ethics is the relation an individual has with itself. This is not to say that there is no social component to ethics, for mastery of and caring for the self is inscribed in a nexus of social and pedagogical relations and aims at developing onself as a better ruler over oneself and other people. Whereas other forms of ethics such as Kantianism focus on the duties and obligations a self has to others, the Greco-Roman model holds that the freedom of individuals (defined not as free will or in opposition to determinism, but in relation to mastery of one's desires) was essential for the overall good of the city and state, and that the person who could best rule himself could best rule other people. On this model, ethics is the deliberative component of free activity and the basis for a prolonged practice of the self whereby one seeks to problematize and master one's desires and to constitute oneself as a free self.

While Foucault does not uncritically affirm Greek culture, and expresses his distaste for their hierarchical and patriarchal society (1982b: pp. 231–2), the unstated normative assumption is that Greco-Roman ethical practice is superior to Christian and modern moral systems. Foucault rarely explicitly states his moral and political preferences. Indeed, the most often made criticism of his work is that he fails to define and defend the implicit normative assumptions of his analyses and politics and hence provides no theoretical basis for his vigorous critiques of domination (see Fraser 1989; Rachjman 1985; Taylor 1986; Walzer 1986; Dews 1987; Habermas 1987a and 1987b). Nevertheless, Foucault seems to suggest that Greek and Roman cultures offer contemporary individuals elements of a model for overcoming modern forms of subjectivity and creating new forms of life that break with coercive normalizing institutions of modernity. Foucault seems to be embracing the reinvention of the self as an autonomous and self-governing being who enjoys new forms of experience, pleasure, and desire in stylized forms. In a rare moment of normative declaration, he proclaims that 'We have to promote new forms of subjectivity through the refusal of this kind of [normalized] individuality which has been imposed on us for centuries' (1982a: p. 216).

But Foucault is adamant that the Greeks do not offer an 'alternative' (1982b: p. 231) for contemporary society, only an example of a non-normalizing morality which modern cultures will have to develop themselves: 'Trying to rethink the Greeks today does not consist of setting off Greek morality as the domain of morality *par excellence* which one would need for self-reflection. The point rather is to see to it that European thinking can take up Greek thinking again as an experience which took place once and with regard to which one can be completely free' (Foucault 1985: p. 7), 'free', that is, of nostalgia for a lost world or a past normative model to reproduce in the present.

Hence, the genealogical importance of Foucault's historical inquiries into ethics would seem to involve the valorization of a form of ethical practice that is non-universalizing and non-normalizing, attentive to individual differences, while emphasizing individual liberty and the larger social context of the freedom of the self. As Foucault says, 'What was missing in classical antiquity was the problematization of the constitution of the self as a subject . . . Because of this, certain questions pose themselves to us in the same terms as they were posed in antiquity. The search for styles as different from each other as possible seems to me to be one of the points on which particular groups in the past may have inaugurated searches we are engaged in today' (1985: p. 12). Ethics here depends not so much on moral norms as free choice and aesthetic criteria and avoids subjectivizing the individual into a normalized, universal ethical subject. The task is not to 'discover' oneself, one's secret inner being, but rather to continually produce oneself. A goal of genealogy here, like before, is to help delegitimize the present through a recuperation of a radically different past. Yet where earlier Foucault sought a vindication of marginalized and excluded groups, here he is analyzing the moral codes of ruling classes, finding among the privileged elite of antiquity a way of life and form of ethics radically different from what one finds in the modern world, and which presents a useful critical perspective on modernity. For Foucault now defines the task of genealogy as an attempt to create a space for freedom where there can be a 'constitution of ourselves as autonomous subjects' (Foucault 1984: p. 43).

Foucault still rejects essentialist liberation models that assume the self is an inner essence waiting to be liberated from its repression or alienation. He contrasts liberation with liberty, and defines the later as an ongoing ethical practice of self-mastery and care of the self. He sees liberty as 'the ontological condition of ethics' and ethics as 'the deliberate form assumed by liberty' (1988b: p. 4). Similarly, the return of the 'subject' in Foucault is not a return to a pre-archaeological – i.e., humanist or phenomenological – concept of the subject endowed with an inner essence or originary will that precedes and stands apart from the social. The subject is still discursively and socially conditioned for Foucault, and still theorized as situated within power relations; the difference is that he now sees that individuals also have the power to define their own identity, to master their body and desires, and to forge a practice of freedom through techniques of the self. What Foucault now suggests, therefore, is a dialectic between an active and creative agent and a constraining social field where freedom is achieved to the extent that one can overcome socially imposed limitations and attain self-mastery and a stylized existence. As Foucault says: 'if now I am interested . . . in the way in which the subject constitutes himself in an active fashion, by the practices of the self, these practices are nevertheless not something that the individual invents by himself. They are patterns that he finds in his culture and which are proposed, suggested, and imposed on him by his culture, his society and his social group' (1988b: p. 11).

Where earlier it could be said that Foucault privileged political issues relating to the theme of power, in his later work he states that 'what interests me is much more morals than politics or, in any case, politics as an ethics' (1984: p. 375). This is not to say that Foucault abandons his past concepts and methods, for all three 'axes' of his studies overlap in his later works on techniques of self: the archaeology of problematizations intersects with a genealogy of the ethical practices of the self. Nor is it to say that the turn to analysis of techniques of the self represents a rejection of his earlier political positions, since ethics for Foucault suggests the struggle of individuals against the forces that dominate, subjugate, and subjectify them. But the analysis of power undergoes an interesting mutation in this stage of Foucault's work. He continues to hold that all social relations are characterized by power and resistance (1988b: pp. 11–12), but he distinguishes now between power and domination, seeing domination as the solidification of power relations such that they become relatively fixed in asymmetrical forms and the spaces of liberty and resistance thus become limited (1988b: p. 12).

In the later Foucault, emphasis on technologies of the self decentres the prior emphasis on power and domination. Yet, it would be a mistake to think that domination disappears altogether in this stage of his work. First, one finds an emphasis on gaining power and domination over oneself, of subduing and mastering one's desires and body in a self-relation of 'domination–submission' and 'command–obedience' (Foucault 1986a: p. 70). Here the conflict between power and the autonomy of the self is overcome as freedom is defined as mastery of and power over oneself. Second, in his history of ethics, Foucault foregrounds the domination of men over women. He constantly stresses that the Greco-Roman project of self-mastery is a strictly male concern from which women are excluded, or, if they are included at all, it is only in order to be a better servant for the man (see 1986: pp. 22–3, 47, 83–4, 154–6) – although in Roman culture women gained a greater degree of equality with the increased importance of the marriage institution (1988a: pp. 75–80). Thus, while feminist critiques of Foucault rightly point out that his early and middle works fail to confront power in the form of male domination (see the essays in Diamond and Quinby 1988), his later works on ethics discuss to some extent gender differences and male domination.[4]

Furthermore, we find that critics like Megill (1985) and Wolin (1986) exaggerate the Nietzschean aestheticism in Foucault's work, since the concepts of aesthetics of existence and care of the self imply some form of reflexive practice, acquired habits, and cognitive capacities.[5] As Foucault emphasizes in his later works, the aesthetic stylization and practice of freedom these technologies of the self may involve are impossible without self-knowledge and rational self-control. While Foucault sometimes may have privileged the aesthetic over the cognitive component of the constitution of the self, we find a shift within the later Foucault away from an emphasis on creating one's life as a work of art toward a care of the self where he moves ever closer to some of the Enlightenment positions he earlier described under the sign of social coercion. Indeed, the later Foucault sometimes sounds almost Kantian in his later embrace of the Enlightenment 'historico-critical attitude' and its discourse of autonomy, in his concern for the question 'What are we today?', in his emphasis on the formation of oneself as a thinker and moral agent, and in his conception of philosophy as a project of critique (Foucault 1984: pp. 42ff.).[6]

Yet there are several undertheorized aspects of Foucault's later writings. While Foucault signals in places that an ethics of self-mastery and care of the self has a social dimension involving how the governing of the self is integrated into the governing of others, he does little to bring this out. He thus has no social ethics or theory of intersubjectivity – a problem we shall note in other postmodern theorists. We therefore find an individualistic turn in Foucault's later works where his earlier emphases on the politics of genealogy are submerged in the project of care for the self and where individual differences – 'the search for styles [of existence] as different as possible from each other' – are emphasized over social and political solidarity.[7] Symptomatically, the social or cultural field is defined as something that is 'imposed' rather than a positive field for self-constitution.

If Foucault intends his ethics to have a substantive social and political dimension, it is not clear how and when self-constitution leads to social contestation nor why care of the self – especially in our present culture dominated by therapeutic and media industries – does not lead to narcissistic self-absorption and a withdrawal from the complexities and vicissitudes of social and political life. We are not arguing for any false separation between ethics and politics for, certainly, the struggle against the disciplinary archipelago within each one of us is an important political act and on this count ethics can be seen as an extension of Foucault's earlier micropolitical concerns. But this struggle has to be placed in a larger sociopolitical context that Foucault only hints at and does not specify; and the emphasis on personal ethics should be supplemented with a social ethics that is lacking in Foucault.

In general, while Foucault has developed an interesting new perspective that overcomes some of the problems of his genealogical stage, such as speaking of political resistance on one hand and rejecting the category of the subject on the other, he creates for himself a whole new set of problems. In particular, he does not adequately mediate the shift from technologies of domination to technologies of the self and fails to clarify the connections between ethics, aesthetics, and politics. He did not, therefore, accomplish his task 'to show the interaction between these two types of self' (Foucault 1982c: p. 10), between the constituted and constituting self.

Thus, he leaves untheorized the problem of how technologies of the self can flourish in our present era which, as he claims, is saturated with power relations. His attempts to situate discursive shifts within a social and historical setting remain vague and problematic (for example, his attempt to 'explain' the social and political forces behind the Roman cultivation of the self; see 1988a: pp. 71–95). Moreover, Daraki notes (1986), there is a symptomatic displacement of politics and democracy in Foucault's study of the Greeks. His focus is solely on sexuality and the techniques of self-constitution rather than on the Greek practices of democratic self-government. Foucault stresses that mastery of the self is essential for mastery of others, but nowhere discusses the constitution of the self through democratic social practices. This omission points to a typical ignoring of democracy, a word he rarely employs, which points to his decentring of politics and his individualistic tendencies, since democracy is a socially constituted project. And Foucault downplays the importance of the demise of the city state in the transition from Greece to Rome, as if the disappearance of democracy was not a key factor in the 'withdrawal into the self' in Rome which Foucault himself presents as a key feature of the era.

Foucault's continued refusal to specify alternative modes of subjectivity and social organization to those of modernity, and to develop a normative standpoint from which to criticize domination and project alternative forms of social and individual organization undermines the critical import of his work. Against conventional Foucault scholarship, Gandal (1986) persuasively argues that Foucault resists specifying his values and normative beliefs not because he feared reproducing power (Foucault understood that everything is more or less cooptable), but because he was concerned strictly with the strategic uses of his ideas, rather than their justifications. While Gandal provides a lucid account of Foucault's politics, his apologetics fail to grasp that Foucault's refusal to specify his normative commitments, whatever the practical efficacy of his positions, forces him into vague formulations, as when it prevents him from clarifying what our freedom should be from and for.

2.4 Foucauldian Perspectives: Some Critical Comments

Foucault's work has had a profound impact on virtually every field in the humanities and social sciences. Undoubtedly, one of the most valuable aspects of his work is to sensitize theorists to the pervasive operations of power and to highlight the problematic or suspicious aspects of rationality, knowledge, subjectivity, and the production of social norms. In richly detailed analyses, he demonstrates how power is woven into all aspects of social and personal life, pervading the schools, hospitals, prisons, and social sciences.

Following Nietzsche, Foucault questions seemingly beneficent forms of thought and value (such as humanism, self-identity, and utopian schemes) and forces us to rethink them anew. Where Nietzsche showed how the highest values have the lowliest 'origins', for example, how morality is rooted in immorality and resentment, and how all values and knowledge are manifestations of the will to power, Foucault exposes the links between power, truth, and knowledge, and describes how liberal–humanist values are intertwined with and supports of technologies of domination. Foucault's work is a powerful critique both of macrotheorists who see power only in terms of class or the state, and microtheorists who analyze institutions and face-to-face interaction while ignoring power altogether.

For all its virtues, however, Foucault's work also suffers from a number of limitations. While Foucault came to acknowledge some positive aspects of Enlightenment reason, he failed to follow suit for the institutions and technologies of modernity. His critique of modernity remains too one-sided in its focus on repressive forms of rationalization and fails to delineate any progressive aspects of modernity (see Merquior 1985; Walzer 1986; Taylor 1986; Habermas 1987a). On Foucault's scheme, modernity brings no advances in medicine, democracy, or literacy, but only in the efficacy of domination. While Habermas' characterization of Foucault as a 'young conservative' (1983) is problematic and itself one-dimensional (see Fraser 1989: pp. 35–54), he has correctly observed that Foucault describes all aspects of modernity as disciplinary and ignores the progressive aspects of modern social and political forms in terms of advances in liberty, law, and equality (see 7.32).

In general, Foucault's writings tend to be one-sided. His archaeological works privilege discourse over institutions and practices, his genealogical works emphasize domination over resistance and self-formation, and his later works analyze the constitution of the self apart from detailed considerations of social power and domination. The shift from technologies of domination to technologies of the self is abrupt and unmediated, and Foucault never adequately theorizes both sides of the structure/agency problem. He leaves behind his earlier political positions for a 'politics as ethics' and shifts the focus from analysis of social institutions to analysis of medical and philosophical texts of antiquity, never returning to analysis of the present era and its urgent political issues.

Moreover, while Foucault has argued that power breeds resistance and has on occasion pointed to tactics of resistance, there is no adequate description of resistance, the scope, detail, and rigour of which approaches the analysis of technologies of domination. To put it another way, a *genealogy of resistance* remains to be written as a full-scale study and historical perspective in its own right. Interestingly, in his later essay 'The Subject and Power' (1982a: pp. 210–11), Foucault proposes an alternative method of studying power relations: from the perspective of resistance to power rather than the exercise of power. This is similar to the proposal of Antonio Negri (1984) who analyzed class struggle from the perspective of the 'self-valorization' of workers against capital.[8] But Foucault never followed through on this proposal, nor did he ever adequately specify the meaning of the terms struggle, force relations, resistance, and opposition, the same problem for which he chastized Marxist analyses of class struggle (Foucault 1980a: p. 208). In his later work he might have theorized political resistance as a form of technologies of the self, as a creative response to coercive practices, but, as we have been arguing, Foucault's later work lacks substantive political dimensions.

On Foucault's account, power is mostly treated as an impersonal and anonymous force which is exercized apart from the actions and intentions of human subjects. Foucault methodologically brackets the question of who controls and uses power for which interests to focus on the means by which it operates. Whatever new light this perspective sheds in its emphasis that power operates in a diffuse force-field of relations of subjugation and struggle, it occludes the extent to which power is still controlled and administered by specific and identifiable agents in positions of economic and political power, such as members of corporate executive boards, bankers, the mass media, political lobbyists, land developers, or zealous outlaws in the Pentagon and White House.

While Foucault opens up a space for rethinking power and political strategies, he provides very little positive content with which to fill it and has no means whatsoever for a normative grounding of the critique of domination. Since his emphasis is on the microlevel of resistance, Foucault does not adequately address the problem of how to achieve alliances within local struggles or how an oppositional political movement might be developed. If indeed it is important to multiply and autonomize forms of resistance to counter the numerous tentacles of power, it is equally important to link these various struggles to avoid fragmentation. The question becomes: how can we create, in Gramsci's terms, a 'counter-hegemonic bloc'? This is a question which concerns Guattari, Laclau and Mouffe, some feminists, and Jameson, but to which Foucault has no response. At times, he seems to recognize the problem, as when he speaks of the 'danger of remaining at the level of conjunctural struggles' and 'the risk of being unable to develop these struggles for lack of a global [!] strategy or outside support' (1980a: p. 130). But he then dodges the problem, retreats to an insistence of the efficacy of 'specific struggles', and speaks as though larger macrostruggles would somehow take shape on their own accord apart from the strategies and intentions of human subjects.

Moreover, Foucault rarely analyzes the important role of macro-powers such as the state or capital. While in *Madness and Civilization* and *Discipline and Punish* he occasionally points to the determining power of capitalism, and in *The History of Sexuality* he sees the state as an important component of 'bio-power', macrological forces are seriously undertheorized in his work. In Foucault's defence, it could be argued that his intention is to offer novel perspectives on power as a diffuse, disciplinary force, but his microperspectives nevertheless need to be more adequately conjoined with macroperspectives that are necessary to illuminate a wide range of contemporary issues and problems such as state power (as manifested in oppressive laws or increasingly powerful surveillance technologies) and the persistence of class domination and the hegemony of capital.

As Poulantzas (1978) observes, Foucault seriously understates the continued importance of violence and overt repression. For Poulantzas, by contrast, '*State-monopolized physical violence per-manently underlies the techniques of power and mechanisms of consent: it is inscribed in the web of disciplinary and ideological devices; and even when not directly exercized, it shapes the materiality of the social body upon which domination is brought to bear*' (1978: p. 81). Poulantzas does not deny the validity of Foucault's perspective of disciplinary power, he only insists that it wrongly abstracts from state power and repression which, for Poulantzas, are the conditions of possibility of a disciplinary society. As we shall see, the neglect of macrotheory and political economy is a recurrent lacuna of all postmodern theory (see Chapter 8).

In order to more satisfactorily analyze the totalizing operations of macropowers, Foucault would have to modify his 'theory-as-tool-kit' approach and adopt a more systemic mode of analysis. In fact, there are numerous places in his texts where he lapses into totalizing claims and positions and tries to theorize certain types of unities or systems. One often finds highly general statements about power and domination that apply to all societies: 'in any society, there are manifold relations of power' whose existence depends on the production and circulation of 'a certain economy of discourses and truth' (Foucault 1980a: p. 93). Similarly, he has spoken about relations of power whose 'interconnections delineate general conditions of domination' where 'domination is organised into a more-or-less coherent and unitary strategic form' (1980a: p. 142). He has even referred to 'the global functioning of . . a *society of normalisation*' (1980a: p. 107).

Thus, Foucault utilizes global and totalizing concepts as he simultaneously prohibits them, resulting in a 'performative contradiction' (Habermas). Our quarrel with Foucault is not that such generalized statements or analyses are fallacious or misconceived, for we shall argue in favour of forms of systemic theory, but rather that they are inconsistent with his strident attacks on 'the tyranny of globalising discourses'. To the extent that disciplinary powers assume a 'global functioning', their analysis will require a form of global or systemic analysis. Like other poststructuralists, Foucault fails to distinguish between legitimate and illegitimate kinds of totalities and macrotheories, for example between open and heterogeneous modes of analysis that situate seemingly discrete particulars within a common context of determination, and homogeneous modes which obliterate differences among diverse phenomena. Foucault, in fact, employs both kinds of analysis, while polemicizing against totalizing thought *tout court*. If his analysis of a 'regularity in dispersion' in *The Archaeology of Knowledge* is an example of a complex and open system, his all-out attack (until his 1980s writings) on modernity, rationality, and knowledge is an example of a closed and reductive approach. In many ways,

Foucault violates his own methodological imperative to 'respect differences'.

Thus, Foucault is beset by competing theoretical commitments. He is a conflicted thinker whose work oscillates between totalizing and detotalizing impulses, discursive and bio-politics, destroying the subject and resurrecting it, assailing forms of domination but eschewing normative language and metadiscourse. He sometimes attacks the Enlightenment and modern theory *in toto* while at other times aligning himself with their progressive heritage. His later positions seek a cultivation of the subject in an individualistic mode that stands in tension with emphasis on political struggle by oppressed groups.

Ironically, this thinker often associated with the postmodern ended his career affirming Enlightenment criticism and Greek ethics while entrenched in the study of antiquity and writing in the style of a classicist. Throughout various times Foucault employed a rhetoric of the postmodern, referring to new forms of knowledge and the dawn of a new era in *The Order of Things*, to a new form of postdisciplinary and posthumanist rights in *Power/Knowledge* (1980a: p. 108), to new bodies and pleasures in *The History of Sexuality*, and to 'new forms of subjectivity' in a later essay (1982a: p. 216). Moreover, in his later work he embraces philosophy as a project of critical reflection on the contemporary era, on 'this precise moment in which we are living' (1982a: p. 216). Yet, Foucault ultimately abandoned the pathos of the postmodern to descend into the dusty archives of antiquity. He thereby not only retreated from 'an enigmatic and troubling "postmodernity"' (Foucault 1984: p. 39), he became something of a classicist and modernist with Kantian elements, while continuing the postmodern project of rejecting universal standpoints in order to embrace difference and heterogeneity. Thus, we find a complex, eclectic mixture of premodern, modern, and postmodern elements in Foucault, with the postmodern elements receding ever further into the background of his work.

As we turn now to Deleuze and Guattari, we shall find that they adopt many similar positions to Foucault, but also offer quite different perspectives on power, subjectivity, modernity, and politics, as well as providing other models of postmodern thought, writing, and living.

Notes

1. This empathy is demonstrated in the conclusion to *Madness and Civilization* (1973a), in *I, Pierre Rivière* (1975b), and in the introduction to *Herculine Barbin* (1980c).

2. Foucault has his own specialized periodizing discourse. He rarely uses the term 'modernity' and tends to speak instead of the 'modern age' which he distinguished from the Renaissance and classical eras, as well as the unnamed era that succeeds it which could be called, literally, postmodern. We sometimes collapse Foucault's distinction between the classical and modern eras to speak of his 'critique of modernity', since the disciplinary and normalizing powers of the modern era begin in the classical era. Moreover, Foucault rarely mentions and nowhere adopts the discourse of the postmodern. In response to one interviewer's question about postmodernity, Foucault says, 'What are we calling postmodernity? I'm not up to date . . . I do not understand what kind of problem is common to the people we call postmodern or poststructuralist' (Foucault 1988d: pp. 33–4). Of course, Foucault might be speaking ironically or playfully here and may know more about these discourses than he is letting on. Whether Foucault is knowledgeable of these developments or not, there are salient postmodern aspects to his thought and he periodizes a postmodern break in history. In the final chapter of *The Order of Things*, and in a 1967 interview (1989: p. 30), he says, 'I can define the modern age in its singularity only by opposing it to the seventeenth century on one hand and to us on the other; it is necessary, therefore in order to be able to continuously establish the division, to make the difference that separates us from them surge up under each of our sentences.' He then says the 'modern age . . . begins around 1790–1810 and goes to around 1950'.

3. Nietzsche's perspectival theory, however, did not commit him to relativism of the kind that all values are equally good or plausible, since he believed that the perspectives of the 'higher types' were superior to those of the 'lower types' and he even appealed to life, instincts, and the will to power to attempt a non-arbitrary grounding of his positions. Foucault certainly does not develop a normative philosophy of the *Übermensch*, but like Nietzsche he does not believe all perspectives are equally valid, rejecting conventional views of history and philosophical theories such as phenomenological theories of the subject, for example, as erroneous, and privileging Greek ethics over Christian morality.

4. Yet Foucault never developed a critical analysis of patriarchy in modern culture and nowhere developed a critique of the family as an institution that oppresses women and children.

5. Wolin (1986) commits a genetic fallacy, reducing Foucault's problematic to that of his two major philosophical sources, Nietzsche and Heidegger. Wolin follows Megill in accepting overly aestheticist readings of all three thinkers. In particular, Megill and Wolin exaggerate the primacy of aestheticist motifs in the early Foucault and fail to note the shift in the last works and interviews from the rhetoric of almost all

Foucault commentators of an aesthetics of existence to that of care of the self and practices of freedom. We find that most interpreters of Foucault who miss this shift tend to totalize marginal asides into general positions. Aestheticism is a perpetual temptation for Foucault, but he ultimately rejects it in turning to stress the importance of care of the self, Enlightenment autonomy, and the practices of freedom (see Foucault 1984; 1988b; 1988c).

6. Foucault is careful, however, to separate the Enlightenment, which for him has redeeming aspects, from humanism, which he believes does not, and to reconstruct Enlightenment critique in non-universalizing and non-transcendental forms (see 1984: pp. 43–6).

7. The political omissions in the later Foucauldian analyses are especially surprising since, as Gandal notes (1984: p. 134), Foucault continued to work on political problems such as prisons until the end of his life.

8. For a trenchant critique of monolithic domination models of the Frankfurt School and the alternative perspectives of 'Italian New Left' theorists such as Negri and Tronti who focus on workers' resistance to capital, see Cleaver 1979. For a Foucauldian analysis of the history of prisons that focuses on practices of resistance by various confined groups, see O'Brien 1982.

Chapter 3

Deleuze and Guattari: Schizos, Nomads, Rhizomes

> We live today in the age of partial objects, bricks that have been shattered to bits, and leftovers . . . We no longer believe in a primordial totality that once existed, or in a final totality that awaits us at some future date (Deleuze and Guattari 1983: p. 42).

> A theory does not totalize; it is an instrument for multiplication and it also multiplies itself . . . It is in the nature of power to totalize and . . . theory is by nature opposed to power (Deleuze 1977a: p. 208).

Gilles Deleuze and Félix Guattari have embarked on postmodern adventures that attempt to create new forms of thought, writing, subjectivity, and politics. While they do not adopt the discourse of the postmodern, and Guattari (1986) even attacks it as a new wave of cynicism and conservativism, they are exemplary representatives of postmodern positions in their thoroughgoing efforts to dismantle modern beliefs in unity, hierarchy, identity, foundations, subjectivity and representation, while celebrating counterprinciples of difference and multiplicity in theory, politics, and everyday life.

Their most influential book to date, *Anti-Oedipus* (1983; orig. 1972) is a provocative critique of modernity's discourses and institutions which repress desire and proliferate fascist subjectivities that haunt even revolutionary movements. Deleuze and Guattari have been political militants and perhaps the most enthusiastic proponents of a micropolitics of desire that seeks to

76

precipitate radical change through a liberation of desire. Hence, they anticipate the possibility of a new postmodern mode of existence where individuals overcome repressive modern forms of identity and stasis to become desiring nomads in a constant process of becoming and transformation.

Deleuze is a professor of philosophy who in the 1950s and 1960s gained attention for his studies of Spinoza, Hume, Kant, Nietzsche, Bergson, Proust and others. Guattari is a practising psychoanalyst who since the 1950s has worked at the experimental psychiatric clinic, La Borde. He was trained in Lacanian psychoanalysis, has been politically active from an early age, and participated in the events of May 1968. He has collaborated with Italian theorist Antonio Negri (Guattari and Negri 1990) and has been involved in the 'autonomy' movement which seeks an independent revolutionary movement outside of the structures of organized parties. Deleuze and Guattari's separate careers first merged in 1969 when they began work on *Anti-Oedipus*. This was followed by *Kafka: Toward a Minor Literature* (1986; orig. 1975), *A Thousand Plateaus* (1987; orig. 1980), and numerous independent works by each author.

There are many interesting similarities and differences between their work and Foucault's. Like Foucault, Deleuze was trained in philosophy and Guattari has worked in a psychiatric hospital, becoming interested in medical knowledge as an important form of social control. Deleuze and Guattari follow the general tenor of Foucault's critique of modernity. Like Foucault, their central concern is with modernity as an unparalleled historical stage of domination based on the proliferation of normalizing discourses and institutions that pervade all aspects of social existence and everyday life.

Their perspectives on modernity are somewhat different, however. Most conspicuously, where Foucault tended toward a totalizing critique of modernity, Deleuze and Guattari seek to theorize and appropriate its positive and liberating aspects, the decoding of libidinal flows initiated by the dynamics of the capitalist economy. Unlike Foucault, Deleuze and Guattari's work is less a critique of knowledge and rationality than of capitalist society; consequently, their analyses rely on traditional Marxist categories more than Foucault's. Like Foucault, however, they by no means identify themselves as Marxists and reject dialectical methodology for a postmodern logic of difference, perspectives, and fragments. Also, while all three foreground the importance of theorizing micro-structures of domination, Deleuze and Guattari more clearly address the importance of macrostructures as well and develop a detailed critique of the state.

Further, where Foucault's emphasis is on the disciplinary tech-nologies of modernity and the targeting of the body within regimes of power/knowledge, Deleuze and Guattari focus on the colonization of desire by various modern discourses and institutions. While desire is a sub-theme in Foucault's later genealogy of the subject, it is of primary importance for Deleuze and Guattari.[1] Con-sequently, psychoanalysis, the concept of psychic repression, engagements with Freudo-Marxism, and the analysis of the family and fascism play a far greater role in the work of Deleuze and Guattari than Foucault, although their critique of psychoanalysis builds on Foucault's critique of Freud, psychiatry, and the human sciences.

In contrast to Foucault who emphasizes the productive nature of power and rejects the 'repressive hypothesis', Deleuze and Guattari readily speak of the 'repression' of desire and they do so, as we shall argue, because they construct an essentialist concept of desire. In addition, Deleuze and Guattari's willingness to champion the liberation of bodies and desire stands in sharp contrast to Foucault's sympathies to the Greco-Roman project of mastering the self. All three theorists, however, attempt to decentre and liquidate the bourgeois, humanist subject. Foucault pursues this through a critical archaeology and genealogy that reduces the subject to an effect of discourse and disciplinary practices, while Deleuze and Guattari pursue a 'schizoanalytic' destruction of the ego and superego in favour of a dynamic unconscious. Although Foucault later qualified his views on the subject, all three theorists reject the modernist notion of a unified, rational, and expressive subject and attempt to make possible the emergence of new types of decentred subjects, liberated from what they see to be the terror of fixed and unified identities, and free to become dispersed and multiple, reconstituted as new types of subjectivities and bodies.

All three writers have shown high regard for each other's work. In his book *Foucault* (1988; orig. 1986 p. 14), Deleuze hails Foucault as a radically new thinker whose work 'represents the most decisive step yet taken in the theory-practice of multiplicities'.

For his part, Foucault (1977: p. 213) claims that Deleuze and Guattari's work was an important influence on his theory of power and has written a laudatory introduction to *Anti-Oedipus*. In his review of Deleuze's work in 'Theatrum Philosophicum' (1977: pp. 165–96), Foucault praises him for contributing to a critique of Western philosophical categories and to a positive knowledge of the historical 'event'. Modestly downplaying his own place in history, Foucault even claims (1977: p. 165) that 'perhaps one day, this century will be known as Deleuzian'. In the dialogue 'Intellectuals and Power' (Foucault 1977: pp. 205–17), Foucault and Deleuze's voices freely interweave in a shared project of constructing a new definition of theory which is always–already practice and 'local and regional' in character.

In this chapter we follow the odyssey of Deleuze and Guattari's work from Deleuze's early attempts to construct a radical Nietzschean philosophy of difference and Guattari's essays on micropolitics to their collaborations in *Anti-Oedipus* and *A Thousand Plateaus*. Their works subvert the distinction between philosophy and art and are playful in spirit and innovative in form, yet they are also quite serious in their philosophical and political goals. Their writings attempt to theorize a dynamic world of becoming comprised of desiring 'intensities' and non-totalizable multiplicities. This world is described through their key concepts of schizos, nomads, and rhizomes and we read these figures as presenting a postmodern theory and politics of desire that attempts to critically analyze modernity and facilitate the construction of some new, unspecified, postmodern/postcapitalist social order.

3.1 Deleuze's Nietzsche

What I detested more than anything else was Hegelianism and the Dialectic (Deleuze 1977b: p. 112).

There is no being beyond becoming, nothing beyond multiplicity, neither multiplicity nor becoming are appearances or illusion (Deleuze 1983: pp. 23–24).

While Sartre was claiming that Marxism is 'the unsurpassable philosophy of our time' and Althusser was working to establish it as a 'rigorous science', other intellectuals in France during the 1960s were turning elsewhere for an alternative to Marx, Hegel, dialectics, and the phenomenological tradition which culminated in the work of Merleau-Ponty. Theorists such as Foucault, Deleuze, and Derrida were searching for a new theory of difference, a non-dialectical theory which theorized difference on its own terms, freed from any unifying or synthesizing schemes. The political context for this turn from Marxism involved the revulsion on the left from the dogmatic and reactionary character of the Communist Party and the complexity of political forces operating in May 1968. Both factors led many French intellectuals to break from Marxist discourse as too rigid a framework for analyzing social reality. But Nietzsche's work provided the positive example and inspiration for theorizing a new logic of difference fundamental to poststructuralism and postmodernism (see 1.2).

While Nietzsche's thought was already introduced in France by thinkers such as Gide, Bataille, Klossowski, and Blanchot, it was Deleuze's *Nietzsche and Philosophy* (1983; orig. 1962) that promoted Nietzsche as a coherent philosopher and new figurehead of French theory during the 1960s and 1970s (Bogue 1989). Deleuze's own turn to Nietzsche came at a time in his career when he was studying various anti-rationalists that appealed to him after his classical training in the rationalist and scholastic traditions. Deleuze became fascinated with 'authors who seemed to form a part of the history of philosophy, but who escaped from it in one respect, or altogether: Lucretius, Spinoza, Hume, Nietzsche, Bergson' (Deleuze and Parnet 1987: pp. 14–15). These thinkers were united by a 'secret link which resides in the critique of negativity, the cultivation of joy, the hatred of interiority, the exteriority of forces and relations, the denunciation of power' (Deleuze 1977b: p. 112).

As Descombes observes (1980: p. 152), Deleuze can be read as a Nietzschean-inspired post-Kantian who attempts to follow through on Kant's critical philosophy which boldly attacked traditional concepts of Western rationality such as soul, world, and God, but was uncritical of other central concepts like Beauty, Truth, and the Good, values which Nietzsche thoroughly problematized in his genealogies. Like Nietzsche, Deleuze holds that the role of philosophy is a critical one: 'Philosophy is at its most positive as critique: an enterprise of demystification' (Deleuze quoted in Descombes 1980: p. 153).

In *Nietzsche and Philosophy*, Deleuze reads Nietzsche as a

radical critic of systematic, totalizing, and nihilistic modes of
thought, trying to advance beyond Platonism, French rationalism,
and German dialectics. A key focus of the book is Nietzsche's
attack on dialectical thought and his construction of an alternative
theory of difference, becoming, and valuation rooted in a theory
of natural and biological forces. Eliding his own voice with
Nietzsche's, Deleuze celebrates plurality and attacks dialectics as a
totalizing and reductionistic mode of thought.

On Deleuze's interpretation, Nietzsche holds that reality consists of differing quantities of forces, the dynamic phenomena that
constitute the world, driven by an inner will. Renouncing atomist
metaphysics and static philosophies of Being, Nietzsche claims
that forces exist in antagonistic relations with one another, relations of domination rooted in hierarchical patterns of command
and obedience. Any body, 'chemical, biological, social, or political', is defined as a relationship between dominant and dominated
forces. As is evident in the human realm of 'higher' and 'lower',
'active' and 'reactive' types – those who affirm existence and
promote values of strength and those who disparage it from a
morality of weakness – different quantities of force lead to
qualitatively different phenomena. The will to power, which differentiates living forces, is the most encompassing principle of reality.
Although the will to power is also a synthesizing force, creating
diverse relations and underlying everything, the plurality of forces
in the world is irreducible. 'The monism of the will to power is
inseparable from a pluralist typology' (Deleuze 1983: p. 86).

Nietzsche's pluralism is radically different from the dialectical
theory of difference. On Deleuze's reading, Hegel and other
dialecticians claim that reality is generated through the antagonistic construction of polar opposite phenomena, through the
'labour of the negative'. Ostensibly, this is a dynamic interpretation of the world, but Deleuze sees it as a theological outlook
where differences are always subsumed to an underlying unity,
contradictions always seek a higher synthesis, and movement
ultimately results in stasis and death. Lost in scientific abstractions
and mired in a logic of identity, dialectics is 'unaware of the real
element from which forces, their qualities and their relations
derive' and is blind to 'the far more subtle and subterranean
differential mechanisms' (1983: p. 157) that constitute reality
through the will to power. Only genealogy can given an adequate

account of the differential nature of values and the world; dialectics remains 'a perpetual misinterpretation of difference itself, a confused inversion of genealogy' (ibid.).

Deleuze's study is an illuminating reading of Nietzsche's enigmatic aphorisms and fragments; his book makes explicit implicit ideas, developing some of Nietzsche's ideas beyond what Nietzsche himself had done (for example, Nietzsche's theory of active and reactive forces) and, ironically, bringing them together in a systematic reading of a thinker who many see as resolutely unsystematic. It is in Nietzsche, in large part, that Deleuze finds an alternative to dialectical thought, one that affirms difference apart from a relation to a 'higher' unity, and a notion of desire (in its affirmative capacity) as productive and creative, rather than as suffering, lack, and negativity. Deleuze also shares Nietzsche's basic attitudes toward philosophy. For both thinkers, the task of philosophy is to criticize the verities of Western philosophy; to reject stable identities and affirm difference, chance, chaos, and becoming; and to overcome nihilism and create new forms and possibilities of thought and life, which requires, in large part, a revaluation of the creative capacities of the body in its primordial forces and desires.

Hence, Nietzsche's thought was indispensable for Deleuze's early construction of a postmodern epistemology that is non-essentialist, non-representational, pluralist, anti-humanist, and 'resolutely anti-dialectical' in character. The dynamism of Nietzsche's account of power and his valorization of active forces is transcoded in Deleuze's early works and collaborations with Guattari as a theory of constitutive desire that champions desire's productivity and condemns the social forces that seek to weaken and immobilize it. Nietzsche's attack on all philosophies of Being and his dynamic view of a world in constant flux, transformation, and becoming was immensely influential on their concepts of desire and their critiques of Western philosophy. The critical function of Nietzsche's philosophical demystification is realized in Deleuze and Guattari's later nomadic thought which explodes all forms of generalized order, totality, hierarchy, and foundational principles, and attacks the philosophical imperialism of 'state-thought'. Nietzsche's emphasis on affirmative thought animates the efforts of their later writings to create new concepts and values without nostalgia for the old.

Nietzsche's critique of representation was also influential for Deleuze and Guattari and postmodern theory. This critique has two different components: (1) an attack on realist theories that claims subjects can accurately reflect or represent the world in thought without the mediations of culture, language, and physiology; (2) a *Lebensphilosophie* which privileges the body and its forces, desires, and will over conscious existence and representational schemes. The first theme assails the subject–object distinction of modern epistemology where a neutral and objective world is mirrored in the receptive mind of a passive subject. Rejecting this view, postmodern theorists argue that the perception of the world is mediated through discourse and a socially constructed subjectivity. Theorists such as Deleuze and Guattari and Lyotard argue on behalf of the dynamic and indeterminate aspects of reality which representationalist schemes try to fix and stabilize through foundations of knowledge. Their philosophy of desire also attacks representation in the broader sense of totalizing discourses, humanist frameworks, and cognitive schemes in general. They see these as derivative from primordial states of affective existence and as repressive totalizations of difference and bodily 'intensities', or punctuated bursts of desiring energies.

In his subsequent books *Différence et répétition* (1968) and *Logic of Sense* (1989; orig. 1969), Deleuze no longer 'explicates' (in his transformative way) the thought of others, but now speaks in his own voice, working out his philosophy of difference in complex detail through innovative stylistic forms. In *Différence et répétition*, where he combines the genres of science fiction and detective story, his project is to overturn Plato and Kant. Plato laboured to distinguish between the realm of ideas and their copies in the physical world, and between good and bad copies, stigmatizing bad copies as simulacra that caused ontological confusion and threatened the world of ideal forms. Deleuze attempts to deconstruct the opposition between essence and appearance and to recuperate the phenomena that Plato tries to repress – difference, impermanence, contradiction, non-identity, and simulacra.

Against Kant's transcendental idealism which tried to uncover the *a priori* categories of the mind that make sense experience possible while being divorced from it, Deleuze championed an empirical and sensual realm of dynamic intensities and a mode of thought which is aconceptual, non-representational and unconscious. Where Kant's faculties of the mind tried to establish the identity of the subject and a common-sense representation of the object, Deleuze develops the category of 'difference in itself' that eludes apprehension by common sense and representation by concepts.

In *Logic of Sense*, Deleuze attempts to write a 'logical and psychoanalytic novel' in thirty-four different sections, or 'series'. Each series analyzes a different paradox and Deleuze's analyses range from the Stoic theory of universals to the 'nonsense' works of Lewis Carroll. Once again, Deleuze's focus is on criticizing identity logic and privileging the prerepresentational realms of bodies and their intensities over representational schemes of meaning. Deleuze describes a primal realm of undifferentiated bodies from which emerge the structures of the ego and superego. He connects the nonsense texts of Carroll to the discourse of schizophrenics and analyzes schizophrenic experiences of language and the body. For schizophrenics, words enter the body as animate, corporeal, fragments of nonsense and leave the body as unarticulated phonic waves. In a parallel way, schizophrenics experience the body both as a random jumble of fragmented parts, and as a solidified, unindividuated, mass which Deleuze terms, borrowing from Antonin Artaud, the 'body without organs'.

As Deleuze was developing a theory of desire and a new postmodern philosophy of difference that broke with Western totalizing and representational schemes, Guattari was working within radical political organizations, a psychiatric clinic, and was participating in groups devoted to studying institutional forms of domination. As is evident from a collection of his published papers from the 1950s and 1960s, *Psychanalyse et transversalité* (1972), some of which are collected in *Molecular Revolution* (1984) Guattari was experimenting with efforts to merge Freud and Marx and produce new micropolitical theories. In his chronological overview of these early essays, Stivale (1984) distinguishes four periods in Guattari's development: essays written up to 1968 where he develops a theory of the nature of the group within the psychiatric institution; essays written between 1969 and 1972 where he formulates a machinic theory of desire; essays on molecular politics from 1973 to 1978 that theorize the micropolitics of desire and construct a theory of semiotics using Hjelmslevian linguistics; and the post-1979 essays on schizoanalysis and radical politics. Among Guattari's major concerns is the social constitution of the individual libido, capitalism as a world system that creates new forms of control as it erodes old ones, and a sharp critique of leftist bureaucratic structures.

Despite their different approaches, backgrounds, and focuses, Deleuze and Guattari found a common rallying point in creating a revolutionary philosophy and politics of desire and their collaboration process began in 1969 with work on *Anti-Oedipus*.

3.2 *Anti-Oedipus*: Psychoanalysis, Capitalism, and Normalization

> The problem for capitalism is to link . . . energy in a world axiomatic which always opposes new interior limits to the revolutionary power of decoded flux (Deleuze and Guattari 1983).

Anti-Oedipus, the first volume of *Capitalism and Schizophrenia*, was a *succès de scandale* for its radical political positions; its critique of state and party worshipping forms of Marxism; its assault on Lacanian psychoanalysis at the apogee of its influence; and its dramatic poststructuralist attacks on representation, interpretation, the modern subject, and 'the tyranny of the signifier'. In contemporary social conditions where psychoanalysis has perhaps become a state religion and therapists state priests, some writers see the book as the 'modern counterpart' (Bogue 1989) of Nietzsche's *The Anti-Christ*. Deleuze and Guattari's emphases in their earlier work are readily identifiable in this collaboration and merge in interesting ways.

As we shall read it, *Anti-Oedipus* attempts to provide a materialist, historically-grounded, Foucauldian-inspired critique of modernity with a focus on capitalism, the family, and psychoanalysis. Their work attempts to subvert all theoretical and institutional barriers to 'desiring-production' in order to create new postmodern 'schizo-subjects' who 'unscramble the codes' of modernity and become reconstituted as nomadic desiring-machines. Their positive alternative to psychoanalysis, schizo-analysis, can be read as a postmodern theory/practice that deconstructs modern binaries and breaks with modern theories of the subject, representational modes of thought, and totalizing practices. Schizoanalysis articulates new postmodern positions organized around the concepts of plurality, multiplicity, and decentredness, and attempts to help create new postmodern forms of thought, politics, and subjectivity.

3.2.1 Desire, Modernity, and Schizoanalysis

Deleuze and Guattari start from the Reichian axiom that 'desire is revolutionary in its essence' (1983: p. 116). As revolutionary, desire upsets and subverts any form of society, or 'socius'. They rewrite Reich's theory within a postmodern context that interprets desire as decentred, fragmented, and dynamic in nature. Desire 'operates in the domain of free synthesis where everything is possible' (1983: p. 54) and it always seeks more objects, connections, and relations than any socius can allow, pursuing 'nomadic and polyvocal' rather than 'segregative and biunivocal' flows. Thus, the first order of business for a society is to tame and repress desire, to 'territorialize' it within closed structures. 'To code desire . . . is the business of the socius' (1983: p. 139).

Moreover, Deleuze and Guattari assert that desire, like power for Foucault, is fundamentally positive and productive in nature, operating not in search of a lost object which would consummate and complete it, but out of the productive plenitude of its own energy which propels it to seek ever new connections and instantiations. Hence, desire cannot be theorized in Hegelian, Freudian, or Lacanian terms as lack – 'an idealist (dialectical, nihilistic) conception' (1983: p. 25) – and is better theorized as a kind of dynamic machine. Deleuze and Guattari insist that this is no mere metaphor, that desire actually is a machine: it produces things ('alliances' and reality itself), it runs in discontinuous fluxes and 'break-flows', always making connections with ('partial') objects and other desiring-machines.

The emphasis on desire as the primary reality of subjective and social being signals a shift away from modern theories of representation, totality, and subjectivity. As Deleuze defined it (Deleuze and Parnet 1987: p. 78), desire 'is the system of a-signifying signs with which fluxes of the unconscious are produced in a social field.' Unlike 'signifying semiologies', a – signifying semiotics operates prior to representation, linguistic schemes, and social regulative codes.[2] A-signifying semiotics 'do not produce effects of meaning and ... are capable of entering into direct relations with their referents' (Guattari 1984: p. 290). Desire is the constant production of affective and libidinal energy generated by the unconscious in various types of 'syntheses'. Seeking inclusive rather than exclusive relations, desire is a free-flowing physical energy that establishes random, fragmented, and multiple connections with material flows and partial objects. There is no enunciating subject of desire, nor any proper object of desire, '[f]luxes are the only objectivity of desire itself' (Deleuze and Parnet 1987: p. 78). The unconscious 'is not essentially centred on human subjectivity. It partakes of the spread of signs from the most disparate social and material flows' (Guattari 1979: p. 46).

Hence, mental representation of this reality is thoroughly derivative and rationalist schemes of representation and interpretation are rejected as repressive impositions that fix and stabilize desiring flows, and thereby dam creative energies. The thrust of their attack on psychoanalysis is that it transforms machinic desire into a passive theatre of representation that confines desire within the circumscribed field of Oedipus and the family. Opposing such schemes, Deleuze and Guattari call for 'direct contact [of desire] with material or semiotic fluxes' (Guattari 1984: p. 105) and they seek a-signifying sign machines without 'despotic signifying semiologies' (ibid., p. 140). Deleuze and Guattari's position is quite different from other poststructuralists such as Derrida in that they feel the primacy of the signifier is too confined to linguistic representation and they draw distinctions between different kinds of semiotic systems.

This poststructuralist characterization of desire as incessant flux echoes Nietzsche's theory of the will to power, Lacan's emphasis on libidinal instability, Derrida's idea of dissemination, and Foucault's conception of productive power. The notion of desiring-machine works to deconstruct traditional dichotomies between subjective and objective, reality and fantasy, vitalism and mechanism, and base and superstructure. Against these dualisms, Deleuze and Guattari substitute a monist theory which claims that desire creates all social and historical reality and is part of the social infrastructure. Their materialist theory, therefore, pushes Freud beyond the boundaries of the family and into a larger social field, and Marx into a production reality that is 'immediately invested by desire'. Thus, they combine a macroanalysis of 'molar' social machines with a microanalysis of the body and its 'molecular' desiring-machines. The materialism of Deleuze and Guattari analyzes cultural, familial, and psychological developments in terms of the dynamics of the capitalist economy, but the economy itself is rooted in the materiality of desire and its physical forces.

Anti-Oedipus attempts a historical analysis of the ways in which desire is channelled and controlled by different social regimes. The process of repressing desire by taming and confining its productive energies is termed 'territorialization' and the unchaining of both material production and desire from socially restricting forces is called 'deterritorialization' or 'decoding', where the decoding of repressive social codes allows desire to move outside of restrictive psychic and spatial boundaries. Ironically, rather than pursuing a genealogy of institutions in the style of Nietzsche or Foucault, privileged figures in their work, Deleuze and Guattari employ Marx's method of a retrospective narrativization of history from the standpoint of the most historically differentiated social structure, capitalism. Capitalist society is the realization of the Oedipalization, schizophrenic, and commodification tendencies that threaten to explode all precapitalist societies. Deleuze and Guattari interpret modernity as a capitalist modernity and grant a kind of intelligibility and continuity to history that other postmodern thinkers reject. Sharply diverging from Foucault, they characterize this trajectory as a 'universal history' and they seek a 'general theory of society' based on a 'generalized theory of flows' of desire, significations, and material goods (1983: p. 262). Also like Marx, they periodize history into discernible stages, identifying relevant lines of continuity and discontinuity. Moreover, they analyze capitalism in terms of the conflictual dynamics that potentially undermine its economic system.

But they transcode their Marxist theories within a Nietzschean and Freudian context to speak of libidinal 'social machines' rather than modes of production and to analyze 'social flows' rather than structural relations. For Deleuze and Guattari, there are three main stages of history, three fundamental types of social machines, each being a different system for representing and regulating the production of goods, needs, and desire. Succeeding the 'primitive territorial machine' and the 'despotic machine', the 'capitalist machine' retains the state apparatuses created by despotic society and begins a new system of control of material and psychic existence.

In its 'cynical' desacralization of the premodern world, capitalism dissolves all premodern forms of alliances and filiations, shatters all restrictions to economic development, and thereby radically extends the decoding process. Where previously social flows were coded and overcoded, the capitalist mode of production is based on decoded flows that result from the dynamic movement of unrestrained economic production. Capitalism leads to the break-up of the feudal guild system in favour of 'free' exchange and production, replacing feudal estates with private property through commodification and the unfettering of commercial exchange. Capitalism extends market relations everywhere and creates a growing division of labour, producing the private individual with an ego/superego, as well as social and psychic fragmentation. In a double movement of liberation and alienation, capitalism produces abstract labour on one side (the terrain of political economy) and abstract desire on the other (the terrain of psychoanalysis).

Capitalism subverts all traditional codes, values, and structures that fetter production, exchange, and desire. But it simultaneously 'recodes' everything within the abstract logic of equivalence (exchange-value), 'reterritorializing' them within the state, family, law, commodity logic, banking systems, consumerism, psychoanalysis and other normalizing institutions. Capitalism substitutes for qualitative codes an 'extremely rigorous axiomatics' that quantitatively regulate and control all decoded flows. Capitalism re-channels desire and needs into inhibiting psychic and social spaces that control them far more effectively than savage and despotic societies.

On this point too, their analysis of capitalism is similar to that of Marx, who saw how capitalism 'liberates' workers, but only to deliver them over to new and more intense forms of exploitation, and also to Marcuse, who theorized capitalism in terms of the 'repressive desublimation' of desire. Indeed, the dialectic of deterritorialization and reterritorialization is perhaps most evident in the shift to consumer society where the psychological barriers of Protestantism necessary for an earlier form of capital accumulation became a barrier to further accumulation as capitalism began to manipulate people's needs and desires as well as exploiting their labour power. But while Marcuse analyzed this dialectic only in terms of the consumer culture of late capitalism, Deleuze and Guattari see it as the inherent logic of modernity.

For Deleuze and Guattari, the most significant example of capitalist deterritorialization is the production of the schizophrenic. In their analysis, schizophrenia is not an illness or biological state, but a potentially liberatory psychic condition produced within capitalist social conditions, a product of absolute decoding. As a psychic decentring process whereby subjects escape from the bourgeois reality principle, its repressive ego and superego constraints, and its Oedipal traps, the schizophrenic process poses a radical threat to the stability and reproduction of capitalism. But capitalism attempts to block its revolutionary potential as decoded flow. For Deleuze and Guattari, the schizophrenic process is the basis for a postmodern emancipation, which is to say, an emancipation from the normalized subjectivities of modernity, and they see the schizo-subject as the real subversive force in capitalism, 'its inherent tendency brought to fulfillment, its surplus product, its proletariat, its exterminating angel' (1983: p. 35).

The method whereby Deleuze and Guattari analyze the production and circulation of desire in society is termed 'schizoanalysis'. Schizoanalysis is the antithesis of psychoanalysis and rationalist Marxist politics, providing an initial articulation of a postmodern epistemology and politics that would be more fully developed in *A Thousand Plateaus* (see 3.3). Against Marxism, schizoanalysis begins with the primacy of desire and the unconscious over needs, interests, and material production. Here, of course, it follows psychoanalysis, but it operates, as we have seen, with a different conception of the unconscious, neither structural, symbolic, nor representational, 'but solely machinic and productive', a free-flowing machine rather than a closed and deterministic system. Schizoanalysis opposes the plethora of mechanisms, discourses, institutions, specialists, and authorities that block the flows of the unconscious. Deleuze and Guattari refer to the deterritorialized body as the 'body-without-organs'. The body-without-organs is not an organless body, but a body without 'organization', a body that breaks free from its socially articulated, disciplined, semioticized, and subjectified state (as an 'organism'), to become disarticulated, dismantled, and deterritorialized, and hence able to be reconstituted in new ways.

Thus, schizoanalysis has various theoretical and political tasks that can be characterized as postmodern. Theoretically, it attempts a decentred and fragmented analysis of the unconscious investments of individual and group desire in all spheres of society, theorizing how the flows of desire work, how they become integrated into repressive hierarchies and structures such that subjects come to desire their own repression, and how they can again become productive desiring-machines.

Politically, schizoanalysis attempts to destroy all unified and rigid segments of subject and group identity (comprised of 'molar lines'), while facilitating the formation of deterritorializing lines of flight ('molecular lines') on 'planes of consistency' where the body-without-organs can be produced. In their primordial state, desiring-machines are 'molecular units' without purpose or intentionality, a-signifying and non-representational in character. They are distinguished from the 'molar aggregates' which include large social machines such as economic and political institutions and the family. Under historical conditions of repression, molecular units are transformed by molar aggregates where they receive form, function, and purpose, such as when they are normalized into gender and class identities. Hence, 'molar' signifies hierarchy, stratification, and structuration, and is loosely associated with macrostructures, while 'molecular' signifies unfixed, deterritorialized, and nomadic movement which occurs on the microphysical plane of productive desire.

With regards to the individual, schizoanalysis seeks to dissolve the ego and superego and to liberate the prepersonal realm of desire that molar and representational structures repress, the libidinal flows that exist 'well below the conditions of identity' (Deleuze and Guattari 1983: p. 362). It seeks, in effect, to destroy modern identities and to create new postmodern desiring subjects. Where psychoanalysis neuroticizes, producing subjects who conform to authority and law and are repressed in their desire, schizoanalysis schizophrenicizes, opening up the lines of movement of desire away from hierarchical and socially imposed forms. For Deleuze and Guattari, the paradigm of the revolutionary is not the disciplined party man, but the schizo-subject, the one who resists the capitalist axiomatic, rejects Oedipus, unscrambles the social codes, and breaks through the walls of reterritorialization into the realm of flows, intensities, and becoming, thereby threatening the whole capitalist order. They concur with Laing and Cooper that revolutionary action requires an 'ego-loss' (Laing) or type of 'personal disintegration' (Cooper), a 'radical dissolution of fascist egoic structures that one is brought up to experience oneself in' (Cooper 1971: p. 60). For Deleuze and Guattari, the ego is 'part of these things we must dismantle through the united assault of analytical and political forces' (Deleuze and Guattari, quoted in Seem 1975: p. 176).

Hence, their postmodern rejection of the subject is more radical than Foucault's, who later attempted to rehabilitate modern notions of reason and subject. But they are frequently misunderstood to be saying that they actually celebrate schizophrenia, when in fact they qualify their position: 'We do not at all think that the revolutionary is schizophrenic or vice versa. On the contrary, we have consistently distinguished the schizophrenic as an entity from schizophrenia as a process ... This explains why we have only spoken of a schizoid pole in the libidinal investment of the social fields, so as to avoid as much as possible the confusion of the schizophrenic process with the production of a schizophrenic' (1983: p. 379). The schizophrenic process, in other words, is a decentring process that fascist, paranoid, or repressed individuals need to undergo in order to become revolutionary, but there are limits to the process beyond which one self-destructs, becoming a 'schizophrenic'. There must be a 'breakthrough' without a total 'breakdown' (1983: p. 278), a destructive transition which Deleuze and Guattari attempt to analyze in various aspects (1983: pp. 362–363). Hence, the vibrant schizo-subject is distinguished from the dysfunctional schizophrenic.

On this point, at least in relation to Foucault who empathized with the mad, criminal, and marginal of all kinds, they show themselves to be somewhat guarded: 'Marginals have always inspired fear in us, and a slight horror' (Deleuze and Parnet 1987: p. 139). Hence, in subsequent works (see Deleuze and Parnet 1987: pp. 137ff.; Deleuze and Guattari 1987: pp. 161ff.), they warn us about deterritorializing too quickly, both at the macrolevel of blowing up the state and the microlevel of the individual, where a too sudden or rapid line of flight can turn into a line of destruction or suicide.

Making desire pass from the paranoid, fascist pole to the 'schizorevolutionary' pole 'could not be accomplished without overthrowing power, without reversing subordination' (Deleuze and Guattari 1983: p. 367). With Foucault, Deleuze and Guattari agree that traditional workers' and leftist organizations are bankrupt and a 'new politics' requires micropolitical forms of struggle.

3.2.2   The Micropolitics of Desire

> Let a thousand machines of life, art, solidarity, and action sweep away the stupid and sclerotic arrogance of the old organizations! (Guattari and Negri 1990: p. 132).

Like Foucault, Deleuze and Guattari articulate a postmodern politics that draws the practical consequences of the poststructuralist critique of subjectivity, totality and representation (in its epistemological and political senses). Their concept of micropolitics is an attempt to rethink political strategies in light of developments in capitalism toward a consumer, media, and therapeutic society. They build on the theoretical advances made by the Reichian interpretation of fascism and draw from the political experiences of 1968 which created a new vision of revolution and led many theorists to embrace the new social movements and politicize everyday life.

As Foucault observes (1983: p. xiii) in his introduction to *Anti-Oedipus*, a central concern of the book is with the growth of fascism, not so much in authoritarian political movements, such as led by Hitler and Mussolini, but within each one of us, the fascism that flowers 'in our heads and in our everyday behaviour, the fascism that causes us to love power, to desire the very thing that dominates and exploits us.' Fascism is the ultimate form of modern power – 'without doubt capitalism's most fantastic attempt at economic and political reterritorialization' (Deleuze and Guattari 1983: p. 258). But where traditional Marxist analyses interpreted fascism strictly in terms of the state, overt political repression, and the crisis of capitalist accumulation, Deleuze and Guattari focus on fascism mainly as a deformation in desire and a subjective psychological condition produced in capitalist social conditions.

Following Reich, Deleuze and Guattari argue that genuinely radical politics cannot simply make rational appeals to subjects concerning the nature of their oppression and provide cogent reasons why they should overthrow their oppressors. A politics of class struggle must be superseded by a politics of desire that struggles at every microlevel where fascism and capitalism instantiate themselves to impede the flow of revolutionary forces and produce reactionary or fascist subjectivities. 'Hitler got the fascists sexually aroused. Flags, nations, armies, banks get a lot of people aroused. A revolutionary machine is nothing if it does not acquire at least as much force as these coercive machines have for producing breaks and mobilizing flows' (Deleuze and Guattari 1983: p. 293). A traditional rationalistic macropolitics leaves the terrain of desire, culture, and everyday life uncontested, precisely the spaces where subjects are produced and controlled, and where fascist movements originate. Capitalism not only exploits labour power, it works its way into the desiring economy of every subject. Deleuze and Guattari hold that the love of or acquiescence to power is not a problem of ideology, but of desire and its unconscious investments. Individuals desire their own repression when their libidos are cathected to powerful and destructive emotional sources or symbols, or demagogic leaders, rather than to political groups, ideologies, and values which promote their interests.

Hence, Deleuze and Guattari deconstruct the traditional oppositions between objective and subjective, politics and everyday life, since one's subjectivity is produced as a political operation and, conversely, changing one's everyday existence becomes a political act with potentially radical consequences. Consequently, the opposition between reformist and revolutionary tactics is problematized, and they argue that so-called 'local' or 'reformist' actions can have explosive consequences that lead to the questioning of the totality of power, such as occurred during the May 1968 events in France.

Deleuze and Guattari do not deny the need for class struggle; rather they argue that class does not exhaust the multiple forms of oppression and struggle and that important preconditions must be met before a real class struggle can be achieved – the creation of revolutionary forms of desire. In Guattari's words (1984: p. 62), the class struggle and the struggle in relation to desire 'need not be mutually exclusive'. In their collaborative work, Guattari and Negri reject the opposition between 'centre' (class) and 'margin' (students, women, etc.) which works to subordinate diverse political groupings to the fictive unity and primacy of a working class and they emphasize the need for new political alliances that decentre the position of labour. Yet while they hold that 'the discourses of workers' centrality and hegemony are thoroughly defunct' (1990: p. 122), and the traditional working classes 'no longer represent a social majority' (1990: p. 127), they continue to utilize reconstructed concepts of class and class struggle.

Thus, Deleuze and Guattari reject any firm distinction between the macropolitical and micropolitical. They argue that 'politics is simultaneously a *macropolitics* and a *micropolitics*' (1987: p. 213) insofar as every society has both repressive molar aggregates and molecular elements that intersect in complex ways (as fascism is both a macro- and micropolitical phenomenon). Hence, it is the totality of capitalist society that must be changed. They are much clearer on this point than Foucault, who often exhibits a veritable phobia of the macro.[3]

One of the central contributions of schizoanalysis is to underline the contingency of desiring formations within radical political groups. Similar to Sartre's reflections (1976) on the fragility of all revolutionary movements, where 'groups-in-fusion' ultimately collapse in seriality, Deleuze and Guattari warn that revolutionary struggles can fail since 'groups and individuals contain micro fascisms just waiting to crystallize' (1987: p. 9). They reject the Marxist revolutionary programme because it fails to grasp the primacy of the unconscious as the ultimate locus of repression and to understand that conflicts and divisions occur not only within social life, but within the subject and group itself, a disunity between the preconscious investments of class goals and interests and the far more powerful unconscious investments of desire. Since these investments are different and not necessarily compatible, it is quite possible to have subjects who are 'revolutionary' in their class interests and objectives, but reactionary or fascist in their modes of desire.

Hence, political groups must also wage permanent struggle within their own ranks. Revolutionary groups that fail to liberate desire in the process of political struggle and reproduce hierarchy and authority remain 'subjugated groups', while those groups with molecular libidinal investments are 'subject groups'. These are not rigid distinctions, since the same individual can participate in both groups (e.g., Lenin) and the same groups can simultaneously exhibit both characteristics (e.g., the surrealists).[4] The political problem is how to combat 'the deadly inclination' that makes a group pass from revolutionary libidinal investments to merely preconscious revolutionary investments, or to reformism, or even to authoritarianism. To whatever extent possible, therefore, revolutionary politics must avoid the 'molar pole' of investment, with its paranoid, structured lines of movement, stratified flows of desire, and reactionary or fascist social character, and stay within the 'molecular pole' with its schizophrenic intensities, decoded flows, and revolutionary social investments.

Given their goal not to reproduce authoritarianism within revolutionary groups, Deleuze and Guattari break with the Leninist conception of the universal intellectual, the avant-gardist party, and its centrist model of organization. Deleuze commended Foucault (1977: p. 209) for drawing the consequences of the critique of representation at the political level by repudiating the universal intellectual who 'represents' all oppressed groups and by insisting that individuals or groups should be autonomous and speak for themselves. Not surprisingly, Guattari renounces traditional leftist party organizations – Socialist, Communist, Eurocommunist – as bureaucratically deformed and antithetical to the destratification of desire in individuals and radical groups. He seeks alternative, decentralized forms of organization that maximize freedom, democracy, and creativity, as defined in more detail in his collaboration with Negri.

While there are salient postmodern aspects to these micro-political strategies, Guattari divorces his project from postmodernism. In his essay 'The Postmodern Dead End' (1986) he decries the postmodern as a cynical and reactionary 'fad', a 'new ethics of non-commitment' that paralyzes radical politics at a time when social repression and ecological crises are dramatically mounting. Guattari agrees with postmodernists that a 'certain idea of progress and of modernity has gone bankrupt', but he observes that 'in its fall it has dragged along all confidence in the notion of emancipation through social action' (1986: p. 40). He concedes we are in a novel historical situation, but he strenuously resists the idea of a 'postmodern condition' which he considers 'to be the very paradigm of every sort of submission, every sort of compromise with the existing status quo' (1986: p. 40). The postmodern suspicion of positive programmes for social action and emancipation, such as he finds in the work of Baudrillard and Lyotard, is a 'mere trap' for rejecting all forms of politics and hence for supporting the present state of affairs. Favouring activist strategies, Guattari – as we shall see is true of Laclau and Mouffe and Habermas – reaffirms modern political values and calls for a 're-invention of democracy', a project that is 'greatly facilitated' by a positive appropriation of new media and communication technologies by micropolitical groups.

Turning now toward the second volume of *Capitalism and Schizophrenia, A Thousand Plateaus*, we find that Deleuze and Guattari have by and large settled their score with modernity and psychoanalysis to embark on an affirmative voyage, a sustained celebration of difference and multiplicity which can be read as a practice of a new type of postmodern text, theory, and politics.

3.3 *A Thousand Plateaus* for the Postmodern!

> In truth, it is not enough to say 'Long live the multiple', difficult as it is to raise the cry. No typographical, lexical, or even syntactical cleverness is enough to make it heard. The multiple *must be made* (Deleuze and Guattari 1987: p. 6).

> Find your body without organs. Find out how to make it. It's a question of life and death, youth and old age, sadness and joy. It is where everything is played out (Deleuze and Guattari 1987: p. 151).

A Thousand Plateaus sets forth a postmodern theory of non-totalizable multiplicity based on the concept of the 'rhizome', their new term for deterritorialized movement. While this second volume of *Capitalism and Schizophrenia* continues the politics of difference and desire of *Anti-Oedipus*, there are also some key changes. These include a more detailed analysis of linguistics, semiotics, the schizo-subject and the state; a far greater range of material (geological, historical, anthropological, etc.); and a replacement of the molar/molecular opposition with a triadic scheme of rigid lines, supple lines, and lines of escape, where 'lines' refers to the spatial, material, and psychological components that constitute or deconstitute a society, group, or individual. But, unlike the polemically encumbered *Anti-Oedipus, A Thousand Plateaus* is mainly concerned with a positive application of postmodern thinking that analyzes the rhizomatic nature of natural, social, and personal reality.

Like *Anti-Oedipus, A Thousand Plateaus* employs avant-garde writing techniques such that the 'form' of the book becomes part of its 'content' or, rather, these distinctions break down. While *Anti-Oedipus* is a schizo-text that reproduces the delirium it analyzes through a frenzied collage of theoretical and literary figures, it nonetheless retains a certain narrative structure. *A Thousand Plateaus* uses similar bricolage techniques, but abandons any semblance of narrative or argument exposition in favour of a random, perspectival juxtaposition of chapters, or 'plateaus' (Gregory Bateson's term), comprised of complex conceptual flows. These plateaus range promiscuously across diverse topics, time frames, and disciplinary fields and are to be read, the authors suggest, in any order (with the proviso that the 'conclusion', a 'dictionary' of terms, is to be read last).

In *A Thousand Plateaus*, Deleuze and Guattari multiply the terms for their analysis – schizoanalysis, rhizomatics, pragmatics, diagrammatism, cartography, micropolitics – in order to prevent their position from stabilizing in an ideology, method, or single metaphor. If the business of philosophizing is to invent new concepts, as Deleuze believes, that is precisely what they do, making their work multiply in a myriad of conceptual matrices. As Patton points out (1984: p. 61), these concepts are not to be understood in the traditional philosophical sense where interior thought mirrors exterior reality, but are meant to be 'lines of intensities, which react upon the flow of everyday thought, forming relays between artistic, political, and other practices'.

A Thousand Plateaus is organized around the distinction between 'arborescent' and 'rhizomatic'. The 'arborescent model of thought' designates the epistemology that informs all of Western thought, from botany to information science to theology. It is well known that Western thought has long relied on the metaphor of the mirror, whereby reality is translucently reflected in consciousness (see Rorty 1979). Deleuze and Guattari argue that the Western tradition has a second major metaphor, that of the tree, whereby the mind organizes its knowledge of reality (provided by the mirror) in systematic and hierarchical principles (branches of knowledge) which are grounded in firm foundations (roots). These allow arborescent culture to build vast conceptual systems that are centred, unified, hierarchical, and grounded in a self-transparent, self-identical, representing subject. The leaves that flower on such trees have names like Form, Essence, Law, Truth, Justice, Right, and Cogito. Plato, Descartes, and Kant are arborescent thinkers who seek to eradicate temporality and multiplicity in universalizing and essentializing schemes. Information science is arborescent thought, using the imagery of command trees to hierarchize data in centred systems, and so is Chomskyean linguistics, which proceeds by sentential linear division according to the principle of dichotomy.

In contradistinction to arborescent thought, rhizomatics intends to uproot philosophical trees and their first principles to deconstruct binary logic. It seeks to extirpate roots and foundations, to thwart unities and break dichotomies, and to spread out roots and branches, thereby pluralizing and disseminating, producing differences and multiplicities, making new connections. Rhizomatics affirms the principles excluded from Western thought and reinterprets reality as dynamic, heterogeneous, and non-dichotomous. A rhizome method decentres information into divergent acentred systems and language into multiple semiotic dimensions. The affinities of Deleuze and Guattari to Derrida are strong in their mutual attempts to subvert dichotomous conceptual schemes and the essentializing, totalizing, and foundational modes of thought that binary thinking allows. Like Derrida, they interpret all of Western philosophy in terms of such schemes and valorize difference, although Deleuze has singled out the modern empiricist tradition as able to think in terms of plurality and multiplicity (see Deleuze and Parnet 1987: pp. vii–viii). Moreover, Deleuze and Guattari reject the textual idealism characteristic of extreme deconstructionist thought and emphasize the materiality of desire and rhizomatic linkages of thought to the world of flows.

Privileging botanical metaphors, Deleuze and Guattari employ the term rhizome to designate the decentred lines that constitute multiplicities. As a 'subterranean stem', the rhizome is opposed to the root and the radicle. Unlike the root-tree structure that limits and regulates connections among its aspects, rhizomes are non-hierarchical systems of deterritorialized lines that connect with other lines in random, unregulated relationships. These relations form on a 'smooth' space that is open-ended rather than on a 'striated' space of closed boundaries. Crabgrass, ants, wolf packs, motorcycle gangs, and schizos are examples of rhizomes roaming deterritorialized spaces. Nature is a rhizome, where 'roots are taproots with a more multiple, lateral, and circular system of ramification, rather than a dichotomous one' (Deleuze and Guattari 1987: p. 5). Kafka writes rhizome texts that open up language to multiple paths of desire, Nietzsche's aphorisms are perspectival rhizomes, and *A Thousand Plateaus* itself is a rhizome-text that flows in a myriad of directions. There is no beginning or end to rhizomatic lines, they are always in the middle of dynamic movement; hence they form multiplicities that change in character when their line compositions change, lacking any identity or essence.

On a rhizomatic analysis, the subject is like a hand, comprised of multiple lines. There are three basic kinds of lines. First, the 'rigid segmentary line', a molar line that constructs fixed and normalized identities within various social institutions by way of binary oppositions. Here individuals are constructed in binary identities such as bosses or workers, male or female, white or black, and any combination thereof. The second line, the supple segmentary line, is a molecular movement away from molar rigidity which disturbs its linearity and normalcy, as when cracks occurs in the facade of one's identity, or one begins cracking up. On Deleuze and Guattari's interpretation (1987: pp. 26–38) Freud's famous analysand, the Wolfman, was stranded on this line seeking a way out, but Freud tried to reterritorialize him on Oedipal molar lines. Finally, there are 'lines of flight', the full-fledged deterritorializing movements away from molar identity where cracks becomes ruptures and the subject is shattered in a process of becoming-multiple. This is the plane of creativity and desire, and also of death and destruction. Castaneda's Don Juan was reborn on these lines, and Artaud and countless others died on them.

Rhizomatics is defined in opposition to a Marxist analysis of structures and contradictions, which Deleuze and Guattari believe may be adequate for an analysis of molar formations, but is unable to theorize the more important molecular levels of society and their lines of flight. The events of May 1968 provide an important example of the limitations of a Marxist macroperspective. For Deleuze and Guattari, the eruption of revolutionary struggle was incomprehensible to politicians, parties, unions, and many leftists because the 'objective conditions' for such struggles were not ripe; the class contradictions and crises in capital, in other words, had not yet reached a crisis stage. At a micropolitical perspective, however, crisis was indeed brewing as large numbers of people, in particular students, had become intolerant of institutional bureaucracy and alienation in everyday life. From a rhizomatic perspective, these events are readily foreseeable and intelligible. Not having fit the orthodox revolutionary models, and developing outside the authority of party leaders, the struggles of May were rejected as diversionary or immature, rather than being embraced as the necessary preconditions for a real macropolitical revolution.

Deleuze and Guattari also distinguish their position from Foucault's microanalytics of power on two essential counts (1987: p. 531). First, they claim that the 'assemblages' on which deterritorialized lines form are fundamentally assemblages of desire, rather than power. Rhizomes are inherently flat and non-hierarchical; they break up, scatter, and disseminate. They only become organized as unities, foundations, and hierarchies by dominant sociolinguistic powers, tyrannical signifiers, political despots, the authorities of the normalizing institutions, or a host of micropractices of everyday life. Power is epiphenomenal to the flow of desire. Second, and consequently, the lines of flight are fundamentally positive and creative, rather than lines of resistance or counter-attack. On this point, they out-Nietzsche Foucault by insisting, in accordance with Deleuze's earlier position, that desire is purely affirmative, and not a desire to resist another force. Within this framework, Foucault employs a reactive theory that binds desire to lack and dyadic relations of struggle and resistance.

As the philosophy of authentic multiplicities, which are analyzed without being related to a lost unity or totality, rhizomatics seeks to 'expose arborescent pseudomultiplicities for what they are' (Deleuze and Guattari 1987: p. 8) – derivative constructions comprised of stratified rhizomes. All of reality is constituted as multiplicities; unities, hierarchies, and structures are only colonized rhizomes. Hence, even macrostructures are rhizomatic and they distinguish between arborescent and rhizomatic multiplicities. The assumption here is similar to Foucault who sees macrostructures such as the state to be derived from a complex field of micropowers (school, army, hospital, asylum, and so on). Hence, for Deleuze and Guattari, although the modern political system is a unified whole, 'it is so because it implies a constellation of juxtaposed, imbricated, ordered subsystems' (1987: p. 21). Similarly, fascism cannot become a totalitarian macropower without organizing a vast pre-existing molecular field of desire, and dominant languages emerge as a homogenization of linguistic heterogeneity. But the distinction between arborescent and rhizomatic multiplicities is not a rigid opposition, since arborescent structures have rhizome lines, just as rhizomes have points of arborescence that portend the emergence of bureaucracy, hierarchy, or fascism.

Hence, rhizomatics analyzes the various flows of society and looks for lines of escape which can be further deterritorialized in political struggle, as well as the rigid or supple lines that stratify micropolitical struggles and threaten their revolutionary character. Against the determinism of extreme postmodern theorists such as Baudrillard, rhizomatics emphasizes that 'there is no social system that does not leak in all directions' (1987: p. 204), and hence that multiple paths of escape and transformation are possible. For Deleuze and Guattari, 'power centres are defined much more by what escapes them or by their impotence than by their zone of power' (1987: p. 217). In contrast to the centralized power of the church, for example, there is a constant flow of sins and transgressions. Similarly, escaping the legal system of the state are a proliferation of infractions and criminalities. Women fleeing the patriarchal family, homosexuals throwing off the straitjacket of heterosexual conformity, and people of colour attacking racist ideologies are further examples of lines of flight from molar lines and a process of 'becoming minority'.

Rhizomatics is a form of 'nomadic thought' opposed to the 'State thought' that tries to discipline rhizomatic movement both in theory (e.g., totalizing forms of philosophy) and practice (e.g., police and bureaucratic organizations). Universalist state thought is exercized through 'state machines' and nomad thought combats them through its own 'war machines' such as rhizomatics. These metaphors are drawn from the history of military battles between the state and nomads, which Deleuze and Guattari describe in great detail (1987: pp. 351–473). As an arborescent institution, the state attempts to control flows of all kinds – populations, commodities, money, etc. and so to vanquish nomadism. In response, nomads attempted to destroy the cities and states through micro operations such as rioting and guerilla warfare. Against the myth that nomads were technologically primitive, Deleuze and Guattari claim the nomads were innovators on many different levels, including technology, weaponry and the art of war. Through such innovations, the nomads developed effective war machines for use against the state, but the state appropriated these machines for its own insatiable goals of conquest.

Hence, the model for a postmodern 'warfare' which seeks not literally to spread violence but to liberate difference and intensities from the grip of state machines, is the premodern nomad tribes that roamed deterritorialized spaces while resisting the efforts of state powers to subdue them. As they previously lionized schizo-subjects, Deleuze and Guattari now champion nomads. Nomadic movement is a metaphor to describe the way intensities circulate on the body-without-organs and a normative goal for the post-modern subject who should 'keep moving, even in place, never stop moving' (1987: p. 159). Nomads provide new models for existence and struggle. The nomad-self breaks from all molar segments and cautiously disorganizes itself. Nomad life is an experiment in creativity and becoming, and is anti-traditional and anti-conformist in character. The postmodern nomad attempts to free itself of all roots, bonds, and identities, and thereby resists the state and all normalizing powers.

Thus, like Foucault who valorized the Greek concept of self-mastery, Deleuze and Guattari find a model for the postmodern subject in premodern societies. Like Nietzsche, they employ warrior models as ideals of freedom, although they eschew Nietzsche's militarist celebration of war. For Deleuze and Guattari, the schizo, rhizome, and nomad are all variations on the postmodern theme of breaking with repressive, representational identity and producing the fragmented, libidinal body. Schizos withdraw from repressive social reality into disjointed desiring states, nomads roam freely across open planes in small bands, and rhizomes are deterritorial-ized lines of desire linking desiring bodies with one another and the field of partial objects. Hence, schizos, nomads, and rhizomes represent emancipated, non-fascist modes of existence and all are translated into theoretical models (schizoanalysis, nomadology, and rhizomatics) that map the flows of desire within social machines and combat totalizing modes of thought and social regulation.

Again, these concepts represent only part of the conceptual machinery that Deleuze and Guattari put into motion. The postmodern character of their work is not to be identified with any one concept or model, but the very multiplication of concepts and models and the attempt to connect rhizomatic conceptual lines with other multiplicities. It is the thousand plateaus of different levels of analysis, concepts, and multiplicities that is distinctly postmodern in their work. While much modern theory operates from a conceptual centre and employs stable concepts within unifying, linear, and hierarchical modes of thought that seek to represent the real, Deleuze and Guattari operate on a multiplicity of levels, from mutating conceptual planes, eschewing finalized systems for rhizomatic thought experiments.

Thus, in the second and last volume of *Capitalism and Schizophrenia*, we see that while Deleuze and Guattari have introduced new themes and concepts, have expanded the range and detail of some aspects of their analysis, and have altered their writing style, the fundamental positions of their work calling for a politics of desire have not changed and it is to a final assessment of these positions that we now turn.

3.4   Critical Reservations: Bodies Without Politics?

Using postmodern microanalytical methods, Deleuze and Guattari provide critical theorizations of modernity from the perspectives of the social management of desire, the unconscious, and the body as this occurs at the molecular levels of society. Unlike nearly all postmodern theorists, they theorize modernity as a capitalist modernity and creatively engage Marxist discourse rather than simply denouncing it as a terroristic master narrative. Through a kind of Freudo-Marxist theory that privileges a Nietzschean theory of the body, they foreground important issues concerning the production and control of desire by the culture, media, and therapeutic industries of advanced capitalism. They drsw links between capitalism and the control of needs and desire, between political and libidinal economy. They also theorize the ways that states control and channel desire into repressive paths, posing the problem in terms of the struggle between centralizing state machines and nomadic war machines.

Deleuze and Guattari thereby call attention to the problem of creative and vital existence in a global capitalism predicated on the narcoticization and robotization of its subjects. They emphasize the importance of combatting the ('paranoiac') personality type that requires rigid centredness, authority, stability, and obedience, the kind of subjects that cannot tolerate the difference of others and march readily in fascist movements. Like Foucault, their work is highly political in character, drawing out the politics of language, desire, and everyday life. While they express a scepticism toward the emancipatory projects of modernity, this does not harden into a pessimistic rejection of the possibility of social change. Rather, they effectively problematize old liberation models which privilege obsolete concepts of revolutionary transcendence by underlining the contingency of radical movements and the ambiguity of desire. For Deleuze and Guattari, desire is neither inherently good nor bad, only dynamic and productive; desiring-machines can travel along the path of becoming-revolutionary as well as becoming-fascist; lines of escape can turn into lines of liberation or destruction.

The 'emancipation' that Deleuze and Guattari frequently speak of, therefore, is always an uncertain and incomplete project where success is never guaranteed. While they attack all forms of statist thought, they avoid the opposite extreme of a naive anarchism that breaks with all models of organization at both the level of politics and the body. At the bodily level, they seek the body-without-organs that operates on a 'smooth plane' of self-organization; at the political level, they seek non-hierarchical forms of organization which connect various microstruggles without reducing them to a homogenizing form that eradicates their character as multiplicities, a form of connection that Guattari (1984) calls, in one of its senses, 'transversality'.

Yet, unlike Foucault and nearly all other postmodern theorists, Deleuze and Guattari posit a dialectic of macro- and micropolitical struggle. The macrological struggle against the state and mode of production is impossible without resisting micrological sites of domination and normalization, just as micrological struggles against the various institutions of control are ultimately powerless without transforming the larger economic and political forces that shape them.

While Deleuze and Guattari's concepts and models offer important perspectives for radical theory and politics, we believe that their development of these themes is problematical. They are committed to a metaphysical concept of desire, claiming that desire is 'inherently revolutionary', that it has a fundamental nature, essence, or intentionality which is to be creative and productive, rather than manipulated and repressed. This view of desire, however, remains a dogmatic assumption that does not successfully refute the theories of desire as lack.

There is, in fact, a tension between essentializing and historicizing impulses in Deleuze and Guattari's account of desire. On the one hand, they analyze desire as socially and historically constituted; yet on the other hand, they appeal to a historically invariant nature of desire as productive and multiplicitous which different social regimes repress and which could perhaps be liberated. They do not consider the possibility that even the characteristics of multiplicity and productivity of desire might also be historically conditioned, might be distinctly modern creations. There remains a fundamental realm of desire in their theory therefore, that is ontological rather than cultural in nature, a position which Foucault rejects in his more rigorously historical framework.[5]

Thus, Deleuze and Guattari produce not only a modern narrative history of social representations of desire, but also a postmodern metaphysics. Their notion that everything is constructed in rhizomatic form leads them to adopt organicist models of behaviour ('become like a plant') and to make dubious naturalist claims such as the statement that 'thought is not arborescent' in nature (1987: p. 15). But how do Deleuze and Guattari know this? Why is this claim correct, as opposed to, say, the structuralist claim that the mind naturally organizes reality according to binary divisions, or the narrativist claim that it organizes reality in stories and temporal sequences? Apart from dubious appeals to the discontinuous nature of brain's synapses (ibid.), we are not told.

We also question the productivist mode of discourse Deleuze and Guattari employ. While we find the concepts of nomads and rhizomes suggestive, the discourse of machine and production, meant to destroy the notions of the subject as a rational ego and desire as lack, does not seem as useful. Since this discourse stems from the capitalist factory model of repressed and alienated labour, it's curious that Deleuze and Guattari, whatever their philosophical intentions, would resort to it to discuss problems of freedom, creativity, and autonomy. Baudrillard's critique of Marxism as a 'mirror of production' (1975) that reflects the system it seeks to destroy readily applies to Deleuze and Guattari's productivist imaginary.

More generally, such productivist discourse suggests that Deleuze and Guattari have uncritically assimilated the modernist ethos of incessant self-transformation, becoming, and psychic instability. Their positions are the theoretical and ethical equivalent of a futurist painting. If we can speak of frenzied, permanent self-revolution as the Deleuzo-Guattarian 'ethic', it is not clear that this position radically breaks from capitalist and consumerist behaviour. Just as one does not need a new car or wardrobe every year, one does not constantly need a new subjectivity. While there is much to say in favour of personal growth and development, and even psychic decentring as Laing and Cooper suggest, there are also positive forms of identity and stability, which also require experimentation, such as having consistent progressive political commitments and maintaining some core characteristics of creative subjectivity. Deleuze and Guattari might counter that one could freely desire stable commitments and selfhood, but this qualification conflicts with and considerably weakens their thesis that desire is a protean machine.

If Deleuze and Guattari are right about the machinic nature of desire, their concept seems to militate against the project of constructing a new social or communal order. The notion of unstable and nomadic desire subverts the micropolitical organizations and postmodern society that ensures its liberation. But if a new society were possible, then some form of social constraints, such as rules, norms, laws, morals, and even authority would be necessary. Guattari (1984: p. 86) anticipates this criticism by insisting that 'desire is not necessarily disruptive and anarchic', and is compatible with forms of (non-repressive) social control and planning and even science, but how nomadic desire is compatible with new forms of social organization is not specified, nor do Deleuze and Guattari ever state what kind of social codes they would accept as legitimate. Their possible response, however, might be to sketch out a theory of norms that do not normalize and regulative codes that are self-constitutive or democratically defined within local communal networks.

Such a perspective points to a decentring of ethics in favour of aesthetics that is typical of postmodern theory. Like Foucault, Deleuze and Guattari fail to articulate a normative position. Whereas Foucault failed to account for the legitimacy of radical politics, Deleuze and Guattari have no theory of why revolutionary desire is preferable over fascist desire. Deleuze and Guattari do not explicitly call for an aesthetic transformation of life as Foucault sometimes did, but such a project is implied in their efforts to creatively engage desire and transform everyday life. By focusing on the problem of liberated desire, Deleuze and Guattari have undertheorized the issues of intersubjectivity and the social. They have no account of how social bonds form and how these could be fostered within and outside of a revolutionary movement. While they certainly do not advocate a solipsistic retreat of individuals into their private desiring-machines, and they emphasize the need to overcome familial and other privatized boundaries to open up the desiring process to the whole social field, their account of intersubjectivity is exceedingly thin and abstract. Intersubjective relations, when discussed at all, are conceived in terms of imbricated machines or criss-crossing rhizomatic lines.

Throughout their work, Deleuze and Guattari exhibit a paranoid phobia of signification and rationality in order to celebrate the a-signifying, nomadic existence of desiring flows. Human beings are liberated when they are 'able to behave as *intentionless phenomena*' (Deleuze and Guattari 1983: p. 368). Ultimately, there is no need to produce revolutionary subjectivity in any of its traditional forms (radical needs, interests, or consciousness) since desire 'does not "want" revolution, it is revolutionary in its own right' (Deleuze and Guattari 1983: p. 116). There are no ideological battles to be fought and won, no critical consciousness to achieve, no basis for political agency; politics primarily involves the liberation of desiring bodies from which everything apparently will follow.

Like the early Foucault, Deleuze and Guattari tend to equate personal identity, rationality, and reflexivity with a totalizing repression of singular libidinal states. Deleuze and Guattari are even more extreme than Foucault, however, since they do not adopt his qualified stance toward rationality and the Enlightenment. Moreover, while Foucault espoused a bio-politics with similar aims as schizoanalysis, he also espoused a politics of discourse struggle and signification that Deleuze and Guattari dispense with in favour of an exaltation of desire. In all three theorists, we see a postmodern replay of the aestheticist tradition of modernity which stigmatized reason, normalcy, and social convention, seeking refuge in art, the body, and highly individualized modes of being.

Turning now to our next theorist, Jean Baudrillard, we shall see the first explicit attempt to construct a conception of postmodernity as a new epoch in history. In the process, we shall leave behind a concern with the substantive material reality of desire, power, and social institutions, and enter into the abstract, vertiginous, dematerialized Baudrillardian world of simulations and hyperreality.

Notes

1. In response to an interviewer's query if he accepts the Deleuzian notion of desire, Foucault replies 'no, definitely not', and says that his work focuses not on desire but 'the question of truth, of telling the truth ... and the relation between "telling the truth" and forms of reflexivity, of self upon self' (1988d: pp. 32–3). Hence, for Foucault's later genealogical project, it became critical to theorize representational and epistemological schemes of truth, how subjects come to know and speak the truth about themselves, questions which are quite foreign to Deleuze and Guattari's focus on how to liberate the machinic unconscious from all blockages.

2. For a detailed explication of the semiotic theory informing *Anti-Oedipus*, see Guattari (1979: pp. 73–107).

3. This is particularly evident in some of Guattari's essays (1984) such as 'Plan for the Planet' and 'Capitalist Systems, Structures and Processes' (with Eric Alliez) where he develops notions such as 'integrated world capitalism', analyzes relations between state and economy, and theorizes the totalizing power of capitalism that requires molecular revolution at a global level.

4. While Deleuze and Guattari posit innumerable oppositions in their works, one cannot easily deconstruct them since every time they create an opposition they immediately qualify and destabilize it, replacing the disjunctive 'or' with the conjunctive 'and'. As they say, 'We employ a dualism of models only in order to arrive at a process that challenges all models' (1987: p. 20).

5. For another argument that Deleuze (Guattari is not mentioned) has an essentialist concept of desire, see Butler (1987: pp. 205–17). Our account differs from Butler's in that we see a tension between the essentialist and historicist aspects of Deleuze and Guattari's concept of desire.

Chapter 4

Baudrillard en route to Postmodernity

Jean Baudrillard has emerged as one of the most high-profile postmodern theorists. He has achieved guru status throughout the English-speaking world and his works are rapidly being translated into Spanish, Italian, German, and other languages as well. Baudrillard's acolytes praise him as the 'talisman' of the new postmodern universe, as *the* commotion who theoretically energizes the postmodern scene, as *the* supertheorist of a new postmodernity.[1] Moreover, whereas Foucault and Deleuze and Guattari never adopted the discourse of the postmodern, Baudrillard eventually identified with the postmodern turn and was crowned as a high priest of the new epoch. Furthermore, Baudrillard has developed the most striking and extreme theory of postmodernity yet produced and has been highly influential in cultural theory and discussions of contemporary media, art, and society.

A professor of sociology at the University of Nanterre from the 1960s until 1987, Baudrillard provided a series of provocative analyses of objects, signs, and codes in the consumer society in his early works. These writings attempted to synthesize the Marxian critique of political economy with semiology and were part of many attempts to revitalize revolutionary theory in the aftermath of the 1960s. He then carried out a sharp critique of Marxism in *The Mirror of Production* (1975; orig. 1973) and provided alterna-

111

tive, arguably postmodern, perspectives on contemporary society in *L'échange symbolique et la mort* (1976). In a series of widely discussed books and articles in the 1970s and 1980s, Baudrillard attacked the fundamental presuppositions of modern theory and politics, while offering postmodern perspectives.

We shall not attempt to survey the full range of Baudrillard's themes here;[2] instead we shall focus on his analysis of modernity (4.1), on his turn to postmodern perspectives (4.2), and on his move toward metaphysics and nihilistic cynicism in the 1980s (4.3). We shall indicate in these discussions what we see as the major contributions and limitations of his project. Baudrillard is especially important for postmodern theory because he has gone further than anyone in articulating a concept of postmodernity. Since the discourses of the postmodern in social theory, politics, philosophy, cultural theory, and so on, frequently derive pathos and resonance from the notion that we are in a new postmodern age or paradigm, the development of a theory of postmodernity is a key component of a full-blown postmodern theory. How well does Baudrillard succeed in developing a new theory of postmodernity?

4.1 Exploring Modernity

[Modernity is] a characteristic mode of civilization, which opposes itself to tradition, that is to say, to all other anterior or traditional cultures: confronting the geographic and symbolic diversity of the latter, modernity imposes itself throughout the world as a homogeneous unity, irradiating from the Occident (Baudrillard 1987a: p. 63).

All postmodern theorists relate their new perspectives to analysis and critique of modernity. As we have seen, Foucault by and large presents modernity as a process of increasing rationalization, 'normalization', and domination, while Deleuze and Guattari characterize it as an oppressive territorialization of desire into constrictive social structures and repressed personalities that nevertheless multiplies rhizomatic lines of escape. In his early writings, Baudrillard theorized modernity in terms of an analysis of the system of objects, the consumer society, media and information, modern art, contemporary fashion, sexuality and thought.

His first published book, *Le système des objets* (1968), investigates the new system of mass consumption bound up with the explosive proliferation of consumer goods and services. The project operates within the framework of a subject–object dialectic where the subject faces a world of objects which attract, fascinate, and sometimes control the individual's perception, thought, and behaviour. The analyses presuppose the theory of the commodification of everyday life under capitalism advanced by Marxists like Lukács and semiological theories in which objects are interpreted as signs that are organized into systems of signification.[3]

Baudrillard's ambitious task is to describe the contours and dominant structures of the new system of objects while indicating how they condition and structure needs, fantasies, and behaviour. *Le système des objets* is animated by a sense that he is describing a *new* social order which he characterizes as a 'new technical order', 'new environment', 'new field of everyday life', 'new morality', and new form of 'hypercivilization'. The framework of a perceiving and desiring subject facing a world of objects and signs will define the trajectory of Baudrillard's thought through the present. Consequently, his first book begins his project of describing the ways that subjects relate to, use, dominate – or are dominated by – the system of objects and signs which constitute our everyday life.

Baudrillard's second book, *La société de consommation* (1970), studies the system of objects organized into a consumer society, while *For a Critique of the Political Economy of the Sign* (1981; orig. 1972) attempts to synthesize Marxian political economy with semiology and structuralism. His topics concern such modern phenomena as the new domestic environments, cybernetics and contemporary architecture, pop art and contemporary painting, and media and information. Baudrillard's first three works can be read as sketches for developing a neo-Marxian social theory that synthesizes Marxism with semiology. Yet Baudrillard begins distancing himself from Marxism in the *Critique* and unequivocally breaks with it in his subsequent book *The Mirror of Production* (1975; orig. 1973) where he claims that Marxian political economy can neither be applied to traditional societies, nor does it provide adequate perspectives on contemporary society – a claim that we shall take up in Chapter 8.

At this point in his theoretical itinerary, Baudrillard's work revolves around a fundamental distinction between premodern societies structured by symbolic exchange and modern societies structured by production. Let us, then, explicate this fundamental divide in history before turning in 4.2 to a discussion of the transition between modernity and postmodernity which constitutes for Baudrillard an equally momentous rupture in history.

4.1.1   From Symbolic to Productivist Societies

In all societies prior to modern society, exchange is conducted through a series of symbolic transactions not yet coded as 'value'. Value emerges only with capitalism which distinguishes between use value and exchange value in its system of political economy. This system constitutes a fundamental rupture with the complex systems of symbolic exchange and inaugurates an exchange of goods according to the laws of the market, governed by quantitative measures of exchange. Political economy thus replaces the concreteness of symbolic exchange with the abstractions of exchange value in which money and a market economy constitute a new realm of value (Baudrillard 1981: pp. 63ff.). Henceforth, value is determined by the laws of political economy and as the system of political economy expands, the entire world is rationalized and functionalized in accordance with the imperatives of capital accumulation. Thus abstract values – money, capital, exchange value – rule society and reduce complex symbolic systems to the nexus of the cash register and its quantitative measures. Within the system of political economy, value is articulated as use value (utility of objects), exchange value (monetary worth, commercial value), and statutory value, or what Baudrillard calls 'sign value'.

To Marx's distinctions between use value and exchange value, Baudrillard adds an analysis of sign value, whereby commodities are valued by the way that they confer prestige and signify social status and power. Baudrillard claims that Marx champions use value as the utopian other to exchange value, without realizing that use value itself is a construct of the system of exchange value which produces a rationalized system of needs and objects that integrate individuals into the capitalist social order. Marx's 'radical' theory for Baudrillard thus simply reproduces the logic of political economy. Baudrillard attempts to undo the opposition between exchange and use value where use value serves as the 'alibi' of exchange value insofar as it is posited as the ahistorical outside of historical systems of exchange, rooted in natural, unalienated human needs. On Baudrillard's scheme, it doesn't matter that needs are true or real, and that labour is free or unalienated, since such concepts are locked within productivist logic. The genuine revolutionary alternative, as espoused by Baudrillard, is a symbolic exchange that breaks with all utilitarian imperatives and revels in the Dionysian energies of play and festival.

While Baudrillard's reading arguably distorts Marx's work (see Kellner 1989b: pp. 33ff.), for our purposes here it is interesting to note that Baudrillard generally agreed with Marx that modernity is a system of political economy rooted in an abstract order of value. For Baudrillard, the system of political economy rationalizes objects and needs, producing a system of objects and a rationalized subject which reproduces the system of labour and consumption through satisfying its needs. Consequently, political economy is not merely a code for economic organization in any society whatsoever, but describes the particular order of the capitalist economy, of an economy organized around production, and thus is equivalent to modernity itself, read under the sign of Marx (production) and Weber (rationalization).

In these texts of the early and mid-1970s, Baudrillard therefore presupposes a fundamental dividing line in history between symbolic societies – that is, societies fundamentally organized around symbolic exchange such as gift-giving, festivities, religious rituals and so on – and productivist societies (that is, societies organized around production). He thus rejects the Marxian philosophy of history which posits the primacy of production in all societies and he repudiates the Marxian concept of socialism. Baudrillard argues that Marxism does not break radically enough with capitalist productivism, offering itself merely as a more efficient and equitable organization of production rather than as a completely different sort of society with a different logic, values, and life activities.

4.1.2 Symbolic Exchange, Micropolitics, and Cultural Revolution

Thus, in effect, Baudrillard is positing – or dreaming of – another break in history as radical as the rupture between symbolic societies and capitalism which would constitute a return to symbolic societies as his revolutionary alternative. Henceforth, he would oppose, in one way or another, his ideal of symbolic exchange to the logic of production, utility, and instrumental rationality which governs capitalist (and existing socialist) societies. Symbolic exchange stands for a variety of heterogeneous activities, including 'The exchange of looks, the present which comes and goes, prodigality, festival – and also destruction (which returns to non-value what production has erected, valorized)' (1981: p. 207).

Baudrillard seems to be arguing that by engaging in symbolic exchange which is caught up neither in use values nor exchange values, one escapes domination by the logic of political economy, and is able to subvert the logic of a system which demands that all activity have specific uses, values, and purposes. Instead Baudrillard suggests that symbolic exchange provides a mode of activity that is more radically subversive of the values and logic of capitalism than the sort of practices advocated by Marxists which he claims are but a reflex of the 'mirror of production' (for example, worker's control, socialization of the means of production).

In *The Mirror of Production*, Baudrillard links symbolic exchange with the cultural revolutionary projects of the time, locating his oppositional ideal in the revolt of marginal groups like blacks, women and gays, who supposedly subvert the code of racial or sexual difference, and thus are more radical and subversive than socialists who operate within the code of political economy. At this point, Baudrillard advocates a politics of difference and of margins whereby those groups who affirm their own values and needs over and against these of the dominant society are seen as more radical than groups which operate within the codes and logic of contemporary societies. This politics of margins and differences was also related to the micropolitics advocated by Foucault, Lyotard, Deleuze and Guattari, and others in France at the time. Micropolitics would focus on the practices of everyday life and would involve revolution in lifestyle, discourse, bodies, sexuality, communication, and so on that would provide the preconditions for a new society and would emancipate individuals from social repression and domination. Baudrillard never went as far as Lyotard or Deleuze and Guattari in advocating an unleashing of desire as the basis of radical politics – and would later come to explicitly criticize and even mock this position in *Forget Foucault* (1987; orig. 1977). But, in effect, he was at one time close to their position of locating political change and radical politics in the microspheres of society and everyday life, rather than in class struggle, the workplace, or the state.

Moreover, while Baudrillard was calling for a cultural revolution and total revolution (1975: pp. 130ff.), he never explicitly formulated any concrete vision or practice of revolution, other than some reflections on urban grafitti as a form of political resistance (Baudrillard 1976: pp. 118ff.). Thus his micropolitics are rather vague and empty. His ultra-left politics of the time are really no more than slogans which position his theory as 'ultra-revolutionary'. But, it is not clear what this revolution could accomplish in view of the hegemony of the dominant codes that he described. In fact, there is extreme tension between his advocacy of cultural revolution and his descriptions of the system's ability to absorb all oppositional practices. For a cultural revolution would produce new practices, institutions, signs, codes, values, and so on, but in Baudrillard's theory all practices and signs are controlled by and absorbed into the almighty code – a typically vague and undertheorized term. Thus, the only practice that he can really recommend is total refusal, total negativity, and the utopia of radical otherness (Baudrillard 1975: pp. 130ff., *passim*).

Like Foucault and Deleuze and Guattari, Baudrillard's politics at this time circulate in the trajectory of ultra-leftist '*gauchiste*' discourses which purport to be more radical and revolutionary than traditional Marxism. Such *gauchistes* took ultra-left positions and operated outside of the major left parties, either forming splinter parties or groups, or acting as an extra-parliamentary opposition. Baudrillard and other French thinkers of the period, deeply influenced by the heterogeneous uprisings of May 1968, decisively broke with Marxian working-class politics and sought alternative perspectives for revolutionary politics. Yet he never succeeded in articulating any concrete and specific political perspectives and in his later works turned away from political reflection and critique altogether.

4.2   From Modernity to Postmodernity

> Simulation is no longer that of a territory, a referential being or a substance. It is the generation by models of a real without origins or reality: a hyperreal (Baudrillard 1983a: p. 2).

> Today it is quotidian reality in its entirety – political, social, historical and economic – that from now on incorporates the simulatory dimension of hyperrealism (Baudrillard 1983a: p. 147).

Although Baudrillard does not adopt the discourse of post-modernity until the 1980s when it became *the* fashion in some circles, his 1960s and 1970s work contains many proto-postmodern themes focusing on the consumer society and its proliferation of signs, the media and its messages, environmental design and cybernetic steering systems, and contemporary art and sign culture. Baudrillard's narrative concerns the end of the era of modernity dominated by production, industrial capitalism, and a political economy of the sign contrasted to the advent of the era of a postmodernity constituted by 'simulations' and new forms of technology, culture, and society. These postmodern texts leave behind his earlier analysis of the consumer society and abstract his categories from political economy altogether, which he believes is no longer relevant to contemporary societies.

4.2.1   The Holy Trinity: Simulations, Implosion and Hyperreality

> Information dissolves meaning and the social into a sort of nebulous state leading not at all to a surfeit of innovation but to the very contrary, to total entropy (Baudrillard 1983b: p. 100).

We are now, Baudrillard claims, in a new era of simulation in which computerization, information processing, media, cybernetic control systems, and the organization of society according to simulation codes and models replace production as the organizing principle of society. If modernity is the era of production controlled by the industrial bourgeoisie, the postmodern era of simulations by contrast is an era of information and signs governed by models, codes, and cybernetics. Baudrillard describes 'the passage from a *metallurgic* into a *semiurgic* society' (1981: p. 185) in which signs take on a life of their own and constitute a new social order structured by models, codes, and signs. 'Radical semiurgy' describes the dramatic proliferation of signs which come to dominate social life.

Baudrillard never specifies the economic forces or social groups behind this process and thus advances a sort of techno-logical determinism whereby models and codes become the primary determinants of social experience. In a society of simu-lations, the models or codes structure experience and erode distinctions between the model and the real. Using McLuhan's concept of implosion, Baudrillard claims that in the postmodern world the boundary between image or simulation and reality implodes, and with it the very experience and ground of 'the real' disappears.

In 'TV World', for instance, the image or model of the Doctor (the simulated Doctor) is sometimes taken for the Real Doctor; thus Robert Young, who played Dr Welby, received thousands of letters asking for medical advice and later appeared in ads where he advised readers on the wonders of decaffeinated coffee. Raymond Burr successively played lawyer Perry Mason and detective Ironside and received thousands of letters asking for legal advice in the 1950s and detective aid in the 1960s. Soap opera villains and villainesses must hire bodyguards to go out in public to protect them from irate fans angered by their shenanigans in television world.

Hyperreality thus points to a blurring of distinctions between the real and the unreal in which the prefix 'hyper' signifies more real than real whereby the real is produced according to a model. When the real is no longer simply given (for example as a landscape or the sea), but is artificially (re)produced as 'real' (for example as a simulated environment), it becomes not unreal, or surreal, but realer-than-real, a real retouched and refurbished in 'a hallucinatory resemblance' with itself (Baudrillard 1983a: p. 23). For Baudrillard the models of the United States in Disneyland are more real than their instantiations in the social world, as the USA becomes more and more like Disneyland (1983a: pp. 25ff.). The hyperreal for Baudrillard is a condition whereby models replace the real, as exemplified in such phenomena as the ideal home in women's or lifestyle magazines, ideal sex as portrayed in sex manuals or relationship books, ideal fashion as exemplified in ads or fashion shows, ideal computer skills as set forth in computer manuals, and so on. In these cases, the model becomes a determinant of the real, and the boundary between hyperreality and everyday life is erased.

With the advent of hyperreality, therefore, simulations come to constitute reality itself. In the 1980s, TV programmes appeared in the USA which directly simulate real-life situations such as *The People's Court* which re-enacts the trials and tribulations of the petty bourgeoisie, while TV evangelists simulated religion and Ronald Reagan simulated politics. In this universe, the simulation models become more real than the actual institutions, and not only is it increasingly difficult to distinguish between simulations and reality, but the reality of simulation becomes the criterion of the real itself.

In the postmodern mediascape, boundaries between information and entertainment, images and politics, implode. As many commentators have pointed out, TV news and documentary assume more and more the form of entertainment, using dramatic and melodramatic codes to frame their stories. CBS's news magazine show *57th Street* begins with a collage of iconic images of the news correspondents who are presented as if they were characters in a sitcom or weekly drama, while MTV, *Entertainment Tonight*, and various talk shows utilize the frames of news commentators to disguise culture industry hype as 'facts' and 'information'. The TV tabloid news programme *USA Tonight* replicates the structure of the popular national newspaper *USA Today* and presents around thirty short news/entertainment bytes as the day's news. The result is what has been called 'infotainment' in which boundaries between information and entertainment collapse.

A similar implosion between politics and entertainment is evident in recent political campaigns where image is more important than substance, and political campaigns become increasingly dependent on media advisors, public relations 'experts', and pollsters who have transformed politics into image contests, or sign struggles. Analysts of the 1988 American Presidential campaign agree that television advertising, photo-opportunities, debates and other media events which presented the candidate's image played the major role in the election (discussed in Kellner 1990).

The concept of implosion thus becomes a key component of Baudrillard's postmodern social theory. The Western industrial world was previously marked by 'explosion', by expanding production of goods, science and technology, national boundaries, and capital, as well as by the differentiation of social spheres, discourse, and value. Marx and Engels' *Communist Manifesto* (1978) describes the explosion of industrial capitalism with its revolutionizing and expanding of productive forces, new modes of transportation and communication, and colonization of the world. Modernity's explosions thus included new technologies, product differentiation, and a constant proliferation of goods and services.

Baudrillard's theory of implosion describes a process of social entropy leading to a collapse of boundaries, including the implosion of meaning in the media and the implosion of media and the social in the masses (1983b). The dissemination of media messages and semiurgy saturates the social field, and meaning and messages flatten each other out in a neutralized flow of information, entertainment, advertising, and politics. Baudrillard argues that the masses become bored and resentful of their constant bombardment with messages and the constant attempts to solicit them to buy, consume, work, vote, register an opinion, or participate in social life. The apathetic masses thus become a sullen silent majority in which all meaning, messages, and solicitations implode as if sucked into a black hole. The social thus disappears and with it distinctions implode between classes, political ideologies, cultural forms, and between media semiurgy and the real itself (Baudrillard 1983a and 1983b). Baudrillard is not only describing a series of implosions (that is, between politics and entertainment, capital and labour, or high and low culture) but is claiming that the society in its entirety is implosive.

The Baudrillardian universe of simulacra without referents can therefore be read as an effect of the poststructuralist critique of meaning and reference taken to an extreme limit where the effluence of simulacra replaces the play of textuality or discourses in a universe with no stable structures in which to anchor theory or politics. Indeed, in many of his writings, the universe seems to be without boundaries and in a vertiginous flux where all the old boundaries and distinctions of philosophy, social and political theory, and capitalist society are imploded into an undifferentiated flux of simulacra.

Unlike Deleuze and Guattari who strive to develop a materialist theory of desire and who insist that 'the real is not impossible; it is simply more and more artificial' (1983: p. 34), Baudrillard claims that reality vanishes altogether in a haze of images and signs. Yet Baudrillard also suggests that there is a quite precise and important borderline between the previous and the current social order, between modernity and postmodernity, and his claims to novelty and originality are dependent on the belief that he is up to something new, that he is catching some new social conditions and phenomena, that he is moving rapidly beyond previous thinking, boundaries, and politics.

4.2.2   Baudrillard vs. Foucault

By the late 1970s, Baudrillard apparently wished to position his theory as the most avant-garde position. While he earlier drew upon and cited Foucault's work,[4] in *Forget Foucault* (1987a; orig. 1977), written at the height of Foucault's fame, Baudrillard carried out an aggressive critique of theoretical positions which he had previously utilized. This is a key text in Baudrillard's development where he abandoned his previous commitments to a politics of symbolic transgression and cultural revolution, moved into a more nihilistic, cynical, and apolitical theoretical field, and radically questioned the validity of basic concepts in critical social theory. In this same text, Baudrillard also attacks Freudo-Marxian theories of desire, as popularized by Deleuze, Guattari, and Lyotard, and thus differentiates himself from his chief competitors in the French cultural scene in the battle for the hyper-avant-gardist position.

Baudrillard interprets Foucault as a theorist who could not take the postmodern turn and remained within the classical formula of sex and power. For all his innovative theorizing, Foucault 'comes to a halt right at the threshold of a current revolution of the system which he has never wanted to cross' (Baudrillard 1987a: p. 16). Baudrillard takes Foucault's eloquent discussions of power as a sign that he has described an obsolete era: 'What if Foucault spoke so well to us concerning power ... only because power is dead? Not merely impossible to locate because of dissemination, but dissolved purely and simply and in a manner that still escapes us, dissolved by reversal, cancellation, or made hyperreal through simulation' (1987a: pp. 11–12).

Baudrillard proposes that we forget Foucault because his theory is obsolete in a postmodern era of simulation and determination by models, codes, information, and media where the classical referents of social theory disappear. Foucault saw that power is complex and pluralized, but he failed to see that it has become completely abstract, no longer located in any institutions what-soever, be they macro or micro. For Baudrillard, power is no longer disciplinary, but a dead power which moves through the indeterminant circulation of signs. Power becomes a simulacrum, 'it undergoes a metamorphosis into signs and is invented on the basis of signs' (Baudrillard 1987a: p. 59).

While Baudrillard fails to indicate the ways in which Foucault provides postmodern perspectives on power (see 2.2 below), we concur with him that Foucault's wide-ranging analyses of power omit any discussion of key contemporary mechanisms of power and social reproduction: media, consumption, fashion, leisure, and semiotics. Because he has said nothing of these important phenomena, Foucault's analysis of society and power lacks crucial dimensions. The virtue of Baudrillard's work is to provide an alternative per-spective on contemporary society concerning the ways in which signs and images function as mechanisms of control within contemporary culture. But in espousing an amnesiac repudiation of Foucault, Baudrillard goes too far and fails to appreciate the heterogeneous character of contemporary forms of power, which include media, signs, and codes, but also spectacle, discipline, surveillance, sexism, racism, torture and other modes of social control.

We see here, in fact, how some postmodern theory adopts a simplistic logic of either/or, rather than a more multiperspectival approach. As Nietzsche argued, a multiplicity of perspectives provides a richer approach to phenomena than a single-optic perspective.[5] Thus, while Baudrillard provides a corrective to Foucault's neglect of semiotic or media power, Foucault's work is a useful counter to Baudrillard's implosive analysis. Where Baudrillard asserts that all oppositions and lines of differentiation implode, Foucault shows how discipline and power segregates, differentiates, creates hierarchies, marginalizes, and excludes. Foucault also demonstrates the ways in which power creates know-ledge, disciplinary mechanisms, and subjects in his analysis of institutions, practices, and discourses, while Baudrillard simply offers an abstract semiotic theory of power. An adequate theory of power, therefore, would forget neither Baudrillard nor Foucault and would theorize, in a contextualist manner, the multiple forms of power in contemporary society.

For example, in some contexts, a particular mode of power may dominate, while in other places multiple modes may operate in an overdetermined way. In the Soviet Union, for instance, repressive state power served for decades to keep the population under surveillance and control. In the United States, by contrast, a combination of state power, media spectacles, and the fascination of commodities and affluence provided a multiplicity of forms of social control. With the relaxing of oppression in the Soviet Union, the media are assuming new functions, fascinating the population, for instance, with spectacles of Communist Party corruption, debates in the new parliament, and far-reaching political changes. In addition, the media have been used to create hegemony for *perestroika* by positively portraying Gorbachev's policies. For instance, 'liberalized' Soviet media were subtly used in the spring of 1990 to attack Lithuanian and other independence movements by limiting media discourse to those who wanted to preserve the USSR's national unity and who attacked nationalist 'separatism'. The media are thus shifting in the USSR from serving as an instrument of dull, oppressive state ideological power, to a more sophisticated force of integration and containment. Consequently, theories of power must be able to utilize multiperspectival approaches subtle enough to theorize changing configurations of power, domination, and social struggle.

For Baudrillard, the mutation of power into the dead power of floating signs in a media and information society makes power into a phenomenon so dispersed, abstract, and dematerialized that it is impossible to chart its trajectories, structures, relations, and effects. Foucault, by contrast, charts the trajectories of power and the ways that power functions in institutions, discourses, and practices. Yet, as we have noted, Foucault never specifies on whose behalf power operates. Indeed, both Baudrillard and Foucault neglect political economy and thus are not able to analyze how the mode of production and social relations produce power relations, that is, relations of domination and subordination. Neither Foucault nor Baudrillard delineate any actually existing power structure, or cite which groups or sectors control the prisons, media, or government and for what purposes.

A multiperspectival social theory, however, is concerned with delineating the interconnections between the economy, polity, society, culture, and everyday life and with analyzing how these dimensions form a complex social system. Foucault's perspectives on prisons, medical and psychiatric institutions, and various discourses and practices illuminate important regions of social life that are often neglected by social theory. Likewise, Baudrillard's emphasis on cultural semiotics, simulacra, cybernetics, and postmodern culture provides important perspectives for conceptualizing our present society of mass media and high technology. But neither Foucault nor Baudrillard come close to providing adequate perspectives for a critical social theory of the present age. Both are too one-sided, reductive, and blind to the continuing importance of the economy, state, race and gender domination, neglecting a wide range of economic, environmental, and political issues. Thus against the one-sidedness of Foucault's and Baudrillard's perspectives, we are calling for a multiperspectival social theory that will incorporate their analyses in a broader and more comprehensive theory, while rejecting their excessively one-sided perspectives on contemporary society (see Chapter 8).

In *Forget Foucault*, Baudrillard broadens his attack beyond Foucault to include his contemporaries Deleuze and Guattari and Lyotard while calling into question the validity of micropolitics (1987a: pp. 25ff.). Where these theorists claim that power is decentred and thus requires multiple forms of struggle waged at local levels of society, Baudrillard claims that molecular politics also is to be rejected on the grounds that power is more dispersed and pulverized than even Foucault and Deleuze and Guattari postulate, and thus is impossible to struggle against. Baudrillard argues that the emphasis on unleashing desire and investing it in a multitude of new objects merely replicates the ethos of capitalism (1987: p. 25). He also believes that social determination takes place precisely on the microlevels celebrated by Deleuze and Guattari and warns against fetishizing a domain that is controlled by models and codes, proclaiming: 'Beware of the molecular!' (1987: p. 36).

Forget Foucault also contains a new delineation of an opposition between production and seduction – a new Baudrillardian 'strategy' which would become a topic of his next book *Seduction* (1990; orig. 1979). For a while, until he tired of it, seduction replaced symbolic exchange as his privileged oppositional term to the world of production and utility. Baudrillard opposes seduction as an artistocratic 'order of sign and ritual' to the bourgeois ideal of production and valorizes artifice, appearance, play, and challenge against the deadly serious labour of production. Baudrillard interprets seduction not primarily in the sense of enticing someone to have sexual intercourse, but as a ritual and game with its own rules, charms, snares, and lures. His writing regresses at this point into a premodern neo-aristocratic aestheticism dedicated to idiosyncratic modes of thought and writing with frequent lapses into conservative thought. Henceforth, his texts are more idiosyncratic, personal, and fragmentary, exhibiting a new amalgam of metaphysics, story telling, and *aperçus* concerning the contemporary scene. Moreover, Baudrillard gives up all modes of radical politics and enters into a post-political phase of analysis.

4.3   Postmodernity, Metaphysics, and Postpolitics

> If being nihilist is to privilege this point of inertia and the analysis of this irreversibility of systems to the point of no return, then I am a nihilist.

> If being nihilist is to be obsessed with the mode of disappearance, and no longer with the mode of production, then I am a nihilist. Disappearance, aphanisis, implosion, Fury of the *Verschwindens* (Baudrillard 1984b: p. 39).

In Baudrillard's post-1976 writings, political economy, the media, and cybernetics coalesce to produce a world of simulacra and new technologies which could be interpreted as an altogether new type of postmodern society. Yet until 1980 – and to some extent thereafter as well – Baudrillard persisted in describing the contemporary social scene as 'our modern society', 'modern times', and 'our modernity' (Baudrillard 1976: pp. 7ff., *passim*). In an article 'On Nihilism', first delivered as a lecture in 1980, he describes for the first time his own theory as an analysis of 'postmodernity'. Here, he presents 'modernity' as 'the radical destruction of appearances, the disenchantment of the world and its abandonment to the violence of interpretation and history' (1984b: p. 38). Modernity is now characterized as the era of Marx and Freud, the era in which politics, culture, and social life were interpreted as epiphenomena of the economy, or everything was interpreted in terms of desire or the unconsciousness. These 'hermeneutics of suspicion' employed depth models to demystify reality, to reveal the underlying realities behind appearances, the forces that constituted the facts.

The revolution of modernity was thus a revolution of meaning grounded in the secure moorings of the dialectics of history, the economy, or desire. Baudrillard scorns this universe and claims to be part of a 'second revolution, that of the twentieth century, of postmodernity, which is the immense process of the destruction of meaning, equal to the earlier destruction of appearances. Whoever lives by meaning dies by meaning' (1984b: pp. 38–9). The postmodern world is devoid of meaning; it is a universe of nihilism where theories float in a void, unanchored in any secure harbour. Meaning requires depth, a hidden dimension, an unseen substratum, and a stable foundation; in postmodern society, however, everything is 'obscene', visible, explicit, transparent, and always in motion. The postmodern scene on this account exhibits signs of dead meaning and frozen forms mutating into new combinations and permutations of the same. In this accelerating proliferation of signs and forms, there is an ever growing implosion and inertia, characterized by growth beyond limits, turning in on itself, and collapsing into inertia.

Unlike the active nihilism posited by Nietzsche (1967: pp. 17ff.), Baudrillard's nihilism is without joy, without energy, without hope for a better future: 'melancholy is the fundamental tonality of functional systems, of the present systems of simulation, programming and information. Melancholy is the quality inherent in the mode of disappearance of meaning, in the mode of volatilisation of meaning in operational systems' (1984b: p. 39). In fact, Baudrillard's postmodern mind-set exhibits a contradictory amalgam of emotions and responses ranging from despair and melancholy, to vertigo and giddiness, and nostalgia and laughter. Analysis of the 'mode of disappearance' constitutes a rather original contribution and indeed Baudrillard has been true to this impulse to describe without illusions or regret what is disappearing in our society and culture.

In an interview 'Game with Vestiges', Baudrillard (1984a) again describes his thought in terms of the postmodern, and continues to describe the disappearance of the central items in previous social theories. After the destruction of meaning and the referentials and finalities of modernity, postmodernism is described as a response to emptiness and anguish which is oriented toward 'the restoration of a past culture'. It tries 'to bring back all past cultures, to bring back everything that one has destroyed, all that one has destroyed in joy and which one is reconstructing in sadness in order to try to live, to survive. Really, that is the tendency. But I hope it won't finish there. I hope there is a solution that is more original than that. For the moment one really doesn't see it [*Laughter*]' (1984a: p. 24).

Baudrillard claims that in the sphere of art every possible artistic form and function has been exhausted. Theory too has exhausted itself. Thus, the postmodern is 'characteristic of a universe where there are no more definitions possible . . . It has all been done. The extreme limit of these possibilities has been reached. It has destroyed itself. It has deconstructed its entire universe. So all that are left are pieces. All that remains to be done is to play with the pieces. Playing with the pieces – that is postmodern' (Baudrillard 1984a: p. 24).

In this universe, all art – and presumably theory, politics, and individuals – can do is to recombine and play with the forms already produced. At other times, however, Baudrillard criticizes the attempt to resurrect old disciplines, forms, and ideas in a postmodern pastiche or play with remnants.[6] Indeed, Baudrillard does radically break with previous theory and politics in postulating a 'catastrophic' rupture with modernity into an entirely new social situation. His theory became increasingly idiosyncratic in the 1980s with its own distinctive language, positions, and style. Yet he never adequately describes or theorizes the assumed absolute break between the modern and the postmodern eras and thus never develops a theory of postmodernity which adequately periodizes, characterizes, or justifies claims concerning an alleged break or rupture within history. Consequently, his notion of postmodernity is grossly undertheorized and lacks adequate contextualization. Baudrillard's theory tends to be abstract, one-sided, and blind to a large number of continuities between modernity and postmodernity, as well as to numerous depressing realities and problems of the present age. The first high tech social theorist, Baudrillard reproduces certain trends of the present age which he projects into a simulation model of the future as now.

4.3.1   Metaphysical Turn: Baudrillard in the 1980s

The universe is not dialectical: it moves toward the extremes, and not towards equilibrium; it is devoted to a radical antagonism, and not to reconciliation or to synthesis. And it is the same with the principle of Evil. It is expressed in the cunning genius of the object, in the ecstatic form of the pure object, and in its victorious strategy over the subject (Baudrillard 1988: p. 185).

During the 1980s, rather than developing a theory of post-modernity, Baudrillard turned to metaphysics, and progressively displaced what might be read as his analysis of postmodernity with metaphysical ruminations concerning the new relation between the subject and object in the contemporary scene. His 1983 text *Les stratégies fatales* (translated 1990) is full of delphic pronouncements concerning the ultimate nature of things such as: 'Things have found a way to elude the dialectic of meaning, a dialectic which bored them: they did this by infinite proliferation, by potentializing themselves, by outmatching their essence, by going to extremes, and by obscenity which henceforth has become their immanent purpose and insane justification' (Baudrillard 1988b: p. 185). For Baudrillard, objects (the masses, information, media, commodities, and so on) have surpassed their limits and have eluded control by subjects. We shall see in the next section that Baudrillard interprets the alleged great divide in our historical destiny in terms of a reversal of the respective roles of the subject and the object though his metaphysical visions are connected with his analysis of the contemporary era.

Fatal Strategies attempts to develop what might be called a postmodern metaphysics which delineates a scenario where the subject has lost the battle to dominate the object which had hitherto marked the trajectory of Western metaphysics, science, and politics. Metaphysics was traditionally the attempt to conceptualize ultimate reality and for modern philosophy the subject/object dichotomy provided the framework for metaphysical investigation. The philosophy of subjectivity maintained the superiority of subject over object and modern metaphysics legitimated this superiority. According to Baudrillard, this game is over and the subject should abandon its pretensions to gain sovereignty over the object world.

Baudrillard's metaphysics is saturated with irony and is influenced by Alfred Jarry's pataphysics, 'the science of imaginary solutions'. Like the universe in Jarry's *Ubu Roi, The Gestures and Opinions of Doctor Faustroll*, and other literary texts, as well as in Jarry's more theoretical explications of pataphysics, Baudrillard's world is a totally absurd place in which objects rule in mysterious ways, and people and events are governed by absurd and ultimately unknowable interconnections and by predestination (French playwright Eugène Ionesco is another good source of entry into this space). Baudrillard follows Jarry in inventing a world in line with the fantasies, hallucinations, and projections of its creator. Like Jarry's, Baudrillard's universe is ruled by surprise, reversal, blasphemy, obscenity, and a desire to shock and outrage.

Thus while modern metaphysics is deadly serious, Baudrillard's postmodern metaphysics is more ironic, playful, and pataphysical. Yet there is a fundamental difference between Jarry's and Baudrillard's pataphysics. Jarry's subjects – Ubu Roi, Faustroll and others – heroically, albeit foolishly, try to master the universe and remake reality according to their imaginary designs, ambitions, and desires. But for Baudrillard, the subject has been defeated, the reign of objects has commenced, and we had better recognize the new rules of the game and make the necessary adjustment to the triumph of the object.

Pataphysics aside, it seems that Baudrillard is trying to end the philosophy of subjectivity which has controlled French thought since Descartes by going over completely to the other side. Descartes' evil genius was a ruse of the subject which tried to seduce him into accepting what was .not clear and distinct. But Descartes was able to master his subjectivity and to prevail over doubt and confusion. By contrast, Baudrillard's evil genius is the object itself, which is much more malign than the merely epistemological deceptions of the subject faced by Descartes, for it constitutes a fatal destiny that demands the end of the philosophy of subjectivity. Thus, Baudrillard goes much further than Foucault, Deleuze and Guattari, and other contemporary theorists in renouncing subjectivity and taking up the position of the object.

In *Fatal Strategies*, Baudrillard repeats several times one of his favourite mottoes – itself hidden menacingly in the cover of the book – '*le crystal se venge*', which suggests that in the new high tech society objects have now taken over and dominate the hapless subject. With some irony, Baudrillard recommends that individuals should thus surrender to the world of objects, learning their ruses and strategies, and should give up the project of sovereignty and control. In this strange metaphysical scenario, the problematics of reification – which has stood at the centre of

Western Marxism – comes to a bizarre end. Whereas earlier critical modern theorists – like Lukács, the Frankfurt School, Sartre, and others – worried about the decline of subjectivity and the processes whereby humans were becoming thinglike, reified, Baudrillard reverses this evaluation. Instead, he proposes that we become more like things, like objects, and divest ourselves of the illusion and hubris of subjectivity. Likewise, he proposes that it is useless to try to change or control the world and that we should give up such subjective strategies and adopt the 'fatal strategies' of objects (1983c: pp. 259ff. and 1988b: pp. 185ff.).

A fatal strategy pursues a course of action or trajectory to its extreme, attempting to surpass its limits, to go beyond its boundaries. Proliferation of information in the media, cells in cancer, sex in pornography, and the masses in contemporary society are all fatal strategies whereby objects proliferate, metastasize to extremes, and in going beyond all hitherto conceivable limits produce something new and different. During the 1970s when Baudrillard first proposed these fatal strategies he seemed to believe that pursuing the logic of the system to its extremes would cause the system to turn into something else and thus provide the radical transformation desired by those who sought a new society. For instance, he wrote: 'a system is abolished only by pushing it into hyperlogic, by forcing it into an excessive practice which is equivalent to a brutal amortization. "You want us to consume – OK, let's consume always more, and anything whatsoever; for any useless and absurd purpose"' (1983b: p. 46). Such strategies hardly caused capital any hardships and obviously were not going to subvert or transform the system and by the 1980s Baudrillard gave up postulating any specific goals or political projects.

Indeed, it is not clear why, in *Fatal Strategies*, Baudrillard recommends that we follow the ruses and trajectories of objects. It is not clear if this is a survival strategy, an ironic and comical intervention, or even a pataphysical put-on. Yet in his interviews and subsequent writings he seems quite serious about this project and continues to advocate these odd fatal strategies. Baudrillard can be read as taking the contemporary scientific view that matter is active and dynamic to pataphysical extremes where he anthropomorphizes objects as having ruses and strategies of their own. Where he claims to be repudiating the position of the subject, he in fact simply transposes it to the realm of the object. Where over a century ago Marx demystified the fetishistic character of commodity production in capitalist society, in which the value of objects appears as inherent in the objects themselves, rather than a result of exploitative social relations that extract surplus value from the working class, Baudrillard reveals himself today to be the supreme fetishist of the object world. He executes faithfully the goal of the capitalist imaginary – to reverse the roles of subject and object. Baudrillard gives to objects autonomous powers such that they seem to circulate independent of social relations of production, and he turns subjects into objects without creativity and efficacy of action. The potentially progressive critique of the domination of subjects by their own fetished and alienated object creations, or of the hubris of the subject in terms of the exploitation of animal, human, and natural life, is forfeited in the abstraction of objects from the labour process and in the denial of subjective agency. Baudrillard's evisceration of the subject precludes analysis of the responsibility and ability of subjects to collectively transform the present social structures and relations of production.

Such a development obviously takes Baudrillard beyond conventional politics and indeed beyond any imaginable politics altogether. While *Fatal Strategies* is certainly Baudrillard's most bizarre text, it is also original and ambitious. His succeeding works, however, either repeat or even pastiche previous positions (*La gauche divine*, 1985, *L'autre par lui-même*, 1987, translated as *The Ecstasy of Communication*, 1988), and *La transparence du mal* (1990), or abandon the form of theoretical argumentation altogether in favour of the genres of travel reports (*America*, 1987; translated 1988), or memoirs (*Cool Memories*, 1987; translated 1990) which revel in random asides, personal observations, and aphoristic insights. Those readers who journey through Baudrillard's 1980s writings thus encounter the same theoryscape, first set forth in his metaphysical scenario *Fatal Strategies* and then recycled in succeeding interviews, travelogues, notebooks, and essays. His writings thus take on a postmodern style which pastiches his previous texts, mixes together various subject matters, and eventually provides a frozen, glaciated hyperrealization of texts increasingly more Baudrillardian than Baudrillard, in which he endlessly reproduces his favourite ideas.

4.3.2 The End of History

> A painful thought: that beyond a certain precise moment in time, history is no longer real. Without realizing it, the whole human race suddenly left reality behind. Nothing that has occurred since then has been true, but we are unable to realize it. Our task and our duty now is to discover this point or, so long as we fail to grasp it, we are condemned to continue on our present destructive course (Canetti, *The Human Province*).

Much of Baudrillard's postmodern theory involves conceptualizing the end or disappearance of production, the real, the social, history, and other key features of modernity. He is constantly quoting Canetti's remarks that at a certain moment the human race has dropped out of history and entered a new posthistorical existence (Baudrillard 1987a: pp. 67f.; 1987b: *passim*). This process constitutes an ecstasy of history 'in the primal sense of that word – a passage at the same time into the dissolution and the transcendence of a form' (Baudrillard 1987a: p. 68). Baudrillard's discussion of the end of history exemplifies his 1980s obsession with the mode of disappearance, with a description of the demise of the key concepts of modernity. For modernity, history was its substance and ethos: modernity was a process of change, innovation, progress, and development. Moreover, history was the repository of hopes of the epoch; it would bring democracy, revolution, socialism, progress, and well-being for all. All of this has now disappeared, Baudrillard suggests, with the end of history.

Yet he claims that history is (barely) kept alive in a state of simulation, as a series of special effects or a toy (Baudrillard 1987a: pp. 68f., p. 134). History is not dead in the way God was once pronounced dead. Rather: 'Suddenly, there is a curve in the road, a turning point. Somewhere, the real scene has been lost, the scene where you had rules for the game and some solid stakes that everybody could rely on' (Baudrillard 1987a: p. 69). For Baudrillard, there are no longer any stable structures, nexuses of causality, events with consequences, or forms of determination through which one could delineate historical trajectories or lines of development. Everything instead is subject to indeterminism and an unpredictable aleatory confluence that produces vertigo.

Baudrillard provides his most detailed account of the end of history in 'The Year 2000 Has Already Happened' (1988a). He poses three different interpretations as to how history might have come to an end. His first hypothesis derives from astrophysics, and has to do with the possibility that the increasing speed with which the universe is expanding will accelerate the movement of history to such an extent that it will eventually vanish 'into a hyperspace where it loses all meaning' (1988a: p. 36). His second hypothesis also derives from the physical sciences, but the scenario is the inverse of the first. Drawing on the concept of entropy, Baudrillard suggests that if society, the masses, reach a state of absolute passivity and boredom, history will implode into a state of inertia and stagnation (1988a: pp. 37f.). His third hypothesis derives from technology, and suggests that in a situation of technological perfection, entities will cease being what they were previously. Thus music, as we presently know it, could conceivably disappear as stereophonic perfection increases. Other phenomena could similarly disappear as they become perfected. As a result, we would enter a qualitatively new field of experience, as we leave the real of history for that of simulation (1988a: p. 40).

Baudrillard suggests that we face a new, futureless future in which no decisive event can await us, because all is finished, perfected, and doomed to infinite repetition: the eternal recurrence of the same as the postmodern fate of the West. He claims that frenetic attempts to gather and circulate information and to record historical events are symptomatic of a desperate awareness that there is no more history to come, that we are frozen in a glacial present in which time is annihilated (1988a: p. 43). He concludes: 'It remains for us to accommodate ourselves to the time left to us, which is seemingly emptied of sense by this reversal. The end of this century is before us like an empty beach' (1988a: p. 44).

Interestingly, Baudrillard's postmodern theory of the end of history shares a lineage with certain conservative, postindustrial theories which make similar claims. As Claus Offe (1988) points out, theories of *post-historie*, such as those of the conservative German sociologists Gehlen and Schelsky, rule out the possibility of future global alternatives to the 'technological society' which these theorists, along with Baudrillard, see as the fate of the West. Theories of post-history utilize a model of a self-reproducing, perfected apparatus of control and functionality similar to that maintained by celebrants of the technological or cybernetic society and Baudrillard. More recently, the neo-conservative State Department house intellectual Francis Fukuyama (1989) published an article 'The End of History?' which suggests that Western liberal democracies, having won out over communism as the most viable social system, provide the ideal model for society and that all other ideas are bankrupt and obsolete. Consequently, in proposing notions of the end of history, the radical Baudrillard aligns himself with a conservative tradition of passive and apologetic thought that envisages no alternatives to the existing order of society.

'The Year 2000' thus reveals Baudrillard's thought to be frozen in static images of the end of history, obsessively fixated on a vision of entropy and sterile repetition: precisely the modality of his own work of the 1980s. This sense of stasis and ennui is especially evident in *Cool Memories* which repeat over and over Baudrillard's favourite ideas in the form of slogans which soon become platitudes. Many of Baudrillard's articles after *Cool Memories* tend to be eccentric commentaries on issues of current interest such as Heidegger and the Nazis, drugs, the 1986 French student movement, the 1987 stock market crash, and contemporary art. These articles combine some acute sociological insight with clichéd commonplaces, repetitions of his pet ideas, and downright distortions and sophistries. This is symptomatic of Baudrillard's work of the late 1980s which combines some incisive observation with sheer nonsense and with racist, sexist, and misanthropic ravings. He does not provide any significant new perspectives or ideas and his project appears to have reached a cul-de-sac.

This is particularly evident in what is perhaps his most ambitious paper of the 1980s, 'Transpolitics, Transexuality, and Transaesthetics'. This paper, delivered in May 1989 as a keynote address to the first conference in the United States devoted to Baudrillard, attempts to summarize his current position and to sketch out some new points of departure.[7] The paper evokes the utter exhaustion of all possibilities in art, sexuality, and politics and recommends assuming a 'delirious point of view' adequate to the 'delirious state of things'.

'Transaesthetics' refers to a process in which aesthetics permeates the economy, politics, culture, and everyday life, and thus loses its autonomy and specificity. Artistic forms have proliferated to such an extent that they permeate all commodities and objects so that by now everything is an aesthetic sign. All aesthetic signs coexist in a situation of indifference and aesthetic judgement is impossible: 'We are all agnostics when it comes to art: we no longer have any aesthetic convictions, we do not profess any aesthetic doctrine or we profess them all (which is the case of the agnostic toward religion).' Within the art market, prices have become so exorbitant that they too no longer signify relative values of the works but simply point to an 'ecstasy of value', in which value, like cancer, metastasizes uncontrollably beyond all boundaries and limits.

These reflections lead Baudrillard to postulate a new stage of simulacra, a new stage of value, beyond the trilogy of value postulated in his earlier study of simulations (1983a). Previously, he had postulated a natural stage of value, a mercantile stage of value, and a structural stage of value which creates a society of simulation. After these stages in the history of simulacra and value, Baudrillard claims that we are entering a new 'fractal stage of value'. He writes that:

> To the first [stage] corresponded a natural referent, and value evolved in reference to a natural use of the world. To the second corresponded a general equivalent and value evolved in reference to a logic of merchandise. To the third corresponds a code and value unfurls itself in reference to an *ensemble* of models. To the fourth stage, which I will call the fractal stage, or also, the viral stage, or still, the irradiated state of value, there is no longer a referent at all. The value irradiates in all directions, filling in all interstices, without bearing reference to anything whatsoever except by way of mere continuity.

At this fractal stage, there is no longer any natural equivalent of value, nor any structural equivalent that can be calculated as one did the price or sign value of commodities. Rather, there remains only:

> a sort of epidemic of value, a general metastasis of value; a sort of proliferation and problematic dispersal. In order to be rigorous, one should not use the word value any longer since this kind of gearing up and chain reaction nullifies all evaluation. It is once more the same as in microphysics. The reckoning of value in terms of beautiful or ugly, good or evil, true or false is as impossible as the simultaneous calculus of a particle's speed and position. Each particle follows its own movement, each value or fragment of value shines momentarily in the

sky of simulation, then disappears into the void, according to a broken line which will only cross other lines occasionally. It is the very schema of fractals and it is the present schema of our culture.

Typically, Baudrillard does not define in any more detail this 'fractal' stage of value and it is not clear how this stage differs from the third stage of simulation. He discusses, first, a 'fractal multiplication of body images' in which individuals can combine any number of models into a new body that erases previous divisions of race, class, gender, or specific looks. His prototype is Michael Jackson who has lightened his skin and undergone plastic surgery to diminish racial differences between black and white and who has also scrambled gender differences between male and female by combining appearances and behaviour traditionally associated with both sexes. Transvestites and transsexuals who undergo sex change operations are also examples for Baudrillard of transexuality in the new age of fractals.

We are currently, therefore, in what Baudrillard calls 'the post-orgy state of things' after everything is liberated, everything is possible, utopia is realized, everything can and has been done, and all we can do is to assemble the fractal pieces of our culture and proceed to its extremities, to its hypertelos beyond previous boundaries and limits. The postmodern condition is thus for Baudrillard a play with all of the forms of sexuality, art, and politics, combining and recombining forms and possibilities, moving into 'the time of transvestism'. 'In fact', he writes, 'the regime of transvestism has become the very basis of our institutions. One will find it everywhere: in politics, in architecture, in theory, in ideology, even in science (it would be very interesting to analyze transvestism in scientific theories, in art and on the chess board of politics.)'

4.3.3   Aporia and Blindspots

Reflection on this article provides insight into the striking limitations of Baudrillard's current theoretical position. First, his notion of the fractal stage of value is highly undertheorized. He says little to explicate this stage of value and his examples are not particularly helpful. It is not certain why he chooses the term 'fractal' – invented in 1975 by IBM mathematician Benoit Mandelbrot who was looking for a term to describe the measurement of irregular shapes in nature – to characterize the current stage of value. Further, it is not clear to what extent Baudrillard builds on current scientific discourse of the fractal or simply coins his own concept. Typical of his 1980s work, the concept serves more as a slogan than as a theoretical concept and is given little precise analysis, explication, or illustration. Indeed, it is not certain that Baudrillard really understands contemporary scientific theory at all. Rather, he constantly uses scientific metaphors like black holes, Moebius strips, and catastrophe theory in idiosyncratic ways to characterize current social conditions, but his use of these notions is often not appropriate or particularly illuminating.

Furthermore, Baudrillard's analysis operates on a excessively high level of abstraction. He fails to make key distinctions and engages in misplaced abstraction. For instance, Ron Silliman pointed out in his response to Baudrillard at the Montana conference that Baudrillard failed to distinguish between tranvestism and transexuality. Transvestites play at dressing as members of the opposite sex and enjoy the 'gender fucking' and subversion of dress codes; transsexuals, by contrast, are often tortured and suffering individuals who can appear uncomfortable in either sex – as evidenced by the high rate of suicides of those who undergo sex change operations. But human suffering is erased from Baudrillard's semiological universe which abstractly describes certain sign spectacles abstracted from material underpinnings.

The same bad abstraction appears in his travelogue *America* (1988d). Baudrillard speeds through the desert of America and merely sees signs floating by. He looks at Reagan on TV and sees only his smile. He hangs out in southern California and concludes that the United States is a 'realized utopia'. He fails to see, however, the homeless, the poor, racism and sexism, people dying of AIDS, oppressed immigrants, and fails to relate any of the phenomena observed to the vicissitudes of capitalism (he denies that capital ever existed in America!), or to the conservative political hegemony of the 1980s. Baudrillard's imaginary is thus a highly abstract sign fetishism which abstracts from social relations and political economy in order to perceive the play of signs in the transvestite spectacles of the transaesthetic, transsexual, and transpolitical. Baudrillard's 'trans' manoeuvres, however, are those of an idealist skimming the surface of appearances while speeding across an environment which he never contextualizes, understands, or really comes to terms with.

Indeed, Baudrillard's erasure of the fundamentality of sexual and racial differences is highly insensitive and even grotesque. Most blacks and people of colour experience virulent racism in the United States and the fact of racial difference – Baudrillard to the contrary – remains a salient feature of contemporary US society. Most blacks do not achieve the media fame and wealth of a Michael Jackson and cannot easily mix racial and sexual features in new configurations. As is obvious to anyone who has lived for any length of time in the United States, racial oppression and difference is a deep-rooted feature of contemporary US society from which Baudrillard abstracts in his 'theory' of fractal value.

Indeed, Baudrillard's current positions are profoundly superficial and are characterized by sloppy generalizations, extreme abstraction, semiological idealism and oft repeated banalities, such as: we are in a 'post-orgy condition' of simulations, entropy, fractal subjects, indifference, transvestism, and so on, *ad nauseam*. If he were merely expressing opinions or claiming to present a possible perspective on things, one would be able to enjoy his pataphysical meanderings, but Baudrillard's writing is increasingly pretentious, claiming to describe 'the real state of things', to speak for the masses, and to tell 'us' what we really believe. For instance, the essay on 'Transaesthetics' opens with the declamation:

> It is commonly held that the avant-garde no longer exists, whether this avant-garde is sexual, political or artistic; that this movement which corresponds to the linear acceleration of a history, to an anticipatory capacity and henceforth of a radical critique in the name of desire, in the name of the revolution, in the name of the liberation of forms, that this revolutionary movement has come to a close. Essentially this is true. This glorious movement which is called modernity did not lead us to a transmutation of all values, as we had once dreamed, but to a dissemination and involution of value which resulted in a state of utter confusion for us. This confusion expresses itself, first and foremost, by our inability to grasp anew the principle of an aesthetic determinacy of things, might it be political or sexual.

Baudrillard thus contradicts himself in denying that reality exists any longer in an era of simulations and hyperreality, and then constantly appealing to 'the real conditions of things today'. Note also the glib references to 'this is true' and 'utter confusion' that has resulted 'for us', while pointing to 'our inability' to perceive this or that. The easy complicity of Baudrillard and the masses, him and 'us', is pretentious and hypocritical in addition, for the implication of the whole lecture is that he really understands what is going on while 'we' remain confused and deluded. His positions are grounded in mere subjective intuition or ironic play which he wants to pass off as profound truths and which his gullible followers appropriately praise. Despite postmodern critiques of totalizing thought, Baudrillard represents totalizing thought at its worst and despite critiques of representational thought which is confident that it is describing reality as it is, Baudrillard foists his musings and asides as insight into the very heart of things.

On the other hand, Baudrillard's superficiality and banality replicate much of the superficiality and banality of contemporary culture and provide his writings with a certain resonance and potential usefulness. In fact, Baudrillard and postmodern social theory have achieved a certain notoriety because of their pathos of the new. Arguably, the intense interest in postmodern theory ultimately derives from fascination with our present moment, with the current social situation in which we find ourselves and its often surprising developments and events. Yet in articulating the new, postmodern theory – especially that of Baudrillard and his followers – tends to degenerate into sloganeering and rhetoric without any systematic or comprehensive theoretical position. With Baudrillard and other postmodernists, theory itself is 'postmodernized', adapting to the speed, fashions, superficiality, and fragmented nature of the contemporary era. Theory thus becomes a hypercommodity, geared to sell and promote the latest fashions in thought and attitudes. While for some postmodern theorists – for example, Lyotard – renunciation of systematic social theory is a methodological postulate, we suspect that for Baudrillard it is a sign of laziness or theoretical burnout. Rather than working out his ideas systematically, or with any care or detail, Baudrillard writes increasingly in an aphoristic shotgun fashion, shooting out the same ideas at the same targets until they become increasingly clichéd and predictable.

Curiously, Baudrillard is parasitical on precisely what he denies: history and social reality. Although he rejects notions of both the social and the real, he is constantly commenting on the contemporary social scene and whatever value and effects his work possess is parasitic on the saliency of his observations. He constantly uses the term 'original situation' to denote a sense of the novelty of the current social situation and the need for new theories. He also uses the sociological tropes of no longer, obsolete, and no more, which presuppose that one has grasped a shift, a change, from one situation to another. For instance, 'The Ecstasy of Communication' (1983c) is structured around a contrast between 'then' and 'now'. Then was the time of the scene, depth, alienation, and authenticity; now is the time of the obscene, surface, and the ecstasy of communication in which the subject is fragmented into a series of communications networks.

Yet it is precisely contemporary events and experiences which Baudrillard's 1980s texts completely fail to articulate. Reading his Fall 1986 lecture 'Anorexic Ruins', presented in New York at a conference on 'The End of the World' (1989b: pp. 29f.), is highly instructive in reference to the events of the late 1980s in Europe and elsewhere. Baudrillard repeats his slogans concerning the end of history, reading history as a set of anorexic ruins. One such ruin is the Berlin Wall which he sees as a lifeless image of a once 'hot' history, now serving as a sign of history coming to an end (1989b: pp. 35ff.). The dramatic tearing down of the Wall in late 1989 and ecstatic celebrations of the end of an era and beginning of a new one, of course, render Baudrillard's lugubrious ruminations on frozen history rather comical. The great postmodern prophet also misses the coming turmoil in the communist world, writing:

> The hysteria of change conceals the hysteresis of processes, especially that of the historical process, which in truth does not discontinue but rather extends and persists through inertia and thus seems quite tranquil in its own course. The meters measuring history have come to a standstill in the east with communism; in the West, with a 'liberal' society discomfited by its own excess. Under such circumstances there is no longer any stake in original political strategies. The one who enters the scene just when the meters stop stands a good chance of remaining at that point and letting history idle (1989b: p. 40).

Fortunately, the people of Eastern Europe and the communist world were not misled by Baudrillard and instead devised original and often heroic political strategies which caused important historical developments and effects (see our analysis of '1989' in Chapter 8). Curiously, Baudrillard's erasure of history and political economy in a way privileges his own discipline of sociology which seems to be capable of grasping true and real sources of change in such things as signs and codes, the trajectories of objects, the destiny of the masses, and so on. So Baudrillard is a sociologist *malgré lui* and his anti-sociology is really a covert sociology. Yet it is probably more accurate to describe Baudrillard's work as a trans-sociology, as a science fiction fantasy of a potential future, of a coming state of affairs. This is indeed a useful way to read Baudrillard: as a dystopic projection of a possible future which can be read alongside Huxley, Orwell, and cyberpunk fiction.

Moreover, it is increasingly clear that Baudrillard *is* transpolitical, beyond all political determinations and positions. In the 1989 Montana lecture, he states that just as everyone is now a transsexual, so too have 'we suddenly become transpoliticals, that is to say beings politically indifferent and undifferentiated, politically androgynous and hermaphroditic, having digested and rejected the most contradictory ideologies and knowing only how to wear the mask. We even have become, without realizing it, perhaps, political drag queens.'

Baudrillard's 'we' is a superficial homogenizing device that occludes differences and erases complexity (Beware of 'We'!). Moreover, Baudrillard to the contrary, some of us have maintained a distinct political identity, but it is probably the case that the above passage accurately describes Baudrillard's own transpolitical indifference. While he is still often read in the English-speaking world as a leftist, in fact, Baudrillard has gone so far into hyperreality that it is undecidable whether he is now really on the left or right. Baudrillard himself denies whether such political distinctions really have any meaning. Yet he chooses to focus his more overt political polemics against the French left and expresses occasional scorn toward ecologists, peace activists, feminists, and others generally deemed progressive.[8]

At bottom, therefore, we would suggest that the Baudrillard of the 1980s is best read as 'transpolitical' and as difficult to categorize in traditional political models. Yes, Baudrillard is beyond left and right and traditional political determinations – though his political asides have the pungent flavour of a neo-Nietzschean aristocratic aestheticism which is hardly unknown to French culture. Although Baudrillard provides many stimulating aspects toward developing a comprehensive theory of postmodernity, of a new historical epoch, ultimately his efforts remain woefully under-theorized and inadequate to interpret the momentous changes that he suggests are taking place. Consequently, while Baudrillard's work takes us en route to developing a theory of postmodernity, it ultimately fails to deliver the goods.

Yet much of Baudrillard's early and middle work is extremely valuable for illuminating some of the development of contemporary techno-capitalist societies. His early writings contain novel syntheses of Marxian political economy and semiology, producing a political economy of the sign and incisive perspectives on the consumer and media society. His middle works on simulation, hyperreality, and implosion are often brilliant and capture the turn toward simulation and hyperreality in contemporary capitalist societies. These categories have been immensely productive in analyzing contemporary media and cultural trends. But his most extreme postmodern theory often takes contemporary trends as finalities. He exaggerates the extent to which postmodern simulation and hyperreality constitute the contemporary society and his erasure of political economy mystifies the continuing domination of capital. On the other hand, the extent to which new forms of simulation, cyberspace, and technologically produced realities in the forms of computer games, designer foods and cosmetics, artificial awareness modules, and other curiosities are currently being introduced suggests some dramatic future transformations which Baudrillard's categories anticipate.[9]

Baudrillard's best work can therefore be read along with the novels of J. G. Ballard, Philip Dick, William Gibson, and cyberpunk fiction as projecting visions of futuristic worlds which illuminate the present high tech society. These novels concretize postmodern categories and Baudrillard himself has been influenced by some of this fiction.[10] Unfortunately, in the 1980s, Baudrillard has neither pursued his studies of simulation and hyperreality, nor opened any exciting new theoretical perspectives. He has the curious habit of discarding his best ideas and abandoning his most promising research perspectives. In the middle 1970s, for example, he dropped his fascinating syntheses of semiology and political economy, and made the fatal mistake of breaking with political economy. In the 1980s he dropped his studies of simulation and turned to metaphysics and transpolitics.

During the period of Baudrillard's theoretical collapse, however,

Jean-Francois Lyotard entered into a prolific period, producing a variety of postmodern perspectives, and it is to Lyotard's work that we now turn.

Notes

1. See Kroker and Levin 1984: p. 6 and the 'Notes on Contributors' in Kroker *et al.*, 1989: p. 265.
2. For further discussion of Baudrillard's work, see Kellner 1989b and Best 1989b.
3. On the Lukácsian problematic of the commodification and reification of the totality of life under contemporary capitalism, see Lukács 1971. The Frankfurt School had also discerned the importance of commodities and consumption in the reproduction of capitalist societies, but although the starting point and perception is similar, Baudrillard's work eventually will differ from these predecessors in his use of the categories of semiology to explore the commodity world. On the Frankfurt School analyses of commodification and the consumer society, see Kellner 1989a.
4. In *L'échange symbolique et la mort*: pp. 193ff., Baudrillard draws on several of Foucault's major works, citing them as 'masterful analyses of the true history of our culture, the Genealogy of Discrimination' (1976: p. 195). The entire book resonates with Foucauldian notions of the disciplinary society, the normalization of the body, etc. All the more curious that Baudrillard would soon tell us to *Forget Foucault* (1987a).
5. In *The Will to Power*, Nietzsche writes (1967: p. 330): 'That the value of the world lies in our interpretation ... that every elevation of man [*sic*] brings with it the overcoming of narrower interpretations; that every strengthening and increase of power opens up new perspectives and means believing in new horizons – this idea permeates my writings.'
6. See Baudrillard 1986a where he distances himself from what he describes as a postmodern resurrection of philosophy (p. 32) and a postmodern 'patchwork' of old values and ideas (p. 38). In another interview, he states that his theories of simulations and fatal strategies are more than a mere postmodern theory: 'In the notions of simulacrum, seduction and fatal strategy, there is something metaphysical at stake (without wanting to be too serious) that the postmodern reduces to an effect of intellectual fashion, or to a syndrome of the failure of modernity. In this sense, the postmodern is itself actually post-modern: it is itself only a model of superficial simulation, and designates nothing else but itself. These days, that assures it a long posterity' (1989b: p. 5).
7. At the May 1989 conference featuring 'Baudrillard in the Mountains', Baudrillard provided the main address to which poet and former *Socialist Review* editor Ron Silliman responded. Thanks to Silliman for providing us with Baudrillard's talk and his response. This paper is the

centrepiece of Baudrillard's *La transparence du mal* (1990) which merely collects his recent shorter pieces.

8. While many perceive Baudrillard as a leftist radical, in fact, he has published several of his 1980s books in a series edited by 'new philosopher' entrepreneur Bernard-Henri Lévy who helped lead the cavalry of the New Right in attacks on Marxism and the left which were held responsible for the Gulag and other political atrocities.

9. See magazines such as *High Frontiers, Mondo 2000, Reality Hackers, Processed World* and some of the more mundane computer and high tech publications for examples of new technologies and artifacts representative of Baudrillard's postmodern categories.

10. See, for instance, his analysis of Ballard's *Crash*, collected in *Simulacres et simulation* (Baudrillard 1981: pp. 165ff.). Baudrillard also helped edit the Beauborg Cultural Centre publication *Traverses* which frequently contains futuristic articles and special issues on such topics as hyperrealism, simulacra, computers, robots, and so on.

Chapter 5

Lyotard and Postmodern Gaming

In many circles, Lyotard is celebrated as *the* postmodern theorist *par excellence.*[1] His book *The Postmodern Condition* (1984a; orig. 1979) introduced the term to a broad public and has been widely discussed in the postmodern debates of the last decade. During this period, Lyotard has published a series of books which promote postmodern positions in theory, ethics, politics, and aesthetics. More than almost anyone, Lyotard has championed a break with modern theory and methods, while popularizing and disseminating postmodern alternatives. As a result, his work sparked a series of intense controversies that we address in this and the following chapters.

Above all, Lyotard has emerged as the champion of difference and plurality in all theoretical realms and discourses, while energetically attacking totalizing and universalizing theories and methods. In *The Postmodern Condition, Just Gaming* (1985; orig. 1979), *The Differend* (1988; orig. 1983) and a series of other books and articles published in the 1980s, he has called attention to the differences among the plurality of 'regimes of phrases' which have their own rules, criteria, and methods. Stressing the heterogeneity of discourses, Lyotard has, following Kant, argued that such domains as theoretical, practical, and aesthetic judgement have their own autonomy, rules, and criteria. In this way, he rejects notions of universalist and foundationalist theory, as well as claims that one method or set of concepts has privileged status in such disparate domains as philosophy, social theory, or aesthetics.

146

Arguing against what he calls 'terroristic' and 'totalitarian' theory, Lyotard thus resolutely champions a plurality of discourses and positions against unifying theory.

Many of Lyotard's positions are of fundamental importance for contemporary postmodern theory and in this chapter we shall discuss those ideas which we find to be most central to current controversies and debates. Since his career encompasses almost four decades of diverse theoretical activity, our focus necessarily will be selective and will ignore many of his interesting interventions in theory, aesthetics, and politics. While we shall point to some important shifts in Lyotard's works from the standpoint of postmodern theory, there is also a continuity to his development. For at all stages, Lyotard sharply attacks modern discourses and theories, while attempting to develop new discourses, writing strategies, politics, and perspectives.

This chapter will delineate the circuitous paths through which Lyotard took up and developed the discourse of the postmodern. Accordingly, we shall see how his early works led him to adopt postmodern positions (5.1) and then examine his full-blown postmodern texts (5.2 and 5.3). While we attempt to sympathetically present Lyotard's postmodern perspectives, we also point to some of their aporia and limitations (5.4). At stake is whether Lyotard provides an adequate critique of modern discourses and theory, an acceptable postmodern epistemology, and a viable postmodern politics.

5.1 Drifting with Marx, Freud, and Nietzsche: Early Writings

> What is important in a text is not what it means, but what it does and incites to do. What it does: the charge of affect it contains and transmits. What it incites to do: the metamorphoses of this potential energy into other things – other texts, but also paintings, photographs, film sequences, political actions, decisions, erotic inspirations, acts of insubordination, economic initiatives, etc. (Lyotard 1984b: pp. 9–10).

Lyotard was born in Versailles in 1924 and studied philosophy and literature at the Sorbonne. Active in trade union politics, his first essays in the late 1940s and early 1950s were primarily on political themes. Philosophically, he was influenced by Husserl and his first book produces a clear and sympathetic introduction to *La phéno-*

ménologie (1954). Just before the Algerian war, he taught and was politically active in Algeria. Radicalized by the Algerian experience, Lyotard became politically engaged upon his return to France and joined the group *Socialisme ou Barbarie*.[2] During this period, he wrote many articles for left journals and was active in the French anti-war movement.

Cornelius Castoriadis was the major theoretician of the 'Socialism or Barbarism' group. When he developed a fundamental critique of Marxian theory which he claimed was no longer adequate to describe contemporary conditions, a segment of the group, including Lyotard, split and formed an organization around the journal *Pouvoir ouvrier* in 1964. In 1966, Lyotard broke from this group and later said: 'A stage of my life was ending, I was leaving the service of the revolution, I would do something else, I had saved my skin' (1988b: p. 49). Lyotard turned to theoretical studies and began preparing himself for an academic career. Yet as a lecturer at Nanterre University, he became involved in the May 1968 student movement and was active in oppositional politics for some years.

In 1971, Lyotard received his dissertation with the text *Discours, figure*; he became a philosophy professor at Vincennes University in the early 1970s where he was a popular teacher and prolific writer, receiving recognition as a professor emeritus in 1987. His early works – *Discours, figure* (1971), *Dérive à partir de Marx et Freud* (1973), *Des dispositifs pulsionnels* (1973), and *Economie libidinale* (1974) – exhibit a profound kinship with Deleuze and Guattari, sharing a Nietzschean philosophy of forces, intensities, and affects which he develops as a philosophy and politics of desire. Deeply influenced by Marx and Freud, Lyotard breaks with Marx in his early texts and turns – temporarily – to a highly aggressive Nietzschean philosophy of affirmation. His theory is also more strongly informed by aesthetic concerns than the works which we have so far examined and he has published widely on art and aesthetics.[3]

5.1.1 Discours, figure

> This book protests that the given is not a text, that there is within it a density, or rather a constitutive difference, which is not to be read, but to be seen: and that this difference, and the immobile mobility which reveals it, is what is continually forgotten in the process of signification (Lyotard 1971: p. 9).

Discours, figure begins Lyotard's polemic against theoretical discourse and contains his first systematic attempt to develop new theoretical perspectives. The study is complemented by a series of essays from the same period, *Dérive à partir de Marx et Freud*, some of which is translated in *Driftworks* (1984b).[4] *Discours, figure* contains a series of criticisms of Saussure, Lacan, Hegel, Merleau-Ponty, Freud, and other theorists, while developing a new transgressive aesthetics and mode of writing. David Carroll's term 'paraesthetics' (1987) seems useful to describe this enterprise which turns art against theory by using the figures, forms, and images of art to subvert and overthrow theoretical positions.

Rejecting the textualist approach which privileges texts and discourses over experience, the senses, and images, *Discours, figure* defends the claims of the senses and experience over abstractions and concepts. Lyotard describes his text as a 'defence of the eye' (1971: p. 11), and his deep immersion in visual arts informs his position. Criticizing the devaluation of the senses in Western philosophy since Plato, Lyotard attempts to dissolve the 'penumbra which, after Plato, speech has thrown like a grey veil over the sensible, which has been constantly thematized as less-than-being, and whose side has very rarely truly been taken, taken in truth, since it was understood that this was the side of falsity, of scepticism, of the rhetorician, the painter, the *condottière*, the libertine, the materialist' (Lyotard 1971: p. 11).

Criticizing the pantextualism of some poststructuralists, Lyotard declares that: 'one does not at all break with metaphysics by putting language everywhere' (1971: p. 14). Pursuing Derrida's critique of philosophy, he argues that Western philosophy has been organized around a set of binary oppositions between discourse and figure, the discursive and the sensible, saying and seeing, reading and perceiving, and universality and singularity. In each case, the former position traditionally has been privileged and Lyotard attempts to defend the devalued member of the binary set. Opposing the primacy of language advocated in many semiotic theories, Lyotard champions figure, form, and image – in other words, art and imagination – over theory. *Discours, figure* is dense and highly complex with its first half polemicizing against 'imperialistic' semiotics and Hegelian theory, while the second half presents the first sketch of his philosophy of desire which champions bodily forces, intensities, and what he calls 'energetics'. The first half draws heavily on phenomenology, especially Merleau-Ponty, to criticize formalist linguistic theories and speculative metaphysics, while the second half draws on Freud to develop a philosophy of desire, a position that would later be developed by Lyotard in more Nietzschean terms.

Desire for Lyotard in *Discours, figure* is divided into a negative, disruptive, transgressive force which subverts reality to gain its ends and a more positive, affirmative force which affirms certain words, sounds, colours, forms, and objects. He claims that both senses appear in Freud (1971: p. 246), and he reads Freud as a theorist of the disruptive and transformative nature of desire. For Lyotard, Eros, the life instincts, and Thanatos, the death instincts, are intertwined in Freud's theory of the unconscious and Freud stresses that it is undecidable whether desire in a given instance is destructive or unifying, negative or positive. In fact, he suggests that Eros and Thanatos are both always present in desire.

Where Deleuze and Guattari denounce forms of fascist desire, Lyotard, at this stage, celebrates all desire (positive and negative) for providing intensities of experience, liberation from repressive conditions, and creativity. Further, art and figure are the privileged vehicles of desire which are deemed to be disruptive and transgressive, as well as affirmative of life energies which they articulate in figural forms. Disruptive desire is thus most immediately found in art which attacks the existing regime of reason, order, and convention. For Lyotard, desire in what Freud calls the 'primary processes' (direct, libidinal, unconscious, instinctual processes governed by the pleasure principle) finds direct expression in figures. In addition, art articulates unconscious desire which follows the ruses of displacement, condensation, and metaphoric transformation.

Discourse, by contrast, follows what Freud describes as 'secondary processes' (that is, processes governed by the reality principle) and proceeds by the rules and rational procedures of the ego. Desire which is articulated into discourse is bounded and structured by the rules of language. Discourse is thus more abstract, rationalized, and conventional than the figures of desire. Consequently, Lyotard links discourse with theory that freezes, immobilizes, and paralyzes the flow and intensities of desire (1971: pp. 11ff.; see also Lyotard 1974: pp. 9ff. and the partial translation in Lyotard 1975).

Lyotard thus attempts to redeem images, forms, and figures

from their critique, or devaluation, by both rationalist and textualist discourse theories. Scott Lash (1988: pp. 313ff.) argues that the distinction between discourse and figure itself provides the foundation for a postmodern aesthetics as a 'figural regime of signification'. In Lash's reading, the modern sensibility is primarily discursive, privileging words over images, sense over nonsense, meaning over non-meaning, reason over the irrational, and the ego over the id. The postmodern sensibility is, by contrast, figural, and privileges a visual over a literal sensibility, figure over concept, sensation over meaning, and immediacy over more mediated intellectual modes. Lash suggests that Susan Sontag's 'new sensibility' and championing of an 'aesthetics of sensation' over an 'aesthetics of interpretation' anticipates a postmodern aesthetics which can be conceptually grounded through Lyotard's distinction between discourse and figure.

Deleuze and Guattari praised Lyotard's critique of the signifier and privileging of the figural element (1983: p. 243). They agree with Lyotard that even in written language there is a primary asignifying element which escapes language and semiotic chains to flow into the realm of intensities. Further, they commend Lyotard for reversing the order of signifier and figure, breaking with the view that makes the figure dependent on the signifier and instead tying signification to the realm of the figural (Deleuze and Guattari 1983: p. 244). For Lyotard and Deleuze and Guattari, then, it is not a matter of privileging the signifier over the signified, but of championing the 'flux-schiz' or the 'break-flow' over signifying schemes (ibid.).

Interestingly, Lyotard provides a quite different analysis of images from Baudrillard. While images in contemporary society for Debord and Baudrillard became increasingly abstract, commodified, and divorced from social reality in the form of spectacles or simulations, for the early Lyotard the image is the very figure of plenitude, of pulsating desire, of singularity. Debord and Baudrillard analyze how images manipulate desire into commodified consumption and other modes of social conformity, while Lyotard privileges image and figure as forces that intensify life and the flow of desire. Lyotard thus operates with something of a romanticism of the image or figure at this point, while attacking language and theory. He tends to divorce images from their actual process of social production and reception, and uncritically champions images and figures *per se* as vehicles of desire and intensities. This perspective neglects the way that capitalism exploits images and exhibits a lack of social theory and critique which we find to be a recurrent problem in Lyotard's work.

Yet Lyotard's *Discours, figure* is deconstructive as well, and does not simply champion figure over discourse, or seeing over saying. Lyotard wishes to allow figure to enter and shape discourse, as well as to develop a mode of writing that is a figuring, 'to paint with and in words' (1971: p. 53). Consequently, he champions imagery, polysemic poetic tropes, and ambiguity in writing, valorizing poetry as a model for all types of writing. The goal is to disrupt abstract theoretical discourses with figural discourse and to overthrow hegemonic discourses with new discourses that employ transgressive literary strategies. Thus *Discours, figure* is protopostmodern without naming the conceptual space of the new discourse that Lyotard is searching for 'postmodern', or systematically labelling the theoretical discourses under attack as 'modern'.

5.1.2 *Lyotard's Nietzschean Drift: Libidinal Economy and the Politics of Desire*

> If one had to enumerate the shores from which this boat set adrift and distanced itself: a certain Freud; a certain Marx; a general notion of critique ... an idea of transgression which belongs to the same sphere of *critique* (Lyotard 1973: p. 9).

Lyotard's early texts exhibit a complex, even convoluted, trajectory. *Discours, figure* and most of the texts collected in *Dérive à partir de Marx and Freud* participated in the May 1968 ultra-left discourse of critique, deconstruction, demystification, reversal, and revolutionary transformation. The post-1968 texts through 1970 continued – as with his earlier writings – to be sympathetic to Marx and positively employed Marxian discourse and critical strategies in the form of *gauchisme* or ultra-leftism. In the interview 'On Theory' (1984b; orig. 1970), Lyotard characterizes theory in typically Marxian terms claiming that 'the function of theory is not only to understand, but also to criticize, that is, to call in question and *overturn* a reality, social relationships, the relationships of men with things and other men, which are clearly intolerable' (1984b: p. 19; orig. 1970). In the interview, Lyotard criticizes Althusser and orthodox Marxism, while defending a left-variant whose goal was to undermine dominant discourses, practices, and institutions as part of a thoroughgoing social critique and transformation. Lyotard shared this ultra-left politics of negation, though by the early 1970s he was to abandon this project and would critique theoretical discourse itself.

In the Preface to the collection of essays *Dérive*, translated in *Driftworks* (1984b), Lyotard attacked the revolutionary discourse of critique, negation and deconstruction. The Preface 'Adrift' begins with a typically Lyotardian attack on modern reason and unifying philosophical schemes, while valorizing intensity, fragments, plurality, singularity and drifting. He polemicizes against the demand for unity and coherence in theoretical discourse, arguing that such a battle is 'a battle for reason, for unity, for the unification of diversities, a quibbling battle which no one can win for the winner is already and has always been reason' (Lyotard 1984b: p. 11). In the ultra-revolutionary rhetoric of the day, he explains: 'We don't want to destroy capital because it isn't rational, but because it is. Reason and power are one and the same thing. You may disguise the one with dialectics . . . but you will still have the other in all its crudeness: jails, taboos, public weal, selection, genocide' (ibid.).

This wildly anti-theoretical animus is also directed against the project of critique and the language of dialectics. Criticizing and negating, he suggests, is infinite and useless, never coming to an end. During this period Lyotard is, in his own metaphor, 'drifting', searching for a new way of thought and practice. His break with more conventional radical theories have set him adrift and he is attempting to affirm the very absence of a fixed theoretical and political position. As he later put it: 'Only by my not mourning my powerlessness could another way of thinking be sketched out, I thought without justification, just as at sea a swimmer incapable of opposing the current relies on drifting to find another way out' (Lyotard 1988b: p. 54).

Rejecting the discourse of critique and negation, Lyotard adopts instead a Nietzschean affirmative discourse within a politics and philosophy of desire. This project is worked out in *Economie libidinale* (1974), Lyotard's most extreme break with modern discourses and most violent critique of theory, reason, and the discourses of modernity. The text is, along with *Anti-Oedipus*, the most striking example of the micropolitics of desire and the critique of representation. Like Deleuze and Guattari, Lyotard presents an affirmative philosophy of desire which celebrates the circulation, flows, intensities, and energetics of desire.

Thus, strictly speaking, *Economie libidinale* should not be read as a 'Freudo-Marxian' text. Lyotard's libidinal economy turns Marx against Freud, Freud against Marx, and Nietzsche against both. Lyotard has now drifted away from Marx into the turbulent theoretical currents of a Nietzschean vitalism. As with Deleuze and Guattari, Lyotard claims that desire is bound and fixed into oppressive forms through the family, workplace, economy, and state. In binding desire to authoritarian social forces, it is deintensified with an ensuing loss of life energies and vitality. Like Deleuze and Guattari, Lyotard thus embraces a sort of Nietzschean vitalism, a philosophy of life (*Lebensphilosophie*) that affirms the free flowing of life energies.

The goal of libidinal economy, like schizoanalysis, is to describe the flows, intensities, and territorializations of desire, to liberate the flows of desire, and to unleash desire in its full and glorious varieties and intensities. Theory itself binds desire by congealing it into fixed categories, values, and modes of thought and behaviour. Even critical theory which operates by critique and negation often merely negates and fails to affirm desire, to produce actual intensities. Libidinal economy thus offers a new type of theory and practice that is purely affirmative, that attempts to provide the outlines of a new (anti)theoretics and politics of desire.

The process of cultivating intensities, Lyotard believes, is best achieved by a certain sort of art and writing. Against the semiotic sign, Lyotard advocates the 'tensor', a conduit for desire that does not terminate in a unitary and identical meaning but which generates libidinal effects (1974: pp. 57ff.; partially translated in Lyotard 1989: pp. 1ff.). The notion is similar to what Derrida calls 'dissemination' and Kristeva 'semiosis', except that Lyotard is more interested in the proliferation and intensification of libidinal effects rather than merely the multiplication and dispersion of signification.

In his essays of the period, Lyotard provides some concrete examples from the realms of art and politics of how certain artistic and political practices can positively liberate desire and create new flows and intensities. He tends to privilege avant-garde art as the most efficacious mode of producing intensities, evoking libidinal effects, just as he earlier privileged figure over discourse. In an article on John Cage, 'Several Silences', Lyotard valorizes the surges of tension, intensities, 'dissonances, stridences, positively exaggerated, ugly, silences' in Cage's music (Lyotard 1984b: p. 92; orig. 1972. A 'libidinal economy' of artistic production will describe how the devices of the work provide effects, either blocking or facilitating flows and intensities of desire. Lyotard valorizes singular intensities, rather than the musical structure, composition, or effects of the work as a whole, arguing that: 'To hear this event is to transform it: into tears, gestures, laughter, dance, words, sounds, theorems, repainting your room, helping a friend move' (1984b: p. 93). As a positive example of libidinal intensities and effects he says: 'I can testify to the fact that a black cat (Lhermite) heard Kagel's *Music for Renaissance Instruments*: bristling of whiskers, fluttering of ears, prowling in the vicinity of the listening room. The intensity of noise-sound – an urge to produce something' (ibid.).

Thus it is libidinal effects, the intensifying and flow of desire, which are at stake in libidinal economy. In an article on Adorno from the same period, Lyotard claims: 'What brings us out of capital and out of "art" (and out of the *Entkunstung*, its complement) is not criticism, which is language-bound, nihilistic, but a deployment of libidinal investment. We do not desire to possess, to "work", to dominate ... What can they do about that?' (Lyotard 1984b: p. 136; orig. 1972). We see here that the aesthetic practices of the libidinal economy are related to political practices, to a micropolitics of desire, which champions the production of intensities. From this postmodern perspective, activities that produce intensities, that free and intensify the flow of desire, are embraced over modern politics which are concerned with such things as rights and justice. In several essays of the period, Lyotard gives examples of such a politics of desire. In an article 'Notes on the Return and Kapital' which takes up Deleuze's challenge of providing an 'intensive reading of Nietzsche' that unleashes the intensities in theoretical texts, Lyotard concludes:

> More important than political leftism, closer to a concurrence of the intensities: a vast subterranean movement, wavering, more of a ruffle in fact, on account of which the law of value is dis-affected. Holding up

production, uncompensated seizures (thefts) as modalities of consumption, refusal to 'work,' (illusory?) communities, happenings, sexual liberation movements, occupations, squattings, abductions, productions of sounds, words, colours, with no 'work of art' intentions. Here are the 'men of profusion', the *'masters'* of today: marginals, experimental painters, pop, hippies and yippies, parasites, madmen, binned loonies. One hour of their lives offers more intensity and less intention than three hundred thousand words of a professional philosopher. More Nietzschean than Nietzsche's readers (Lyotard 1978a: p. 53; orig. 1973).

Lyotard links here a postmodern micropolitics of desire to a Nietzschean politics of intensities and finds vehicles of this politics in the contemporary political scene (see also Lyotard 1977: pp. 24–5; orig. 1972). Yet he will soon abandon this utopian politics of desire which sees subversive desires exploding everywhere. First, in *Economie libidinale*, Lyotard seemed to abandon politics altogether, or to reject all existing political positions, and then he turned to a politics of justice and discourse which we shall discuss below. His early works thus pursued a politics of bodily affirmation to its extremes and Lyotard eventually saw the limitations of this position and moved toward a politics of justice.

In *Libidinal Economy*, Lyotard splits decisively with Marxism and those contemporaries who do not break sharply enough with Marx. His critique emerges in a dialogue with Baudrillard and Deleuze and Guattari whom he describes as close 'brothers' to his own positions: 'There is a *movement* in Baudrillard with which we feel as synchronized and copolarized with our own positions. Very close to us, you only have to read him. Yet far from us, because that which governs the approach of this brother remains for us weighed down by the mortgage of theory and of critique' (Lyotard 1974: p. 128). Baudrillard is too rationalistic and trapped in the modern problematics of truth and representation, rejecting the Marxist theory, for example, on the grounds that he has discovered a better, truer theory (see Baudrillard 1981 and 1975). Moreover, for Lyotard, Baudrillard's privileging of symbolic exchange over production rests on a nostalgic idealization of archaic society. Despite Baudrillard's rejection of naturalism in theory, of attempts of political economy to naturalize historically produced forms of behaviour, Lyotard suggests that there is a bit of naturalism in Baudrillard which repeats the ethnographic figure of the noble savage and good symbolic exchange which is opposed to bad production (1974: p. 130) – a critique which he repeats in *The Postmodern Condition* where he writes that Baudrillard 'is haunted by the paradisaic representation of a lost "organic" society' (1984a: p. 15).

According to Lyotard, Baudrillard shares with Marx and other radical modern theorists a 'fantasy of a region that is exterior' where radical desire would be the motor of (revolutionary) forces opposed to production. This myth of a 'non-alienated' region is also transposed by Baudrillard into a myth that radical, marginalized outsiders are found in modern society. Thus, 'the *subversive reference*, that of the good savage and good hippy is for him [Baudrillard] present *positively* in modern society, not only *negatively* as Marx imagined the proletariat' (1974: p. 132). As we have just seen, Lyotard himself had earlier championed an affirmative subversive politics with references in the contemporary society, but now he condemns this as yet another 'religious fantasy' and affirms a 'desperate' politics without a region: 'Perhaps, as for politics, *we will still desire and always be desperate*' (that is, since 'we', Lyotardians, lack a positive subject of revolution) (1974: p. 133).

Lyotard believes that Castoriadis (1974: pp. 142ff.), like Baudrillard, is too caught up in the theoretics of representation, truth, production, religious politics, and thus modernity and its practices. Lyotard, by contrast, is positioning his own theory (in the style common to the competitive French intellectual scene of the day) as the most radical and avant-garde theory that surpasses all previous discourses and politics – an ultra-radical and avant-gardist ethos that would lend itself to the postmodern turn which he would take by the end of the decade. He is attempting to break more radically with modernity than anyone, to enter a new space for which he still has not found the term postmodern.

Economie libidinale is Lyotard's most extreme attempt to go beyond all previous theory, to develop a radically new theory, to open new theoretical space in a celebration of textual effects over meanings and valorization of the body, desire, and intensities. The text attacks modern theory from Hegel and Marx through semiotic theory and Baudrillard. Almost everyone, including Lyotard himself, found the book to be a theoretical dead-end, trapping its author in a series of untenable positions. While he criticized the naturalism of Marx, Baudrillard, and others, it is hard to see how his own relentless Nietzschean vitalism escapes naturalistic traps, celebrating desire and its intensities as the Great Other of blockage, repression, inhibition, and fixation. Furthermore, desire for Lyotard functions much like labour for Marx through creating a world, becoming alienated, and then struggling for liberation in the revolutionary scenario. In a similar fashion, so too does desire for Lyotard invest itself in a world of objects, become alienated, and then struggles for release in subversive and emancipatory eruptions. Thus, just as the proletariat overcomes alienation within labour, so too does libidinal economy attempt to emancipate desires and intensities from their alienation.

Economie libidinale thus seems to commit Lyotard to a naive naturalism in which the expression, articulation, and effects of all desire, beyond good and evil, were valorized, making it impossible to distinguish between fascist and revolutionary, or regressive and emancipatory desire. Later he would replace this amoral naturalism with a linguistic turn and ethic of justice which broke with his earlier vitalistic metaphysic and Nietzschean affirmation of life energies.

We believe that Lyotard's totally affirmative version of Nietzsche's vitalism caricaturizes and distorts Nietzsche's own thought which operates with a dialectic of yes and no, affirmation and negation, and not just pure affirmation.[5] It is also questionable whether one can escape theory and reason from within the highly theoretical discourse of Lyotard's *Economie libidinale* with its abstractions, implicit claims to truth and validity, and complex rhetoric and linguistic demands. Thus the project of *Economie libidinale* is aporetic and in a 1976 article collected in *Rudiments païens*, he speaks of the philosophy of desire merely as a *façon de parler*, a way of speaking (Lyotard 1977: p. 130). In a Preface to a new edition of *Des dispositifs pulsionnels*, Lyotard refers to his earlier work as a 'metaphysics of desire or of drives' which is merely a *coup*, a polysemic word that could describe them as a blow, a shock, a bolt of thunder, or, more modestly, a discursive intervention (1980: p. iii). In conversations with Jean-Loup Theabaud in 1977/8, published in 1979 as *Au Juste*, Lyotard concedes that his *Economie libidinale* is highly dogmatic and represents a failed attempt to develop a philosophy of forces. The text is primarily rhetorical, he admits, and works largely on the level of persuasion (1985: p. 4).

Lyotard recognizes that this philosophy of will and desire cannot yield a political philosophy, confessing: 'It is not true that one can do an aesthetic politics. It is not true the search for intensities or things of that type can ground politics, because there is the problem of injustice. It is not true, for example, that once one has gotten rid of the primacy of the understanding in its knowing function, there is only aesthetic judgement left to discriminate between the just and the unjust. Aesthetic judgement allows the discrimination of that which pleases from that which does not please. With justice, we have to do, of necessity, with the regulation of something else' (1985: p. 90).

In his search for a new standpoint to develop a philosophy of justice and judgement, Lyotard turned to philosophy of language, replacing the discourse and politics of desire with a theory and politics of language. Lyotard breaks ranks with the micropolitics of desire championed by his comrades Deleuze and Guattari and never returns to these perspectives. He rejects, therefore, the sort of aestheticized politics typical of much postmodern theory and is one of the few postmodern theorists who takes seriously the problematics of justice. The issue of injustice and justice drives him to reflect on the nature of political judgement and the question of prescriptives. These problems in turn lead him to his study of Kant and his later philosophical perspectives. Yet we shall see that this turn in his itinerary propels him to develop a postmodern politics of discourse and not simply to return to modern politics. Lyotard's earlier works can be read in retrospect as linguistic experiments which sought certain effects but which were ultimately deemed unsatisfactory. Henceforth the focus of his critique from the mid-1970s to the present is on 'metalanguage', on totalizing theories, and his strategies are linguistic, providing new ways of theorizing, talking, and writing. In a mid-1970s article 'One of the Things at Stake in Women's Struggles', Lyotard proposes inventing new guerilla strategies of discursive skirmishes and raids, inventing new theory fictions, new modes of feminine writing (1989). The enemy is masculist metalanguage, totalizing theory that empowers and legitimates masculine and class rule. Against hegemonic and homogeneous masculine discourses, Lyotard calls for a 'patchwork' of minority discourses, of ways of speaking differently. For 'men in all their claims to construct meaning, to speak the Truth, are themselves only a minority in a *patchwork* where it becomes impossible to establish and validly determine any major order' (1989: pp. 15–16).

5.1.3   *Paganism, Just Gaming, and the Postmodern Turn*

After *Economie libidinale*, Lyotard published a series of literary/ philosophical experimental texts and some writings on art between 1977 and 1979, when he made his postmodern turn. His early writings had probed, questioned, subverted, transformed, and even attempted to obliterate theoretical discourse (for example, as in *Economie libidinale*). Yet, Lyotard sought other ways of presenting 'theoretical' positions, utilizing literary experiments, writings about art, philosophical dialogues, and 'rudimentary' essays before returning to theoretical treatises and discourse with *The Postmodern Condition*. Indeed, his literary texts *Récits tremblant* and *Le mur du pacifique* make theoretical points, as do his philosophical dialogues.

'Lessons in Paganism' (Lyotard 1989; orig. 1977) is a philosophical dialogue with himself in which he first sets forth his new 'pagan' philosophy and satirically attacks the 'new philosophers' who were then engaging in a polemic against Marxism and the 'master thinkers' – such as Hegel and Marx – who were supposedly responsible for the Soviet Gulags and other horrors of contemporary society. 'Paganism' breaks with the modern concern for truth and certainty. Yet it manifests a concern for justice and this turn to an explicit philosophy of justice constitutes a decisive shift from Lyotard's previous amoral vitalistic perspectives. He suggests that all discourse is narrative and focuses his lessons on analysis of narrative. Narratives take place in specific narrative contexts and their references are other narratives. For paganism there are no privileged narratives, no metatheories of truth or grand historical narratives. Thus he suggests that Marxism and other Enlightenment theories are historical narratives, stories about the historical process (1989: pp. 126ff.) and not themselves the ground or truth of history. In practice, the Marxian metanarrative justifies 'the history recounted by Communist Power' and thus legitimates existing communist regimes (1989: p. 128). Lyotard attacks this narrative while valorizing the oppositional narratives of opponents to the Communist regime. He thus prefigures the attack on 'grand narratives' in *The Postmodern Condition* which valorizes 'little narratives' and the proliferation of narratives in our culture.

Lyotard argues that 'theories themselves are concealed narratives' and that 'we should not be taken in by their claims to be valid for all time' (1989: p. 130). Most of 'Lessons in Paganism', however, mocks the 'new philosophers' (1989: pp. 141ff.) and does not fully explicate his conception of 'justice'. This issue becomes central to *Just Gaming*, a dialogue with Jean-Loup Thébaud, where Lyotard continues to criticize modern theory which he contrasts with his 'paganism'. The French title *Au Juste* could be read as *Towards Justice* and it is important to read the English title as *just* gaming, in the sense of playing the game of the just, rather than as merely gaming in a frivolous way. Justice involves playing by the rules and preserving the autonomy of rules in different language games (theory, ethics, aesthetics, and so on).

Just Gaming also contains an attack on Enlightenment universality (Lyotard and Thébaud 1985: pp. 11ff.) and belief in absolute criteria for judgement. Now Lyotard describes paganism as 'the denomination of a situation in which one judges without criteria' (1985: p. 16). 'Justice', therefore can only be local, multiple, and provisional, subject to contestation and transformation. All discourses are theorized as moves in language games (1985: pp. 55ff.), and Lyotard argues that just moves are always understood as moves in a context, always tactical, always taking into account the context in which they appear. Lyotard describes this pagan discourse as merely giving instructions whose validity is always limited to a specific context. Thus political discourses always proceed context by context, case by case, move by move in local, specific, and strategic interventions.

Much of the dialogue consists in discussion of what constitutes prescriptive discourse and how one could justify specific prescriptions. Lyotard insists on the distinction between descriptive and prescriptive statements, on the incommensurability between is and ought, arguing that prescriptives are specific and individual and simply do not allow universalizability. We are condemned to making prescriptives, – 'one cannot live without prescriptions' – but must make them one by one and without appealing to ontology or claiming universality (1985: pp. 59, 99, *passim*).

The dialogue thus concludes with the idea of a plurality of justices and a 'justice of multiplicities', with Lyotard arguing:

Yes, there is first a multiplicity of justices, each one of them defined in relation to the rules specific to each game. These rules prescribe what must be done so that a denotative statement, or an interrogative one, or a prescriptive one, etc., is received as such and recognized as 'good' in accordance with the criteria of the game to which it belongs. Justice here does not consist merely in the observance of the rules; as in all the games, it consists in working at the limits of what the rules permit, in order to invent new moves, perhaps new rules and therefore new games (1985: p. 100).

Lyotard lays the basis here for a postmodern politics of multiplicities, pluralities, and marginalities. In an article 'On the Strength of the Weak' (1978b; orig. 1976), he proposes a politics of intervening within existing language games, subverting rules, principles, and positions within hegemonic discourses. His models are the Sophists who attacked master discourses, discourses of truth, and who fabricated ruses within dominant discourses. Against certain oppositional currents of the time (Baudrillard and others), Lyotard suggests that it is impossible to imagine an exteriority to hegemonic discourses and that one must occupy these discourses and destabilize them, using the rules of the hegemonic discourse against other discourses. For example, he suggests posing paradoxes, paralogies, or pointing to aporia within hegemonic discourses in any given field in which one operates (for instance, philosophy, literary criticism, economics) in order to disturb, trouble, and undermine them.

In a sense, Lyotard is reducing politics to rhetoric, attempting to dismantle a politics of truth which seeks universality and certainty, replacing it with a self-consciously 'sophistic' politics of cunning, of strategies, of subtle subversion that is local, modest, provisional, and centred on the rhetorical effects of discourse. In a curious way, Lyotard comes close to liberal reformism, which he reconstructs, however, in a postmodern fashion. Against modern conceptions of justice, which aim at producing a just society through transformation of macrostructures based on a general theory of justice, Lyotard proposes a justice of multiplicities, rooted in micropolitics.

Lyotard is different from other postmodern theorists that we have examined in that he concentrates on the ethical and political discourse of justice as the main focus of his postmodern politics. Yet, as with other theories of postmodern politics which we have examined, Lyotard's programme is highly schematic and undeveloped, containing slogans and programmatic gestures that were never adequately theorized. In any case, Lyotard's postmodern politics is now and henceforth a politics of discourse, of struggle within language games. Political struggle for Lyotard is a matter of discursive intervention within language, contesting rules, forms, principles and positions, while offering new rules, criteria, forms of life, and perspectives. The struggle takes place within a given language game (such as politics, philosophy, and art), and perhaps between these language games. Yet Lyotard insists that there is no overarching language game, no privileged discourse, no general theory of justice within which struggles between different language games could be adjudicated. Justice in each case will be the matter of a provisional judgement which allows no generalization of universal rules or principles. Yet certain principles ideally operate in just language games. One must agree that disagreement, as well as putting in questions and challenging, always be allowed or else there is terror and not justice. One must also agree that no one language game can adjudicate between competing language games nor can specific principles or rules be appealed to which will automatically settle disputes or resolve differences.

Lyotard concedes at the end of *Just Gaming* that 'the justice of multiplicity' is 'assured, paradoxically enough, by a prescriptive of universal value. It prescribes the observance of the singular justice of each game such as it has just been situated' (Lyotard and Thébaud 1985: p. 100). Lyotard's *interlocateur* Thébaud points to the paradox in his position that he is 'talking like the great prescriber himself' and the dialogue ends with laughter. The laughter covers over an as yet unacknowledged Kantian turn in Lyotard that he would thematize explicitly in the 1980s. Before turning to this development in Lyotard's thought, however, let us focus on his postmodern turn and his motives for championing postmodern discourse.

5.2 *The Postmodern Condition*

The society of the future falls less within the province of a Newtonian anthropology (such as structuralism or systems theory) than a pragmatics of language particles. There are many different language games

– a heterogeneity of elements. They only give rise to institutions in patches – local determinism (Lyotard 1984a: p. xxiv).

In a footnote to *Just Gaming* it is stated that Lyotard

> proposes introducing a distinction between the modern and the post-modern ... Postmodern (or pagan) would be the condition of the literatures and arts that have no assigned addressee and no regulating ideal, yet in which value is regularly measured on the stock of experimentation. Or, to put it dramatically, in which it is measured by the distortion that is inflicted upon the materials, the forms and the structures of sensibility and thought. Postmodern is not to be taken in a periodizing sense (Lyotard and Thébaud 1985: p. 16).

In this interesting aside, in which Lyotard uses the term post-modern for the first time, the postmodern is associated with the pagan, with the absence of rules, criteria, and principles, and with the need for experimentation, and producing new discourses and values. In his next text, *The Postmodern Condition*, Lyotard turns affirmatively to postmodern discourse and sharpens his polemical attack against the discourses of modernity while offering new postmodern positions. In the text, he attempts to develop a postmodern epistemology which will replace the philosophical perspectives dominated by Western rationalism and instrumental-ism. Subtitled *A Report on Knowledge*, the text was commissioned by the Canadian government to study

> the condition of knowledge in the most highly developed societies. I have decided to use the word *postmodern* to describe that condition. The word is in current use on the American continent among sociolo-gists and critics; it designates the state of our culture following the transformations which, since the end of the nineteenth century, have altered the game rules for science, literature, and the arts (Lyotard 1984a: p. xxiii).

Following our distinctions between postmodernity as a sociohistorical epoch, postmodernism as a configuration of art after/against modernism, and postmodern knowledge as a critique of modern epistemology, it would be more accurate to read Lyotard's text as a study of conditions of postmodern knowledge, rather than of the postmodern condition *tout court*, for the text does not provide an analysis of postmodernity, but rather compares modern and postmodern knowledge.[6] Indeed, like Foucault, Lyotard's focus is more on a critique of modern knowledge and a call for new knowledges than on developing analyses of post-modern forms of society or culture.

In fact, Lyotard is the only theorist we are examining who fails to produce critical perspectives on modernity as a socioeconomic phenomenon. Consistent with his postmodern epistemology, he never theorizes modernity as a historical process, limiting himself to providing a critique of modern knowledge. Thus modernity for Lyotard *is* modern reason, Enlightenment, totalizing thought, and philosophies of history. Failing to develop analyses of modernity and postmodernity, these notions are undertheorized in his work and shifts postmodern theory away from social analysis and critique to philosophy. Lyotard thus carries through a linguistic and philosophical turn which renders his theory more and more abstract and distanced from the social realities and problems of the present age.

For Lyotard, there are three conditions for modern knowledge: the appeal to metanarratives to legitimate foundationalist claims; the inevitable outgrowth of legitimation, delegitimation, and exclusion; and a desire for homogeneous epistemological and moral prescriptions. Postmodern knowledge, by contrast, is against metanarratives and foundationalism; it eschews grand schemes of legitimation; and it is for heterogeneity, plurality, constant innovation, and pragmatic construction of local rules and prescriptives agreed upon by participants, and is thus for micropolitics. The postmodern therefore involves developing a new epistemology which responds to new conditions of knowledge, and the main focus of the book concerns the differences between the grand narratives of traditional philosophy and social theory, and what he calls postmodern knowledge which he defends as preferable to modern forms of knowledge.

To legitimate their positions, modern discourses, Lyotard claims, appeal to metadiscourses such as the narrative of progress and emancipation, the dialectics of history or spirit, or the inscription of meaning and truth. Modern science, for instance, legitimated itself in terms of an alleged liberation from ignorance and superstition, as well as the production of truth, wealth and progress. From this perspective, the postmodern is defined 'as incredulity toward metanarratives', the rejection of metaphysical philosophy, philosophies of history, and any form of totalizing thought – be it Hegelianism, liberalism, Marxism, or positivism.

The metanarratives of modernity tend, Lyotard claims, toward exclusion and a desire for universal metaprescriptions. The scientist, for instance, provides a paradigmatic example of modernity's propensity toward exclusion (1984a: p. 80). Lyotard argues that the modern act of universalizing and homogenizing metaprescriptives violates what he considers the heterogeneity of language games. Furthermore, he claims that the act of consensus also does violence to heterogeneity and imposes homogeneous criteria and a false universality.

By contrast, Lyotard champions dissensus over consensus, diversity and dissent over conformity and consensus, and heterogeneity and the incommensurable over homogeneity and universality. He writes:

> Consensus does violence to the heterogeneity of language games. And invention is always born of dissension. Postmodern knowledge is not simply a tool of the authorities; it refines our sensitivity to differences and reinforces our ability to tolerate the incommensurable (1984a: p. 75).

Knowledge is produced, in Lyotard's view, by dissent, by putting into question existing paradigms, by inventing new ones, rather than assenting to universal truth or agreeing to a consensus. Although Lyotard's main focus is epistemological, he also implicitly presupposes a notion of the postmodern condition, writing: 'Our working hypothesis is that the status of knowledge is altered as societies enter what is known as the postindustrial age and culture enters what is known as the postmodern age' (1984a: p. 3). Like Baudrillard, Lyotard thus associates the postmodern with the trends of so-called 'postindustrial society'. Postmodern society is for Lyotard the society of computers, information, scientific knowledge, advanced technology, and rapid change due to new advances in science and technology. Indeed, he seems to agree with theorists of postindustrial society concerning the primacy of knowledge, information, and computerization – describing postmodern society as 'the computerization of society'.

For Lyotard, as for theorists of 'postindustrial society', technology and knowledge become the main principles of social organization.[7] On the other hand, Lyotard does not – like Daniel Bell and others – claim that his postmodern society is a postcapitalist one, stressing early in his study how the flow and development of technology and knowledge follow the flow of money

(1984a: p. 6). Yet Lyotard does not adequately analyze the relations between technology, capital, and social development and cannot in principle do this because of his rejection of macrotheory – a point that we shall expand in 5.4.

5.3 Between Kant and the Postmodern: *The Differend*

The differend is the unstable state and instance of language wherein something that must be able to be put into phrases cannot yet be ...
What is at stake in a certain literature, in a philosophy, or perhaps even in a certain politics, is to bear witness to differends by finding idioms for them (Lyotard 1988c: p. 13).

In *The Differend*, Lyotard takes a philosophical turn and elaborates a 'philosophy of phrases' that provides a new linguistic twist to his emerging postmodern theory. Curiously, Lyotard's development reverses the movement of poststructuralism. While previously poststructuralists such as Barthes and Kristeva proceeded from a stage favouring language and the signifier to one privileging the body and desire, Lyotard has moved in the reverse trajectory. His earlier work championed the body, desire, and intensities over language. In his later work, however, he privileges language and philosophy.

In his 1980s texts, Lyotard turns from more general analyses of language and society to more philosophical discourse. His philosophical turn is unique within the postmodern theory that we have examined. While Lyotard played to some extent to the postmodern trends of the 1980s, collecting some 'letters' and essays in a collection *Le postmoderne expliqué aux enfants* (1986),[8] his energies were focused most intensely in developing postmodern philosophical positions. The full range of his philosophical interrogations are too complex for us to discuss here, so we shall limit ourselves to aspects of *The Differend* which contribute to developing a postmodern philosophy.

In *The Differend*, Lyotard gives up the concept of language games which he replaces with the concept of 'regime of phrases'. In a conversation with his translator George Abbeele, Lyotard indicates that study of Wittgenstein's *Philosophical Investigations* helped purge him 'of the metaphysics of the subject'. 'Thereafter, it seemed to me that "language games" implied players that made use of language like a toolbox, thus replicating the constant arrogance of Western anthropocentrism. "Phrases" came to say that the so-called players were on the contrary situated by phrases in the universes those phrases present "before" any intention' (1984c: p. 17).

This project of divesting his theory of the subject allies Lyotard with Baudrillard's similar project which can be contrasted to the later Foucault's concept of self-mastery and Deleuze and Guattari's search for new subjectivities. That is, both Baudrillard and Lyotard wanted to develop theories that did not appeal in any way to subjects, while Foucault, Deleuze, and Guattari wanted to produce new subjectivities. The total erasure of the subject is evident in the style and feel of *The Differend* which is Lyotard's most technical, sombre, and complex philosophical text.

The book is concerned with the conditions of justice and is deeply influenced by Kant, Wittgenstein, and linguistic philosophy. Most of the text is devoted to language analysis, often of a highly technical and sophisticated nature. He states that 'the time has come to philosophize' (1988c: p. xiii) and does exactly that. In particular, Lyotard attempts to 'rephrase the political' by developing a philosophy of phrases which take the phrase as the basic unit of theory and the linking of phrases as its task. Lyotard once again appeals to the heterogeneity of regimes of phrases and the undesirability of translating one kind into another (that is, prescriptives into descriptives), or of appealing to a metatheory whereby phrases could be ordered, systematized or adjudicated.

While Lyotard describes the late works of Kant and Wittgenstein as 'epilogues to modernity and prologues to an honourable postmodernity' (1988c), he does not develop what he means by 'an honourable postmodernity' and does not systematically take up the discourse of the postmodern in the text. Presumably it is the differend itself which is the principle of an honourable postmodernity: 'As distinguished from a litigation, a differend would be a case of conflict, between (at least) two parties, that cannot be equitably resolved for lack of a rule of judgement applicable to both arguments. One side's legitimacy does not imply the other's lack of legitimacy. However, applying a single rule of judgement to both in order to settle their differend as though it were merely a litigation would wrong (at least) one of them (and both of them if neither side admits this rule)' (1988c: p. xi).

Modern discourses utilize metadiscourses of truth and judgement to adjudicate between specific disputes. Lyotard – pursuing his earlier polemic against universalist discourse – argues that such procedures inevitably oppress the weak and suppress minority discourses. Like Foucault's genealogy, Lyotard's philosophy of the differend would articulate differences, giving voice to minority discourses and would thus preserve rather than suppress differences. Applying this analysis to his earlier concept of justice, he argues that while one must judge without universal prescriptives, one should seek the differences and listen for the silences that betoken differends; then one should seek to allow the mute voices to speak and to articulate the principles or positions that oppose the majority discourses. One thus comes to accent and tolerate differences and seeks a plurality of reasons rather than one unitary reason.

While maintaining this postmodern emphasis on plurality, multiplicity, difference, and otherness, Lyotard articulates these principles in terms of the theory of Kant and other modern philosophers, thus investing his work with an (unarticulated) tension between modern and postmodern discourses. Much of the text involves commentary on Kant, Hegel, and modern philosophy, often using modern discourses to make his points. In this way, he 'deconstructs' hard and fast oppositions between the modern and the postmodern – which raises the question of the extent to which Lyotard's recent work is postmodern. Indeed, many of Lyotard's 1980s texts are commentaries on Kant and mark a surprising turn to a thinker identified traditionally as an archetype of Enlightenment rationalist philosophy.

Lyotard's Kant is the philosopher of the three critiques with the unbridgeable gaps between theoretical and moral judgement, descriptive and prescriptive phrases – a position followed by Lyotard for some years now. He reads the third critique as an attempt to bridge this gap, a project he interprets in terms of linking different regimes of phrases. Lyotard also follows Kant's position that there can only be an Idea of justice, community, mutual understanding, and the like which can serve as a regulative ideal, but which cannot generate substantive criteria or universal judgements in specific cases. Disregarding Kant's transcendental and universalist moments, Lyotard instead wishes to valorize the critical Kant, the Kant of the critiques of the three faculties of judgement, theoretical, moral, and aesthetic.

Lyotard sees a structural parallelism between Kant's three faculties and genres of judgement and Wittgenstein's language games, all of which are governed by their own rules and criteria. He goes further than these theorists, however, by positing an ineluctable heterogeneity in discourse, assuming that there will always be differences which cannot be assimilated to universal or general criteria. In *The Differend*, he also suggests that the modern 'we' of human solidarity, community, and universality is inexorably fissured and shattered. After Auschwitz, he argues, there can be no more pretence that humanity is one, that universality is the human condition. Rather, fragmentation in groups and competing interests is the postmodern condition and agonistics is thus an inevitable aspect of contemporary life.

Lyotard builds his theory on an agonistics that presupposes that social and cultural life will always be divided among differing positions, and that conflict in language is an inevitable situation. The notion of a differend attempts to ensure that precisely these differences be articulated, that minority and oppositional views be put into language and affirmed in social discourses. Totalitarian discourses, by contrast, attempt to silence other voices and discourses by advocating general rules or criteria which exclude marginal and oppositional voices. Lyotard's postmodern theory thus affirms the differend as the very principle of justice whereby all are allowed to speak and enter the terrain of social agonistics.

The other Kantian moment that shapes his latest position is Kant's aesthetics of the sublime. The sublime for Lyotard is precisely that which cannot be put into words, that which resists presentation in conventional forms and words, that which requires new language and forms. Once again, avant-gardist aesthetic notions are central for his theoretical and political positions and again it is Kant, with his theory of the sublime, that provides the reference point for Lyotard's aestheticized theory and politics and his political aesthetics.

In general, we find that the differences between *The Postmodern Condition, The Differend*, and his other 1980s works are not particularly striking and we do not believe that his 1980s works produce any major advances over *The Postmodern Condition* and *Just Gaming*. The turn to Kant and the 'philosophy of phrases' provides a new philosophical gloss to his postmodern perspectives, but do not provide any significant new departures. Yet Lyotard's linguistic turn calls attention to the importance of language in constituting subjectivity, politics, and our everyday life. His agonistics and emphasis on dissensus suggest that conflicts also take place in language and that contesting existing discourses is an important component of social criticism and transformation. His concept of the differend points to the need to articulate differences between competing theoretical and political positions; the concept suggests some of the ways that differences are glossed over and suppressed in everyday interaction through the more powerful imposing their discourses and practices on subordinate groups who are unable to articulate their needs and positions in the hegemonic discourse.

Lyotard's politicizing of phrasing and speaking attempts to destabilize existing relations of domination and contributes to the politics of language established by Orwell, Marcuse, Foucault, Habermas, and others. The politics of difference which he advocates has been taken up by a variety of groups and theorists which we shall discuss in 6.3; we also discuss some of Lyotard's contributions in 7.4 where we address the Lyotard–Habermas debate. Next, however, we want to indicate some of the problems that we find in his thought.

5.4 Postmodern Aporia

Lyotard's work points to some fundamental aporia in certain French postmodern theories. His 'war on totality' rejects totalizing theories which he describes as master narratives that are somehow reductionist, simplistic, and even 'terroristic' by providing legitimations for totalitarian terror and suppressing differences in unifying schemes. Yet Lyotard himself is advancing the notion of a postmodern condition which presupposes a dramatic break from modernity. Indeed, does not the very concept of postmodernity, or a postmodern condition, presuppose a master narrative, a totalizing perspective, which envisages the transition from a previous stage of society to a new one? Doesn't such theorizing presuppose *both* a concept of modernity and a notion of a radical break, or rupture within history, that leads to a totally new condition which justifies the term *post*modern? Therefore, does not the very concept 'postmodern' seem to presuppose both a master narrative and some notion of totality, and thus periodizing and totalizing thought – precisely the sort of epistemological operation and theoretical hubris which Lyotard and others want to oppose and do away with?

Against Lyotard, we might want to distinguish between master narratives that attempt to subsume every particular, every specific viewpoint, and every key point into one totalizing theory (as in Hegel, some versions of Marxism or Parsons) from grand narratives which attempt to tell a Big Story such as the rise of capital, patriarchy, or the colonial subject. Within grand narratives we might want to distinguish as well between metanarratives that tell a story about the foundation of knowledge and the narratives of social theory that attempt to conceptualize and interpret a complex diversity of phenomena and their interrelations, such as male domination or the exploitation of the working class. We might also distinguish between synchronic narratives that tell a story about a specific society at a given point in history, and diachronic narratives that analyze historical change, discontinuities, and ruptures. Lyotard tends to lump all large narratives together and thus does violence to the diversity of narratives in our culture.

Furthermore, Lyotard is inconsistent in calling for a plurality and heterogeneity of language games, and then excluding from his kingdom of discourse those grand narratives which he suggests have illicitly monopolized the discussion and presented illegitimate claims in favour of their privilege. One is tempted to counter Lyotard's move here with an injunction to 'let a thousand narratives bloom', although one would need to sort out some differences between these narratives. One should distinguish between empowering and disabling narratives, for example, and should provide a critical position towards conservative, fascist, idealist, and other theoretically and politically objectionable narratives.

In fact, Lyotard is caught in another double bind *vis-à-vis* normative positions from which he can criticize opposing positions. His renunciation of general principles and universal criteria preclude normative critical positions, yet he condemns grand narratives, totalizing thought, and other features of modern knowledge. This move catches him in another aporia, whereby he wants to reject general epistemological and normological positions while his critical interventions presuppose precisely such critical positions (such as the war on totality).

In our view, a more promising venture would be to make explicit, critically discuss, take apart, and perhaps reconstruct and rewrite the grand narratives of social theory rather than to just prohibit them and exclude them from the terrain of narrative. It is likely – as Jameson argues – that we are condemned to narrative in that individuals and cultures organize, interpret, and make sense of their experience through story-telling modes (see also Ricoeur 1984). Not even a scientistic culture could completely dispense with narratives and the narratives of social theory will no doubt continue to operate in social analysis and critique in any case (Jameson 1984d: p. xii). If this is so, it would seem preferable to bring to light the narratives of modernity so as to critically examine and dissect them, rather than to simply prohibit certain sorts of narratives by Lyotardian Thought Police.

It appears that when one does not specify and explicate the specific sort of narratives of contemporary society involved in one's language games, there is a tendency to make use of the established narratives at one's disposal. For example, in the absence of an alternative theory of contemporary society, Lyotard uncritically accepts theories of 'postindustrial society' and 'postmodern culture' as accounts of the present age (1984a: pp. 3, 7, 37, *passim*). Yet he presupposes the validity of these narratives without adequately defending them and without developing a social theory which would delineate the transformations suggested by the 'post' in 'postindustrial' or 'postmodern'. Rejecting grand narratives, we believe, simply covers over the theoretical problem of providing a narrative of the contemporary historical situation and points to the undertheorized nature of Lyotard's account of the postmodern condition. This would require at least some sort of large narrative of the transition to postmodernity – a rather big and exciting story one would think.

In fact, if Lyotard was consistent with his epistemology, he wouldn't play the 'post' game at all, for the terminology of 'post' involves one in a historical, sequential discourse that implies a master narrative, totalizing periodizations, and historical, sequential thinking – all modes of modern thought which Lyotard attacks. Occasionally, he takes note of this dilemma and attempts to extricate himself by trying to provide a different sense to the 'post' in postmodern – such as in the appendix to the English translation of *The Postmodern Condition*. In other texts from the period, Lyotard concedes that ' "postmodern" is probably a very bad term because it conveys the idea of a historical "periodization". "Periodizing", however is still a "classic" or "modern" ideal. "Postmodern" simply indicates a mood, or better a state of mind' (Lyotard 1986–87: p. 209). Yet here too Lyotard is merely engaging in a verbal subterfuge and seems to want to exploit the prestige of the postmodern (which, after all, he helped to promote and which in turn promoted his work), while extricating himself from some of the theoretical commitments of 'post' discourse and from justifying one's use of the discourse.

It probably makes most sense to limit the term postmodern in Lyotard's discourse to postmodern knowledge, to a discourse and practice that breaks with modern knowledge. At different points, he valorizes such precursors of postmodern positions as the Stoics, Aristotle and Greek philosophy, Augustine, modern theorists such as Diderot and Kant, and, of course, Nietzsche. He limits critiques of modernity to modern knowledge with some critical asides against capital without analyzing the relationships between capitalism and modernity. In fact, from a strictly Lyotardian postmodern perspective, it seems wrong to operate with unitary notions of a postmodern condition, scene, or whatever, for it would seem to be more in the spirit of postmodern thought (and more accurate!) to talk of postmodern scenes, trends, and texts which are themselves multiple, heterogeneous, and often contradictory. One could also argue that theories of postmodernity greatly exaggerate the alleged break or rupture in history from which they gain their currency and prestige. Indeed, neither Baudrillard nor Lyotard nor any other postmodern theorist has adequately theorized what is involved in a break or rupture between the modern and the postmodern. And Lyotard in principle is prohibited from producing a theory of postmodernity of this kind by his postmodern epistemology which explicitly renounces grand narratives and macro social theory.

In a sense, Lyotard's celebration of plurality replays the moves of liberal pluralism and empiricism. His 'justice of multiplicities' is similar to traditional liberal pluralism which posits a plurality of political subjects with multiple interests and organizations. He replays tropes of liberal tolerance by valorizing diverse modes of multiplicity, refusing to privilege any subjects or positions, or to offer a standpoint from which one can choose between opposing political positions. Thus he comes close to falling into a political relativism, which robs him of the possibility of making political discriminations and choosing between substantively different political positions.

His emphasis on a multiplicity of language games and deriving rules from specific and local regions is similar in some respects to an empiricism which rejects macrotheory and analysis of broad structures of domination and oppression. Limiting discourse to small narratives would prevent critical theory from making broader claims about structures of domination or to legitimate critical claims made about society as a whole. His 'wonderment at the variety of language games' and exhortation to multiply discourses, to produce more local narratives and languages, also replicates the current trend in academia to multiply specialized languages, to produce a diversity of new jargons. As we argue in Chapter 8, postmodern discourses themselves can be interpreted as an effect of a proliferating academic specialization and imperative to produce ever new discourses for the academic market. Against such academic pluralism, we advocate the production of a common, vernacular language for theory, critique, and radical politics that eschews the jargon and obscurity that usually accompanies the production of specialized languages.

5.4.1 Language Games, Consensus, and the Fetishism of Difference

In opposition to Lyotard's one-sided celebration of differences, fragmentation, and dissensus in agonistic language games, we would argue that in both the theoretical and political spheres it is sometimes valuable to stress differences, plurality, and hetero-geneity, while in other contexts it may be preferable to seek generalities, common interests, and consensus. While in some contexts in which consensus is produced it may be forced and oppressive, it does not seem accurate to characterize all attempts at consensus as terroristic or oppressive. Likewise, in regard to Lyotard's championing paralogy over consensus, there seem to be at least some situations in which consensus might be preferable to paralogy, just as there might be some contexts in which attempts to capture commonality might be preferable to articulating differ-ences and dissent. Mobilizing progressive forces against reactionary programmes like US intervention in the Middle East, or conservative attempts to curtail abortion rights, requires producing consensus that some actions (i.e. aggressive military intervention) are wrong while rights like women's control of their own bodies are legitimate. In a discussion of the relation between postmodernism and feminism, Fraser and Nicholson (1988) argue that one needs totalizing narratives that traverse the lines of race, gender, and class if one wants to engage in radical social theory and politics. They argue that Lyotard's justice of multiplicities 'precludes one familiar, and arguably essential, version of normative political theory: identification and critique of macrostructures of inequality and injustice which cut across the boundaries separating relatively discrete practices and institutions. There is no place in Lyotard's universe for critique of pervasive axes of stratification, for critique of broad-based relations of dominance and subordination along lines like gender, race and class' (Fraser and Nicholson 1988: pp. 377–8).

As we have seen, Lyotard rejects macrotheory and fetishizes difference and paralogy while stigmatizing such things as totality, grand narratives, consensus, and universality. Against this reductive epistemology, certain postmodern theorists (for example Rorty) operate with a more contextual epistemology which derives epistemological criteria from specific tasks, goals, and topics. Such a 'conceptual pragmatism' is consistent with the spirit of Lyotard's emphasis on a plurality of language games, but conflicts with his prescriptions against certain kinds of social theory by allowing grand narratives as well as localized ones.

Consequently, against Lyotard, one could argue that in some contexts it is necessary and desirable to use holistic modes of thought to grasp certain empirical trends, to make connections between various realms of experience, to contextualize events and institutions, and to target centres of oppression and domination. However, due to Lyotard's polemic against totality and grand narratives, it is impossible – or undesirable – in principle for him to conceptualize totalizing social trends. Yet this epistemological position disables social theory and raises questions concerning the validity and effects of such a position. We would argue that just because some narratives of legitimation are highly dubious, politically suspect, and unconvincing does not entail that we should reject *all* grand narratives – that is, all traditional philosophy and social theory which has systematic and comprehensive aims (see Kellner 1989a and Best 1989a). Consequently, we propose that critical social theory today should conceptualize both macrostructures and differences, both centralizing and decentralizing trends and institutions. Similarly, in political theory and practice, we believe that it is sometimes preferable to stress plurality and the preservation of differences, while in other contexts it is preferable to produce alliances and to articulate common interests.

The general problem with Lyotard's thought is that he is too one-sided and dogmatic. For Lyotard, the social bond *is* language; to speak *is* to fight; 'a person *is* always located at "nodal points" of specific communication circuits'; consensus *is* oppressive; 'invention *is* always born of dissension', and so on (Lyotard 1984a: pp. 10, 15, 75: own emphasis). Against such apodictic and dogmatic essentialist positing, one could argue that the social bond involves social relations, needs, sympathetic attractions, and libidinal bonds as well as language. To speak is to communicate, to reach mutual understanding, to articulate new ideas, to come to understand new things, to come to consensus and agreement, as well as to argue and fight. Consensus, as we have argued, may be oppressive or life-enhancing, while invention and new knowledges may come through cooperative social activity as well as dissension and paralogies. A person is a body and desires, a set of social relations, and many other things besides a nodal point of communication circuits. Lyotard always, it seems, insists on reducing his positions to one-sided and dogmatic posits rather than developing more comprehensive positions. To be sure, his emphases often call attention to phenomena and aspects of experience suppressed in many philosophical theories, but it does not seem to be preferable to replace the tradition's one-sided and reductive positions with Lyotard's.

An underlying problem with Lyotard's writings, symptomatic of much postmodern theory, is the absence of a viable social and political theory and it is to this problem that we now turn.

5.4.2   *Sociological and Political Deficits*

The Differend – and in some ways all of Lyotard's work – exhibits a major theoretical and political limitation: the lack of social theory and comprehensive social analysis and critique. Ironically, a theory that in its early phases sought life, intensities, and concretion has become increasingly abstract and theoretical. Lyotard's work has progressively distanced itself from concrete social critique and analysis, while his philosophical proclivities have always prevented him from developing a comprehensive social theory. However, without a theory of contemporary society, postmodern theory such as Lyotard's is condemned to implicitly assume a model of society that often replicates existing models. We have seen that Lyotard uncritically adopts the model of postindustrial society in *The Postmodern Condition* and inadequately theorizes the social bond as language in that book. Thus, ironically, Lyotard lacks an adequate theory of the postmodern condition, of a new postmodern society, of postmodernity as a new epoch in history. He focuses instead on postmodern knowledge, on developing a critique of modern philosophy and constructing a new postmodern one. While he claims in *The Differend* and other 1980s texts that he is trying to contribute to an understanding of the contemporary politico-historical situation (1989: p. 393), his contributions here are rather minor.

Indeed, there is a sociological deficit that runs throughout postmodern theory. Postmodern theories of language often omit or downplay concrete communication practices and while Lyotard – unlike some other postmodern theorists – does stress the importance of a pragmatic dimension of language analysis, his stress on agonistics covers over the problem of how understanding is produced in language, how language helps produce intersubjectivity and mutual understanding (see Chapter 7). Indeed, notions of community, intersubjectivity, and understanding are lacking in Lyotard. He also tends to reduce politics to an ethical notion of justice, although, otherwise, he fails to develop an ethics in his work – a lack characteristic of all postmodern theory.

These theoretical lacunae are damaging to Lyotard's politics and exposes some limitations of micropolitics in general. By reducing justice to the justice of multiplicities which is necessarily for him local, provisional, and specific, one cannot develop more general theories of justice or normative positions whereby one can criticize a social system as a whole. Surely both the bureaucratic communist societies and the rapacious capitalist societies which were dominant in the 1980s demand systematic social criticism and fundamental restructuring, but such critical positions are disallowed in principle by Lyotard's micropolitics.

We shall return to the issue of the sociological, political, and ethical deficits of postmodern theory in the following chapters and take up the issue again in the conclusion to our studies. Next, however, let us turn to discuss some postmodern theorists who have more explicitly attempted to develop a postmodern politics, in particular Jameson, Laclau and Mouffe, and postmodern feminist theories, as well as those advocating a postmodern politics of identity and difference.

Notes

1. Wolfgang Welsch has tirelessly promoted Lyotard in Germany as the exemplary postmodern theorist of plurality, heterogeneity, and difference; see, especially, Welsch 1988. Bennington (1988) has presented him as a major theorist and though explicating what we are considering as postmodern positions chooses not to interpret him systematically as a postmodern theorist – our task in this chapter.

2. The 'Socialism or Barbarism' group attempted to develop a non-dogmatic approach to Marxism and developed a theory of state capitalism which they used to condemn the Soviet Union; eventually key members of the group turned against Marxism itself. On the development of Socialism or Barbarism, see Poster 1975; for Lyotard's later critique of Castoriadis see Lyotard 1974: pp. 147ff.

3. We see the early Lyotard primarily as a thinker who adopts aesthetic figures and strategies to subvert and reconfigure theory. In his later work, as we shall see, he turns to more traditional philosophical discourse and strategies, though the relation between philosophy and art is a theme that runs throughout his works.

4. The selections in the English translation *Driftworks* sets Lyotard's works adrift from their moorings in Marx and Freud during the early 1970s. Lyotard drifts away from Marx at this point, and will later drift away from Freud as well, turning to more traditional philosophical figures as his 'references'.

5. Lyotard understands Nietzsche as proposing a purely affirmative Dionysian thought. Lyotard's (imaginary) Nietzsche is beyond representation, 'the corruption of yes and no', and 'theological discourse'. Nietzsche is read by Lyotard purely as a philosopher of intensities, as a purely affirmative philosopher of life. Yet in *The Twilight of the Idols*, Nietzsche writes: 'Formula of my happiness: a Yes, a No, a straight line, a *goal*' (1968: p. 27; a formula repeated in *The Anti-Christ* published in the same volume just cited, p. 115). Moreover, this late text (1888) and the posthumous *Will to Power*, based on notes predominantly from the last years of Nietzsche's literary life, contain often violent critiques and

negations of philosophy, religion, and morality, as well as of all the idols of modernity, of the present age (for specific citations of the fundamentality of negation in Nietzsche's project see sections 24, 57, 417, 465, and 1021 of *The Will to Power*). Nietzsche always combined a 'yea' and a 'no', affirmation and negation. Lyotard tries his best to present a truly affirmative philosophy, but it too is marked by the language of negation in his mix of satire, irony, and theoretical violence which he inflicts on Marx, semiology, and others in *Libidinal Economy* which is an ultra-critical, aggressive, and, one might argue, ultra-theoretical text which claims to reject all critique and theory.

6. Many interpreters wrongly see Lyotard as a theorist of postmodernity. Conner, for instance, writes that Lyotard provides an account 'of the emergence of new forms of social, political and economic arrangement', of the 'emergence of postmodernity out of modernity' (1989: p. 27). We argue, on the contrary, that Lyotard is best read as a critic of modern knowledge and advocate of postmodern conditions of knowledge who fails to make a sharp distinction between modernism and postmodernism in the arts and has very little on a 'social, economic and political postmodernity'.

7. We shall provide critical reflections on the relations between postmodern theory and theories of postindustrial society in our concluding chapter (8.2). Lyotard's citing of the connections between his work and theories of postindustrial society provide an admission of the complicity between these theories (though, of course, we shall also later stress the differences as well).

8. There is something condescending in Lyotard's 'lessons on paganism' which provide 'instructions' to contemporaries on contemporary political situations, in the tone taken in his dialogue with Thébaud where he positions himself as master, and in his 'explaining' postmodernism to 'children'. While he calls for more modest, provisional, and minor discourses, his own discourses tend to be discourses of the master, mastering, and masterly discourses. De Laurentis (1987: p. 69) also criticizes what she sees as a condescending use of women in his theory and opportunistic attitude toward feminism.

Chapter 6

Marxism, Feminism, and Political Postmodernism

The differences, fragmentation, and heterogeneity celebrated by some postmodern theorists is replicated in the plurality of postmodern positions and warring factions between and within different camps. If we abstract from many of these differences, we see that postmodern theory is polarized around two conflicting wings. Baudrillard, Kroker, and others espouse an extreme postmodernism that repudiates modern theory and politics while heralding a postmodern rupture in history. Laclau, Mouffe, Jameson, Fraser and Nicholson and other feminists, by contrast, adopt postmodern positions while stressing continuities between the present age and modernity. For these dialectical thinkers, the discourse of the postmodern is a borderline discourse between the modern and postmodern that allows a creative restructuring of modern theory and politics.

In part, these two wings can be seen as different responses to the failure of radical politics in the 1960s. Some theorists (Foucault, Deleuze and Guattari, Laclau and Mouffe, Jameson, and many feminists) worked to develop new forms of radical politics; others returned to an old liberal politics refurbished with new labels (Lyotard); while still others (Baudrillard) eventually gave up on politics altogether and declared the end of society, politics, the masses, and history.

In this chapter we discuss the positions of Jameson, Laclau and Mouffe, and some attempts to combine feminism with postmodern theory and a politics of identity and difference that seeks to

181

constitute, differentiate, and in some cases link radical political identities. All of these theorists repudiate the cynicism and nihilism of extreme postmodernists and engage postmodern positions to reconstruct radical politics. We begin by comparing the conflicting positions of Jameson and Laclau and Mouffe with regards to the relation between Marxism and postmodernism (6.1 and 6.2). While embracing socialist politics, Laclau and Mouffe reject Marxism and turn to postmodern theory and the modern liberal tradition to redefine the socialist ideal in terms of 'radical plural democracy'. Jameson, by contrast, asserts the supremacy of Marxist theory over all challengers and attempts to absorb the best insights of poststructuralist and postmodern theory into an updated Marxian theory of the present age. Other theorists have been synthesizing postmodernism with feminist theory and producing a new politics of difference and identity (6.3). At stake in this chapter is the extent to which political appropriations of postmodern theory do or do not help reconstitute radical politics.

6.1   Jameson's Postmodern Marxism

> The idea is to create a mediatory concept, to construct a model which can be articulated in, and descriptive of, a whole series of different cultural phenomena. This unity or system is then placed in relation to the infrastructural reality of late capitalism (Jameson 1989: p. 43).

Fredric Jameson is at the forefront of attempts to engage Marxist literary and cultural criticism with the postmodern debates. A professor of literature and humanities, his work has been a sustained effort not only to critically confront poststructuralism and postmodernism, but to assimilate their contributions to an enriched Marxian cultural theory. Jameson's most systematic and influential study, 'Postmodernism, or the Cultural Logic of Late-Capitalism' (1984a), is a panoramic sweep of the postmodern cultural scene and a provocative attempt to relativize postmodernism as a stage in the development of capitalism, thereby asserting the supremacy of Marxist theory over all competitors. Of the major postmodern theorists, Jameson is one of the few to theorize postmodernism as a broad cultural logic and to connect it to the economic system of late capitalism. He sees 'the whole global, yet American postmodern culture [as] the internal and superstructural expression of a whole new wave of American military and economic domination throughout the world' (1984a: p. 57) and insists that 'every position on postmodernism in culture ... is ... an implicitly or explicitly political stance on the nature of multinational capital today' (1984a: p. 55). Following Marx's analysis of modernity, Jameson wants to grasp postmodernism and late capitalism dialectically, 'as catastrophe and progress altogether' (1984a: p. 86).

Jameson's interventions in the debates over postmodernism are not accidental or cynical attempts to exploit current trends, but a necessary consequence and logical progression of his earlier work (see Kellner 1989c). Already in *Marxism and Form* (1971: p. xix) he was calling for a 'postindustrial Marxism' that can address the present stage of 'postindustrial monopoly capitalism' in the United States. Here we see his first attempt to synthesize Hegelian Marxism and New French Theory, a project he continued in *The Prison House of Language* (1972). By 1975, Jameson had embraced the 'end of modernity' thesis and his first explicit references to postmodernism occur in his early 1980 articles on film (see Jameson 1981b; 1982). His attempt to develop a theory of postmodernism is also linked to the project developed in *The Political Unconscious* (1981a) where his general goal was to trace the stages of capitalist development and the parallel development of the rise and fall of the bourgeois subject and its expressions in literary forms. In his discussions of postmodernism, consequently, we find what he conceives to be the latest stage in the odyssey of the subject, its schizophrenic and fragmentary disintegration within contemporary postmodern culture.

Jameson's postmodern Marxism is the first attempt to combine Marxian and postmodern positions, contextualizing postmodernism within the development of capitalism, while engaging postmodern positions in order to rethink Marxist theory and politics in the contemporary era. While this is a highly original and interesting merger, we will ask if Jameson's commitments to postmodernism and Marxism are compatible and what advantages and disadvantages result (6.1.2).

6.1.1   Postmodernism as the Cultural Logic of Capital

Jameson agrees with Baudrillard, Lyotard, and Kroker and Cook that there has been a fundamental break in the social and cultural organization of contemporary society, and that we are now in the midst of a postmodern condition. But unlike these theorists, he holds that postmodernism can be best theorized within the framework of neo-Marxian theory. Postmodernism is not merely a new aesthetic style, but rather a new stage of 'cultural development of the logic of late capitalism' (1984a: p. 85). It is the cultural dominant of late capitalist society, eclipsing modernist styles in various art forms and creating new forms of consciousness and experience that predominate over older modern forms.

On Jameson's account, postmodernism signals a number of cultural shifts. These include the breakdown of a firm distinction between high and low culture; the canonization and cooptation of modernist works such that they lose their critical and subversive edge; the near-total commodification of culture leading to the abolition of critical distance through which one can challenge capitalism; the end of the problematics of anxiety, alienation, and bourgeois individualism in the radical fragmentation of subjectivity; a debilitating presentism that erases both the historical past and a sense of a significantly different future; and the emergence of a disorienting postmodern hyperspace. This catalogue of postmodern cultural experience has obvious overlaps with other postmodern theories: like Foucault, Jameson attempts to resist presentism and to recover the historical past; like Deleuze and Guattari, he analyzes the schizophrenic breakdown of the subject and the colonization of the unconscious by capitalism; like Baudrillard he holds that postmodernism is a culture of images and simulacra that projects a vast hyperreality; and like Baudrillard and Lyotard, he emphasizes the fragmentary character of postmodern culture. Moreover, the poststructuralist emphasis on instability and indeterminacy is played out in Jameson's analysis of postmodern space which, *prima facie*, is indecipherable and unmappable.

Of course, there are also significant differences between Jameson and other postmodern theorists. Jameson rejects the anti-Marxism common to nearly all poststructuralists, as well as their dismissal of totalizing methods (see below). Unlike Deleuze and Guattari,

Jameson analyzes the unconscious primarily in linguistic and narrative terms, rather than as a desiring-machine, interpreting it in terms of ideological content rather than operational form. Consequently, where Deleuze and Guattari reject hermeneutics and the classical problematics of ideology critique, Jameson defends a Marxist hermeneutics and declares that the 'political interpretation of literary texts ... [is] the absolute horizon of all reading and interpretation' (1981a: p. 17). Against Lyotard, he holds (1984d) that master narratives have not disappeared, rather they thrive underground in the form of allegories that structure the 'political unconscious'.

In turn, Lyotard (1984d) assails Jameson's 'totalizing dogmas' and claims that, by its very nature, one cannot attribute any characteristics to the unconscious, political or otherwise, and that its meanings are inexhaustible, indefinable, and non-totalizable. With postmodern discourse theory, Jameson agrees (1981a: p. 35) that history 'is inaccessible to us except in textual form', but, in opposition to its more idealist versions, he argues that history is nevertheless '*not* a text, not a narrative, master or otherwise'. Rather, 'history is what hurts' and 'its alienating necessities will not forget us, however much we might prefer to ignore them' (1981a: p. 102). He also polemicizes against the randomizing effects of poststructuralist acausal theories of society and history and adopts an Althusserian model of overdetermination of the social totality. Moreover, he has a view of history as a coherent narrative of class struggle that sharply contrasts with Foucault's emphasis on discontinuous epistemic shifts.

Jameson's theory of postmodernism draws upon Ernest Mandel's *Late Capitalism* (1975), which argued that the present consumer or postindustrial phase of capitalist development, far from contradicting Marx's earlier analysis, in fact represents a purer, more developed, and more realized form of capitalism. Late capitalism extends commodification dynamics to virtually all realms of social and personal life, penetrating all spheres of knowledge, information, and the unconscious itself. Following this scheme, Jameson claims that each stage of capitalism has a corresponding cultural style. Hence, realism, modernism, and postmodernism are the cultural levels of market capitalism, monopoly capitalism, and multinational capitalism.[1]

In characterizing postmodernism as the cultural dominant of

late capitalism, Jameson also employs Raymond Williams' (1977) distinction between emergent and dominant cultural forms and provides a more adequate account of postmodernism as a historical rupture than do radical postmodernists such as Baudrillard or Lyotard. In his essay 'Postmodernism and Consumer Society' (1983: p. 123) Jameson states: 'Radical breaks between periods do not generally involve complete changes of content, but rather the restructuration of a certain number of elements already given: features that in an earlier period or system were subordinate now become dominant, and features that had been dominant again become secondary'. This analysis has the virtue of emphasizing the discontinuous nature of the transition to postmodern cultural forms, while also drawing continuities with what preceded them and contextualizing postmodern developments within the larger framework of capitalism itself. Moreover, Jameson provides an answer to the frequent objection to the term 'postmodern' that its supposed new features are already aspects of modernism and hence do not warrant the prefix 'post-', since these features change significantly enough in the shift from a cultural subdominant to dominant to warrant a new periodization that emphasizes discontinuity with past forms and styles.

Thus, unlike Baudrillard who sees the postmodern as a rupture in history, Jameson sees it as a stage in the development of capitalist society. Jameson's analysis of discontinuity is therefore much closer to that of Foucault who analyzed discontinuity as a reconfiguration of a prior logic and described historical ruptures in terms of continuity and discontinuity. Moreover, against Lyotard who posits a new postmodern condition while rejecting all aspects of totalizing analysis, Jameson demonstrates that the theorization of postmodernism requires a narrativizing and periodizing framework that situates it within a larger historical context, which Jameson interprets in terms of a higher and purer phase of commodification.

Jameson insists on the irreducible heterogeneity of postmodern culture and resists the monolithic projection of the concept onto all forms of cultural production. The claim that postmodernism is a cultural dominant means that countervailing logics and tendencies still prevail in a complex 'force-field'. Nevertheless, in order to measure the plurality of postmodern culture, a general context is required. 'I have always felt . . . that it was only in the light of some conception of a dominant cultural logic or hegemonic norm that genuine difference could be measured and assessed' (Jameson 1984a: p. 57). Indeed, one of the most provocative aspects of Jameson's work on postmodernism is his attempt, in the manner of a surrealist juxtaposition, to connect the most disparate phenomena, such as the theoretical critique of hermeneutic depth models and the two-dimensional, depthless space of some postmodern archi-tecture, within the context of the capitalist mode of production.

Thus, Jameson argues that the analysis of postmodern culture requires a kind of totalizing methodology that postmodern theor-ists reject as reductionist. Throughout Jameson's work, he has defended totalization on two basic counts: (1) difference itself cannot be genuinely understood outside of a relational and sys-temic context; (2) a totalizing analysis is necessary to map the homogenizing and systemic effects of capitalism itself. On this last count, Jameson argues, the poststructuralist emphasis on differ-ence, particularity, and heterogeneity can serve as an obfuscating fiction which, on the one hand, reifies singularity and specificity, and, on the other hand, diverts attention away from the tendencies of capitalism toward sameness, uniformity, and generality, such as are expressed in mass production and consumption, propaganda, mass media, social conformity, and global market relations.

From Jameson's point of view, the burden of argument is placed on poststructuralists to provide a convincing account that differ-ence and heterogeneity are so radical as to stand outside of relational contexts, to be somehow compromised through all possible forms of totalizing procedures. In Jameson's view, the problem is not with employing a totalizing mode of analysis, but rather with instantiating a too abstract totality and constructing interconnections which are too simple, direct, and unmediated. The real issue – if one is to avoid an idealism which divorces social levels from one another and from economic processes – concerns the use of adequate mediations, of constructing a sufficiently sophisticated framework which can map the full complexity of cultural texts and social practices in a non-reductive way.

Jameson does not always theorize these mediations, however, or grasp them in an adequate way, and sometimes produces a too monolithic model of postmodernism as a hegemonic form of contemporary culture. No doubt, there are a variety of arguably postmodern forms such as the subsumption of political discourse to the codes of entertainment and advertising. One could also point to paradigm shifts within various theoretical and artistic fields where postmodern theory has challenged old assumptions about truth, subjectivity, reason, the work of art, and so on. But we find Jameson's claim that postmodernism is a cultural dominant to be overly totalizing in the sense that it exaggerates some tendencies – such as hyperreality or schizophrenia – which may only be emergent rather than dominant. Like extreme postmodernists, Jameson tends to inflate insights that apply to limited sectors of contemporary social life into overly general concepts representing all social spheres, thereby failing to analyze each sector in its specificity.

6.1.2   Cognitive Mapping and Cultural Politics

While Jameson's 'Postmodernism' essay contains suggestions of the difficulties facing radical politics in a postmodern society, his primary focus is on the new spatial disorientation in postmodern society, where the inability of subjects to map the urban space (such as demonstrated in Kevin Lynch's *The Image of the City*) is a manifestation of a larger and more serious problem of their inability to position themselves individually and collectively within the new decentred communication networks of capitalism and its 'local, national, and international class realities'. Jameson argues that postmodern space vitiates capacities to act and struggle. Postmodern hyperspace 'has finally succeeded in transcending the capacities of the individual human body to locate itself, to organize its immediate surroundings perceptually, and cognitively map its position in a mappable external world' (Jameson 1984a: p. 83).

Hence, Jameson privileges a spatial politics where individuals would be able to map their place within society and the world: 'a model of political culture appropriate to our own situation will necessarily have to raise spatial issues as its fundamental organizing concern' (1984a: p. 89). He attempts to put Lynch's work to use in a larger national and global framework and he therefore calls for a new postmodern aesthetic and politics of 'cognitive mapping', a politics of aesthetic representation with a pedagogical and didactic intent. In a postmodern culture where critical distance is abolished, cognitive mapping provides 'one possible form of a new radical cultural politics' (Jameson 1984a: p. 89).

It is not clearly demonstrated, however, why 'spatial issues' should constitute the 'fundamental organizing concern' of a postmodern politics rather than, say, the reconstitution of historical memory which is an important element of Foucault's genealogy. Nor does Jameson propose any specific mapping strategies for postmodern space. In 'Third World Literature in the Era of Multinational Capitalism' (1986), he presents Third World novels as examples of how literature might provide cognitive maps for their nations, insofar as they illuminate the place of the individual within the society and a given set of political demands. But it is not clear how politically effective such novels could be, nor what relevance they could have under conditions of consumer capitalism with its image-saturated culture and cooptive powers. Hence it is not clear, on Jameson analysis, why such cognitive mapping strategies could not also be absorbed or disarmed. Finally, he does not consider the possibility that postmodern space is no more difficult to map than an earlier modern space, which he never theorizes.

The general concern of cognitive mapping, however, grasping capitalist society as a systemic whole, is an extension of Jameson's earlier Lukácsian theory of narrative and here we see a key line of continuity between his earlier and later work. For both Lukács and Jameson, narratives make connections between events and contextualize them within a larger milieu outside of which they are incomprehensible. Narrative enables us to grasp 'the lost unity of social life, and [to] demonstrate that widely distant elements of the social totality are ultimately part of the same global historical process' (Jameson 1981a: p. 226). For Lukács and Jameson alike, narrative is a fundamental expression and realization of the 'aspiration to totality' (Lukács). Politically, Jameson believes that the concept of totality is of utmost importance. 'Without a conception of the social totality (and the possibility of transforming a whole system), no socialist politics is possible' (Jameson 1988b: p. 355). Lacking the category of totality, political struggles are doomed either to reformism (transforming only isolated aspects of the capitalist system) or reproduction of repressive dynamics (as sexism or bureaucracy lingers on in 'existing socialist societies').

One can interpret the call for cognitive mapping as an answer to the poststructuralist critique of representation. Jameson argues that cognitive mapping does not represent the world in the classical mimetic sense, but rather transcodes it through historically conditioned frames. He implicitly points to the debilitating effects of Lyotard's microtheory and politics and of Baudrillard's acquiescence to 'playing with the pieces' of culture. Moreover, he is rejecting the uncritical poststructuralist claim that the world is non-representable to insist that while we may never perfectly or completely apprehend it, we still live within 'a mappable external world' whereby we can gain significant knowledge of social reality. Once we've mapped – both aesthetically and theoretically – and begun to understand the new cultural and sociopolitical field, we can devise radical cultural politics and other political strategies.

But precisely what type of political strategies and groupings does Jameson call for? Generally, his privileging of Marxist politics leads him not to a dogmatic workerism, but rather to a politics of alliance that is similar to the postmodern embrace of new social movements. This position is first sketched out in a footnote to *The Political Unconscious*, where Jameson argues that while a micropolitics would make some sense in a highly centralized France, the situation in the USA is one of extreme fragmentation and hence the political goal must be to build alliances between diverse groups of people. 'The privileged form in which the American left can develop today must therefore necessarily be that of an *alliance politics*; and such a politics is the strict equivalent of the concept of totalization on the theoretical level' (Jameson 1981a: p. 54). The indiscriminate attack on totality within American conditions would mean 'the undermining and the repudiation of the only realistic perspective in which a genuine left could come into being in this country' (ibid.).

In his essay '*History and Class Consciousness* as an "Unfinished Project"' (1988a). Jameson further develops this position. Basing his theory on the work of Lukács, Jameson argues that the experience of feminists, blacks, gays, and other oppressed groups all offer important perspectives, or standpoints, toward a critical theory of capitalism. The task of a cultural politics is 'to make an inventory of the variable structures of "constraint" lived by the various marginal, oppressed, or dominated groups – the so-called "new social movements" fully as much as the working classes – with this difference, that each form of privation is acknowledged as producing its own specific "epistemology", its own specific view from below, and its own specific truth claim' (Jameson 1988a: p. 71).

But this should not be read as a liberal or poststructuralist espousal of a relativist or pluralist position: 'It is a project that will sound like "relativism" or "pluralism" only if the identity of the absent common object of such "theorization" from multiple "standpoints" is overlooked', the determination of structures of constraint within late capitalism (ibid.). Hence, advocating a new standpoint theory, Jameson emphasizes the specificity of each group's experience of domination and privation, while asserting the ultimate commonality of their oppression within late capitalism, thereby implying an alliance politics and some sort of engagement with the new social movements. Precisely how this alliance can be produced and what the nature of this engagement is remains unspecified.

Yet unlike postmodern theorists, Jameson nonetheless seems committed to a more traditional class politics. In 'Periodizing the 60s' (1984b: p. 209), for example, we find the evocation of a new form of proletarianization and class struggle that interprets the 'new subjects of history' within the framework of classical Marxism. Thus, there is a tension in Jameson's writings, theoretically, between the privileging of Marxism as the master discourse and the perspectivism of standpoint theory. Politically, there is tension between a traditional class politics and a more pluralist alliance politics. Jameson could resolve this tension by taking the neo-Marxist stance that while a radical politics requires struggles on numerous fronts, the class struggle retains ultimate importance – a position that Laclau and Mouffe reject as essentialist (see below). Whatever position Jameson upholds, he has not established that the complexification and fragmentation of 'the working class' under postwar and postindustrial conditions does not inalterably change the composition of class relations and politics. Any further clarification of his position should state how the 'proletariat' can be expected to become a unified subject again (if indeed it ever was) and why it should remain the epicentre of political struggle.

There are further tensions created in Jameson's work due to his attempts to blend postmodern and Marxian theory. He uses Marxism to contextualize postmodernism as a new cultural logic of capitalism and adopts postmodern positions to theorize late capitalist culture as a culture of images, simulacra, fragmentation, pastiche, and schizophrenia. But these postmodern positions are sometimes incompatible with or detract from his Marxist positions. This is the case when he adopts a Baudrillardian implosion of the subject–object dialectic (Jameson 1989: p. 47). This results in the demise of critical subjectivity and undermines a Marxian theory of praxis and a belief in the practical efficacy of the subject. Such claims, we believe, are examples where Jameson is seduced by the siren song of extreme postmodernism and exaggerates certain cultural tendencies. Moreover, as is most evident in his analysis of the Bonaventure Hotel, Jameson sometimes privileges a postmodern culturalist analysis over a Marxian political economy analysis and thereby obscures the economic and class determination of culture that he otherwise wants to foreground (see Davis 1985).

Jameson's *Aufhebung* of postmodernism into Marxism helps him to analyze new social and cultural changes and to rethink Marxism in light of these conditions, but at the occasional cost of the coherence and cogency of his theory. His work is an example of the potential hazards of an eclectic, multiperspectival theory which attempts to incorporate a myriad of positions, some of them in tension or contradiction with each other, as when he produces an uneasy alliance between classical Marxism and extreme postmodernism. An attempt to develop a more consistent postmodern theory and politics apart from Marxism characterizes the work of Laclau and Mouffe to which we now turn.

6.2 Laclau and Mouffe: Between the Modern and Postmodern

> Our central problem is to identify the discursive conditions for the emergence of a collective action, directed towards struggling against inequalities and changing relations of subordination (Laclau and Mouffe 1985: p. 153).

Ernesto Laclau and Chantal Mouffe apply poststructuralist theory toward a critique of Marxism and a rethinking of political theory and practice along radical pluralist and democratic lines. On their understanding, the entire Marxist tradition – from Marx to Gramsci to Althusser – suffers theoretically and politically from a reductionistic logic that precludes an understanding of the differential and plural nature of society, the autonomy of various oppressed groups, and the open and contingent character of all political identity and struggle. They analyze society through a discourse theory that emphasizes the discursive constitution of social reality and draws from a wide range of theorists in the realm of philosophy, linguistics, and social and political theory. While they adopt poststructuralist, postmodern, and postmarxist positions, they resist the nihilism and cynicism symptomatic of extreme postmodern theory and attempt to reconstruct the radical tradition on a more satisfactory basis.

Thus, their political positions are quite different from those of Baudrillard or Lyotard, but similar in some ways to Foucault and Deleuze and Guattari in their commitment to radical politics. Unlike these latter thinkers, however, Laclau and Mouffe work towards a reconstruction of modern political values. Their project can be compared to Habermas in that they see modernity as 'an unfinished project' which carries many positive developments and values that need to be salvaged and extended. But they are far more critical of Enlightenment universalism and rationalism than Habermas, and far more positive toward poststructuralist and postmodernist theory which they employ to reconstruct modern politics. Specifically, they criticize essentialist positions that construct universal or *a priori* essences of phenomena such as society, history, or the subject, and foundationalist attempts to ground theory in a stable foundation from which theoretical systems can be built. Hence, in Mouffe's words (1988: p. 33), their project could be defined as 'both modern and postmodern'.

Laclau is a social and political theorist originally from Argentina who now teaches in Britain and frequently lectures in North America. He is the author of numerous essays and of *Politics and Ideology in Marxist Theory* (1977). Mouffe was born in Belgium and has studied with Althusser. She has written and lectured extensively on the topics of class, ideology, politics, and hegemony and is the editor of *Gramsci and Marxist Theory* (1979). Both are primarily concerned with developing a non-reductionistic form of radical democratic theory and politics that combines post-Althusserian with neo-Gramscian perspectives. Ultimately, this project would lead them toward a 'surpassing' of the Marxist tradition and to embrace a 'post-Marxism without apologies' (Laclau and Mouffe 1987), a position anticipated in the earlier work of each thinker, but only fully developed in their collaborative effort *Hegemony and Socialist Strategy*.

6.2.1 Hegemony and the Marxist Tradition

During the 1980s, Laclau and Mouffe joined the growing chorus of voices proclaiming the crisis in Marxism where Marxist discourse is declared to be of little or no use in theorizing society and perhaps a barrier to changing it. For Laclau and Mouffe, Marxism displays a 'monist aspiration' to capture the essence and underlying meaning of history, whose intelligibility is provided by the concepts of labour and class struggle, and whose logic works itself out with iron necessity through a strict succession of evolutionary stages. They believe Marxism reduces the complexity of social reality to the issues of production and class and resolves a multiplicity of 'subject positions' (class, race, sex, nationality, and generation) to class positions. When Marxists address the plural nature of social groups, they attempt to subsume them to a 'class alliance' (Lenin) or a 'historical bloc' (Gramsci) that is governed by the working class.

But the conventional truths of Marxism have been confronted by 'an avalanche of historical mutations'. In the postwar period, Laclau and Mouffe argue, new processes of commodification, bureaucratization, and homogenization create a growing politicization of social relations and dissolution of old solidarities and forms of community. These processes result from the increased extension of capitalist relations into personal and social life, the emergence of the Keynesian welfare state, and the proliferation of mass culture and media. They create new forms of resistance and antagonism which are expressed in the new social movements (including feminist, gay and lesbian liberation, peace and ecological, and other groups). These movements demonstrate the complexity of the social field and its antagonisms and point to new political identities that are irreducible to class positions and productivist logic.

To initiate a rethinking of the radical political imaginary, Laclau and Mouffe break with the main tenets of Marxism and critically deconstruct the tradition from the perspective of a key concept, 'hegemony'. They construct a genealogy of the concept and show how it receives various definitions in different historical contexts. The deconstructive thrust of this effort is to demonstrate that 'hegemony' has been used, in the face of increasing social fragmentation which belied the traditional belief in the unity of the working class, to retotalize the social field around the concept of class. Thus, hegemony has been tied to an essentialist logic which posits an underlying essence beneath the diversity of the social field and which ontologizes the working class as the true and universal subject of history.

Yet, Laclau and Mouffe see hegemony as the crucial category whereby, once freed from an essentialist logic, one can comprehend the nature of social reality as plural, complex, and overdetermined, grasp the new social movements as autonomous from class struggles, and appropriate their historical possibilities for constructing the conditions of radical democracy. Once freed from essentialism and rearticulated within a poststructuralist context, hegemony becomes 'a fundamental tool for political analysis on the left' (1985: p. 193). For Laclau and Mouffe, hegemony entails a detotalizing 'logic of articulation and contingency' (1985: p. 85) that refuses the conception of the *a priori* unity or the progressive character of the working class or any other subject position. Rather, cultural and political identities are never given in advance, but must be constituted, or 'articulated', from diverse elements.

Drawing heavily from Derrida and Foucault's poststructuralist views of language, Laclau and Mouffe argue that society is discursively constituted as an unstable system of differences. Sociopolitical identities and the social field in general are never closed and finalized structures; rather, they are open, unstable, disunified, and contingent, always in a process of being articulated in one form or another and always negotiable. But while Laclau and Mouffe reject conceptions of society as a stable and closed totality, they also reject radical poststructuralist theories of indeterminacy which pulverize the social field into radically disconnected fragments. They see such theories as another form of essentialism, an 'essentialism of elements'. Just as society is not a pregiven unity, so it is not a 'heterogeneous ensemble of isolated practices' (Mouffe 1984: p. 142).

Mediating between these conceptions, they employ the term 'nodal points' to theorize the temporary stabilizations of meanings and identities (for example, forms of ethnic or gender identity). They also use the Foucauldian notion of 'regularity in dispersion' to analyze discursive formations. Politically, this means that once the unifying centre of the working class is abandoned, subject positions can be articulated within a 'historical bloc' that wages a 'war of position' against capitalism from multiple perspectives. Laclau and Mouffe see danger on both sides of articulation: 'the totalitarian attempt to pass beyond the constitutive character of antagonism and deny plurality in order to restore unity' and 'the opposite danger of a lack of all reference to this unity' (1985: p. 188). Mouffe, for example, argues (1984: p. 142) that while gender is irreducible to class, women are oppressed both by men and capitalism and so 'there exist objective points of contact between the struggle against women's subordination and anti-capitalist struggle'. For these 'objective points of contact' to become effective political linkages and relations of struggle, however, they must be articulated in a democratic discourse that finds its fullest realization in socialist institutions and relations.

6.2.2   Socialism, Radical Democracy, and Discourse Struggle

> A society where everyone, whatever his/her sex, race, economic position, sexual orientation, will be in an effective situation of equality and participation, where no basis of discrimination will remain and where self-management will exist in all fields – this is what the ideal of socialism for us should mean today (Mouffe 1984: p. 143).

As we have seen, the logic of hegemony entails a pluralist politics that breaks with the essentialist privileging of the working class and engages the multiple struggles of the new social movements. Society is constituted as a complex field of multiple forms of power, subordination, and antagonisms that are irreducible to a single site or fundamental contradiction. Laclau and Mouffe claim that the new social movements pose a challenge to the class reductionism of Marxism and create new possibilities for democracy by calling new forms of power and subordination into question. These movements demand a 'reformulation of the socialist project' (Mouffe 1984: p. 141) which Laclau and Mouffe attempt under the rubric of 'plural and radical democracy'.

By 'plural', Laclau and Mouffe refer to the multiplicity of political identities. This pluralism becomes 'radical' to the extent that these identities are validated as autonomous in nature and are linked in an alliance. Radical pluralism is 'democratic' insofar as no single group or struggle is privileged over another and each extends the bourgeois democratic revolution to all aspects of life. How then does plural and radical democracy relate to socialism in their work? Positioning themselves on the left and trying to resuscitate the ideal of socialism, Laclau and Mouffe criticize capitalism as a repressive social system which 'subordinates' diverse social groups and they adopt an anti-capitalist and pro-socialist politics. Their conception of socialism, however, is significantly different from that of classical Marxism and, like their definition of democracy, is not adequately theorized.

Laclau and Mouffe break with traditional Marxist views of socialism on two counts: they reject a narrow 'workerist' conception of socialism as a struggle for a classless society led by workers and for the creation of a new mode of production, and they reject the revolutionary conception of socialism as a chiliastic rupture with the past. Moreover, they sharply criticize all 'statist' forms of socialism which lead to bureaucracy and suppression of the individual and they emphasize the libertarian dimensions of radical politics. On their conception, socialism is not a radical rupture with the capitalist past, but rather 'a moment internal to the democratic revolution' (1985: p. 156) begun by capitalism. Socialism involves an eradication of hierarchy and inequality in favour of equality and autonomy and an extension of the democratic revolution initiated by the bourgeoisie to all aspects of existence.

Such a view of socialism is premised on a break with classical Marxism and a *rapprochement* with liberal principles. '*The task of the left therefore cannot be to renounce liberal–democratic ideology, but on the contrary, to deepen and expand it in the direction of a radical and plural democracy*' (1986: p. 176). The argument is similar to Eduard Bernstein's (who, however, believed in Kantian universals and had a more concrete political programme) as well as the tactics advocated by contemporary theorists such as Bowles and Gintis (1986). Their conception is also similar to that of Marx, who emphasized the importance of freedom, democracy, and self-management. What is most unique about their position is their use of a poststructuralist apparatus to defend the values of socialism and democracy. Indeed, they write as if the connection between democracy and socialism were a new invention requiring a poststructuralist logic of hegemony, rather than an emphasis already present in Marx, albeit lost in subsequent distortions of his thought.

While Laclau and Mouffe fail to acknowledge the obvious problems of taking the reformist road to socialism, which must eventually confront the wall of power that is not likely to peace-fully relinquish its hold, their engagement with liberal discourse is a correction of a serious defect in Marx's work and virtually the entire Marxist tradition. While Marx dismissed moral language as bourgeois ideology or superfluous for a Communist society that theoretically will eliminate what Hume has called 'the circum-stances of justice', Laclau and Mouffe rightly see that liberal–democratic discourse is necessary for radical politics insofar as it provides a language which can articulate and defend the needs and political demands of individuals and groups. The concept of 'rights', for example, has been indispensable in bringing about progressive social changes, and socialism by itself provides no adequate alternative language (see Bowles and Gintis 1986).

But, for Laclau and Mouffe, liberal discourse can and must be given a leftist articulation for its dual task of constructing a positive conception of a postcapitalist world and initiating a counter-hegemonic struggle with the New Right. Under the direction of Thatcher and Reagan/Bush, the right has appropriated and mono-polized moral and political discourse to its own advantage, de-fining democracy in a way compatible with the destruction of the welfare state and a return to *laissez-faire* capitalism and atomistic individualism. But democracy, like all other terms, is a 'floating signifier' which can be articulated in any number of directions and must be redefined within a socialist context. The traditional leftist subordination of cultural issues to infrastructural matters has had disastrous consequences, insofar as 'the whole vast field of culture and the definition of reality built upon the basis of it ... was left free for the initiative of the right' (1985: p. 174). Hence, for Laclau and Mouffe, radical politics must abandon its narrow productivist logic and adopt a cultural politics that struggles over the discursive conditions of identity formation as a precondition to a radical democratic movement.

We can now see the conjuncture of modern and postmodern themes in Laclau and Mouffe's work. Like Habermas, they believe that modernity has emancipatory aspects and they see their work as attempting to deepen the achievements of Western democratic revolutions. All three thinkers adopt a far more positive attitude toward liberal values than Foucault, who tended to equate them with ruses for enhanced domination. Unlike Habermas, however, Laclau and Mouffe criticize the universalist character of Enlightenment reason and adopt substantive poststructuralist and post-modernist positions. Postmodern theory informs their work through a critique of essentialism and foundationalism and the deployment of a logic of difference, multiplicity, and non-hierarchical articulation. Where Habermas sees modern politics and postmodern theory as incompatible, Laclau and Mouffe argue that the positive aspects of modernity and Enlightenment can only be realized through a postmodern logic that abandons the previously essentialist and foundationalist character of modern political values. If, according to Mouffe (1988: p. 33), Enlightenment universalism was once instrumental in the emergence of democratic discourse, it 'has become an obstacle in the path of understanding those new forms of politics, characteristic of our societies today', which demand to be 'approached from a non-essentialist perspective' that sees society, reason and subjectivity as contingent discursive products.

To allay the fears of a rationalist like Habermas, Laclau argues that the rejection of essentialism does not entail nihilism or the abandonment of 'global emancipation'. Rather, it leads to 'an awareness of the complex strategic–discursive operations implied by [the] affirmation and defence' of Enlightenment and Marxist values such as autonomy, emancipation, and radical critique (Laclau 1988: p. 72). Once stripped of their fictitious foundations in myths such as God, Reason, or the laws of History, progressive values must be defended within a pragmatic context that appeals to the non-arbitrary force of sound argumentation and discursive strategies. One might read this later essay by Laclau as an attempt to meet Norman Geras' critiques (1987, 1988) that they have no normative basis for defending progressive values. For Laclau, these values (for example democracy and autonomy) can be defended and legitimated within pragmatic language games – a move similar to Lyotard and Habermas. In fact, Laclau and Mouffe reject the characterization of their work as relativist by refusing the position that all viewpoints are equally valid (1987: pp. 83ff.) For Mouffe (1988), there are no absolute standards of legitimation of ethical principles, but within a particular moral tradition one can draw distinctions between just and unjust actions and principles and criticize exercizes of arbitrary power.

Paradoxically, Laclau and Mouffe see postmodern philosophy as providing the 'foundations' that modern philosophies are not able to supply, in other words, the non-arbitrary, normative justifications that Habermas cannot see coming from postmodern positions and which Foucault and others refuse to specify. One of the valuable lessons of Laclau and Mouffe's work is to show that postmodern theory does not entail a rejection of modern political commitments to freedom, democracy, and mass political struggle. They try to mediate between those who reject Enlightenment rationality as conservative and those who equate rationality with terror. Rationality and Enlightenment values remain important aspects of radical politics, but only if shorn of their universalist and essentialist cast. In Mouffe's words (1988: p. 44), 'far from seeing the development of postmodern philosophy as a threat, radical democracy welcomes it as an indispensable instrument in the accomplishment of its goals'. Similarly, Laclau (1988: p. 80) claims that postmodern theory 'further radicalizes the emancipatory possibilities offered by the Enlightenment and Marxism' such as the emphases on autonomy and political struggle.

6.2.3   Beyond Marxism? – The Limits of Discourse Theory

Laclau and Mouffe offer a comprehensive and rigorous application of poststructuralist and postmodern concepts to social and political theory. Their work is an instructive example of the relevance postmodernism and deconstructionism can have for social and political theory – such as the dismantling of metaphysical formulations of history, society, and the subject – while avoiding the nihilism, apoliticism, and anarchism commonly associated with postmodern theories. By rethinking social and political issues within a postmodern logic of difference, they help to clarify the multiplicity of subject positions, both throughout society and within each political group itself, and hence the impossibility of achieving democratization of society through certain totalizing models that ignore these complexities. Their discourse theory perspective is also valuable for emphasizing the need for struggle over the meaning of terms such as democracy and rights in order to articulate new political identities. Despite these contributions, we nevertheless find their work to be problematic on a number of counts, of which we shall focus on three: their reading of the Marxist tradition, their use of discourse theory, and their theories of democracy, socialism, and alliance politics.

As documented by Ellen Wood (1986) and Norman Geras (1987, 1988), Laclau and Mouffe systematically misread Marx and the Marxist tradition. Marx's own positions are conflated with subsequent distortions of his thought by theorists in the Second and Third International. Laclau and Mouffe foist onto Marxism a *tout court* technological determinism where the economy is 'an autonomous and self-regulated universe' (1985: p. 80) which operates according to 'endogenous' laws and with 'no indeterminacy resulting from political or other external interventions' (1985: p. 76). Similarly, Marx is said to hold that the productive forces of society are 'neutral' technical forms that develop teleologically according to their own laws, logically separate from overall social relations. As a result, the political formation of the working class is a strictly mechanical effect of developments in the economic base.

In fact, one of Marx's central contributions was to destroy the ahistorical and technicist concept of the economy (such as propogated by bourgeois political economy) and to theorize the capitalist mode of production from historical and political perspectives. Marx insisted that the economy and productive forces of society, far from 'neutral', are shaped within relations of class struggle. He explicitly stated (1973: p. 86) that 'political economy is not technology'; rather it is undissociable from social and political dynamics. While Marx sometimes adopted scientistic and mechanistic language, he never defined the 'laws' of history as anything more than tendencies (see Kellner 1983; Little 1986), and his historical writings demonstrate that he did not reduce classes and political relations to mere epiphenomenal roles and did not believe in the inevitability of proletariat revolution. Nor did he ever posit a mechanistic stage theory of history or deterministic historical teleology (see Best 1991).

Moreover, Laclau and Mouffe fail to observe that critiques of reductionism, essentialism, and teleological visions of history and the proletariat have already been made from within the Marxist tradition. Much of their analysis replicates earlier critiques of the Second and Third International Marxism by the so-called 'Western Marxists'. But while Korsch, Lukács, Gramsci, *et al.* criticized the distortions of the Marxist tradition, Laclau and Mouffe polemicize against Marxism in general. It is ironic, therefore, that arch-deconstructors Laclau and Mouffe produce an essentialist and monistic reading of a complex and heterogeneous Marxist tradition. Even more ironic, they claim themselves to be post-Marxists when in fact they make significant use of Marxist categories and analysis throughout *Hegemony and Socialist Strategy*, most evidently in their interpretation of the new social movements as political responses to changes in capitalist economic, political, and technological forms.

In addition to their reading of Marxism, we find their use of discourse theory problematic. As Perry Anderson has noted (1984), discourse theory tends to radically undermine the notion of causality and to dissolve historical and social determinacy into randomness and indeterminacy. Appeals to historical and social intelligibility, causal regularity, explanatory mechanisms, and so on, are rejected in favour of emphases on the openness and contingency of the social field. Poststructuralist theories therefore, lead to the 'randomization' of history and society. This criticism applies to Laclau and Mouffe in qualified form. While Geras (1987, 1988) wrongly claims that Laclau and Mouffe construct an inflexible alternative between mechanical determination and radical indeterminacy failing to see how they allow for certain forms of order or coherence in society and political identities in their theory of 'nodal points', he rightly observes (1988: p. 39) that they level political forces such that everything has equal weight. Out of a fear of 'essentialism', Laclau and Mouffe do not raise the problem of whether some articulatory agents or practices might be more central than others in attaining political hegemony and achieving a socialist transformation of capitalist society.

But are all articulatory practices equally determinant or are some more critical than others? Would struggles for sexual liberation be as important as workers' struggles in changing the present system? As Nicos Mouzelis observes (1988), Laclau and Mouffe have no theoretical means for addressing such questions. Their position is informed by the 'anarcho-voluntarist fantasy that every link [in a political chain] is, in every place and time, equally weak, equally appropriate as a point of application for one's critical energies' (Polan 1986: p. xxvi). Specification of such differences need not rely on *a priori* assumptions of the essence or nature of society and its agents; rather it should be the result of historically specific empirical analysis of political events and contexts.

While Laclau and Mouffe's theory is useful for understanding the difficulty of forming a political alliance, they provide little analysis of how that alliance can be achieved and sustained, around what issues it coalesces, and what forms it could take. On their view, political subjects are constituted in and through liberal–democratic discourse. Hence, in a Habermasian vein, they define political struggle as 'a proliferation of public spaces of argumentation' where democratic advances are made to the extent struggles are mediated by and fought on behalf of democratic discourse.

As is evident in their analysis of the mass media and consumer culture (1985: pp. 163–4), they are too uncritical of the formidable problems the dissemination of democratic discourse encounters in capitalist culture, such as the problems of ideology raised by critical theory, the problems of the manipulation of desire discussed by Deleuze and Guattari, or of the fascinations of consumer culture as theorized by Debord and the early Baudrillard. While democratic discourse may indeed have a 'subversive logic' that encourages people to demand their entitled rights and freedoms, they fail to analyze the ways in which capitalism can coopt or defuse these effects.

The issue is not, as Wood and Geras claim, that they reduce everything to discourse, since objects are no less real for receiving their intelligibility through discourse and Laclau and Mouffe are quite explicit that discourse includes both linguistic and non-linguistic realities. The problem, rather, is that they collapse non-discursive into discursive conditions and privilege discourse over practices and institutions. Criticizing Foucault, Laclau and Mouffe reject the distinction between discursive and non-discursive as redundant because all practices are discursive in character and every discursive structure overlaps with material institutions and practices. While they are right that there is no firm distinction to be drawn here, the differences should not be conflated since the term 'discourse' alone is too imprecise and misleading, lending itself to idealist usage such as when one speaks, as Laclau does, of the disenfranchisement of peasants from their land as a form of discourse (see Fields 1988: p. 150).

While discourse theory can illuminate the ways in which social contradictions are experienced and played out in political struggles, political economy and analysis of forces of domination and resistance are necessary to analyze the extra-discursive aspects of

society – the state, economic structures, existing political movements, and so on – none of which are adequately theorized by
interpreting them as forms of 'discourse'. But Laclau and Mouffe
have little analysis of such conditions. Moreover, their discourse
theory lacks concrete analysis of the new social movements which
they champion. While they provide a historical context for the
conditions of their emergence, they say little about their goals,
tactics, and forms of struggle.

Similarly, they do not give specific content to the concept of
radical democracy or adequately theorize its imbrication in new
social movements and socialism. In defining democracy in terms of
self-management and equality, they fail to sufficiently distinguish
bourgeois from socialist democracy, a distinction which would
require a detailed theory of economic democracy that carefully
analyzed key terms such as equality and autonomy, rather than
assuming their meaning. Failing to clarify the institutional basis
of a postcapitalist society, they lack an adequate social theory
and conception of socialism. Certainly, socialism is an extension
of bourgeois democracy, but it is also a qualitative break with
it and which demands to be spelled out in detail.

Where Laclau and Mouffe hold that no democracy is possible
'without renouncing the discourse of the universal' (1985: p. 191),
it is arguable that democracy is impossible without the universally
binding character of law, rights, and freedoms (see Bronner 1990),
a point we develop in the Conclusion. And, rather than attempting
to 'surpass' the Marxist tradition as Laclau and Mouffe do, we
believe that it is far better to expand on it and enrich it by
augmenting its fundamental insights with new theories and
methods more adequate for ever changing social conditions (see
Chapters 7 and 8).

Yet Laclau and Mouffe's efforts to reconstitute a new postmodern political theory and practice have found resonance among
a variety of individuals and groups. A large number of feminists,
people of colour, and individuals from different social movements
have appropriated and developed their positions. We shall accordingly examine some attempts to produce a new postmodern
politics of identity and difference influenced by Laclau and Mouffe
and other postmodern theorists.

6.3 Postmodern Feminism and the Politics of Identity and Difference

The political upheavals of the 1960s challenged the classical Marxist conception of class struggle by pointing to the multiplicity of sites and mechanisms of power and domination irreducible to class and exploitation. Emerging within a complex and highly differentiated political context, the new movements (environmental, feminist, sexual liberation, black and brown power, Native American, peace, and local citizens' action groups) attempted to articulate and oppose the specific forms of oppression affecting different groups and individuals. Reflecting on these movements, theorists like Laclau and Mouffe have emphasized the need for multiple forms of struggle, while feminists, Jameson and others have stressed the importance of cultural politics and the politics of everyday life as an important force of social change.

In the 1980s, the concerns of the political movements of the period generated distinctive emphases on the politics of gender, race, ethnicity, and subject positions which have often been understood within the rubric of 'postmodern politics'. Consequently, marginalized groups and individuals have been attracted to postmodern theory to articulate the specificity of their positions and to valorize their differences from other groups and individuals. In fact, postmodern politics have been theorized under the banners of both the 'politics of identity' and 'politics of difference'. The politics of difference has emerged as a project of building new political groupings with categories neglected in previous modern politics such as race, gender, sexual preference, and ethnicity; identity politics attempts to mobilize a politics based on the construction of political and cultural identities through political struggle and commitment. In relation to the postmodern theories we have examined, there are some tensions between the notions of a politics of difference and a politics of identity, although they can be interpreted as different ways of talking about similar concerns. The tensions stem from the ambiguity of the word 'identity', which has a negative connotation within postmodern theory insofar as it implies a repressive identity logic (associated with Hegel and Marxism) that reduces heterogeneity to homogeneity. 'Identity' also has a positive connotation insofar as it involves a forging of political identity from one's historical and cultural background, and one's gender, class, and ethnic status. Both these overdetermined sources of individual subjectivity and different political groupings have been termed 'subject positions'.

Hence, while there are real conflicts over the issues of identity and difference in contemporary theory and politics, there is no logical incompatibility between a politics of difference and a politics of identity since a politics of identity can emphasize the numerous forces that constitute one's political identity and the importance of validating the specificity of different political groups. Laclau and Mouffe, for example, emphasize the importance of political plurality, but, against the kind of emphases we find in many other postmodern theorists, they also stress the importance of constituting political identities, which are to be articulated within a radical political alliance. Conversely while one could discuss the political projects of Foucault and Deleuze and Guattari in terms of a politics of difference, since they champion heterogeneity, multiplicity, and marginality, one could not associate them with a politics of identity since on Nietzschean grounds they tend to equate identity with social normalization and psychic repression. In fact, one of the central problems of their work is the failure to address the importance of developing radical forms of political consciousness and identity which they de-emphasize in favour of creating new forms of desire, pleasure, or unconscious intensities.

In general, many individuals and groups have been drawn to postmodern theory and politics because modern theory devalued their own subject positions and neglected their vital concerns. Feminists, for example, have quite rightly been suspicious of modernity and modern theory and politics. Feminists tend to be critical of modern theory because the oppression of women has been sustained and legitimated through the philosophical underpinnings of modern theory and its essentialism, foundationalism, and universalism. In particular, the humanist discourse of 'Man' at once occludes important differences between men and women and covertly supports male domination of women. Humanist discourse postulates a universal essence as constituent of human beings which operates to enthrone socially constructed male traits and activities (such as reason, production, or the will to power) as essentially human. In such modern discourses, men are the paradigm of humanity, while women are the other, the subordinate sex (de Beauvoir 1953; orig. 1949).

Following the tropes and strategies of Western metaphysics, the binary opposition between men and women constructs two antithetical sets of characteristics that position men as superior and women as inferior. This scheme includes dichotomies between rational/emotional, assertive/passive, strong/weak, or public/private. These are strategic oppositions which privilege men in the superior position of the hierarchy and women in the inferior position, as the second sex. Such ideological discourses, which go back as far as Plato and Aristotle, justify the domination of women by men, enslaving women in domestic activities, and excluding them from public life and the voice of reason and objectivity.

Because of these ideological mechanisms, deconstructionist, poststructuralist, or postmodern theories which attack universalism, essentialism, foundationalism, and dichotomous thinking were obviously useful to feminists and anyone else suspicious of the imperial and problematic claims of modern philosophy. As Hutcheon notes (1989), feminist and postmodern discourses can mutually inform one another. Feminism encourages postmodern theory to articulate the critique of the humanist universal 'Man' as a discourse of male domination, thereby producing a more differentiated analysis of the production of subjects in terms of gender identities. There are also profound similarities between postmodern and feminist deconstructions of reason, knowledge, the subject, and forms of social domination. And not surprisingly, the postmodern emphasis on plurality, difference, otherness, marginality, and heterogeneity has had immense appeal to those who have found themselves marginalized and excluded from the Voice of Reason, Truth, and Objectivity. So postmodern theory, on this level – as a critique of modernity and modern discourses – is of use to feminism and other social movements, providing new philosophical support and ammunition for feminist critique and programmes.

Yet, modern categories have also given women weapons to fight against their oppression. Patriarchal structures and ideology that predated capitalist modernity have taken on specific modes of functioning within capitalist social relations to perpetuate the subordination of women to men in the newly created public and private spheres, in the factory and workplace, and in the bourgeois family. Modern categories such as human rights, equality, and democratic freedoms and power are used by feminists to criticize and fight against gender domination, and categories of the Enlightenment have been effectively mobilized by women in political struggles and consciousness-raising groups; indeed, the very discourse of emancipation is a modern discourse.

On the other hand, many modern political movements relegated women's concerns to the margins. Women were not able to vote and participate in the bourgeois movements of representative democracy until the twentieth century. Although women early on played important roles in the socialist movement, the marriage of Marxism and feminism has not always been a happy one.[2] In view of the ambivalent heritage of modernity for feminism and women's liberation, it is not surprising that some feminists would strongly affirm modern positions, while others would call for a new postmodern theory and politics.

Just as there are many, often conflicting, postmodern positions, so too are there a diversity of feminist positions and a variety of different articulations between feminist and postmodern theory. Some feminist theorists consider postmodern theory to be politically disabling for feminism (Hartsock in Nicholson 1990), while others call for syntheses of feminist and postmodern theory (Fraser and Nicholson 1990 and Flax 1990), and Hutcheon (1989) has called attention to affinities and tensions between feminist and postmodern theory. Indeed, in a sense, certain versions of feminism are inherently postmodern, since they, like postmodern theory, valorize differences, otherness, and heterogeneity. The splintering of feminism into a variety of discourses also reflects a postmodern condition of diversity, fragmentation, and plurality. But the relationship between feminism and postmodern theory is not unambiguously positive and we shall thus engage the two discourses, analyzing some of their similarities and differences, and the ways in which they can work together, or against each other.

Within feminism, as Fraser and Nicholson and Flax have argued, certain strands of postmodern theory (Foucault, Derrida, Lyotard) can be used to deconstruct ideologies of male domination and to criticize essentialist feminist theory which often reverses the positive/negative valences in the hierarchies between men and women, with women positioned this time in the superior normative position. Fraser and Nicholson (1990), for instance, use the postmodern emphasis on the social constructedness of discourse, gender, and subjectivity to criticize versions of feminism which assume some sort of essence of women's experience, discourse, or psychology, which is then privileged above its male counterparts. They criticize Chodorow for developing a cross-cultural theory of mothering that fails to analyze the specific constituents of mothering in a given society at a specific point of time. In this case, postmodern theory can be used to validate a certain type of feminist theory (socialist feminism, or materialist feminism) and to criticize essentialist or liberal feminism.

Similarly, certain types of feminist theory can be used to criticize postmodern theory, as when Fraser and Nicholson critique Lyotard's version of postmodern theory as theoretically and politically disabling for (radical or socialist) feminism. They argue that Lyotard's rejection of all grand narratives, all macrotheory, and all critiques of systemic structures like male domination, racism, or class exploitation undermine the struggles of women and oppressed groups who need to grasp the systemic nature of their oppression and justify their rebellions. Lyotard's rejection of metanarratives disables construction of narratives of why inequality or women's oppression is illegitimate and why women's liberation is justified. Rejection of concepts of equality and universality in all forms subverts the project of organizing women and others to fight modes of male domination or for women's rights. Consequently, certain postmodern positions directly contradict political objectives of at least a certain kind of political feminism, as when postmodern polemics against macrotheory undercut the need for more general theories of women's subordination and oppression.

Lovibond (1989) has also presented a feminist critique of the postmodern dismissal of Enlightenment values and modern theory by countering that both are important for the feminist project. In particular, she is worried that a too quick rejection of reason, equality, universal rights, emancipation, and other components of modern theory will deprive feminism of important weapons of struggle. Lovibond points out how Nietzsche and others associated with postmodern theory fall prey to 'an irrationalism whose historical origin lies in reactionary distaste for modernist social movements, and specifically for the movement towards sexual equality' (1989: p. 19). Deriving norms and concepts of justice from local and particular domains is problematical, she suggests, since it is often local domains – like the family, office, or conservative neighbourhoods or towns – that oppress women and negate their rights. Lovibond concludes that the feminist 'movement should persist in seeing itself as a component or offshoot of Enlightenment modernism, rather than as one more "exciting" feature . . . in a postmodern social landscape' (1990: p. 28).

Other feminists are suspicious of the postmodern attack on the subject during an era when women are trying to enhance their subjectivity and gain political rights long denied them (Di Stefano and Hartsock in Nicholson 1990). On the other hand, some feminists argue that far from undermining feminist struggles, the postmodern critique of the subject has great value for them. Where the essentialist view that subject identities are pregiven essences deflects critical attention from the social institutions that form and deform the individual, the anti-essentialist view politicizes the entire social realm by emphasizing the social construction of subjectivity across various social sites. The postmodern emphasis on the multiplicity of power relations entails that struggle must be waged against numerous social sites in the form of a micropolitics. But the postmodern critique can be debilitating in determinist versions such as Baudrillard's which reduces subjectivity to a mechanical effect of power and therefore transforms it into a passive entity that has no responsibility for its own nature and is powerless to change itself and society. To be philosophically adequate and politically effective, the decentring of the subject must be a component of a new theory of agency that theorizes the conditions under which subjects both determine history and are determined by it.

Feminists also argue that postmodern emphases on heterogeneity, difference, micropolitics, and so on can in some cases directly advance the objectives of feminism or other radical political projects. The postmodern emphasis on difference and plurality can help prevent the occlusion of significant differences between men and women and therefore can help articulate the specific needs and interests of women. The postmodern epistemology of Lyotard or Foucault can draw attention to differences between women of colour, women of different races or classes, women of different sexual preferences and ethnicity, or from different regions of the world, so as to preserve and articulate the specifici-

ties of women, and thus avoid reduction to universalizing conceptual schemes – schemes that, in some versions of feminism, too
often privilege the experience of white, first world, academic
women.

Jane Flax (1990) calls for a postmodern feminist theory which
plays off psychoanalysis, feminism, and postmodern theory to take
advantage of their mutual strengths and to overcome their respective weaknesses as she sees them. In general, she criticizes
psychoanalysis from feminist and postmodern perspectives,
questions certain versions of feminism from postmodern and
psychoanalytic perspectives, and interrogates postmodern theory
from feminist and psychoanalytic perspectives. While she is
generally positive toward postmodern theory and even tends to
privilege it, she also offers some interesting criticisms of it. First,
Flax chides postmodern theory for operating too exclusively within
the discipline of philosophy and not carrying out a radical enough
critique of it (1990: pp. 190–4). While there is some truth to this
position, it overlooks the extent to which some postmodern
thought does carry out a radical critique of philosophy and
self-consciously subverts the boundaries between philosophy and
other disciplines – in other words, is not content to remain within
the traditional boundaries of philosophy.

Flax also questions postmodern theory for its lack of adequate
analysis of gender and subjectivity. Her discussion of this neglect
in Rorty, Derrida, and Foucault are telling, though Rorty's and
Foucault's neglect of gender have already been rather systematically criticized.[3] The comments on the questionable use of gender
and characterization of women in Derrida is a refreshing break
from deconstructionist celebrations of Derrida as feminist. Flax
argues that despite Derrida's attack on binary metaphysical
schemes, he operates with a binary distinction between men and
women and a rather metaphysical concept of women – a problem
even more acute in Baudrillard (see Kellner 1989b: pp. 181ff.).

Critical of the postmodern emphasis on selfhood and experience
as totally fragmented and heterogeneous, Flax uses certain
psychoanalytic and feminist notions to develop a theory of subjectivity and agency. Postmodern theory, she claims, lacks proper
appreciation of the role of memory, of history, and of those forces
which form relatively stable 'core' aspects of our personality. By
contrast, she claims, some feminist and psychoanalytic theorists

'stress the central importance of sustained, intimate relations with other persons or the repression of such relations in the constitution, structure, and ongoing experiences of a self' (Flax 1990: p. 229). As opposed to seeing the self through postmodern lenses as merely 'fictive', Flax proposes seeing it as gendered and social, constituted by social discourses and relations that are themselves subject to contestation and change. Thus, like Habermas and against postmodern theory, Flax points to the importance of a theory of intersubjectivity to develop a theory of subjectivity.

Finally, Flax valorizes the postmodern emphasis on difference which she claims decentres white, first world feminism and she calls attention to the constitutive forces of race and the voices of women of colour. Yet in her discussion of difference, she limits herself to race and fails to mention class, lesbianism, or sexual preferences and other salient differences among women. Indeed, one of the central lessons of the last decades is that all radical analysis should attend to gender, race, class, and sexual orientation, that all of these perspectives are integral parts of personal identity and critical theory.

For our project of a multiperspectival social theory, feminism offers important insights into the construction of subjects within gender roles while postmodern theory forces us to attend to differences and heterogeneity between different individuals, groups, and subject positions. Yet an extreme postmodern theory can occlude important common interests and provides no basis for a politics of alliance. Indeed, one of the problems with the new social movements and proliferation of feminist positions is the ensuing fragmentation that articulates differences without also finding common points of convergence. Political struggle can become little more than single-issue politics that only accomplishes short-term gains for different groups while failing to organize various groups into alliances fighting for more general social transformation. On the other hand, postmodern theory can usefully be applied to criticize reductive, essentialist, and problematical forms of feminism, Marxism, or any other theory. Consequently, articulations between postmodernism and feminism can help produce non-reductive and multiperspectival social theories for the present age.

Thus, the dialogues between postmodern theory, feminism, and other attempts to produce a politics of identity and difference can help generate new perspectives for social theory and radical politics today. A feminism modified by Marxism provides a different type of theory from one that ignores Marxism, just as a feminist Marxism will modify the conceptual structure of Marxian theory. Likewise, feminism can modify postmodern theory, just as postmodern notions can help produce different versions of feminism. Together, new configurations of critical perspectives can produce richer versions of social theory and cultural analysis which overcome some of the limitations of past theories.

For instance, a multiperspectival cultural analysis will attend to the dimensions of class, race, gender, and specific social groups in textual analysis and critique. A multiperspectival social theory will also conceptualize multiple axes of power and domination and multiple modes of struggle against them.[4] It is indeed one of the lessons of postmodern theory that we are all constituted in a broad range of subject positions and that we should be aware of the constraints involved in living out class, race, ethnic, regional, generational, sexual, and gender positions. Becoming aware of the various discourses and subject positions that constitute our subjectivity gives us the power to see the multiple constraints that inhibit our thought and action and those oppressive discourses and subject positions that we should fight to eradicate (sexism, racism, classism, and chauvinism of various kinds).

A politics of difference, then, will articulate important differences between groups and individuals, and will articulate crucial issues for a variety of movements and groups that will make possible the creation of more multi-issue political movements in the future. A politics of identity helps to foster the development of political and cultural identities and solidarity through struggling against oppression and for a more just and humane society. There are, of course, limitations to a postmodern politics of identity and difference. Differences can become reified and fetishized, and can produce rigid barriers between individuals and groups, leading to a replication of special interest group politics. Common interests can be obscured in favour of heterogeneity, difference, and fragmentation that ultimately buttresses white male and capitalist domination. Politics also can be redefined into a harmless politics of style and personal identity that leaves relations of domination intact and unchallenged.

In addition, a politics of identity can foster nationalism and chauvinism, leading individuals to believe that their groups and subject positions are superior to others. Yet we believe that a postmodern theory that is politicized and mediated with feminist theory (along with Marxism and other forms of critical theory) can produce a politically useful challenge to traditional theory to help create a new politics for the contemporary age. Politicizing postmodern theory in a creative way could help avoid the dead ends and traps of extreme postmodern theory by overcoming the nihilism and defeatism evident in some varieties of postmodern theory. We find pure postmodern theory without a strong dose of feminism or Marxism to be incapable of addressing concrete political problems. Postmodern theory in its more extreme forms tends to be exactly what it accuses modern theory of being: one-sided, reductionist, essentializing, excessively prohibitive, and politically disabling. We shall return to the question of the ways in which postmodern perspectives can contribute to a critical social theory and radical politics for the present age in the conclusion to this book. First, however, we shall examine the confrontation between postmodern theory and the critical theory of the Frankfurt School that has produced some of the most exciting polemics of the contemporary era.

Notes

1. Some of Jameson's critics, such as Davis (1985), charge him with producing a mechanistic typology where these cultural forms are correlated to economic forms in a highly reductive manner. For a variety of critical positions on Jameson's work, see the articles collected in Kellner 1989c.

2. On the relationships between socialism and feminism, see Rowbotham 1972 and the articles in Sargent 1981.

3. See, for example, Fraser 1989 who develops feminist critiques of Rorty, Foucault, and Habermas.

4. For examples of the former, see Kellner and Ryan 1988 and for the latter see Fraser 1989.

Chapter 7

Critical Theory and Postmodern Theory

During the 1980s Jürgen Habermas and other theorists associated with the critical theory of the Frankfurt School emerged as key critics of postmodern theory.[1] Habermas carried out polemics against Derrida, Foucault, and postmodern theory, while his associates polemicized against Lyotard (Honneth 1985; Benhabib 1984), Foucault (Honneth 1986), Derrida (McCarthy 1989), and other postmodern theorists. The polemics have often obscured some interesting similarities, in addition to important differences, between the postmodern theories and critical theory. Both critical theory and much postmodern theory agree in important ways in their critiques of traditional philosophy and social theory. Both attack the academic division of labour which establishes fixed boundaries between regions of social reality, and both utilize supradisciplinary discourses. Both carry out sharp critiques of modernity and its forms of social domination and rationalization. Both combine social theory, philosophy, cultural critique, and political concerns in their theories and, unlike more academic theories, some versions of both attempt to orient theory toward practice, and discourse toward politics. Both critical and post-modern theory have engaged in heated polemics against each other, and have been synthesized with feminist theory.

There are, of course, many differences between critical theory and postmodern theory. Critical theory generally wants to draw and defend some boundaries, some categorical distinctions, which many postmodernists reject. For example, Baudrillard rejects categories of radical social theory that critical theorists retain, such as those of political economy, class, dialectics, emancipation, and socialism. As we have seen, postmodern theorists like Lyotard generally reject the rationalism, the lust for categorical distinctions and systematization, and the global takes on history and society that are associated with Habermas. And Habermas and other contemporary critical theorists in turn reject the alleged break between modernity and postmodernity that many post-modern theorists (Lyotard, Baudrillard, Kroker, and others) assert.

On the whole, postmodern theorists want to go much further than critical theorists in overthrowing traditional philosophy and social theory and in beginning anew with novel theoretical and political perspectives. Baudrillard, at least, would argue that changes in contemporary postmodern society obliterate in a series of implosions the boundaries that are central to much critical theory (nature and history, the economic and political, true and false needs, high and low culture, emancipation and domination, left and right, and so on). Lyotard and Foucault would criticize the macrotheoretical, global aspects of critical theory in favour of a micrological approach to theory and politics. At stake, then, in confronting critical theory with postmodern theory are the methods, fundamental categories, and distinctions of radical social theory, as well as the historical representation of the present age, its relation to the past and future, and the possibilities, strategies, and forces of radical social transformation.

In this chapter, we analyze the similarities and differences between critical theory and postmodern theory. First, we present the critique of modernity carried out by critical theory which anticipates postmodern critiques (7.1). Then, we discuss the ways in which Adorno anticipates many positions in contemporary postmodern theories, as well as the ways in which his work differs from them (7.2). Next, we discuss Habermas' interventions within the postmodern debates and his defence of modernity as an unfinished project (7.3). Finally, we discuss the current epistemic wars between critical and postmodern theory, carried out by Habermas and his associates against Lyotard as a representative figure of French postmodern theory (7.4).

7.1 Critical Theory and Modernity

> The fallen nature of modern man cannot be separated from social progress. On the one hand the growth of economic productivity furnishes the conditions for a world of greater justice; on the other hand it allows the technical apparatus and the social groups which administer it a disproportionate superiority to the rest of the population. The individual is wholly devalued in relation to the economic powers, which at the same time press the control of society over nature to hitherto unsuspected heights (Horkheimer and Adorno 1972: p. xiv).

The work of the Frankfurt School can be read as an analysis of the vicissitudes of Enlightenment and capitalist modernity, of the fundamental mutation in history caused by the emergence of the capitalist mode of production and Enlightenment reason, combined with a critique of its ideological apologists (Kellner 1989a). The 1930s work of the Institute for Social Research follows the Marxian social theory by making the dynamics of capitalism the key to social development and to the constitution of contemporary society. During this period, the Institute utilized the Hegelian–Marxian method of dialectical analysis to depict the trajectories of contemporary capitalist societies. Their distinctive contribution resides in their analysis of the transition from market, entrepreneurial, nineteenth-century competitive capitalism to the forms of organized state and monopoly capitalism characteristic of the twentieth century. Building on Hilferding's analysis of 'organized capitalism', the Institute theorized some of the ways in which the state and economy merged in contemporary social formations. They analyzed the forms of both democratic and totalitarian state capitalism and the development of new modes of social control and administration.

The critical theorists employed Marxian categories such as commodification, exchange, reification, and fetishism to analyze a wide range of social phenomena and to describe the totalizing tendencies of contemporary capitalism and its new forms of domination. They saw domination in spheres such as mass culture where capitalism's apologists saw mere entertainment, and they saw traces of old forms of oppression where others saw novelty and modernity. For instance, during the 1930s, Adorno constantly emphasized how the seemingly most modern phenomena like jazz, radio music, or Husserl's phenomenology, incorporated archaic elements. A concert, he claimed, replicated primitive ceremonial functions with applause reprising an 'ancient, long-forgotten sacrificial ritual'. (Adorno in Buck-Morss 1977: p. 108). Cults of the individual maestro, the conductor, and instruments also replicated fetishistic tribal cults which celebrated sacred objects or individuals.

For the Institute, capitalist modernity threatened to bring the 'end of the individual'. The new system of state capitalism and bureaucracy, of the culture industries, of science and technology as domination, and of the administration of thought and behaviour produced a one-dimensional society devoid of social alternatives and alternative modes of thought and behaviour. This model of society is similar to the analysis of the institutions, discourses, and practices of modernity developed by Foucault that we discussed in Chapter 2. For Foucault, the end of the individual is interpreted archaeologically as the death of man in an emerging posthumanist framework, and genealogically as the fabrication of the individual within disciplinary technologies. While for critical theory the diminishing of individuality is brought about by the capitalist economy, its culture industries, bureaucracies, and modes of social control, for Foucault the death of man is a discursive event occurring with the emergence of new sciences and discourses, and the sociological fate of the individual in a normalizing, disciplinary society. Although both are critical of Enlightenment reason and humanism, most critical theorists tend to be more concerned to preserve the positive Enlightenment heritage – a point that we shall take up in our discussions of Habermas and his debates with postmodern theory (see 7.3 and 7.4).

The Institute broke up during World War II, and in their 1940s writings Horkheimer and Adorno developed a new analysis of history and culture that anticipated in many ways the postmodern critique.[2] In *Dialectic of Enlightenment*, Horkheimer and Adorno discussed the ways that reason turned into its opposite and produced new rationalized forms of social domination. In their interpretation, a synthesis of instrumental rationality and capital-ism employed sophisticated modes of mass communication and culture, a bureaucratized and rationalized state apparatus, and science and technology to administer consciousness and needs to ensure social integration so that individuals would act in conformity with the system's dictates. Horkheimer and Adorno analyzed the ways that social rationality turns into irrationality; how enlightenment turns into deception; and how the modes of freedom and progress characteristic of modernity turn into domination and regression. They argued that Enlightenment reason becomes totalitarian as it eliminates all competing modes of thought and claims sole prerogatives of truth and validity. In this way, Enlightenment reason is intertwined with 'myth' and emerges as a powerful tool of oppressive social powers which use societal rationalization to erect modes of domination. For instance, the tradition of authoritarian, positivistic, and technocratic social theory justified elite rule (Comte, Saint-Simon, Pareto, Stalin) on the grounds that rulers embodied rationality and had superior knowledge and reason. And as Weber argued, uncontrolled rationalization could turn into a form of bureaucratic and institutional domination, in which bureaucratic elites and institutions justify their power and authority on the grounds of superior knowledge and by claiming that their power embodies the claims of reason itself.

Horkheimer and Adorno thus argued that Enlightenment reason and progress were producing social regression and irrationality with the institutionalization of social domination in the capitalist labour process and economy, bureaucracy, the culture industries, and the ascending hegemony of instrumental thought. In the light of these phenomena, the critical theorists rejected the claims that a technologically advanced society automatically embodied freedom and progress. Indeed, Horkheimer and Adorno followed Walter Benjamin in perceiving archaic aspects in the most modern phenomena and in analyzing anticipations of modernity in archaic phenomena.[3] Horkheimer and Adorno argue that science and instrumental reason have become 'mythical', reproducing the mode of blind obedience and worship of superior powers that were formerly attributed to religion. On the other hand, modern bourgeois subjectivity, patriarchy, and domination could be traced back to Odysseus whose cunning and shrewdness anticipated the bourgeois businessman, while his exploitation and domination of his men anticipated capitalist domination of the working class, and his domination of his wife prefigured bourgeois patriarchy.

In contrast to most postmodern theory, the critical theorists conceptualize modernity in terms of the trajectory of capitalism and Enlightenment reason, as a product of the capitalist economic system, instrumental rationality, and technology. They perceived contemporary social formations to be constituted by a synthesis of capitalism and technology, while many postmodern theorists advanced forms of technological or discursive determinism, whereby language, the media, or forms of technology determine the structure and trajectories of postmodern societies (see our further discussion of this issue in 8.2). Yet, while the critical theorists continued to perceive capitalism as a mode of production that is an important constituent of the current social structure, they never subscribed to any form of economic reductionism in which capital is taken as the sole determining force in the constitution of society and trajectory of history. Instead, they utilized the Hegelian–Marxian dialectical categories of mediation and the relative autonomy of superstructures, thus allowing, against orthodox Marxism, a relative autonomy to the state, culture, various social institutions, and individuals – though they also theorized how these institutions and spheres formed an apparatus of domination.

Most postmodern theorists tend to throw out the very concept of social system and society for more fragmentary analysis, for microanalysis of discrete institutions, discourses, or practices. We have seen that few postmodern theorists have a theory of capitalism, nor do they develop theories of the state and the ways in which state, economy, and culture interact and mutually determine each other. For postmodern theory, by contrast, power is more dispersed, plural, and decentred than in the neo-Marxian analysis of the Frankfurt School – though critical theory too is often fragmentary and their analysis of the economy is often undertheorized (see Bronner and Kellner 1989). Yet, for most postmodern theory, power is frequently dissociated altogether from capital, political economy, or, especially in much of Baudrillard and his follower's work, from social relations and institutions.

On the other hand, in *Dialectic of Enlightenment* and the analyses of one-dimensional, or 'the totally administered society', the critical theorists flatten out the dialectical analysis of modernity in classical Marxism. For Marx and Engels in *The Communist Manifesto*, the bourgeoisie and capitalist modernity were both the best and worst of things: they eliminated feudalism and revolutionized production and life more than any previous social class or project. Capitalist modernity produced new products and technologies, new modes of communication and transportation, a world market and a wealth of new relations and needs. Yet it also produced an oppressed working class, exploitation, and a cycle of crises that Marx and Engels believed would eventually destroy the capitalist system. Consequently, Marx and Engels have a dialectical theory of modernity and ground the possibilities of a better future society in its historical trajectory.

The first generation of the Frankfurt School, by contrast, emphasized the negative and oppressive aspects of modernity. *Dialectic of Enlightenment* short-circuits the Marxist theory of revolution by positing a self-reproducing, stabilized capitalist system without any significant revolutionary opposition. The theory of revolution loses its historical grounding in a revolutionary proletariat and becomes a utopian ideal. Thus, capitalist modernity is, in effect, presented in much critical theory as a self-reproducing and stabilizing system of commodity production and exploitation under the domination of capital. No alternative politics other than individual resistance is posited by Horkheimer and Adorno; consequently, an inadequate politics remains a problem with critical theory to this day.

Postmodern theory replicates some of these problems while introducing new ones. It tends to obscure the continuing constitutive role of capitalism in the production and reproduction of contemporary social formations and splinters power and domination into an amorphous multiplicity of institutions, discourses, and practices. On one hand, this provides a more complex model of contemporary society and its modes of domination than classical Marxism or critical theory. But, on the other hand, by minimizing the continuing power of capital and the state as major forces of domination, some postmodern theory occludes analysis of the major constitutive forces and modes of domination in our contemporary and still capitalist societies. For example, while much postmodern theory correctly points to the power of media and information, it downplays the extent to which ruling groups control and shape these new social forces (see Kellner 1990).

Moreover, as we are arguing, it is not clear that postmodern theory has produced satisfactory theoretical and political alternatives to classical Marxism or critical theory – though it does point to some of their problems and indicates the need for new critical theories and radical politics, a position that we shall take up in the conclusion. As we have seen, most postmodern theory aggressively rejects dialectics and totalizing macrotheory. With their emphasis on difference, fragmentation, plurality, and heterogeneity, post-modernists tend to reject concepts of rationality, totality, consensus, and social system as intrinsically repressive. In so doing, however, they forfeit concepts which can illuminate the actual oppressive aspects and practices of existing societies – capitalist and communist – which are in some ways totalizing and homogenizing. With their emphasis on plurality and fragmentation, postmodern theorists wage a war against totality and system; with their emphasis on microanalysis and politics, the postmodernists by and large reject macrotheory and macropolitics; and with their emphasis on the individual and singularity, many postmodernists reject collective struggle and large-scale social transformation.

Yet one could argue that there are social tendencies today towards both fragmentation and totalization; consequently, we believe that a dialectical theory which attends to both sides of this conceptual opposition can best theorize contemporary social processes and developments. Postmodern theory, by contrast, emphasizes fragmentation as a key feature of texts, subjectivity, experience, and society itself in the postmodern era. Lyotard (1984a) describes and celebrates a plurality of language games, while attacking unitary concepts of reason and subjectivity. He calls for a further pluralization and fragmentation of knowledge and politics on the grounds that totalities, systems, and consensus produce terroristic oppression, while Foucault champions local and fragmentary forms of knowledge and resistance as subversive. For Baudrillard, postmodernism itself can be described as a playing with the fragments and vestiges of past cultures, theories, and ideas (1984b), while Jameson describes the fragmentation of experience and culture in postmodernism.

From the standpoint of developments in contemporary capitalist society, postmodern theory thus can be read as articulating social processes toward fragmentation and heterogeneity and one of its contributions is to illuminate these trends. Yet there are also, arguably, trends towards increased centralization, new totalizations, and new forms of social organization as well. For example, although there is an always proliferating product differentiation in a capitalist consumer economy, there are also trends towards economic concentration, the extension of a world market system, and growing commodification as capitalism penetrates every sphere of everyday life and the totality of the globe from Peking to Topeka. While there are new emphases on cultural differentiation and autonomy, a homogeneous mass consumer and media society is also working to standardize tastes, wants and practices. Bureaucratization and administration also continue to be major trends of contemporary society and postmodern theory tends to obscure these fundamental aspects of our everyday life and social experience.

In effect, postmodern social analysis is highly one-sided, articulating tendencies toward fragmentation (Lyotard) or implosion (Baudrillard) while neglecting, with some exceptions, to properly conceptualize either totalizing forms of domination or resistance to them. While many versions of modern social theory such as Marxism and critical theory might overlook or ignore particularity, plurality, and difference, this is not true of all versions of critical theory. As we shall argue in the next section, Adorno and Benjamin utilize a 'micrological approach' that focuses on particularities and the most microscopic details of everyday experience. Yet critical theorists also analyze the major social processes, the mediating institutions and structures, that help constitute particularities. Using the dialectical category of mediation, critical theory attempts to describe how concrete particulars are constituted by more general and abstract social forces, undertaking an analysis of particulars to illuminate these broader social forces. Consequently, we would argue that a dialectical social theory such as one finds in the best of critical theory provides the most adequate models and methods to analyze the multidimensional processes toward both fragmentation and unification, implosion and differentiation, and plurality and homogenization in contemporary techno-capitalist societies. Much postmodern theory rejects dialectics in principle, however, and thus is unable to conceptualize the dialectic of totalization and fragmentation, de-differentiation and differentiation, homogenizing and individualizing tendencies, which we believe characterize the dynamics of the contemporary moment.

Some postmodern theory – to be sure – also provides illuminating analyses of contemporary events, institutions, and practices. Yet by rejecting dialectics, postmodern theory tends to be more fragmentary and empiricist, failing to articulate significant mediations, or connections, between various social phenomena. The criticial theorists, by contrast, analyze mediations between particularities and totalities, parts and wholes, individual artifacts and events, and social processes and structures. In contrast to the postmodern caricature of dialectics as a mystical and teleological logic of history, dialectics for critical theory is primarily a method for describing relationships between different domains of social reality, such as the economy and state or culture. The category of mediation (*Vermittlung*) is above all an interpretive category for depicting the constituting forces and connections of a given phenomenon, rather than a magical device to overcome antagonisms and produce syntheses (as in some Hegelian versions of dialectics).

Dialectics for critical theory thus describes how phenomena are constituted and the interconnections between different phenomena and spheres of social reality. Furthermore, the category of mediation provides a corrective against the reductive, essentialist theories characteristic of modernity which are the target of the postmodern critique. For instance, critical theorists reject identity thinking that posits an identity of thought and being, as well as rejecting a reflection theory epistemology in which concepts mirror objects or the world. Instead, Adorno and other critical theorists analyze the ways in which thought is a product of discourses, social experiences, and institutions, while society and the world of objects is a product of language, social determination, and human practice. Both postmodern theory and critical theory stress the ways that subject and object, thought and being, are mediated by each other, and thus reject in principle reductive idealist or materialist thought. They also reject essentialism that posits a pure mind or subject which constitutes the world, or which posits a realm of pure thought and reason as the proper domain for philosophy.

In the next section, we indicate how Adorno anticipated much of the postmodern critique of modern theory and offered a dialectical alternative that is more critically and reflexively grounded in the best traditions of modern theory than the more polemical traditions of postmodern theory which tend to reject modern theory *an sich*, without distinguishing between its valuable and destructive legacies. We shall therefore argue that while Adorno anticipates many of the valuable motifs of postmodern theory, he presents them within a philosophical framework which is more satisfactory than that of the postmodern theories which we have so far examined.

7.2   Adorno's Proto-Postmodern Theory

> Philosophy, in view of the present historical situation, has its true interest here where Hegel, at one with tradition, registered his dis-interest: with the non-conceptual, the singular and the particular; with that which since Plato has been dismissed as transitory and insigni-ficant, and upon which Hegel hung the label of 'foul [*faul* – also: lazy, insignificant] existence' (Adorno 1973: pp. 19–20).

> It is not up to philosophy to exhaust things according to scientific usage, to reduce the phenomena to a minimum of propositions . . . Instead in philosophy we literally seek to immerse ourselves in things that are heterogeneous . . . without placing those things in prefabricated cate-gories (Adorno 1973: p. 13).

In general, Adorno is much closer to postmodern theory than Horkheimer, Marcuse, Fromm, and the other members of the Frankfurt School. From the beginning, Adorno engaged in a 'self-liquidation of idealism' which constituted a critique of philosophy quite similar to that later developed by postmodern theory. This critique runs through Adorno's work, ranging from his early 1930s essays, to his 1933 book on Kierkegaard, his polemical critiques of Husserl and Heidegger, and his later *Negative Dialectics* (1966). In this book, Adorno characterizes idealism as a form of rage which wants to subsume the object in the categories of thought, eager to capture and assimilate all that is different from itself. In his major philosophical works, Adorno developed a critique of 'identity think-ing' which posits an identity between thought and being, champion-ing instead a 'non-identity' thesis which preserves the ineradicable difference between thought and its objects.

In his 1931 inaugural address, 'The Actuality of Philosophy', which marked his entry into the philosophy faculty of the University of Frankfurt, Adorno develops a radical critique of philosophy that anticipates many postmodern motifs. He begins: 'Whoever chooses philosophy as a profession today must first reject the illusion that earlier philosophical enterprises began with: that the power of thought is sufficient to grasp the totality of the real' (1977: p. 120). Adorno argues that there can be no philosophical cognition of the totality and that all 'ontological blueprints' which attempt to conceptualize the totality of being are mere veils and illusions. 'True being', according to Adorno, only appears in traces and ruins and any attempt to present existing reality as a true and just order 'only veils reality and eternalizes its present condition' (ibid.).

Today, Adorno claims, philosophy has renounced the earlier project of deriving reality itself from reason, from out of itself. On the other hand, he affirms the critiques of anti-rationalist schools such as neo-Kantian, phenomenological, vitalist, and Heideggerian schools and others being savaged by the critical inquiries of the Vienna School. These critiques have cumulatively undermined philosophy's pretensions to truth and higher knowledge, whether via reason, intuition, or other modes. The 'fragmentation of being' today, Adorno claims, renders any philosophical attempt to conceptualize a unitary being illusory, as well as condemning the project of the unity of the sciences which seeks systematic knowledge of the world. While postmodernists like Baudrillard see these fragments as pieces with which one can play without any hope of developing more mediated and comprehensive analyses, Adorno, by contrast, argues that the task of philosophy is precisely to interpret the fragments portrayed by the individual sciences, so as to provide knowledge of the existing society:

> Philosophy will be able to understand the material content and concretion of problems only within the present standing of the separate sciences. It will also not be allowed to raise itself above such sciences by accepting their 'results' as finished and meditating upon them from a safe distance. Rather, philosophic problems will lie always, and in a certain sense irredeemably, locked within the most specific questions of the separate sciences. Philosophy distinguishes itself from science not by a higher level of generality, as the banal view still today assumes, nor through the abstraction of its categories nor through the nature of its materials. The central difference lies far more in that the separate sciences accept their findings, at least their final and deepest findings, as indestructible and static, where philosophy perceives the first finding which it lights upon as a sign that needs unriddling. Plainly put: the idea of science (*Wissenschaft*) is research; that of philosophy is interpretation (Adorno 1977: p. 126).

The task of philosophy is, first, to construct figures and images which are brought into constellations or combinations that will illuminate aspects of 'unintentional reality' (Adorno 1977: p. 127). Such juxtaposition of thought figures which illuminate social reality is 'the programme of every authentically materialist knowledge' (ibid.). Second, philosophy is to interpret the constellations produced in order to illuminate its object. Philosophy is thus a form of composition or construction combined with interpretation. Adorno followed this model from the 1930s to his death in the late 1960s and provided a wealth of illustrations of this project.

Adorno's concept of philosophy is strongly influenced by aesthetic motifs, yet he did not completely aestheticize philosophy, or collapse philosophy into art or aesthetics. His complex, mediated positions on the relations between art and philosophy are set forth in his first major philosophical text, *Kierkegaard. Construction of the Aesthetic* (1989; orig. 1933). Adorno opens by polemicizing against the tendency to collapse philosophy into art. The task of both is to present and illuminate the real, yet while philosophy utilizes aesthetic construction, it has its own conceptuality, its own truth content (Adorno 1989: pp. 3f.). Adorno also wishes to distinguish philosophy from science. Philosophy's method is dialectical and its goal is to construct 'ideas that illuminate and apportion the mass of the simply existing; ideas around which the elements of the existing crystalize as knowledge' (Adorno 1989: p. 4).

Thus, while Adorno shared later postmodern desires to preserve particularity and to engage in microanalysis, he believes that both philosophy and art construct constellations of ideas and images which can illuminate the particular and the broader social forces and processes which constituted singular entities and events. This method derived from Benjamin who, however, believed that the juxtaposition of phenomena would illuminate both particulars and broader social forces, while Adorno always insisted that it was precisely the work of theory to mediate between particular and general and to construct theoretical categories that would both conceptualize particulars and broader social forces and structures.

In contrast to postmodern theory, Adorno advances a strong concept of truth and defends both philosophy and art as vehicles of cognitive insight. Both philosophy and art for Adorno not only illuminate the real but can help to transform it. In *Kierkegaard*, he writes that the goal of 'a materialism whose vision is focused on "a better world" [is] not to forget in dreams the present world, but to change it by the strength of an image ... whose contours are concretely and unequivocally filled in every particular dialectical element' (1989: p. 131).

Consequently, in contrast to later postmodern theory, Adorno believes that construction and interpretation of constellations of images and ideas can provide social knowledge. But this knowledge pertains to concrete particulars and specific social forces, and is not the vehicle of any universal truth, nor does it claim to describe a metaphysical reality. Rather, theoretical analysis can only provide conceptual knowledge of specific constellations of phenomena, while vindicating the importance and heterogeneity of concrete particulars. Thus, Adorno's notion of philosophy is both deconstructive and reconstructive. He attacks idealist philosophy while providing models of materialist philosophy. Through the construction of constellations of images he hopes to redeem the cognitive function of philosophy. For example, he suggests that analysis of the commodity structure would not reveal a deeper form of being in itself, but rather a historically specific form that permeates contemporary social reality; the functions of philosophy thus are 'inner-historically constituted, non-symbolic ones' (Adorno 1977: p. 128). This practice of concrete sociohistorical analysis and interpretation will liquidate the general and empty categories of philosophy which will be replaced by specific constellations of ideas and images. Such a change in philosophical consciousness and the function of philosophy must proceed, Adorno claims, through a critique of existing philosophy and a more positive relation to sociology and culture which will provide the subject matter for the new philosophy which he envisages.

The synthesis of philosophy, art, and the social sciences will avoid the overly large, generalized, and empty categories of philosophy as well as merely empirical microanalyses of the special sciences. These constellations of historical images are 'models' and 'the *organon* of this *ars inveniendi* is fantasy' (Adorno 1989: p. 131). More precisely: 'An exact fantasy, fantasy which abides strictly within the material which the sciences present to it, and reaches beyond them only in the smallest aspects of their arrangement: aspects, granted, which fantasy itself must originally generate' (ibid.). Such a programme is necessarily experimental and will be validated primarily through its 'fruitfulness', the results that it produces (Adorno 1989: p. 132).

Indeed, Adorno's work over the next several decades was precisely to carry through comprehensive attacks on dominant philosophies while attempting to illuminate cultural and societal phenomena. Unlike much postmodern theory, he believes that philosophy and art can serve as a source of critical knowledge, while deconstructing the overly constrictive and ideological schemes of modern theory. Yet he shares much of the postmodern critique of metaphysics and modern theory, engaging in deconstructive critiques of the hierarchical claims of metaphysical schemes *à la* Derrida, as well as attacking idealist theories of the identity between thought and being.[4] Nonetheless, Adorno's method of deconstructing philosophical antinomies and binary schemes is significantly different than Derrida's. While Derrida carries out a philosophical critique of the limitations of claims for the hierarchy of one term over another in binary metaphysical schemes, Adorno operates in a simultaneously deconstructive and reconstructive vein. That is, while Adorno attempts to subvert philosophical binary oppositions and hierarchies, he also, as we shall see, attempts to reconstruct philosophical concepts such as the subject and truth, and produces constellations that will illuminate socio-historical reality. His formula for this procedure is: 'Interpretation of the unintentional through a juxtaposition of the analytically isolated elements, and illumination of the real by the power of such interpretation; that is the programme of every authentically materialist knowledge' (Adorno 1977: p. 127).

With postmodern theory, Adorno shares a critique of representation and the model of thought as the 'mirror of nature'. Yet Adorno merely problematizes representation rather than dissolving the real in discourse or figures. For instance, in *Negative Dialectics*, he characterizes the particular as standing in a pattern of relations to other particulars in a historically constituted configuration (1973: p. 163). Each particular, then, is a unique configuration of constitutive relations or mediations. Dialectical thought is to produce constellations of figures or ideas which illuminate these particulars. Yet there is always a non-identity between the constellation of ideas and the configuration of the particular.

Consequently, Adorno attempts both to undo conventional philosophical theories, categories, and methods, while producing new models of theoretical critique. In his *Metacritique of Epistemology* (1983), he carries out a critique of foundationalism similar to that of postmodern theory. His target is what he calls *prima philosophia*, first philosophy, or philosophy of first principles or beginnings.[5] The example is Husserl's philosophy which he takes as a symptomatic form of idealism. First philosophy, Adorno claims, seeks a 'pure' starting point, an indisputable foundation for knowledge. It usually finds this anchor in its own subjectivity, methodically cleansed of all extraneous content. It claims that access to this foundation is direct and unmediated and that it is universally valid, fundamental, and enduring. Such a project is impossible, Adorno claims, because all experience and thought is mediated – by language, society, and a set of social relations and objects. There is no pure subjectivity which confronts pure objects: the subject is mediated by its objects and vice versa. Moreover, the alleged foundation is itself at best an abstraction, an idealist posit that fetishizes its own conceptual products. At worst, first philosophy is totalitarian with spirit or subjectivity wanting to contain and dominate everything: 'Since the philosophical first must always already contain everything, spirit confiscates what is unlike itself and makes it the same, its property. Spirit inventories it. Nothing may slip through the net. The principle must guarantee completeness' (Adorno 1983: p. 9).

Adorno argues that the very desire for foundational knowledge is symptomatic of a need for 'absolute spiritual security' characteristic of the bourgeoisie (1983: p. 15). As Fromm showed in *Escape from Freedom* (1941), the bourgeoisie emerged from feudalism eventually triumphant but insecure. As political and economic insecurity mounted in the face of wars, economic crises, political upheavals, and challenges by the working class, bourgeois intellectuals sought security in knowledge, in securing stable foundations for their thought and practice. Early theorists like Descartes, for example, sought absolute certainty in philosophical cognition, in the self-certainty of individual consciousness. Kant, Husserl, and later philosophers merely replicated this urge, assuaging social and economic insecurity with philosophical certainty, grounding thought in a foundation of absolute certain truths and principles.

In 'late bourgeois philosophy', the desire for security becomes even more acute as societal crises and tensions mount. Since bourgeois philosophers contribute nothing to the 'real production of life', the need intensifies to compensate for their alienation and insecurity through the medium of knowledge. Consequently, they attempt to secure absolute foundations for knowledge and to substitute intellectual mastery for material and social mastery. 'By furnishing the principle from which all being proceeds, the subject promotes itself' (Adorno 1983: p. 14). The proclamation of an absolute ground for knowledge thus compensates for their own lack of material grounding, for the groundlessness of their material and social existences. Such justification of foundations for knowledge provide 'entitlements' and 'title deeds' to concepts and ideas which secure and enhance their existence. Thus, *'prima philosophia* becomes property' (Adorno 1983: p. 15) and the successful quest for foundations provides both intellectual security and property upon which the bourgeois philosopher can build her or his existence.

The quest for certainty and foundations is not innocent, however, or merely laughable, for, as Deleuze and Guattari also understood, this epistemic compulsion helps produce authoritarian personalities and provides a fertile ground for fascism and authoritarian governments. For submitting to certainty, to *a priori* and absolute grounds and arguments, provides a personality structure susceptible to control by social authorities. Growing insecurity and failures in the intellectual realm also promote a quest for certainties and security outside of philosophy. As he put it in 'Husserl and the Problem of Idealism', the 'desire to vindicate for truth a superhuman objectivity which must merely be recognized' might also promote recognition and obedience of a superhuman social authority, a superior *Führer* (Adorno 1940: p. 12).

In addition to analyzing why philosophers seek certainty and a foundation of knowledge, Adorno also attempts to provide a diagnosis of the ways in which philosophy fosters belief in the objectivity and existence of universal concepts and general propositions. As a response to the fragmentation and alienation of individuals in bourgeois society, its philosophers provide common concepts and ideal objects called propositions that are objectively existent, binding, and valid for all individuals at all times. The ideal universality of its conceptual fetishes compensates for the lack of a universality of material objects which in a class-divided society are available only to the privileged classes. Anyone, however, can possess the universal concepts and propositions of bourgeois philosophy.

Like commodities in capitalist society, bourgeois concepts are reified and fetishized. Exchange takes place, as in the economy, between concepts found and already produced, which attributes a fetishized power to the objects of thought that appear to be pre-existent, independent, and autonomous. We see here how Adorno combines philosophical and sociological critique to illuminate both social reality and philosophical discourse and follies. He argues that even the most abstract philosophical categories are saturated with social content and that therefore sociological critique is necessary to adequately critique philosophy. On the other hand, philosophical critique provides insights into contemporary social reality and its modes of thought and behaviour. This dual optic thus provides Adorno with a dialectical perspective on both philosophy and society, as well as illuminating their mutual interaction.

As we have suggested, there are many parallels between Adorno and postmodern theory. He vindicates otherness, difference, and particularity as consistently and brilliantly as any postmodern theorist. In a discussion of how first philosophy reduces its foundation to the elementary, Adorno argues that this tendency to immediacy and the elementary represents a 'tendency to regression, a hatred of the complicated, [which] is steadily at work in a theory of origins, thus guaranteeing its affinity with lordship. Progress and demythologization have neither exposed nor extinguished this tendency, but rather have let it appear even more crassly wherever possible. The enemy, the other, the non-identical is always also what is distinguished and differentiated from the subject's universality' (Adorno 1983: p. 20).

Yet Adorno did not want to throw out the concept of the subject, or reject it as an ideological illusion. While he criticized idealist inflation of subjectivity, and materialist reductions, he called for reconstruction rather than rejection of subjectivity, believing that subjectivity was a fundamental component of individuality, of cognitive knowledge and individual practice. Adorno's concept of constitutive subjectivity recognized the objective determinations of the subject, while insisting on its potential autonomy.

Subjectivity was a potential to actualize, a goal to strive for, on Adorno's theory, rather than a pre-existing substratum of essential identity. Creation of a critical and self-reflexive subjectivity was thus an important aspect of Adorno's thought which differentiates it from postmodern theory.

Consequently, unlike postmodern theorists Adorno never completely rejects reason, truth, reflexive subjectivity, or modern philosophy, using reconstructed versions of modern categories. While he does not, as Habermas, completely separate philosophy and art, he dialectically mediates them with each maintaining their own autonomy, though Adorno sees an aesthetic element in all philosophy (constructing ideas, figures, and constellations) and a cognitive function in art (that is, illuminating reality through figures and images). But, as we shall see in the next section, the most distinguished member of the second generation of critical theory, Jürgen Habermas, believes that Horkheimer and Adorno go too far in the critique of modernity and fail to adequately explicate its as yet unfulfilled promises (see pp. 212ff. below). Let us then proceed to Habermas' theory of modernity and confrontation with postmodern theory which produced some of the most controversial philosophical debates of the present moment.

7.3 Habermas and Modernity

> The project of modernity, formulated in the 18th century by the philosophers of the Enlightenment, consisted in their efforts to develop objective science, universal morality and law, and autonomous art according to their inner logic. At the same time, this project intended to release the cognitive potentials of each of these domains from their esoteric forms. The Enlightenment philosophers wanted to utilize this accumulation of specialized culture for the enrichment of everyday life – that is to say, for the rational organization of everyday social life (Habermas: 1981: p. 9).

During the 1980s, Habermas entered into the postmodern debates and sharpened his critical and dialectical analysis of modernity. In his article 'Modernity – An Unfinished Project' (1981), Habermas argued that the various postmodern theories were a form of attack on modernity which had their ideological precursors in various irrationalist and aestheticist counter-Enlightenment theories. In a series of succeeding lectures on *The Philosophical Discourse of Modernity* (1987a), Habermas continued to criticize the German and French postmodern theories. He used standard Marxian methods of ideology critique suggesting that the French postmodern theories, which had their roots in Nietzsche, Heidegger, and Bataille, were aligned with the counter-Enlightenment, and exhibited disturbing kinship with fascism. Against postmodern theories, Habermas defended modernity as an unfinished project which contained unfulfilled emancipatory potential.

From this perspective, Habermas' entire corpus of work can be read as reflections on modernity, on its trajectory, contributions, pathologies, and emancipatory potential. In the following discussion, we shall suggest that Habermas' first published work can be read as an analysis of the origins of modernity, its emancipatory features, and its regressive development in the present era. To some extent, his later work continues this project, predominantly in the domain of philosophy, but also in social theory, cultural critique, and his political interventions. In these ways, Habermas' work can be shown to have a deep continuity with the earlier Frankfurt School despite the different emphases and topics which emerged as a result of his 'linguistic turn' in the early 1970s.

7.3.1 Modernity as Unfinished Project

> The public sphere as a sphere which mediates between society and state, in which the public organizes itself as the bearer of public opinion, accords with the principle of publicity (*Öffentlichkeit*) – that principle of public information which once had to be fought for against the arcane policies of monarchies and which since that time has made possible the democratic control of state activities . . . Public discussions about the exercise of political power which are both critical in intent and institutionally guaranteed have not always existed – they grew out of a specific phase of bourgeois society and could enter into the order of the bourgeois constitutional state only as a result of a particular constellation of interests (Habermas in Bronner and Kellner 1989: p. 137).

One can read Habermas' first major book, *The Structural Transformation of the Public Sphere* (1989a; orig. 1962), as a dissection of capitalist modernity in its transition from early to later forms. The first half describes the rise of what Habermas calls 'the bourgeois public sphere' which provides a realm of free and rational inquiry and discussion that mediates between the state and the private sphere. Habermas describes the rise of literary clubs and salons, newspapers and political journals, and institutions of political debate and participation in the eighteenth century. He thus provides a positive picture of early modernity as an epoch when a certain degree of reason and rational debate was exerted in a liberal and democratic public sphere in which individuals critically discussed their common interests and public concerns.

During this epoch, functions of individuality and citizenship, *l'homme* and *citoyen*, overlapped and individuals could both develop their own capacities and rationally shape their social and political order through activity in the public sphere. This analysis provides the historical matrix of Habermas' later valorization of democracy, communicative action, and rational consensus which finds its origins and model in the earlier bourgeois public sphere. Consequently, unlike most postmodern theory, Habermas finds a valuable legacy in modernity worth preserving and revitalizing. The second half of the book, however, analyzes the decline of the public sphere in late modernity. In an analysis parallel to the sketch of the transition between entrepreneurial, market capitalism and state and monopoly capitalism developed by the first generation of critical theory, Habermas claims that in later developments of capitalist society the state and private corporations took over vital functions of the public sphere which was degenerating into a sphere of domination. Habermas discusses the processes whereby the state and public bureaucracies come to penetrate both the economic realm and the private realm. The state merges with the economy in the era of state or organized capitalism and plays a crucial role in managing the economy and attempting to prevent crisis. At the same time, the state takes over public functions such as education, mediating in social conflicts, and providing social welfare, as well as taking over ownership and control of new media like broadcasting in at least some of the capitalist countries.

In addition, giant corporations enter the public sphere and transform individuals from citizens and discussants of political and cultural events to culture-consuming spectators of political and media spectacles. Habermas traces the rise of new media, advertising, public relations, and corporate control of culture as ways in which private corporations come to assume tremendous power in the realm of the public sphere and displace rational individuals, citizens, and parties as the major political forces. In a sense, Habermas is thus replicating – with much more empirical and historical analysis – the earlier Frankfurt School analysis of the culture industries and the way that the capitalist state and media have come to control ever more realms of contemporary life.

Habermas employs the sort of critical and totalizing social theory eschewed by some postmodernists in order to conceptualize the present age, valorizing the earlier bourgeois public sphere against its decline in contemporary societies. Most postmodern theory, by contrast, attacks the entire trajectory of modernity and sees later decline (*à la* Horkheimer and Adorno) in its origins. In contrast to postmodern theory, Habermas wants to valorize early modernity and to realize its unfulfilled potential. His first book, then, provides important clues as to what aspects of modernity he wishes to preserve and serves to explain why he would oppose later postmodern theories which totally reject modernity.

Habermas' succeeding works (for example, *The Logic of the Social Sciences, Theory and Practice, Knowledge and Human Interests*) can be read in retrospect as attempts to salvage the cognitive promises of modernity via redemption of critical, reflexive, activist modes of thought which combine theoretical construction with empirical analysis, self-reflexivity and critique with theory construction, and theory with practice. Habermas consistently defended a type of modern, critical, emancipatory theory against positivistic and conservative theory. His attempts to combine social science and empirical inquiry with social theory (for example, *Legitimation Crisis, Communication and the Evolution of Society*) strive to update and revise the critical theory of capitalist modernity begun by his predecessors in the tradition of critical theory. Habermas' political interventions (such as his critiques of the irrationalism of some new left politics, of various conservative ideologies, and of resurgence of fascist tendencies; see Habermas 1989b) can also be read as a series of critiques of what he considers anti-modern theories and practices in the contemporary era (for example *Toward a Rational Society, Kleinen Politische Schriften I–VI*).

Habermas, then, is a strong advocate of modernity and defender of what he considers its progressive elements, while criticizing its oppressive and destructive aspects. He does, however, call for a revision of the project of Enlightenment rationality and proposes some reconstructions of the concept of reason and critique of a subject-centred tradition of rationalism. On the other hand, he criticizes all counter-Enlightenment theory as potentially danger-ous, theoretically and politically – a point that is central to his 1980s interventions in the postmodern debates. In his article, 'Modernity versus Postmodernity' Habermas defends the modern differentiation of cultural spheres and development of auto-nomous criteria of value in the fields of knowledge, morality, law and justice, and art (1981: p. 8). He refers to this as the project of modernity which he interprets 'as the efforts to develop objective science, universal morality and law, and autonomous art, accord-ing to their inner logic' (1981: p. 9).

While the project of modernity resulted in part in the coloniza-tion of the life-world by the logic of scientific–technological rationality and domination by a culture of experts and specialists, it also for Habermas has unrealized potential in increasing social rationality, justice, and morality. Progress in social rationality could be achieved through 'undistorted communication' based on a willingness to engage in rational discourse on topics of contro-versy, to allow free and equal access to all participants, to attempt to understand the issues and arguments, to yield to the force of the better argument, and to accept a rational consensus.

From the standpoint of this qualified defence of modernity, Habermas criticizes what he considers to be 'false programmes of the negation of culture', or overly negative attacks on modernity, which fail in his view to recognize its positive contributions and potential. These positions include postmodern theory and Haber-mas concludes with the expression of a fear that 'ideas of anti-modernity, together with an additional touch of premodernity, are becoming popular in the circles of alternative culture', and he advances his own defence of modernity in opposition to these tendencies (1981: p. 14).

Ultimately, Habermas fears that the rejection of reason has

dangerous theoretical and political consequences, and he strives to defend what he considers to be the unfulfilled democratic promises of the Enlightenment. Yet Habermas accepts much of the postmodern critique of modern philosophy, although he undertakes to reconstruct rather than to reject reason. His major work of the early 1980s, *Theory of Communicative Action*, Volumes I and II (1984 and 1987b; orig. 1981), carries out a critique of modern philosophy and social theory while developing an alternative conception of rationality based on his theory of communicative action. He argues that the dominant philosophical perspective of modernity is rooted in a subjectivistic 'philosophy of consciousness' against which he posits an intersubjective philosophy of 'communicative action'. Habermas calls for a 'paradigm shift' from the philosophy of consciousness to a philosophy of communication. The philosophy of consciousness operates with a concept of instrumental rationality rooted in the drive for self-preservation. Habermas distinguishes between instrumental and communicative action. Instrumental action relates means to ends, techniques to goals, without reflection on the rationality or justness of the goals themselves. It is rooted in a subjectivistic project of the domination of nature and lacks an intersubjective dimension. Communicative action, by contrast, is action oriented toward understanding and agreement. Habermas' philosophy of communicative action, in contrast to the philosophy of subjectivity, is rooted in intersubjective communication and is grounded in social solidarity and the utopian potentials of language: to engage in mutual understanding, to forge uncoerced consensus, and so on.

Habermas believes that the paradigm shift which he seeks began in the transition from the philosophy of consciousness to a philosophy of language, begun by Frege and Wittgenstein. But the philosophy of language is also too subjectivistic, Habermas claims, basing its philosophical model on the same ego/object model rather than an ego/alter (self/other) model of communication. Some efforts toward this latter paradigm are also found in the social philosophy of Mead and Durkheim, but their work too is limited in that they failed to develop a theory of communicative action which specifies the conditions under which mutual understanding and consensus are reached. Developing a theory of communicative action, Habermas claims, will help provide a reconstruction of the concept of reason in which rationality is transformed into 'communicative rationality'. Rather than rationality being the feat of the self-enclosed subject attempting to dominate nature, it becomes the result of undistorted communication, the model of which Habermas takes pains to explicate.

Like postmodern theory, Habermas undertakes a vigorous critique of modern reason and philosophy, but adopts a reconstructive rather than purely deconstructive approach. This project is similar to early moves by Horkheimer, Adorno, and Marcuse who also called for a reconstruction of reason and contrasted critical reason with instrumental or positivistic reason.[6] Habermas, however, claims that his critical theory predecessors also remained mired in the philosophy of consciousness, arguing that they – like the postmodernists – lacked a dimension of intersubjectivity and communication which would enable one to develop a more social and less egological theory of subjectivity.

Habermas' *Theory of Communicative Action* also develops a theory and critique of modernity that is both similar to and different from Horkheimer and Adorno and postmodern theory. Habermas' major focus is on Max Weber's theory of modernity as the extension of instrumental rationality into an iron cage of domination with the subsequent fragmentation of meaning and decline of freedom through the growth of bureaucratic rationality. Habermas stresses that Lukács, Horkheimer and Adorno, and other Western Marxists share this interpretation of modernity, anticipating the critiques of Foucault, Baudrillard, Deleuze and Guattari, and other postmodern theorists who also conceptualize and criticize the inner connection between rationalization and modernity. Habermas claims, however, that previous theories criticized this model from within a philosophy of consciousness and, at best, allowed individuals to break through the veil and structures of rationalization to create meaning and increase freedom. By contrast, Habermas believes that his concept of communicative action provides a conceptual scheme whereby one can diagnose pathologies of the 'life-world' (such as its colonization by the system of money and power) and provide cures (for instance, an increase in communication, social participation, and discussion of values and norms to reconstruct society). Communicative action, Habermas believes, allows the preservation of modern values of social rationality, consensus, emancipation, and solidarity, and thus provides a basis for both social critique and reconstruction.

7.3.2   Habermas vs. Postmodern Theory

With postmodern theory, Habermas shares the critique of Western rationality and metaphysics.[7] Yet he insists that critical social theory requires a normative foundation to provide a standpoint to launch effective social critique and to engage in social transformation. Rejecting the earlier Frankfurt School and neo-Marxist tradition of immanent critique, whereby existing societal norms and ideals are used to criticize the suppression of these values in the contemporary era, Habermas argues that such immanent norms have lost their critical force. He claims that 'there are no norms for immanent critique to appeal to,' because 'bourgeois consciousness has grown cynical' and no longer responds to normative critique (Habermas 1976: p. 97). Rejecting the model of immanent critique, he indicates that his theory of communicative action 'proceeds reconstructively, that is unhistorically ... A theory developed in this way can no longer start by examining concrete ideals immanent in traditional forms of life' (Habermas 1987a: p. 383).

Instead of deriving the norms of critique from immanent historical forms, Habermas seeks the basis of a critical standpoint in the universally taken-for-granted features of language and communication. He thus moves towards a quasi-transcendental perspective that derives norms for social critique and the foundation of critical theory from the very structure of language and communication, and the capacities for communication and understanding developed historically in the human species.[8] Since he first took this linguistic and normative turn, however, Habermas' critics claim that he has resurrected a quasi-foundationalist position in his theory of communicative action (Roderick 1986; Rasmussen 1990). Others argue that Habermas conflates understanding and agreement, while reifying a distinction between production and communication (Callinicos 1990). And all of his postmodern critics claim that he uncritically reproduces the heritage of Enlightenment rationalism, glossing over its repressive and terroristic heritage (Lyotard 1984a, *et al.*).

Habermas insists in response that he in fact is critical of Enlightenment rationality, yet wishes to undertake a reconstruction of reason that preserves its progressive features (Habermas, forthcoming). For Habermas, the Enlightenment and rationality provide a dual heritage of both progressive and regressive features: democracy, cultural differentiation and critical reason are for Habermas progressive, while the extension of instrumental rationality to all spheres of life is destructive. Habermas argues that his postmodern critics, and his critical theory predecessors, Horkheimer and Adorno, were too undialectical in interpreting Enlightenment reason primarily as an instrument of domination. In addition, Habermas defends the democratic heritage of modernity and claims that his theory of communicative action provides a philosophical standpoint to defend democracy and to criticize domination and hierarchy. He claims that his ideal speech situation provides procedures for allowing democratic participation in decision-making and that his concept of consensus is a democratic norm of coming to agreement that extends democratic practice.

Thus, the expansion of communicative action is, for Habermas, a progressive contribution of modernity. A postmodern response could be that Habermas downplays the social constituents and constraints on communication. From this perspective, Habermas' idealized notion of consensus could be used to legitimate the manipulation of individuals and suppression of difference through celebrating consensus as the ideal of 'coming to an understanding'. This concept downplays the fact that consensus is often forced and forged by the will of the stronger imposing their will on the weaker. A Lyotardian, by contrast, would stress the importance of articulating and preserving differences to avoid potential repression and manipulation (Lyotard 1984a). Other postmodernists attack the universalism and quasi-foundationalism found in Habermas' concept of the ideal speech situation, rejecting all universals and totalizing theories (Rorty 1984).

Our position, in contrast to both Habermas and his postmodern critics, is that in some situations it is best to engage in dissensus, to challenge hegemonic views, and to preserve differences, while in other contexts it is necessary to reach consensus to promote certain political or ethical goals (see 5.4.1). While Habermas would probably agree with this pragmatic, contextualist position, in fact, the overwhelming emphasis of his theory is on attaining understanding, coming to agreement, and reaching consensus, and he rarely, if ever, points to the value of dissensus and preserving differences. Communicative action for Habermas is fundamentally coming to understanding and agreement, while for Lyotard it is simply to fight, to disagree, to put into question in an agonistic mode. For us, communication involves both dimensions, which we see as of equal importance, and thus we find both Habermas and Lyotard one-sided in their communication theory.

Likewise, we reject both Habermas' universalistic quasi-foundationalism which attempts to ground communicative rationality in the very potentials of language, as well as the aversion to all universals found in much postmodern theory. While Habermas' quasi-evolutionary notion of communicative universals tends to be somewhat abstract, we would stress that values like human rights, equality, freedom, and democracy as historically produced universal values that are invaluable discursive weapons in the struggle for emancipation. While the language of rights demands a universal context where rights apply to all, the universality is a product of historical struggle and is not a locus of a transcendental and essentialist universality, as some human rights theorists claim (though not Habermas who, as far as we are aware, has not developed a theory of rights from his concept of communicative action). Rather, certain societies grant universal rights to their citizens as a result of protracted social struggles. Thus human rights and democratic freedoms should be interpreted as social and political constructs, albeit ones that it is important for individuals and groups to protect and they should not be gratuitously dismissed by postmodern intellectuals.

Yet, we would argue that these (historically constructed) universal rights and freedoms are themselves provisional, constructed, contextual, and the product of social struggle in a specific historical context. Although human rights and democratic values are to be defended and extended, they should not be mystified. Consequently, we would provide a historicist rather than an philosophical foundation for these values, interpreting them as the product of struggle and as the progressive constructs of a specific social–historical situation rather than as essential features of human beings or quasi-transcendental postulates of a specific sort, deriving from language or communication.

Against an extreme postmodern theory, we would reject the

attack of a Lyotard or Baudrillard against all universal rights and values, general normative positions, and democratic notions like consensus. Postmodern theory may be justified in suspecting all foundationalist and universalist claims of hiding special interests and serving particular constellations of power, but the creation of a just society requires establishing certain universal rights like equality, rule by law, freedom, and democratic participation and those postmodern theories which scorn these notions ultimately help conservative powers who are all too willing to put aside democratic rights, freedoms, and values.

Habermas' response would be that it is precisely he who is upholding the democratic values of modernity and that it is postmodern theory which is undermining them. The postmodern critique is inaugurated by Nietzsche who carries out a systematic assault on modernity, including the Enlightenment and reason. Habermas provides a reading of Nietzsche as an aestheticist, as a champion of myth over reason, of Dionysian art over philosophy. Nietzsche's aesthetic programme thus provides a foundation for irrationalism, for a dissolving of reason and the individual in the ecstatic, Dionysian plunge into primal life, erotic abandonment, and aesthetic joy.

This irrationalist philosophical ethos was taken over, according to Habermas, in different ways by Heidegger, Bataille and the postmodernists. One tendency extends from Nietzsche to Bataille to Foucault, while another branches from Nietzsche to Heidegger to Derrida. Habermas suggests that Heidegger and his followers pursue the Nietzschean assault on reason into a premodern mysticism, while Bataille and later postmodern theorists like Foucault develop an irrationalist aestheticism. While Habermas does not take up systematically the complex issue of the relationships between Nietzsche, Heidegger, and fascism, he begins his discussion of Heidegger with citations that indicate how his appropriation of Nietzsche's conception of the *Übermensch* coincides with National Socialism's glorification of the storm-trooper (1987b: p. 132). Habermas also stresses the kinship of the messianic elements of Nietzsche and Heidegger, the pathos of the new, and the attacks on reason. Habermas primarily reads Heidegger, though, as a proponent of a new religion, as an advocate of the dissolution of reason in a primordial experience of being, in a mystical embrace of being itself.

Habermas then claims that similar, though highly unconventional, religiosity is found in Bataille who helped introduce Nietzsche into French thought, while similar critiques of reason are found in Foucault, Derrida, and French postmodern theory. Habermas thus finds a counter-Enlightenment thread running through Nietzsche, Heidegger, Bataille, and French postmodern theory. He warns of the theoretical and political dangers of this affiliation, stressing the kinship between irrationalism and fascism that was earlier the topic of Lukács' *Destruction of Reason* (1980; orig. 1954). But while Lukács defended Marxism and socialism as the necessary antidote to destructive irrationalism, Habermas advocates his theory of communicative action and turns to an inter-subjective paradigm for social theory.

In sum, Habermas criticizes postmodern theory for deserting reason and modernity. Derrida's critique of metaphysics and philosophy of language, he claims, flirts with Jewish mysticism (1987a: pp. 181–2) and irrationalism. Further, Habermas criticizes Derrida for collapsing philosophy into literature, in which philosophy loses its autonomy and is dissolved in rhetoric and literature (1987a: pp. 185ff.). Habermas appreciates Foucault's critiques of subjectivity and the institutions of modernity, but believes that Foucault has no standpoint from which to criticize modern institutions and thus has no basis for an ethics and politics. As we have seen in Chapter 2, Foucault refuses to specify or justify the normative values that implicitly inform his critique of modern practices of domination. Habermas seizes on this as a problem which vitiates Foucault's political criticism.

Though both Foucault and Habermas link knowledge to power and criticize coercive forms of rationality, Habermas also attempts to foreground the normative dimensions of social and political critique within a theory of communicative action. While Foucault, in many contexts, links reason with power and domination *per se*, Habermas distinguishes between different types of reason, differentiating among instrumental, strategic, and communicative reason. Habermas also accuses Foucault of rejecting modernity and Enlightenment, at least in his earlier work, though Habermas sees that Foucault eventually came around to a qualified defence of Enlightenment values in a late essay on Kant (see Habermas 1989b: pp. 173–9).

Indeed, Foucault stated that: 'If I had been familiar with the

Frankfurt School . . . I would not have said a number of stupid things that I did say and I would have avoided many of the detours which I made while trying to pursue my own humble path – when, meanwhile, avenues had been opened up by the Frankfurt School. It is a strange case of non-penetration between two very similar types of thinking which is explained, perhaps, by that very similarity. Nothing hides the fact of a problem in common better than two similar ways of approaching it' (1988d: p. 26). Yet Foucault never says precisely what he might have learned from critical theory, nor what things they have in common, but certainly the critique of rationality as an instrument of domination would be one key similarity.

On the other hand, Foucault would surely reject Habermas' universalist, quasi-evolutionist schemes in favour of problematizations of discourse in concrete sociohistorical sites. He might also agree with Lyotard's critique of Habermas' theory of consensus and would obviously have been offended by Habermas labelling him a 'young conservative' – a mislabelling that Habermas does not take up again in *The Philosophical Discourse of Modernity* where he tends to call postmodern theorists 'irrationalists' or 'anarchists' rather than conservatives. Yet in this book, Habermas' attacks on postmodern discourses frequently assume a guilt by association (with Nietzsche, Heidegger and fascism), and his defences of modernity, the Enlightenment, and the universalist heritage of philosophy and reason, often fail to answer the strongest critiques of these phenomena by Foucault, Derrida, Lyotard, Baudrillard, and others.

On the other hand, Habermas correctly delineates irrationalist and reactionary features of some postmodern theory and its predecessors overlooked by some of its celebrants. His readings, however, of Nietzsche, Heidegger, Foucault, and Derrida have been sharply contested by their defenders (see Rajchman 1988 and the articles in *Praxis Intentional*, vol. 8, no. 4, 1989). Yet many of the attacks on Habermas carry out the same caricature of his views that his critics claim that he perpetrates on postmodern theory. This is unfortunate for we believe that a genuine dialogue between postmodern theory and critical theory could be productive for contemporary philosophy and social theory. But for a fruitful dialogue to take place there must be more open and receptive attentiveness and understanding between these traditions. So far, however, critical theorists have tended to reject postmodern theory and culture in its entirety (see the discussion in Kellner 1989a), while postmodernists, with some exceptions, have polemicized against critical theory, especially Habermas.

7.4   Sibling Rivalries: The Habermas–Lyotard Debate

Most of the focus by those in the tradition of critical theory on the postmodern debate has concerned the attacks by postmodern theory on modernity, reason, Enlightenment, universality, and other concepts which critical theory has utilized, albeit not always traditionally. The critical theory optic on postmodern theory has for the most part focused on postmodern forms of knowledge and their allegedly irrationalist proclivities – rather than on the theories of postmodern society, the media, simulation, and so on. With the exception of Habermas who takes on a broad panorama of postmodern theory, the critical theory response has focused on critiques of Lyotard's *The Postmodern Condition*, and on defences of reason, universality, and normativity against the postmodern attack, and so in this section we shall focus on the debates between Lyotard and the Habermasians.[9]

Seyla Benhabib, for instance, points to a contradiction in Lyotard's programme in which he seems unable to decide if he wishes to maintain a relativist and pluralist heterogeneity of language games or to develop an epistemological standpoint from which he can criticize grand narratives or the 'performativity' legitimation practices of the sciences: 'the choice is still between an uncritical polytheism and a self-conscious recognition of the need for criteria of validity, and the attempt to reflexively ground them' (1984: p. 111). Benhabib suggests that Lyotard does not seem to be able to make the choice, though he leans toward the pluralism and relativism pole – which means he lacks a standpoint from which he can criticize competing positions.

In a related critique, Axel Honneth attacks Lyotard's 'aversion to the universal' (1985). Honneth argues that Lyotard's critique of Habermas' conception of consensus 'betrays not only a misunderstanding of Habermas' discursive ethics, but also displays an aversion against the "general", against any universalism at all, which is so deeply seated that it affects the whole of Lyotard's construction' (Honneth 1985: p. 154). Honneth claims that Lyotard's critique is 'largely based on a mistaken interpretation of Habermas' (and Apel's) principle of dialogue free of domination as a procedure for the repressive unification of all particular interests and needs, instead of seeing in it a way of communicatively testing the degree to which such interests and needs can be generalized. The procedure of discursive ethics does not have its final goal in the determination of common needs, as Lyotard supposes, . . . but rather in intersubjective agreement about just those social norms which allow it to realize differing interests and needs within the common relations of social life' (Honneth 1985: p. 154).

Yet the epistemic wars between Lyotard and Habermas and their followers cover over the similarities between Lyotard and the critical theorists of the Frankfurt School. Lyotard's 'incredulity toward metanarratives' and attack on the legitimizing narratives of modernity are similar in some ways to the Frankfurt School practice of ideology critique. For what are legitimizing narratives if not ideologies which legitimate the institutions, practices, values, and social order controlled by a dominant class? Moreover, the specific metanarratives criticized by Lyotard are like the ideologies previously criticized by the Frankfurt School: Hegel's philosophy of spirit, liberalism, and teleological Marxism. Consequently, there are at least some similarities between critical theory and Lyotard's critique of metanarratives, though Lyotard's war on totality and grand narratives obviously breaks with the Hegelian Marxism of the Frankfurt School.

Both Habermas and Lyotard criticize the dominant legitimating principles of contemporary capitalist societies. In many cases, Lyotard's targets are thus similar to those of critical theory. Indeed, like critical theory, Lyotard attacks capitalism, the culture industries, commodification, imperialism, patriarchy and the bourgeois family, and other familiar targets of neo-Marxian critique. Like the Frankfurt School he also depicts contemporary capitalist society as able to coopt all forms of opposition.[10] Indeed, Lyotard develops critical positions on the contemporary organization of society that are not completely dissimilar from those of critical theory. Lyotard's critique of performativity is akin to the Frankfurt School critique of instrumental reason, to Marcuse's critique of the performance principle, and to critical theory's critique of positivism. These critiques all attack the claims of the sciences to impose their criteria on domains of culture, experience, and everyday life where they are deemed inappropriate and even repressive. Both Habermas and Lyotard thus share a 'critique of functional reason', whereby reason is reduced to an instrument of social reproduction, judged solely by the effectiveness of its performances.

Yet, as noted, it is not clear from what position Lyotard can launch a critique of functional reason as he contrasts the narratives of myth and philosophy to scientific reason. Although he defends the principle of a proliferation of different types of discourse and attacks the pretensions of either a functionalist scientific discourse or grand narrative philosophical discourse to legislate between competing discourses, he really does not have a principle whereby he can criticize specific applications of functional reason. Furthermore, although both Lyotard and Habermas, unlike other postmodern theorists, are interested in the question of legitimation, Lyotard's position is quite ambiguous. Both Habermas and Lyotard oppose the traditional philosophical move in which reason or philosophy derives norms to legitimate knowledge claims out of its own resources. Habermas, however, is concerned to rationally ground norms in communication freed from distortion in which individuals come to a rational consensus without domination. Lyotard can respond to Habermas by claiming that this counterfactual ideal speech situation underplays the extent to which strategic action forces consensus, such that the most powerful or clever force their interests and positions on others. For Lyotard, discourse *is* strategic action, whereby individuals struggle in agonistics against dominant positions. Yet he has no concept of how to reach any sort of understanding or come to any sort of consensus whatsoever.

Although his critiques of reason and totalizing theory might lead one to claim that Lyotard is rejecting reason altogether, occasionally he qualifies his position, making it more similar to critical theory. In a *Theory, Culture and Society* interview, Lyotard calls for a more differentiated critique of the Enlightenment and reason, while citing his admiration for the work of Diderot (1988a: pp. 279ff.; 300) – a position that he had already noted in a 1979 article (collected in Lyotard 1989: pp. 181ff.) This would bring his position in closer proximity to that of critical theory which always attempted to differentiate critical reason (and in Marcuse's case libidinal reason) from more instrumental and conformist reason.

Other interesting similarities between Lyotard and Habermas have also been overlooked in favour of emphasis on their differences. Both Lyotard and Habermas made the linguistic turn in theory and both develop a philosophy of language which stresses linguistic pragmatics and language games, accenting the variety and diversity of language games and forms of judgement, rather than developing a structural or formal linguistics. In semiotic terms, both emphasize *parole*, or speaking, over *langue*, or linguistic system. Both stress that different types of discourse (theoretical, practical, aesthetic, for example) have their own particular rules, norms, and criteria. Habermas, however, advocates a concept of consensus to adjudicate disputes within and among the different realms of discourse, while Lyotard tends to stress differences between 'regimes of phrases' and the situation of the differend in which it is impossible to come to a consensus or even to discover a rule that could adjudicate between different positions.

Yet with Lyotard's 1980s turn to Kant and what might be seen as his neo-Kantian perspectives, there is a curious *rapprochement* with what might be interpreted as Habermas' neo-Kantian perspectives. Both Habermas and Lyotard accept Kant's division of reason into the spheres of theoretical, practical, and aesthetic judgements, and both defend the sort of Kantian cultural differentiation in which each sphere of judgement has its own criteria and validity claims. As for their aesthetic theory, Lyotard unambiguously advocates an aesthetics of the sublime, while accusing Habermas of advocating an aesthetics of the beautiful (1984a: p. 79), thus situating their differences within a Kantian framework – though we agree with Jay (1989: pp. 109ff.) that Habermas' fragments on aesthetics cannot unproblematically be assimilated to an aesthetics of the beautiful. Moreover, although Lyotard earlier stressed the incommensurable differences between regimes of phrases, he later comes to argue that Kant's third critique provides a link between the theoretical and practical spheres (1989: pp. 393ff.) and in *The Differend* is interested in the linkages between phrases and their different regimes.

Furthermore, in his dialogues on paganism (1989) and justice (1985), Lyotard actually seeks consensus and the participants in his literary construct end up agreeing with each other for the most part, thus reinforcing the positions advanced by Lyotard in the dialogues. Consequently, although Lyotard may champion dissensus, his philosophical dialogues enact consensus. Curiously enough, while Habermas defends the distinction between philosophy and literature, his *Philosophical Discourse on Modernity* can be read as a grand narrative that employs literary construction, copious rhetoric, and frequent moral and political passion. While he champions consensus, his text enacts dissensus, attacking both certain forms of modern theory and its postmodern opponent. Habermas' tone is sharply polemical and he rarely searches for common ground or points of agreement, preferring instead to engage in often passionate and sometimes overstated polemics. Thus, although Habermas champions consensus, his recent philosophical texts enact dissensus and agonistics.

Consequently, Habermas and Lyotard are closer to each other in many ways than the usual juxtapositions between them would indicate. While Lyotard criticizes Habermas for his alleged desire for a unitary ground for consensus and a universal social theory, both explicate and defend certain neo-Kantian discriminations of reason and judgement not shared by other postmodern theorists. In a sense the debate between Lyotard and Habermas is a squabble amongst neo-Kantians, for both have come to share a certain neo-Kantian terrain. In contrast to Baudrillard, however, their similarities are rather striking.

In addition, Lyotard and Habermas are closer politically than is sometimes perceived. Lyotard has pursued leftist political motivations in his work from the beginning and while his early ultra-left micropolitics of desire was close to Deleuze and Guattari, his later politics of justice provides a sort of left/liberal politics not found in other postmodern theorists. Lyotard is the only postmodern theorist to pursue the theme of justice and a just society, and this puts him in close company with Habermas who also pursues a politics of democracy in which justice is an explicit component of his ideal speech situation. Further, Habermas like Lyotard, arguably has a discourse theory of politics which focuses on how to come to agreement over differences, how to reach a consensus through discussion and argumentation. Indeed, both Habermas' and Lyotard's discourse politics put in question authority and the magisterial discourses and specify conditions in which marginal discourses could join the conversation and more fully participate in political and other debates. This is an explicit theme of Lyotard's and one could argue, as Honneth (1985) does in the passage we cited above, that Habermas provides a procedural approach which allows marginal voices to participate in decision and consensus. Both thus pursue a sort of left liberal democratic politics of discourse in their post-1980s writings that is different from some of the other postmodern theorists, as well as classical Marxism.

Both Habermas and the later Lyotard therefore are significantly different from the postmodern politics of desire and cultural revolution; both defend justice and a discourse politics, and both are sympathetic to new social movements (see Habermas 1987a: pp. 391ff.). There are, of course, significant differences in theory and politics between Lyotard and Habermas. Habermas strongly emphasizes consensus, while Lyotard stresses dissensus, agonistics, and the differend. Indeed, the notion of the differend is the major theoretical gulf between Habermas and Lyotard. In both the theoretical and political sphere, Habermas generally thinks that it is possible to delineate procedures to adjudicate differences and come to consensus, while Lyotard wants to preserve and articulate differences. Habermas also tends more toward traditional Germanic, systematizing philosophy, while Lyotard is resolutely anti-systematic.

Indeed, in this respect, Lyotard's thought is much more akin to Adorno than Habermas. Both Adorno and Lyotard engage in microanalysis and philosophical critique, while rejecting systematic philosophy. Both carry out a critique of instrumental reason, attack capitalism, and are champions of modernist art. While there are also significant differences between them, Lyotard frequently refers positively to Adorno and often cites him. Although in 'Adorno as Devil', Lyotard criticizes Adorno's philosophy of negation from his then Nietzschean philosophy of affirmation (1973). Lyotard later takes up Adorno more positively, pointing to the kinship between his microanalysis and critique of speculative metaphysics with Adorno (1988c: p. 121). Indeed, *The Differend* is haunted by Adorno's dictum that there can be no more speculative philosophy after Auschwitz. There are several references to Adorno's critique of speculative philosophy and he is privileged throughout the text (see, especially, Lyotard 1988c: pp. 86ff.).

Lyotard's modernist aesthetic is also similar to Adorno's though Adorno tends to ascribe more emancipatory power to art than does Lyotard and does not identify his positions with an aesthetics of the sublime.[11] Although Lyotard is passionately involved in modern art, he neither ascribes to 'authentic art' the cognitive or emancipatory powers that Adorno does. Lyotard has always appraised art for the 'intensities', or feelings, that it produces, rather than for cognitive insights, writing in a recent text: 'What is at stake in aesthetics and art is feeling something oneself or making other people feel something' (1988b: p. 28). For Adorno, the realm of the aesthetic is a realm of free subjectivity in which the subject is fully autonomous and beyond the constraints of instrumental rationality. For Adorno, authentic art is privileged as a powerful cognitive force, as a vehicle of social critique, and as an instrument of liberation. While the early Lyotard championed art and image over theory (in a manner completely foreign to Adorno), later he became more modest in his claims for art. Yet both championed modernist art, while art and aesthetic theory shaped both of their theoretical positions.

Thus, in a sense, the debates between Lyotard and the Frankfurt School can be read as a series of sibling rivalries, as brotherly quarrels between perpetually squabbling kin who, however, share some quite significant similarities and quite precise enemies. It is unfortunate that critical theory and postmodern theory have not engaged themselves more productively in a dialogue with each other, for in a sense they complement their respective strengths and weaknesses. Postmodern theory has distinguished itself by conceptualizing the new forms of technology, culture, and experience which have emerged in recent years. Previously, it was arguably critical theory that was at the cutting edge of radical social theory, through conceptualizing new social conditions, practices, and experiences, and through rethinking radical social theory and politics in the light of these new sociohistorical conditions. If it is the case that new sociohistorical conditions, forms, and experiences have emerged, then critical theory today should obviously analyze, criticize, and conceptualize these phenomena, and should develop and rethink radical social theory and politics in the light of these changes. Most critical theorists, however, have not confronted these challenges, and have either attacked so-called postmodern society and culture *en masse* from traditional critical theory positions, or like Habermas have presented ideology critiques of the postmodern theories while defending modernity. This is unfortunate, for critical theory provides the framework, methodology, and positions which could be used to develop a theory of the new social conditions which, arguably, postmodern theory considers without adequately theorizing.

In conclusion, we want to stress, however, that we find that neither critical theory in any of its versions, nor postmodern theory provide an adequate model for a theory of the present age. We find, for example, that both postmodern theory and Habermas are one-sided and require important corrections and compensations. On one hand, Habermas compensates for a major weakness of postmodern theory that we have examined throughout this book: excessive individualism and the lack of strong concepts of intersubjectivity, communication, and consensus. We find his ego–alter model and strong emphasis on intersubjectivity preferable to the excessive individualism of post-modern theory, though we believe that he exaggerates the desirability of consensus and downplays the importance of dissensus, paralogy, and preserving differences.

Habermas and Lyotard also share certain deficits from our point of view of constructing a critical theory and politics for the contemporary era. Both take a linguistic turn and progressively move toward philosophy and away from social theory. While Habermas' political interventions are exemplary, and while he has been more concerned with the trajectory of classical social theory and with developing contemporary social theory than any of the theorists who we have dealt with in this book, his linguistic and communicative turn has steered him away from developing a critical theory of the present age and toward neo-Kantian philosophical perspectives, developing a theory of communicative action in the realm of theoretical, practical, and aesthetic reason. While the classical critical theorists charted developments within the capitalist system from the death of Marx to the present, updating and reconstructing Marxian theory, Habermas, since *Legitimation Crisis*, has turned to interrogations of philosophy and classical social theory rather than to developing a critical theory of the present age. And Lyotard has undertaken a similar turn, sharing certain deficits with Habermas.

The confrontations between critical and postmodern theory therefore raise questions concerning the proper methodology of social theory, the most illuminating and useful perspectives on the contemporary era, and the appropriate type of radical politics. Thus in the final chapter we shall present some perspectives on a model of social theory and radical politics which draw on both critical and postmodern theory while attempting to overcome their limitations. This will also provide an opportunity to produce a final analysis of the contributions and limitations of postmodern theory.

Notes

1. We discuss the Habermas/Lyotard debates later in 7.4 below; for an earlier discussion of the polemics between postmodern and critical theory, see Kellner 1989a: pp. 167ff.

2. Battle lines over the interpretation of *Dialectic of Enlightenment* have emerged with Habermas criticizing its excessive attack on modernity and proximity to postmodern theory (1984; 1987b), while defenders of Adorno attack Habermas' critique (Wolin 1987; Hullot-Kentor 1989).

3. On Adorno's method, its similarities to Benjamin, and its application, see Buck-Morss 1977 and on Benjamin see Frisby 1987. We disagree, however, with Buck-Morss' claim that the early Adorno was under Benjamin's spell in believing that the mere construction of dialectical images and constellations was sufficient to illuminate phenomena, for we see that even in this early essay, Adorno defines philosophy as interpretation and combines construction of constellations with interpretation in all of his work. Later, of course, Adorno criticized Benjamin precisely for his belief that juxtapositions of images and constellations could adequately illuminate phenomena; see their exchange in *Aesthetics and Politics*, (London: Verso, 1977).

4. For an early example of Adorno's deconstructive/reconstructive project, see the 1932 essay 'The Idea of Natural History', a text first presented to the *Kant-Gesellschaft*, published only after his death (translation in Adorno 1984: pp. 111ff.).

5. Adorno was critical of 'first philosophy' from the beginning: see Adorno 1977: p. 132 and his critique of Husserl which was begun in the 1930s though it was not published until 1956 (Adorno 1982).

6. In *Eclipse of Reason*, Horkheimer proposed distinguishing between 'subjective' (or instrumental) reason and critical reason. Marcuse, by contrast, proposed developing a 'libidinal rationality' which would provide an emancipatory alternative to the repressive reason of the rationalist–subjectivist tradition. His valorization of the 'aesthetic–erotic' dimension of experience puts him closer to Nietzsche and postmodern thought than other critical theorists.

7. Habermas has published a book titled *Nachmetaphysisches Denken* (*Post-Metaphysical Thinking*) (1988) and, like poststructuralist and postmodern theory, has from the beginning criticized metaphysical thinking.

8. In his theories of communication and evolution, Habermas claims that his norms derive from a process of evolution whereby species potentials and capacities are historically produced; this theory of evolution is too complex to go into here, so for our purposes we shall put it aside; for discussion of Habermas' linguistic turn and his theory of evolution, see McCarthy 1978. For a contrast between Dewey's historicist method of social critique and Habermas' quasi-foundationalism, see Antonio and Kellner 1991b.

9. No actual debate between Habermas and Lyotard has taken place. While Lyotard criticized Habermas in *The Postmodern Condition*, Habermas did not address Lyotard in *The Philosophical Discourse of Modernity* or other writings, leading Lyotard to complain that certain French thinkers (such as himself) 'do not have the honour to be read by Professor Habermas – which at least saves them from getting a poor grade for their neo-conservatism' (Lyotard 1984a: p. 73). Habermas' associates, however, have frequently criticized Lyotard.

10. Ernesto Laclau has told us that in a 1987 talk at Miami University, Ohio, Lyotard's political analysis tended to project a vision of a monolithic capitalist society, able to absorb all opposition and otherness, in a gloomy one-dimensional analysis reminiscent of the Frankfurt School.

11. Almost all of the remarks that Lyotard makes concerning postmodern art that is seeking to present the unpresentable, that seeks to create new rules and make new moves, that seeks constant innovation (1984: pp. 71ff.), describe the programme of modernist art more accurately than postmodern art, thus we would insist that Lyotard has a modernist aesthetic which puts him close to the ultra-modernist Adorno.

Chapter 8

Towards the Reconstruction of Critical Social Theory

We have seen that there is a broad array of postmodern perspectives and positions, and that postmodern theories can be employed for quite different theoretical and political ends. Postmodern theories can be used to attack or defend modernity, to reconstruct radical politics or declare their impossibility, to enhance Marxian theory or to denounce it, to bolster feminist critiques or to undermine them. Almost all postmodern theories, however, explode the boundaries between the various established academic disciplines – such as philosophy, social theory, economics, literature – and produce a new kind of supradisciplinary discourse. Postmodern theorists criticize the ideals of representation, truth, rationality, system, foundation, certainty, and coherence typical of much modern theory, as well as the concepts of the subject, meaning, and causality. As Hassan puts it, postmodern theories are part of a culture of 'unmaking' whose key principles include: 'decreation, disintegration, deconstruction, decentrement, displacement, difference, discontinuity, disjunction, disappearance, decomposition, de-definition, demystification, detotalization, delegitimation' (1987: p. 92).

In our critical interrogations, we have stressed the differences between various postmodern theories and have pointed to an important distinction between an extreme wing of postmodern theory that declares a radical break with modernity and modern theory in contrast to another reconstructive wing that uses postmodern insights to reconstruct critical social theory and radical politics. Extreme postmodern theories (Baudrillard, some aspects of Lyotard, Foucault, Deleuze and Guattari) carry out a radical critique of modern theory and politics, calling for new theories and politics for the present age. Reconstructive postmodern theories (Jameson, Laclau and Mouffe, Flax and other postmodern feminists), however, combine modern and postmodern positions in their theoretical and political perspectives.[1]

In conclusion, we wish to argue that extreme postmodern critiques of modernity and of modern theory wrongly abandon the progressive heritage of the Enlightenment, democracy, and social theory along with the dubious features of modernity. We find much postmodern critique to be excessive, abstract, and subversive of theoretical and political projects that remain valuable. Extreme postmodern theorists wish to throw out the notion of critical social theory altogether, denying its metatheoretical assumptions (representation, social coherence, and agency), and even claiming that in contemporary postmodern society 'reality' has dissolved into fragments and subjects are in the process of disappearing (Baudrillard). Other postmodern theorists claim that modern theory is reductive, overly totalizing, and rests on foundationalist myths (Foucault, Lyotard, Deleuze and Guattari, and Laclau and Mouffe). Although these criticisms accurately portray certain features of modern theory, there are theorists within the modern tradition who advance criticisms which anticipate important aspects of the postmodern critiques, while avoiding their excessive rejection of modern theory and modernity *in toto* (see Antonio and Kellner 1991a).[2]

Although there are overly totalizing and positivist currents in almost all modern theory, there are also critiques of positivism, scientism, and reductionism within modern theory itself. A whole tradition of modern theory (i.e., Marx, Dewey, Weber, and hermeneutics) calls for theory to be reflexive and self-critical, aware of its presuppositions, interests, and limitations. This tradition is thus non-dogmatic and open to disconfirmation and revision, eschewing the quest for certainty, foundations, and universal laws (although most modern theory fails to avoid some of these sins). These critical themes in modern theory present a model of theory that is non-scientistic, fallibilistic, hermeneutical, and open to new historical conditions, theoretical perspectives, and political applications. We therefore believe that a critical tradition of modern theory continues to provide perspectives, methods and concepts useful for social theory today and that it is a mistake to totally reject this tradition.

In addition, the best modern social theorists recognize the differentiation and fragmentation within modernity, while also providing a language that addresses its integrative and macroscopic features. The tradition of modern theory has undertaken analyses of the growing complexity of modern societies, analyzing such phenomena as increasing social rationalization, individuation, and differentiation (Marx, Weber, Habermas). It has analyzed macroscopic processes such as commodification, massification, reification, and domination which have constituted modern societies. Indeed, classical social theory has been fundamentally a theory of modernity, analyzing the structures, constituents, and trajectories of modern societies (Antonio and Kellner, forthcoming). The historical task of modern social theory has thus been to analyze the ways that the economy, state, society, and culture interact to form a historically specific type of social organization distinguished from traditional societies. Some modern theorists have stressed the primacy of the economy, others the primacy of the state or bureaucratization, others the function of modern culture and values, and have accorded different structural and causal weight to these different domains, but all the major modern social theorists have attempted to analyze the fundamental structures and processes of modern societies.

Postmodern theorists by and large reject this project. Some, like Lyotard, claim that such totalizing analyses are inevitably reductive and aid totalitarian thinking and political oppression. Others, like Baudrillard, claim that in a hyperfragmented, media-saturated society it is impossible to tell the difference between image and reality, sign and referent, and thus one cannot make the distinctions, connections, and systemic analyses that were previously the mark of classical social theory. For extreme postmodernists, social reality is therefore indeterminate and unmappable, and the best we can do is to live within the fragments of a disintegrating social order.

Even reconstructive postmodern theorists like Jameson tend to theorize the postmodern condition as a bewilderingly complex 'hyperspace'. Postmodern capitalism for Jameson erases previously firm boundaries and distinctions, not only between high and low culture, but between reality and unreality, fiction and history. Postmodern culture produces a crisis simultaneously in values, politics, and experience. But while Jameson feels the situation is portentous, and describes 'a mutation in built space itself ... a mutation in the object, unaccompanied as yet by any equivalent mutation [or adaptive response] in the subject' (1984a: p. 80), he refuses the Baudrillardian pact with reification and calls for new mapping strategies that account for these changes and he attempts to revise aesthetics, theory, and politics accordingly.

We agree with Jameson that the forces of capitalism structure ever more domains of social life, a process that is becoming increasingly transparent and cynical under the regimes of Reagan, Bush, Kohl, and Tory conservatism. Thus, we choose to see postmodern theory not as announcing the end of social mapping *à la* Baudrillard, but as contributing to more sophisticated and contemporary maps which update and revise classical social theory. Postmodern theories map micro and marginal phenomena ignored by much classical social theory and valorize differences, pluralities, and heterogeneities that were often suppressed by the grand theories of the past. But postmodern theory tends to map in fragments and to ignore the more systemic features and relations of social structure that were the focus of modern social theory. We therefore call for critical articulations of modern and postmodern theory which map the broader features of social organization and conflicts, as well as features of fragmentation and various microdomains. Consequently, we reject the postmodern renunciation of macrotheory while attending to some of its proposals for the reconstruction of theory.

Postmodern theorists do not do social theory *per se*, but rather eclectically combine fragments of sociological analysis, literary and cultural readings, historical theorizations, and philosophical critiques. They tend to privilege cultural and philosophical analysis over social theory and thereby fail to confront the most decisive determinants of our social world. Yet we believe – against much postmodern theory – that the project of social theory itself continues to be a valuable one. Just as individuals need cognitive maps of their cities to negotiate their spatial environment, they also need maps of their society to intelligently analyze, discuss, and intervene in social processes. For us, social theories provide mappings of contemporary society: its organization; its constitutive social relations, practices, discourses, and institutions; its integrated and interdependent features; its conflictual and fragmenting features; and its structures of power and modes of oppression and domination. Social theories analyze how these elements fit together to constitute specific societies, and how societies work or fail to function.

Social theories therefore provide guides to social reality, producing models and cognitive mappings of societies, and the 'big pictures' that enable us to see, for example, how the economy, polity, social institutions, discourses, practices, and culture interact to produce a social system. Social theory charts and makes connections between different domains of social reality and theorizes the causal power of different forces such as the economy, state, sexuality, or discourse in social or everyday individual life. Modern social theory contains a tradition that analyzes the big, or macro, structures and relations of society; another tradition focuses on microelements of everyday life, while there have been recent attempts to combine these traditions. We believe in the continuing importance of macrotheory and argue that the postmodern assault on macroanalysis produces aporia and lacunae in the various postmodern theories. Our position is that while it is impossible to produce a fixed and exhaustive knowledge of a constantly changing complex of social processes, it is possible to map the fundamental domains, structures, practices, and discourses of a society, and how they are constituted and interact. Thus, in the rest of this conclusion, we shall argue for supradisciplinary social theories and a combination of micro- and macroanalysis.

We believe that the absence of theoretical analysis of the economy, the state, and the interaction between these domains and society, culture, and everyday life vitiates postmodern theory and leads to an unwarranted renunciation of social theory itself. As we have seen, no postmodern theorist provides an adequate analysis of the economy, of the contemporary developments within capitalism, and many eschew political economy altogether. There are also no systematic accounts of the state in postmodern theory, nor are there any substantive analyses of the relationships between the economy, state, and other social domains and processes. Some postmodern theorists neglect the fundamental role of the media (Foucault), or separate analysis of the media from political economy (Baudrillard). And no postmodern theorist provides a theory of society as a systemic organization, as a mode of production with specific social relations, institutions, and organization.

The postmodern rejoinder to our project would be that we now live in a radically new sociohistorical situation and that the new social conditions render obsolete all theories of the past and call for new modes of theorizing. Our answer is twofold: we believe (1) that this sort of extreme claim has not been substantiated; and (2) that to do so requires precisely the sort of metatheoretical argumentation characteristic of modern theories. Asserting that we are in a completely new postmodernity presupposes an epochal theory of a new stage in history – a rather grand claim given their own critiques of narrative and totalizing analysis – and no postmodern theory has adequately theorized such a rupture (see further discussion in 8.2). Our own position, that we shall argue for in the course of this concluding chapter, is that we are living within a borderline region between modernity and a new, as yet inadequately theorized, social situation. In this transitional era, both modern and postmodern theories are helpful to theorize the continuities with the past and the novel, 'postmodern', phenomena.

In addition, we shall argue that to do properly the sort of cultural and sociopolitical analysis characteristic of postmodern theory requires a theory of society in which one contextualizes the specific phenomena that are the subject matter of the best postmodern theories (such as nexuses of power and knowledge; constel- lations of micropower in psychiatry, medicine, or prisons; simulations and media; and new technologies). To be sure, as Jameson has ably demonstrated (1981a), one can use literary or cultural analyses as dialectical illuminations of socioeconomic dynamics, but such a reading requires their contextualization within a larger field de-lineated by social theory, which is necessary to provide contextualization for any cultural or theoretical analysis. No adequate theory of television, for example, can be developed without a theory of society, and in a capitalist society no adequate social theory can be developed without a theory of capitalism and thus political economy (for development of this argument, see Kellner 1990).

While postmodern theory has successfully challenged Marxian economism, workerism, and statism, it has generally ignored issues of economics and production and has little to say about capital and the state, which arguably remain the most important structural determinants of current society. Postmodern theory wants to decentre the economy in order to focus on microphenomena and although this move might produce some important results, as in Foucault, we would argue that the economy remains a central structuring institution in a capitalist society and that it is a mistake to ignore the economy to the extent evident in postmodern theory. From our perspective, social, cultural, and political theory cannot be divorced from a theory of capitalism and an analysis of the systemic relations between the various levels and institutions of capitalism, both in terms of their independent dynamics and their interconnections within a capitalist mode of production. Thus, we would insist upon the continuing relevance of neo-Marxian theories which attempt to theorize social phenomena in terms of a theory of the contemporary stage of capitalism, though we would argue that the existence of new phenomena, such as those analyzed by postmodern theory, requires extensive reconstruction of all social theories of the past. From this perspective, we find postmodern theory that excludes political economy in principle to be abstract and blind, incapable of adequately analyzing the fundamental processes and developments of the present age.

To be sure, many social theorists have undertaken their mapping functions in clumsy, reductive, essentializing, and problematical ways. In this regard postmodern theory is valuable in warning about some of the dangers and limitations of modern social theory. But we find that the postmodern tendency to reject social theory altogether to be crippling and counter-productive. Yet we believe, despite its limitations, postmodern theory has important contributions for developing a critical social theory and radical politics for the present age. Its challenges to modern theory force social theorists to perceive some of the limitations of past models. Its claims concerning the importance of new sociohistorical conditions require fresh theorizing and revision of previous orthodoxies, and thus promote a potential revitalization of critical analysis of the contemporary era.

More specifically, the contributions of postmodern theory include detailed historical genealogies of the institutions and discourses of modernity and the ways these normalize and discipline subjects (Foucault); microanalyses of the colonization of desire in capitalism and the production of potentially fascist subjects (Deleuze and Guattari); theorizations of mass media, information systems, and technology as new forms of control that radically change the nature of politics, subjectivity, and everyday life (Baudrillard and Jameson); emphasis on the importance of micropolitics, new social movements, and new strategies of social transformation (Foucault, Deleuze and Guattari, Lyotard, Laclau and Mouffe); critiques of flawed philosophical components of modernity (Derrida, Rorty, and Lyotard); and new syntheses of feminist and postmodern theory (Flax, Fraser, and Nicholson).

Nonetheless, as we have argued, there are fundamental flaws in the postmodern theories that have developed so far. Most postmodern theories tend to be reductive, dogmatically closed to competing perspectives, and excessively narrow. Most postmodern theories neglect political economy and fail to present adequately connections between the economic, political, social, and cultural levels of society. Against these deficiencies of postmodern theory, we would call for the reconstruction of social theories that are more multidimensional and multiperspectival. We shall set forth this agenda in the next section.

8.1 For a Multidimensional and Multiperspectival Critical Theory

A multidimensional critical theory will provide an analysis of the relative autonomy of the various levels or domains of social reality and the ways in which they interact to form a specific mode of social organization. A multidimensional critical theory is dialectical and non-reductive. It conceptualizes the connections between the economic, political, social, and cultural dimensions of society and refuses to reduce social phenomena to any one dimension. A dialectical theory describes the mediations, or interconnections, that relate social phenomena to each other and the dominant mode of social organization. A dialectical analysis of advertising, for instance, would theorize its emergence in the capitalist economy and its economic functions and effects; it would also indicate how advertising appropriates certain cultural forms and in turn influences cultural production; and it would analyze the ways in which advertising techniques have been assimilated into and have transformed politics, thus analyzing the interconnections between advertising, the economy, politics, culture, and social life (see Harms and Kellner 1991).

Dialectical analysis thus relates particular social phenomena to the constitutive forces and relations of a society, showing how, on one hand, the structures and dynamics of capitalist society constitute specific phenomena and how their analytical dissection can shed light on broader social forces. From this perspective, analysis of the fundamental features of capitalist socioeconomic processes (commodification, reification, fetishism, etc.) can illuminate phenomena like popular music, while microanalysis of music might in turn illuminate broader social processes. Thus, as with Adorno's analyses (7.2), a dialectical critical theory would preserve particularity, attempting to illuminate specific events and artifacts and the broader, more comprehensive social forces which constitute or constrain them. A dialectical critical theory is also historical, open to historical events and changes, and accordingly revises its theories and politics in the light of such developments.

A critical social theory also detects and illuminates crucial social problems, conflicts, and contradictions, and points towards possible resolution of these problems and progressive social transformation. Critical theory analyzes fundamental relations of domination and exploitation, and the ways that hierarchy, inequality, and oppression are built into social relations and practices. Dialectical critical theory is thus political, relating theory to practice and searching for potentialities for change in a given society. Marcuse's notion of multidimensionality (1964), for instance, appraises existing states of affairs according to their higher potentialities, developing critical standpoints that could discern what aspects of existing society should be negated, or changed, in order to develop a better social organization (see the discussion in Kellner 1984). A multidimensional theory thus sees society as composed of a multiplicity of dimensions and potentialities for social transformation.

A multidimensional critical theory stresses the relative autonomy of each dimension of society and is thus open to a broad range of perspectives on the domains of social reality and how they are constituted and interact. A multiperspectival social theory views society from a multiplicity of perspectives. A perspective is a way of seeing, a vantage point or optic to analyze specific phenomena. The term perspective suggests that one's optic or analytic frame never mirrors reality exactly as it is, that it is always selective and unavoidably mediated by one's pregiven assumptions, theories, values, and interests. The notion of perspective also implies that no one optic can ever fully illuminate the richness and complexity of any single phenomenon, let alone the infinite connections and aspects of all social reality. Thus, as Nietzsche, Weber, and others have argued, all knowledge of reality stems from a particular point of view, all 'facts' are constituted interpretations, and all perspectives are finite and incomplete. A perspective thus involves a specific standpoint, focus, position, or even sets of positions that interpret particular phenomena. A perspective is a specific point of entry to interpret social phenomena, processes, and relations.

Perspectives range from disciplinary optics such as sociology or political science, or competing paradigms within these disciplines, to positions within schools, that provide, for instance, different wings of Marxian or feminist theory, to new individual theories or positions. Sociology, for example, contains perspectives ranging from Marx to Weber to Durkheim to Parsons. Each of these perspectives emphasizes different aspects of the constitution of modern societies, with Marx stressing the importance of the mode of production, Weber emphasizing the importance of bureaucracy, rationalization, and cultural differentiation, Durkheim underlining the importance of social representations and institutions for integrating individuals into society, and Parsons focusing on social roles and practices. All of these perspectives, and other theories as well, contain important contributions to developing a critical theory of society, while each also has its blind spots and limitations. Marxism, for instance, has traditionally been strong on class analysis and weak on gender analysis, while some forms of feminist theory are weak on class analysis. Marxism is strong on class conflict and societal contradictions, while Durkheim and Parsons are weak on these aspects, but strong on analyzing social integration.

Furthermore, disciplinary standpoints like economics, sociology, or philosophy have their own typical strengths and limitations, insights and blindspots. A multidimensional and multiperspectival theory thus looks at society from a multiplicity of vantage points, conceptualizing specific phenomena sometimes from the stand-point of the economy, sometimes from the position of the state, or the intersection of economics and politics. Sometimes Weberian perspectives might provide the most illuminating perspective on a specific phenomenon, while at other times a Marxian perspective, or an intersection of Marxian, Weberian, and feminist perspect-ives might provide the most insightful articulations.

By articulation, we mean the mediation of different perspectives in concrete analyses or developments of theoretical positions. To provide comprehensive perspectives on social phenomena, it is also useful to view events, institutions, or practices from different subject positions. In interpreting instances of class struggle, it is useful to see specific events from the standpoint of both capital and labour, and perhaps from the positions of gender and race as well. Likewise, interpreting cultural texts, like political speeches or films, from different subject positions often provides illumin-ating vantage points and insights missed by more 'neutral', 'object-ive' modes of thought and discourse. Feminist theory, for instance, articulates the subject positions of women and provides insights into dimensions of texts or events often missed by male theoretical standpoints. Taking the perspectives of race, ethnicity, and vari-ous marginal standpoints also provides insights missed by certain perspectives. Different subject positions therefore provide differ-ent perspectives on social and cultural phenomena and a multi-plicity of positions often provides more comprehensive and illuminating analyses. Perspectives are thus specific optics in-formed by theoretical positions. We are therefore not using the term perspective, as a hyperrelativist Nietzschean might, to signify that all standpoints are merely subjective, merely the expression of individual points of view or ways of seeing. Rather, we are using perspective to delineate the range of existing positions available to theory at a given moment in history.

Since there exists no one, true, certain, or absolutely valid perspective in which one could ground social theory today, a critical social theory must be open to new theoretical discourses and perspectives, eschewing dogmatism and closed theories. Multiperspectival theories could bring together perspectives such as critical theory, poststructuralism, postmodern theory, feminist theory, and other major theoretical discourses to produce a radical theory and politics for the present age. This would involve drawing on the specific perspectives advanced within critical theory ranging from Adorno to Habermas, or feminist theory ranging from de Beauvoir to Kristeva. From the political standpoint, a multi-perspectival critical theory would involve bringing people together with various standpoints, articulating their common interests, and respecting their differences – a point that we shall return to in 8.3.

While some of the strains of postmodern theory that derive from Nietzsche stress the importance of a multiplicity of perspectives, postmodern theorists are often inconsistent when they actually carry out their social analysis, often engaging in one-dimensional or reductive analysis, as when Baudrillard looks at the media from a strictly technological perspective. On the other hand, it is often the single-minded pursuit of a given idea or perspective that yields valuable insights for social theory, and thus interpreting society from the standpoint of media, new technologies, or simulacra *à la* Baudrillard may yield important results. But when one is constructing a social theory of the present age, or analyzing complex phenomena like prisons, sexuality, the media, or the family, it is more useful to have a variety of perspectives at one's disposal. Extreme postmodern perspectives thus yield a tunnel vision and restricted conceptual grasp of phenomena if not supplemented by other perspectives.

The value of a multiperspectival critical theory can be illustrated through some examples. Rather than theorizing modernity, for instance, in strictly economic terms (some Marxists), technological terms (McLuhan and Baudrillard), or cultural terms (intellectual historians like Blumenberg and Cahoone), it is important to adopt multiple perspectives on the emergence and development of modernity, analyzing it from the vantage points of a new capitalist economy and industrial revolution, new sciences and technologies, new democratic revolutions and forms of class struggle, new ideas and ideologies, new forms of art, and new forms of experience of space, time, and everyday life.

Similarly, if one wishes to develop a theory of contemporary society, postmodern or otherwise, instead of simply interpreting it from the perspective of discourses and knowledge (the early Foucault and Lyotard), or media and simulacra (Baudrillard), or the cultural logic of capital (Jameson), or a new post-Fordist stage of capitalist development (Harvey), one would examine it from the standpoint of economics, technology, culture, politics, and social developments, while demonstrating how these phenomena are interrelated. Such a theory would conceptualize the connections and interactions between changes in the capitalist mode of production, new forms of politics, new technologies, new aesthetic practices, and new forms of experience.

Likewise, if one wanted to develop a theory of television, it would not be enough to merely interpret it in terms of its technological form, as pure medium, as do McLuhan and Baudrillard, or merely in terms of its content and ideological effects as do some cultural theorists. A multiperspectival position argues that one cannot grasp the full dimensions of television simply by analyzing its determination by political economy alone, or its political functions, or its constitution as a cultural form, though all of these aspects are obviously important. Rather one would need to analyze the interconnections between the political economy of television, its insertion into political struggles of the day, its changing cultural forms and effects, its use of new technologies, and its diverse uses by its audiences in order to produce a comprehensive theory of television. Similarly, reading television texts requires that one use a multiplicity of methods to grasp the various dimensions of the text, including semiotics, ideology critique, psychoanalysis, feminism, and other critical methods (see Kellner 1980 and Best and Kellner 1987; for examples of multiperspectival film analysis see Kellner and Ryan 1988 and Kellner, forthcoming). This requires openness to a multiplicity of types of theoretical discourses and development of multiperspectival analyses.

Postmodern theory, by contrast, is often closed to competing theoretical and political perspectives (see for example Baudrillard's dismissal of Foucault discussed in 4.2.2) and critics of postmodern theory are also often dogmatic and closed to the new postmodern perspectives (some Habermasians and Callinicos 1990). Postmodern theory in general analyzes phenomena mainly from cultural and discursive perspectives, and often in terms of disconnected fragments without grasping systemic interrelationships such as exist between the capitalist state, economy, and mass media. Such fragmented analyses reproduce what Lukács identified as a reification process whereby capitalist ideology prevents individuals from understanding the structures and class relations which constrain their actions and thus prevent them from drawing appropriate political consequences. Foucault, for example, occasionally situates his analysis of disciplinary technologies and normalizing strategies in the context of the capitalist state and economy, but he largely divorces his descriptions of power from this context and never specifies in detail these macroinstitutions. Deleuze and Guattari theorize desire, schizophrenia, and the family in the larger context of the capitalist economy, but they collapse political economy into libidinal economy, and later pursue the fragments of a thousand plateaus. Baudrillard and his followers, by contrast, theorize the production of signs and images apart from capitalist economic strategies and mechanisms and produce idealist culturalist analyses that project their interpretation of a few contemporary phenomena onto the whole of contemporary society. Lyotard, Laclau, and Mouffe focus on discourse and fail to analyze institutions and the economy, and Jameson sketches a systemic analysis of capitalism and foregrounds the importance of culture and economy, but fails to adequately mediate and contextualize his theory.

Thus, postmodern theory tends to be overly culturalist in its perspectives. There is little concrete social and political analysis in postmodern theory, with some postmodern theorists increasingly distancing themselves from all social analysis and critique whatsoever. While Baudrillard's 1970s writings are full of brilliant insights into contemporary social developments, his 1980s works tend to be more metaphysical, fragmentary, and apolitical, or even anti-political. Lyotard has turned progressively to philosophy and away from social analysis and critique. Foucault never provided a concrete analysis of the present age despite numerous methodological indications that this was his goal.

Thus to avoid reductionism and to provide richer and more comprehensive perspectives on contemporary society, one should employ a wealth of perspectives on the economy, polity, society, and culture which reveal how they are constituted and interact and what changes are currently taking place. This requires combining perspectives of classical modern thinkers like Marx, Weber, and Habermas with postmodern theorists like Foucault and Baudrillard. But to avoid mere electicism and liberal pluralism, a dialectical social theory must be aware of certain traps and dangers for a perspectivist epistemology and theory. One must avoid an extreme relativism which holds that 'anything goes'. Some dimensions are more viable and important than others, and some critical theories and methods are more appropriate for specific contexts and problems. Eclectic pluralism fails to specify what phenomena are most salient in specific situations and fails to provide distinctive and strong theoretical analysis that provides novel and innovative ways of seeing. In other words, the task of social theory is not simply to multiply perspectives, but to provide original and illuminating perspectives that call attention to new phenomena, that disclose relationships hitherto obscured, or that even provide new ways of seeing, as when Marx pointed to the relationships between the ruling ideas and the ruling class, or Foucault called attention to the nexuses of power and knowledge in specific disciplines, institutions, discourses, and practices.

One's own goals, context, and theoretical and political orientations will obviously determine which perspectives are most relevant in given cases. Developing a theory of the social functions and effects of television in contemporary US society would require analysis of the relationships between the television industries, the state, and transnational capital, thus political economy would be necessarily privileged in such a project (see Kellner 1990). Analyzing the representations of gender on television would privilege feminist theory, and perhaps psychoanalytic or semiotic theory. Theorizing the 'post-colonial subject' would necessarily involve macrotheory, utilizing broad theories of imperialism, dependency, underdevelopment, and anti-imperialist struggles and movements. Interpreting the impact of advertising on society might require a combination of macrotheory which focuses on the role of advertising in the circulation of capital and production of needs with microanalysis of how individuals and groups process advertising and what effects it has on their thought and behaviour. This could be combined with semiotic and psychological theories of advertising images and identity constitution.

Which and how many perspectives one chooses is thus a function of specific topics and projects. Multiperspectival analyses do not, moreover, rule out strong and focused analyses of specific phenomena or development of a specific perspective. More is not necessarily better for two reasons. First, a detailed and concrete uniperspectival analysis can be far more powerful and illuminating than a highly abstract multiperspectival analysis. Moreover, multiperspectival analyses can be vitiated by indiscriminate use of different perspectives which can lead to confused and unfocused analysis that combines contradictory assumptions and logics. Hence, multiperspectival analysis cannot indiscriminately 'synthesize' various problematics in their entirety, and here the postmodern emphasis on difference and incommensurability is valuable. Rather, multiperspectivalism has to judge in specific cases which aspects of competing theories are or are not useful.

In doing actual theoretical analyses, one must also choose between incompatible perspectives, or reconstruct the perspectives to avoid incoherency. For instance, one must choose between a form of systemic, totalizing thought and the postmodern war on totality. Yet if one chooses systemic analysis, one should also perceive the importance of concrete analyses and, in some contexts, the merging of micro- and macroperspectives. A multiperspectival theory engages the contemporary problem of merging micro- with macroperspectives, as well as using complementary perspectives such as those of Foucault and Baudrillard on power (see 4.2.2), or those of Habermas and Lyotard on the issues of consensus and dissensus (employing the former model in some contexts and the latter in other contexts).

The challenge for critical social theory is therefore to combine its perspectives into an illuminating theory of the present age. Such a project needs the sort of dialectical vision and imagination that was characteristic of the best of critical theory. Developing a dialectical and multiperspectival social theory requires not only bringing together and mediating a variety of theoretical perspectives, but vision of the progressive and regressive features of society, and the respective forces of domination and liberation. It also requires mediating theory and practice, discerning forces and possibilities of progressive social change. Herbert Marcuse, for example, constantly informed his analysis with a vision of liberation and domination that specified the prevalent forms of domination and forces of liberation. At times, his theory was too focused on the forms of domination and underplayed forces of liberation, but during other periods he obtained a more dialectical balance (see Kellner 1984). Marcuse always took specific positions in contemporary theoretical and political debates from the standpoint of a well-articulated theory that enabled him to adjudicate between competing theoretical and political positions.

Since we find ourselves in a different historical conjuncture, with different competing theories and politics confronting us, we cannot merely appeal, however, to Marcuse or any other theoretical position. Rather, comprehensive and salient critical theories and politics of the present age remain to be produced. We have found that postmodern theory is often an obstacle to this project since it does not provide a language to show how aspects and domains of society are interrelated, interdependent, and mediated, preferring to play with fragments (Baudrillard), to renounce macro-theory (Lyotard and, with qualifications, Foucault), to focus on more discrete microphenomena, or discourse analysis (Laclau and Mouffe), or to privilege cultural phenomena to the neglect of economy, society, and politics. Instead of differentiating the various social spheres and their modes of interaction, most postmodern theory collapses the economy, society, state, and culture into an oppressive machine or system of domination, while producing its own form of totalizing theory. While Foucault, for instance, talks of preserving difference and polemicizes against totalizing theories, we have found that in his specific analyses he often evokes a picture of a totalizing system of power/knowledge domination which absorbs all opposition and heterogeneity (see Chapter 2).

Against the postmodern renunciation of social theory, we thus call for its reconstruction. As we argued in Chapter 7, both Adorno and Habermas anticipated and shared important aspects of postmodern theory and the postmodern critique of subjectivity, metaphysics, and society, but undertook to reconstruct subjectivity and theories of history and society rather than to simply reject out of hand these components of modern theory. Although we are calling for the reconstruction of social theory, we do not believe that any given theorist, method, tradition, or style provides *the* model for a critical theory of the present age. Instead, we would support the production of a variety of critical theories of society which would draw upon the best of postmodern theory, while also drawing on the best of modern theory (Marx, Nietzsche, Weber, Dewey, Du Bois, de Beauvoir, and others).

Consequently, we find that many postmodern perspectives are valuable and could be used by a critical social theory of the present age which seeks to avoid the deficiencies of both mainstream social theory and extreme postmodern theory. Against modern theory, defenders of the postmodern turn argue that it is precisely the emphasis on notions of difference that distinguishes postmodern theory and that constitutes its significance for contemporary social theory. Charles Lemert (1990), for instance, argues that the concept of difference championed by postmodern theorists demands that social theory attend to differences in the perspectives of different cultural, racial, gender, and class groupings and determinations, as well as to differences within these groups. On this view, postmodern theory is distinguished by refusal of a cultural imperialism that imposes the views of one's own group or specific biases on the topic of inquiry, and that respects differences and discontinuities which are not absorbed into a homogenizing universal or general theory.

Wolfgang Welsch (1988) also argues that the pluralistic perspectives of postmodern theory constitute an important contribution which has both theoretical and political implications. Welsch argues that the postmodern refusal to privilege a single discourse undermines the dogmatism and reductionism which infects much contemporary social theory. Further, he believes that pluralist perspectives are also valuable for a postmodern politics which refuses to privilege one political subject or focus, instead valorizing a multiplicity of issues and movements. While we too advocate developing a multiperspectival social and political theory, we have been arguing here that there are crucial perspectives missing from postmodern theory and that it is often dogmatic and reductive in spite of its attacks on modern theory for these limitations.

We find, for instance, the postmodern tendencies to reject systemic and historical theory to be problematical. If postmodern discourse is useful describing a diverse set of new and developing circumstances in society, culture, theory, and the arts, no one has adequately theorized these various shifts in their multiple dimensions or developed an adequate theory of postmodernity. Foucault and Lyotard both posit a new postmodern condition but fail to theorize it, limiting their analyses of the postmodern to the realm of new knowledges and discourses. Laclau and Mouffe appropriate aspects of postmodern theory for a theory of radical democracy without a broader cultural analysis such as Jameson attempts and without taking up problems of periodization. Baudrillard and his epigones provide perspectives on new postmodern conditions, but their descriptions are excessively totalizing and one-dimensional, and often lack concrete empirical grounding. These extreme postmodernists also do not confront the central issue of what constitutes a historical rupture or discontinuity, what historical factors caused it, what the lines of continuity and discontinuity are, and whether or not capitalism remains a dominant historical force. Jameson provides perhaps the most adequate analysis of postmodernism as a cultural totality, attempting to analyze its various facets, to contextualize it within a larger social and historical framework, and to theorize it in terms of continuities and discontinuities, but his account also is frequently too totalizing, hyperbolic, and undertheorized. And recent feminist theory has generally appropriated postmodern epistemological concepts without developing substantive postmodern social theories.

We thus argue that no adequate analysis of the imputed break between modernity and postmodernity has yet been produced, nor is there an adequate account of the allegedly new postmodern society. An important part of such an account involves specifying the continuities between modernity and postmodernity.

8.2   Postmodernity, Postindustrial Society, and the Dialectics of Continuity and Discontinuity

> Not all people exist in the same Now. They do so only externally, by virtue of the fact that they may all be seen today. But that does not mean that they are living at the same time with others (Bloch 1977: p. 22).

For many postmodern theorists, it is no longer possible to discern a 'depth dimension', an underlying reality, or structure, as when Marx discovered class interests behind ideology, or Freud discovered unconscious complexes within texts or the actions of individuals. The erasure of depth also flattens out history and experience, for lost in a postmodern present, one is cut off from those sedimented traditions, those continuities and historical memories which nurture historical consciousness and provide a rich, textured, multidimensional present. Some postmodernists, like Baudrillard, postulate a radical presentism, a self-conscious erasure of history which eschews diachronic, historical analysis, and contextualization in favour of synchronic description of the present moment. Foucault resists this anti-historical tendency, however, through his archaeological and genealogical studies, and Deleuze and Guattari also develop historical analyses and contextualization, while Jameson attempts to historicize and contextualize his analyses of postmodernism, though he too fears a loss of history in contemporary postmodern society.

The notion of the end of history (see 4.3) has a certain ideological kinship with theories of the postindustrial society and the end of ideology (Bell 1973). On this account, modern liberal, democratic capitalist societies have produced the formula for social stability and affluence. The ideological passions of the past were irrelevant to the new postindustrial harmony and no dramatic changes or ruptures in history could be expected. The future would thus merely appear as a streamlined version of the present and the passions of history would cool off in the new postindustrial order.

Although postmodern theory does not share the glib optimism of this discourse, it replays many of the themes and positions of theories of the postindustrial society and shares, we would argue, their characteristic limitations and distortions. Both exhibit a form of technological determinism with theorists of the postindustrial society, such as Bell (1973 and 1976), claiming that information and knowledge are the new organizing principles of society, while postmodern theorists ascribe extreme power to new technologies. Baudrillard, for example, reproduces McLuhan's technological determinism in his media theory by claiming that 'the Medium is the Message', thus reducing media to their formal effects while erasing content, possibilities of emancipatory or progressive uses, and alternative media from the purview of his media analysis (see Baudrillard 1983b and the discussion in Kellner 1989b). He assigns a primary role in constituting postmodern society to simulations, codes, models, and new technologies, while completely eliminating political economy from his theory, claiming that 'TV and information in general are a kind of catastrophe in Rene Thom's formal, topological sense: a radical, qualitative change in an entire system' (Baudrillard 1984: p. 18). Such theories posit an 'autonomous technology' (see Winner 1977) which, as with theories of postindustrial society, uphold technology as the fundamental organizing principle of the contemporary society.

Both postmodern theories and those of the postindustrial

society thus make technological development the motor of social change and occlude the extent to which economic imperatives, or a dialectic between technology and social relations of production, continue to structure contemporary societies. Some postmodern and postindustrial theory erases human subjects and social classes as agents of social change and often explicitly renounces hope for radical social transformation. Both – despite the postmodern critique of totality – totalize and project a rupture or break within history that exaggerates the novelty of the contemporary moment and occludes continuities with the past. Both take trends as constitutive facts, seeing developmental possibilities as finalities, and both assume that a possible future is already present. From this perspective, postmodern theory can be seen as a continuation of theories of the postindustrial society in a new context and with new theoretical instruments. These 'post' theories can thus be read as two successive attempts to identify new social conditions and to provide new theoretical paradigms during an era when significant change was forcing theorists to question old paradigms and theories.

Both postmodern and postindustrial theories are explicitly focused against Marxian theory and during the 1970s and 1980s there was much discussion of a 'post-Marxist' turn among former radicals. Baudrillard, Lyotard, Laclau, Mouffe, and others put in question their previous Marxian positions and developed explicit critiques of Marxian theory, which was often taken as symptomatic of the problems with modern theory. Indeed, postmodern theory manifests a 'postie syndrome' of radical rejection of previous positions to create new discourses and theories adequate to the allegedly novel social conditions. The question arises, however, whether the break between modernity and postmodernity is as radical as the posties claim and whether such an alleged rupture constitutes sufficient grounds to reject such social theories as Marxism, critical theory, or feminism.

We would argue that many criticisms of earlier theories of the postindustrial society are relevant to debates over postmodern social theory which shares some of the presuppositions and weaknesses of its predecessor (see Frankel 1987; Poster 1990; and Feenberg, forthcoming, for critiques of theories of the post-industrial society). In some ways, however, postmodern theories might be seen as an advance over theories of postindustrial society by more adequately theorizing the role of culture in the constitution of contemporary societies and the multiplicity of forms of power, though some versions might be interpreted as a regression due to their excessive rhetoric, hyperbole, and lack of sustained empirical analysis. Furthermore, theorists of the postindustrial society tend to subscribe to Enlightenment values of rationality, autonomy, and progress, often with a deep faith in science and technology. Postmodern theorists, by contrast, tend to be sharply critical of the Enlightenment and to affirm opposing values.

Both postindustrial and postmodern social theory, however, greatly exaggerate the alleged break or rupture in history. While postmodern theory gains its currency and prestige from precisely this *coupure*, neither Baudrillard nor Lyotard nor any other postmodern theorist has adequately theorized what is involved in a break or rupture between the modern and the postmodern. Baudrillard and his followers dramatically proclaim a fundamental break in history and the end of a historical era with the advent of a new postmodern era without providing a clear account of the transition to postmodernity and without specifying the continuities between the previous era and the allegedly new one. And Lyotard is prohibited in principle from producing a periodizing analysis of this sort by his postmodern epistemology which renounces grand narratives. Jameson, by contrast, gives a fairly precise periodization of postmodern culture and a detailed account of its differences from the culture of high modernism. Yet although he postulates the existence of a new stage of society in terms of important developments within capitalism, he does not provide a detailed narrative of the transition from the stages of capitalism described by Marx, Lenin, and earlier Marxists, relying on a brief synopsis of Mandel, while providing only a highly general analysis.

Generally speaking, there are three main responses to the claim that we are living in a new postmodern era. One can argue that a rupture has occurred with modernity and that we are in a totally new era, requiring new theories and concepts; this extreme postmodernism thus stresses radical discontinuity (Baudrillard and Kroker and Cook). Second, one could deny that there is any radical rupture with modernity and stress the continuities between modernity and the present (Habermas; Callinicos). This position denies that there are any breaks or major discontinuities with modernity and thus sees postmodern discourse as merely ideological. Third, one could argue for a dialectic of continuity and discontinuity, theorizing the breaks and novelties, as well as the continuities with modernity. This is the position taken by Jameson, Harvey, Laclau, and Mouffe who provide strong critiques of modernity and much modern theory, while undertaking a postmodern turn in theory which builds on and appropriates salvageable aspects of modern theory.

Generalizing from the lacunae and aporia in postmodern theory, one could argue that an adequate theory of postmodernity must historically analyze the alleged postmodern break. If one wishes to claim that a transition from modern to postmodern society has occurred, one must provide an account of the features of the previous social order (modernity), the new social condition (postmodernity), and clarify the postulated rupture or break between them. Furthermore, one should also indicate both continuities and discontinuities between the old and the new, the previous and the current social order. Foucault – unacceptable interpretations of his work to the contrary – constantly engaged in such dialectical analysis (see Chapter 2). Foucault declares: 'One of the most harmful habits in contemporary thought' is 'the analysis of the present as being ... a present of rupture' (1988d: p. 35), without also specifying historical continuities. And Derrida – sometimes celebrated as the voice of rupture, break, otherness, and difference – states: 'I do not believe in decisive ruptures, in an unequivocal "epistemological break", as it is called today. Breaks are always, and fatally, reinscribed in an old cloth that must continually, interminably be undone' (1981a: p. 24).

Against postmodernists who celebrate the radically new and who postulate extreme rupture, discontinuity, and difference, we would argue that one must characterize both the continuities and the discontinuities in the historical process, as well as between different forms of culture, theory, experience, and so on in a given society. While by definition postmodernity is discontinuous with or constitutes a break from previous developments, we reject any periodizing analysis which emphasizes only discontinuity in favour of a dialectical analysis which theorizes the lines of continuity and discontinuity in a transition from one movement or period to another.

Frequently, what is identified as a postmodern development can be seen to be a prototypical modern trait. Thus, the numerous attempts to characterize a postmodernist cultural style in terms of self-reflexivity, ambiguity, indeterminacy, paradox, and so on, fail to see that these characteristics were already defining features of certain modernist movements.[3] From Jameson's perspective (6.1), in contrast, one can still differentiate a postmodern style or period from a modern style or period, even though they may share similar aspects, since certain features may become more prominent, intensified, or qualitatively different in postmodernism. Consequently, as Jameson notes, elements of popular culture can be found in modernist and postmodernist texts, but while a modernist text like Joyce's *Ulysses* may incorporate these elements into its text at certain moments, a postmodernist like Pynchon or Venturi absorbs them 'to the point where the line between high art and commercial forms seems increasingly difficult to draw' (1983: p. 112). With Jameson and against more apocalyptic notions of postmodernism and postmodernity, therefore, we see postmodern culture not as an absolute change which occurs *in vacuo*, but as one that occurs *ab utero*, within the matrix of capitalist modernity.

Raymond Williams' (1977) distinctions between residual, dominant, and emergent cultures, combined with Bloch's notion of non-synchronicity (1977), might help us theorize the specificity of the postmodern. Williams proposes that rather than speaking of stages or variations within culture, we should recognize the internal dynamic relations of any actual process. 'We have certainly still to speak of the "dominant" and the "effective", and in these senses of the hegemonic. But we find that we have also to speak, and indeed with further differentiation of each, of the "residual" and the "emergent", which in any real process, and at any moment in the process are significant both in themselves and in what they reveal of the characteristics of the "dominant"' (1977: pp. 121–2).

Bloch's notion of non-synchronicity indicates that we live in several different times and spaces at once, as when Nazi Germany simultaneously celebrated its mythic past and technological future. Using this concept, one could show how different socioeconomic conjunctures combine premodern, modern, and postmodern features. Using Williams' distinctions, we might want to speak of postmodern phenomena as only emergent tendencies within a still dominant modernity that is haunted as well by various forms of residual, traditional cultures, or which intensify key dynamics of modernity, such as innovation and fragmentation. Our present moment, on this view, is thus a contradictory transitional situation which does not yet allow any unambiguous affirmations concerning an alleged leap into full-blown postmodernity. At this point, it appears premature to claim that we are fully in a new postmodern scene, though one might see postmodern culture and society as new emergent tendencies which require a theoretical and political response and thus a reconstruction of social theory.

Consequently, while postmodern theory has attempted to cross the borderline and to chart the terrain of the new, its claims for an absolute break between modernity and postmodernity are most unconvincing. Although we may be living within a borderline, or transitional space, between the modern and the postmodern, and may be entering a terrain where old modes of thought and language are not always useful, postmodern theory exaggerates the break or rupture in history and thus covers over the extent to which the contemporary situation continues to be constituted by capitalism, gender and race oppression, bureaucracy, and other aspects of the past. Adopting a term of Max Horkheimer's, we prefer to speak of a society in transition rather than a completely new postmodern social formation.

Consequently, the first discussions of postmodernity are vitiated by the failure to distinguish clearly between modernity and post-modernity, and to specify the rupture in society and history that produces the postmodern condition or postmodern society. Such an operation would require detailed theoretical and empirical analysis, and a historical account or narrative of how modernity metamorphosed into the postmodern condition. Theorists who reject master narratives, or diachronic, periodizing social theory, are naturally going to have difficulty producing such a narrative, and thus find themselves in an aporetic situation.

In many instances, postmodernists have simply produced new totalizing theories which covertly presuppose mastery of a complex sociohistorical field, while, sometimes, rejecting discourses of mastery. It is ironic that despite the war against totality by Lyotard and others, theorists identified as postmodern like Foucault and Baudrillard have produced extremely totalizing theories which are often abstract, overly general, and sometimes oversimplify complex historical situations. Certainly these types of totalizing theory *should* be rejected in favour of a more multidimensional and complex social theory.

Furthermore, rather than throwing out concepts of grand narrative, representation, truth, subjectivity, and so on – as do extreme postmodernists – we should reconstruct these notions, taking account of the postmodern critique of modern theory, while recognizing the need for these concepts in order to do social theory, critique, and politics at all. The abandonment of key concepts of modern theory creates intense aporia in postmodern theory and contradictions between their theoretical critiques and actual performances, such as the rational critique of rationality, totalizing rejections of totality, and the subjective hubris of dismissing the category of subjectivity. In addition, postmodern theorists often reject reference, representation, and the very concept of reality, while presupposing an access to social reality, and thus to some ground of reference, in order to make claims about postmodernity. That is, the very statements about contemporary trends or developments made by a Baudrillard or a Lyotard presuppose that they are actually telling us something new or important about society or theory today, that their statements are accurately describing some phenomena, that they are illuminating at least some domain of social reality. This raises the issue of whether commitments to poststructuralism and postmodernism are always compatible.

Baudrillard and Lyotard dramatize different sides of the poststructuralist critique. As noted, Baudrillard problematizes the concepts of reality and representation in postmodern society, yet makes many claims about contemporary social conditions and constantly uses the discourse of the real (see Chapter 4). Lyotard seems comfortable with the concepts of reality and society, yet consistent with his prohibitions against totalizing narratives takes the poststructuralist critique of representation seriously and rarely attempts to represent postmodern society. Consequently, he lacks a social theory. In fact, his obsessive celebration of differences and desire to proliferate language games, art works, knowledges, and so on both reproduces the fundamental tendencies of a protean, fragmenting capitalism and loses the possibility of developing a critical standpoint in the emphasis on gaming and the refusal to privilege specific discourses. Thus we see that certain poststructuralist commitments preclude the development of social theory which is condemned as representational, totalizing, reductive, and terroristic *per se*.

Postmodern theory is also too totalizing in its rejection of modernity. As we argued in Chapter 7, both postmodern and critical theorists have carried out a radical critique of modernity and modern theory, though by comparison, critical theory is more differentiated *vis-à-vis* modernity and more likely to defend aspects of it. While some works of Horkheimer and Adorno approximate the postmodern critique in a radical rejection of the project of modernity itself, other critical theorists like Habermas see an unfulfilled heritage in modernity, the progressive possibilities of democratization, humanization, and individualization yet to be realized. From this perspective, the postmodern critique of modernity is one-sided and overly negative. Some postmodern critiques of modernity provide something of a caricature of modernity, reducing it to Enlightenment metanarratives (Lyotard), an oppressive semiological system which produces a hyperreal system of simulation (Baudrillard), or a 'vast carceral society' (Foucault).

Likewise, most postmodern theory is too undifferentiated in its critiques of rationality. There are different sorts of reason and critical theorists have traditionally distinguished between critical and instrumental reason, separating reason that is critical of existing society from instrumental reason which is part of a rationalizing system of domination. The conflation of instrumental with critical reason leads to an irrationalism that paralyzes social critique and transformation. As Gerald Graff puts it: 'In a society increasingly irrational and barbaric, to regard the attack on reason and objectivity as the basis of our radicalism is to perpetuate the nightmare we want to escape' (1973: p. 417). Thus, rather than simply rejecting reason it is better to develop more differentiated critiques as does critical theory. In contrast to most postmodern theory, this position builds on the progressive heritage of modern theory, while carrying out critiques of ideological discourses which serve conservative and regressive social interests and forms of rationality which contribute to oppression. Critical theory attempts to provide analyses of contemporary society, holding onto the intention that theory provide cognitive illumination of social reality. And yet, as we have argued, it is postmodern theory which has most dramatically conceptualized many of the key novelties and developments of our times.

8.3 Postmodern Politics: Subjectivity, Discourse, and Aestheticism

We have seen that most postmodern theory rejects macropolitics and the modern projects of radical social reconstruction. Extreme postmodern theory, as we have seen, announces the end of the political project in the end of history and society. Such postmodern theories not only lack an adequate social theory, they attack the social as such and tend to reject in principle all social norms, institutions, and practices as oppressive. Foucault, for example, attacks the processes of socialization as normalizing forms of repression, and the early Lyotard and Deleuze and Guattari also attack modes of sociality in these terms. Postmodern theory thus lacks positive notions of the social, failing to provide normative accounts of intersubjectivity, community, or solidarity. Habermas, by contrast, grounds his communication theory in an ego–alter relation that privileges non-coercive forms of inter-subjectivity (1984 and 1987a). Building on the theories of Durkheim and Mead, Habermas attempts to specify forms of communication and interaction free from domination. The earlier Frankfurt School attempted to develop theories of solidarity based on shared human needs, suffering, and interests in emancipation. This approach provided at least the basis for an ethical theory and normative grounds for critiques of existing norms, practices, and social relations (see Kellner 1989a).

Postmodern theory, by contrast, lacks a notion of intersubjectivity and attacks rationality, while calling for new forms of subjectivity and valorizing the production of new bodies, desires, and discourses. Postmodernists frequently claim that the autonomous rational ego of modern theory is disintegrating, or was a myth in the first place, and champion more plural, decentred, and multiple forms of subjectivity. They attempt to decentre and liquidate the modern bourgeois, humanist subject which they interpret as a construct of modern discourses and institutions, while politically valorizing the destruction of the subject.

However, all postmodern theory lacks an adequate theory of agency, of an active creative self, mediated by social institutions, discourses, and other people. Here we find Sartre's notion (1956) of the self as a project useful in his emphasis that creative subjectivity is an accomplishment of a process of self-creation rather than as a given. Yet theories of subjectivity and political agency must be mediated with theories of intersubjectivity which stress the ways that the subject is a social construct and the ways that sociality can constrict or enable individual subjectivity. In addition, an adequate theory of subjectivity should stress the social construction of the subject, its production in discourses, practices and institutions (see Coward and Ellis 1977).

For extreme postmodern theory, however, the subject is not merely a construct, but is a fiction and illusion *tout court*. Similar to structural–functionalist theorists such as Parsons and Luhmann, most postmodern theory sees the subject as a superfluity, a mere node within self-governing technical and semiotic systems. It is argued that in postmodern media and information society one is at most a 'term in a terminal' (Baudrillard 1983d), or a cyberneticized effect of 'fantastic systems of control' (Kroker and Cook 1986). Baudrillard claims (1983b) that subjects have imploded into the masses, while Jameson (1984a) argues that a fragmented, disjointed and discontinuous mode of experience is a fundamental characteristic of postmodern subjectivity. Deleuze and Guattari (1983 and 1987) even celebrate schizoid, nomadic dispersions of desire and subjectivity, valorizing the pulverization of the modern subject. Thus, a contradiction of some postmodern theory is that while theoretically it dispenses with the individual, it simultaneously resurrects it in a post-liberal form, as an aestheticized, desiring monad.

Postmodern politics tends to revolve around the poles of the politics of subjectivity and everyday life contrasted with a political cynicism. Ignoring the reality of phenomena such as substantive grass roots politics in countries like the United States, international forms of solidarity with labour or with liberation movements, the global environmental and peace movements, and other new movements of the present, Baudrillard *et tutti quanti* project their own cynicism onto the masses, declaring them a black hole which absorbs all messages with equal indifference, and consigning the working class into oblivion with the flurry of a few keystrokes. If there is a positive political strategy for extreme postmodernists, it is a fatal strategy of hastening the process of nihilism without also advancing any positive social and political alternatives, as when Kroker and Cook (1986: p. 266) promote nihilism and pessimism 'as the only possible basis of historical emancipation', while having no conception of what could or should emerge from the detritus of modernity. Baudrillard proposes the fatal strategy of imitating the object world and pushing behaviour like consumerism to its extreme, while Deleuze and Guattari urge pushing lines of deterritorialization and schizoid behaviour until normalizing codes and structures of capitalism break down and new psychic identities and political possibilities emerge.

Such tactics risk replicating or intensifying pernicious aspects of capitalism without challenging it, particularly when they lack a positive social and normative vision to guide them. In addition, such postmodern politics are highly indeterminate and on the whole postmodern theorists tend to substitute sloganeering for concrete analysis and political proposals. Postmodern politics reject all ideals and models exterior to the existing system and thus all utopian alternatives. They prefer to push the system to its extremes and perhaps breaking point rather than positing alternative or oppositional strategies. Extreme postmodern theory (such as Baudrillard) rejects all politics whatsoever and most postmodern theory posits a totalizing logic capable of absorbing all potential challenges, and turning opposition against the system to its own advantage.

In our view, no postmodern theorist has formulated an adequate political response to the degraded contemporary conditions they describe. Indeed, extreme postmodern theorists have abandoned politics for an avant-gardist posturing that is bloated with cynicism and opportunism. With the defeat of radical politics in the late 1960s, the collapse of Eurocommunism, and the rise of the New Right which has dominated politics for the last decade, postmodern discourse offered solace for isolated and embittered intellectuals who gave up hope for social change and retired from social involvement to retreat to the academy and in some cases to the stylized hedonism of the 'new intellectuals' (Bourdieu). Generalizing their own sense of isolation and hopelessness, extreme postmodernists declare the end or bankruptcy of liberal and radical values. Going beyond Gramsci, they espouse not only a pessimism of the intellect, but also a pessimism of the will, thereby passing from the extreme of 1960s revolutionary optimism which naively envisioned a new and exciting world on the immediate horizon to the opposite extreme of a 1980s–1990s revolutionary defeatism that cynically derides political commitments *per se*.

These attitudes, representative of the collapse of the post-1968 radical will, lack a historical perspective on the cyclical patterns of mass resistance and quietism. May 1968, after all, erupted within the midst of the 'one-dimensional society' and not even the most prescient minds foresaw the tumultuous events in the Soviet Union and Eastern Europe in 1989. Much postmodern discourse is thoroughly apolitical and deconstructs every opposition except the boundary separating its own isolation within the academy and the outside world.

Yet, we have seen in Chapter 6 that there have been more promising political appropriations of postmodern theory than is found in extreme postmodernists like Baudrillard and Lyotard. The postmodern politics of identity and difference have pluralized political struggles both in terms of the spaces of struggle and the number of oppositional subjects and groups, all of which are deemed to be autonomous from workers' struggles (see for example Laclau and Mouffe 1985). On the positive side, this opening of the discourse and space of the political allows new actors, movements, and ideas to reinvigorate radical politics. Yet, much celebration of 'new social movements' and 'alliance politics' replays old liberal tropes, thus replicating interest group liberalism in new guises.

At its best, the project of a postmodern politics of identity and difference responds to the enormous social and cultural changes which have taken place in the last few decades and provides new subjects, movements, and strategies of social transformation. The positive contribution to radical politics within a reconstructive postmodern theory is the emphasis on the need for reconstruction of society, subjectivity, theory, and culture, and rethinking power and struggle in non-juridical or economistic models. For postmodern theory, social forms are not natural or given but are the products of a historical process which can be changed and transformed. The postmodern emphasis on disintegration and change in the present situation points to new openings and possibilities for social transformation and struggle. The postmodern celebration of plurality and multiplicity facilitates a more diverse, open, and contextual politics that refuses to privilege any general recipes for social change or any particular group. The postmodern theory of decentred power also allows for the multiplication of possibilities for political struggle, no longer confined simply to the realm of production or the state. The idea that power and potential resistance are everywhere may therefore be more exhilarating than depressive and may help politicize new areas of social and personal existence.

Another way of theorizing the nature of the various postmodern political positions is to interpret them as an attack on the modern concept of representation in its many senses. Epistemologically, postmodernists refuse the modern belief that we have unmediated access to reality. All postmodernists reject the metaphor of the mind as a mirror of nature, the object as a neutral datum, and the subject as an aloof observer of the world. In agreement with a critical tradition extending from Kant to Hegel to Nietzsche to twentieth-century pragmatism, postmodernists argue that the mind is constitutive, rather than reflective, of reality. In more extreme versions of this thesis, some postmodernists lapse into a linguistic idealism that denies the world any external reality independent of language or discourse. Postmodernists in literature, painting, photography and other media, however, follow avant-garde modernists in attacking realist forms of representation and its realist biases, attempt to foreground the operation of cultural codes in the construction of reality and subjectivity to replace these with new forms of representation (see Hutcheon 1989). Jameson too attempts to reconstruct the concept of representation as cognitive mapping that situates one's existence within the global space of transnational capitalism.

Existentially, many postmodernists refuse mental representation of any sort as a mediating ballast on the immediacy of the desiring body. Deleuze and Guattari, the early Lyotard, and sometimes Foucault, privilege the physical body over critical cognition and hence align themselves with the *Lebensphilosophie* tradition. In particular, they follow Nietzsche's attack on self-reflection, self-identity, and decadent rationalist culture which deadens the vital physical instincts. Politically, postmodernists refuse the right of political parties or intellectuals to speak on behalf of other individuals and groups. Foucault and Lyotard reject macro-political organizations as repressive totalizations of diverse political groups and Foucault substitutes the 'specific intellectual' who advises and assists local forms of struggle for the 'universal intellectual' who arrogates to him or herself privileged concepts and knowledge.

But we find that there are many serious problems with the forms of postmodern theory and politics which have been produced so far. Critics complain of a fetishism of difference in postmodern theory, or uncritical celebration of single-issue interest group politics, which fails to articulate common issues and universal political values (see Bronner 1990). Furthermore, the emphasis on difference and pluralism in social theory and politics replicates the favoured tropes of liberalism and raises the question of whether postmodern theory is really that new and whether it is a decisive advance over liberal theory. Postmodern theory, like some liberal pluralist theory, has problems theorizing macrostructures and seeing how totalizing tendencies, like capitalism or gender and racial oppression, permeate microstructures and the plurality and differences celebrated in the theory.

Indeed, most postmodern theory, like liberal pluralist theory, is unable to theorize structural causation and the relative weight and significance of causal factors like the economy, state, or other institutions, discourses, and practices. As Althusser has empha-sized, the opposite extreme of mechanistic monocausal theories is a pluralism which effectively denies causation altogether and sees everything to be of equal structural weight. Politically, this sort of pluralism is mystifying and ineffectual, unable to specify key sites of domination and oppression. Furthermore, extreme pluralism fails to indicate major forces or subjects of struggle, or exaggerates the powers of specific oppressed individuals or groups. Lyotard and Rorty, for example, champion a plurality and diversity of voices in a great cultural 'conversation' without realizing that some people and groups are in far better positions – politically, economically, and psychologically – to speak than others. Such calls are vapid when the field of discourse is controlled and monopolized by the dominant economic and political powers. In the world of Lyotard and Rorty, there us no such thing as class or systematically enforced exclusion and oppression. In opposition to this pluralism, Foucault, who otherwise is a causal agnostic, reminds us that asymmetrical power relations constitute knowl-edge and discourse, and that some discursive subjects and posi-tions are more authoritative than others. Similarly, Habermas argues that the conditions of conversation can be distorted from the start, and hence not everyone participates on equal terms. Thus, both liberal pluralist and postmodern theory show an inability to grasp systemic relations and causal nexuses, and mystify various forms of social inequality.

Nor do liberal pluralist and postmodern theory provide us with a means for asking how we can adjudicate between the various claims made in the great conversation. Extreme postmodern theory claims that consensus is impossible and undesirable (Lyotard) and that it is impossible to choose more progressive political positions because distinctions between Left and Right have imploded (Baudrillard). Yet when engaging in politics one has to choose. Are we to accept all voices – Bush, Jackson, Major, and Mandela – as espousing equally valid claims? If not, then how do we discriminate between them? If, as Laclau and Mouffe claim (1985: p. 3), 'the era of normative epistemologies has come to an end', then it is indeed difficult to make such distinctions and here again we see that postmodern theory has crippling political implications.

In addition, both liberalism and postmodern theory de-emphasize community and intersubjectivity in favour of highly individualized modes of being. Both, moreover, fragment society into isolated spheres: much liberal theory bifurcates capitalism into public and private realms, state and civil society, while postmodern theory splits capitalist society into separate and unmediated realms, analyzing culture in isolation from the economy, or politics apart from the conjuncture of business and government. There is, however, a significant difference between liberalism and postmodern theory in that while both apotheosize individualized modes of existence, much postmodern theory rejects the liberal discourse of autonomy and rights which becomes superfluous with the 'death of man'. Indeed, theorists such as the early Foucault see moral discourse only as a ruse of domination through subjectification. Only Laclau and Mouffe have attempted to critically reconstruct liberalism and to push the liberal democratic heritage to a higher level, though their efforts could have the effects of strengthening liberalism and undermining the radical democracy that they seek.

In contrast to the reconstructive wing of postmodern theory which stresses the politics of identity and difference, and perhaps alliances between these forces, extreme postmodern theory tends to promote a micropolitics of desire that is excessively subjectivistic and aestheticized. Despite its dismissal of the subject, we find much postmodern theory to be highly subjectivistic, as is its politics in which the unleashing of subjectivity is privileged in thinkers such as the early Lyotard or Deleuze and Guattari. These subjectivist political positions approximate the sort of spontaneism and anarchism which appeared in the May 1968 events and their aftermath. This politics of subjectivity valorizes desire, pleasure, intensities, and the body over reason, discourse, and intersubjectivity. It celebrates fragmented and libidinal states of being while rejecting such concepts as personal and social identity, unity, or harmony as terroristic and oppressive.

Postmodern theory and politics, in some versions, is highly aestheticized as well as subjectivistic. Much postmodern theory proposes an aesthetic politics that breaks with traditional rationalist politics based on ideology critique, the overcoming of false consciousness, the subordination of art to politics, and a pragmatic concern with the serious business of seizing power. For postmodern theorists such as the early Lyotard and Deleuze and Guattari, capitalism has colonized both our conscious and unconscious existence and the revolutionary project has therefore been defused as individuals are libidinally bound to the present system. In response to these conditions, postmodernists seek a politics of desire where art and desire become fundamental political concerns and tactics.

While postmodern theorists are correct to underline the importance of developing new modes of desire and emancipating the imagination from the ballast of instrumental reason, aesthetics tends to be privileged over theory, rationality, and pragmatic political issues such as coalition building. Such an approach has three main problems: it fails to provide a language to articulate what are arguably indispensable concerns with autonomy, rights, and justice; it is individualist in its emphasis on desire and pleasure; and it is irrationalist in its rejection of theory and rational critique.

The postmodern aestheticization of the subject is simply another way of denying subjectivity as a multidimensional form of agency and praxis, reducing it to a decentred desiring existence. Indeed, postmodern aestheticized subjectivism presents the paradox of a politics of subjectivity without the subject and calls attention to the need for social theory to provide richer accounts of subjectivity. The postmodern repudiation of humanism, without reconstructing its core values, strips the subject of moral responsibility and autonomy. The 'death of man' also spells the death of a moral language whereby the rights and freedoms of exploited, degraded, and repressed people can be upheld and defended. Political action in a world where such language is common coin becomes impossible. On this count, as Wolin observes (1987), postmodernism is a regression behind the progressive advances of the Enlightenment. Of the theorists we have considered, Laclau and Mouffe alone attempt to reconstruct liberal discourse within a postmodern context, while rejecting universality.

Postmodern aestheticism militates against developing theoretical discourses of rights and equality by dissolving the tension between the need to negate this world through art and the imagination and the need to live in and analyze it rationally and ethically. Marcuse, by contrast, offers an alternative to postmodern theory that absorbs its virtues and avoids its flaws. While emphasizing that capitalism has come to control our very instinctual being, and hence granting the importance of new modes of desire and a 'new sensibility', Marcuse insisted on the equal importance of critical theory and reason. Although he supported the New Left, he saw it as a flawed movement which could not effectively challenge power because of its irrationalist biases. A new eros is needed to combat repressive instrumental rationality, but 'the instinctual rebellion will have become a political force only when it is accompanied and guided by the rebellion of reason' (Marcuse 1972: p. 131). Thus, 'the emancipation of consciousness is still the primary task. Without it, all emancipation of the senses, all radical activism, remains blind, self-defeating. Political practice still depends on theory ... on education, persuasion – on Reason' (Marcuse 1972: p. 132). While calling for an aestheticization of life, Marcuse always emphasized the need for a distance between art and life, and qualified the role art could have in a political movement, unable to change reality apart from political education and a mass political movement.

Against the postmodern politics of subjectivity and tendencies to aestheticize politics, we would advocate a politics of alliances, a cultural politics, and a strategic politics which combine micro- and macroperspectives and retain a salient place for critical rationality. Postmodern theory, however, is too subjectivist and aestheticized to develop a politics of alliances which requires theories of needs, interests, consensus, and mediation. Indeed, politics *is* mediation between competing groups, interests and demands; thus, a micropolitics that fails to address the problems of mediation and alliances cannot possibly provide a model for politics in the current situation – a point to which we return in the next section.

Yet, while the postmodern emphasis on micropolitics, new social movements, and a multiplicity of struggles is exciting, their polemic against macrotheory and politics, trade union or economic struggle, and traditional politics is as one-sided and dogmatic as the modern theories which they oppose. While the emphasis on cultural revolution and decentred politics may be useful, it too can be constrictive and disabling for developing mass struggles and movements. Against the neo-liberalism of some postmodern theory, we see a concrete and substantive basis for a radical political alliance to lie in a common anti-capitalist politics. The exploitation and repression of diverse groups and individuals by the capitalist economy and state provides a fundamental point of commonality to unite a myriad of oppressed social groups. While the oppression of women, workers, blacks, Asians, gays and lesbians, and so on, is not reducible to economic conditions, they are all conditioned by them insofar as they live within a capitalist society. The relationship here is not indeterminate, as Laclau and Mouffe suggest, but rather asymmetrical: while capitalism cuts across all social groups, the specific concerns of any one group do not intersect with all other groups (except for environmental groups, though their concerns too are directly related to developments within the capitalist economy).

The privileging of anti-capitalist politics does not entail the privileging of labour and class politics within an alliance, since the dynamics of male domination, racism, homophobia, etc., are not reducible to class oppression and not automatically eliminated with the creation of non-exploitative social relations. The abolition of capitalism, therefore, is a political objective relevant to all oppressed groups, but it is only one step in the creation of a free and democratic society. Most postmodern theory, by contrast, exhibits an anti-utopianism, political pessimism, and renunciation of hopes for radical political change. Much postmodern theory is motivated by disillusionment with liberal ideals of progress and radical hopes for emancipation. For Lyotard, 'there is sorrow in the *Zeitgeist*', while Baudrillard claims that 'melancholy' is the appropriate response to the disappearance of previous eras of history and theoretical–political constructions (1984b: p. 39). Foucault rejects utopian values as just a ruse for expanding present forms of domination, claiming that 'to imagine another system is to extend our participation in the present system' (1977: p. 230).

In contrast to most postmodern theory, Jameson and Laclau and Mouffe argue for the importance of utopian values. Attempting to overcome the Frankfurt School position that reduces mass culture to nothing but a manipulated and degraded realm of commodification, Jameson (1979 and 1981a) draws from Ernst Bloch to claim that mass culture has critical aspects in its utopian impulses for community and yearning for a social life beyond the current forms of alienation. Jameson holds that an adequate hermeneutical theory not only pursues a negative ideological critique and demystification of the text, but also deciphers positive utopian moments in every text in order to reawaken them. Laclau and Mouffe argue that utopian thought on some articulations has repressive implications insofar as it envisages an 'Ideal City' to be socially engineered along lines of consensus. Yet they also claim that the complete rejection of utopianism is debilitating insofar as this leaves the radical project with nothing but sterile 'positivist pragmatism'. Utopian visions, properly qualified, remain important, for 'without "utopia", without the possibility of negating an order beyond the point that we are to threaten it, there is no possibility at all of the constitution of a radical imaginary' (Laclau and Mouffe 1985: p. 190).

It is precisely the political problems with postmodern theory that have made many suspicious of their discourses and perspectives. Political suspicions have to a large extent motivated Habermas' critiques of postmodern theory[4] and the postmodern assault on the various post-1960s' attempts to reconstitute critical social theory have angered many who have participated in these projects. For instance, the theorists of the Birmingham School of Cultural Studies and their allies have attempted to reconstruct theory, subjectivity, and politics in the present age. Stuart Hall particularly objects to Baudrillard and other postmodern theorists' conception of the masses as a passive, sullen, 'silent majority' and their political cynicism and nihilism which he relates to the collapse of the critical French intelligentsia during the Mitterrand era. 'What raises my political hackles', Hall notes, 'is the comfortable way in which French intellectuals now take it upon themselves to declare when and for whom history ends, how the masses can or cannot be represented, when they are or are not a real historical force, when they can or cannot be mythically invoked in the French revolutionary tradition, etc. French intellectuals always had a tendency to use "the masses" in the abstract to fuel or underpin their own intellectual positions. Now that the intellectuals have renounced critical thought, they feel no inhibition in renouncing it on behalf of the masses – whose destinies they have only shared abstractly ... I think that Baudrillard needs to join the masses for a while, to be silent for two-thirds of a century, just to see what it feels like' (1986: pp. 51–3).

Other British cultural theorists find postmodern theory to be equally debilitating in its political implications (see Hebdige 1987; Chambers 1986; McRobbie 1986; and Fiske and Watts 1986). As opposed to Baudrillardian monolithic categories of the 'masses', British cultural studies attempt to analyze society in terms of different classes, groups, and subcultures with their own unique patterns of experience, cultural styles, modes of resistance, and so on in a neo-Gramscian analysis which tries to specify the concrete forces of hegemony and counter-hegemony in a specific sociohistorical conjuncture. Postmodern theory, by contrast, is too abstract and lacks concrete, empirical and sociohistorical analysis. Postmodernists also tend to be self-consciously superficial, preferring to focus their descriptions on the surface, on appearance, and thus fail to conceptualize some of the underlying dynamics of contemporary capitalist societies.

8.4 Theory, Culture, and Politics: Conflicting Models

There will always be antagonisms, struggles and a partial opaqueness of the social: there will always be history (Laclau and Mouffe 1987: p. 106).

The postmodern debates have fostered concern with methodological endeavours and models to be used in contemporary theory. Postmodern theory has distinguished itself by challenging previous methods, theories, and concepts while offering new theoretical and political perspectives. Yet we believe that contemporary events put in question certain aspects of postmodern theory such as the thesis of the end of history, the prohibition against global thought, the attack on macropolitics and mass struggle, and the general sense of malaise and cynicism. In short, we believe that postmodern theory fails to provide the instruments needed to analyze its own moment in history and the events of the 1980s in which it rose to international prominence.

Despite postmodern claims concerning the end of history and society, the 1980s were a decade of unparalleled historical turmoil and change. Although the new conservative hegemonies in the United States, Britain, Germany, and elsewhere during the beginning of the decade produced a sense of historical glaciation and malaise – as did the dreary Stalinism in the Soviet bloc – contestations of the conservative hegemony, its own debacles, and the dramatic upheavals in the communist world produced historical transformations and upheaval as significant as the events of 1848, or the era of democratic revolutions in the late eighteenth century.

Indeed, 1989 alone saw the collapse of Soviet communism with electoral victories of democratic forces in Poland, the renunciation of bureaucratic communism in Hungary, and nine months of dramatic demonstrations and struggles which forced the collapse of communism in East Germany, culminating in the dramatic tearing down of the Berlin Wall. Then in rapid succession, demonstrations in Czechoslovakia led to the collapse of a communist government, while bloody revolts in Romania led to the overthrow of the communist regime there and the execution of a hated dictator. Turmoil continued in the Soviet Union itself and dramatic political changes punctuated continued repression, nationalist upheaval, and often surprising liberalization. In China, the world observed exciting demonstrations for democratization in Tiananmen Square and then brutal oppression of the democratic movement by a still oppressive Stalinist regime.

Late 1989 and 1990 have continued this era of political upheaval and surprise. The criminal US invasion of Panama, the release of Nelson Mandela and the beginnings of hoped-for changes in South Africa, the electoral defeat of the Sandinistas in Nicaragua and demobilization of the Contras, continued upheaval in the communist bloc, and rapid movement toward reunification in Germany make this the most tumultuous and dramatic political period of the postwar era. Changes in East–West relations, the apparent end of the Cold War, new political realignments and transformations, the Iraqi invasion of Kuwait and US-led military intervention in the Middle East, resulting in the Gulf War, as well as the unanticipated dramas of tomorrow, all require critical comprehensive and systemic theories of society to articulate and make sense of these momentous events. Adequately conceptualizing the present historical moment requires the type of systemic, comprehensive theory of society with practical intent associated with the classical theorists of modernity (Marx, Dewey, Weber), as well as with the earlier stages of the Frankfurt School. A critical theory of society provides both a theory of the contemporary moment and a historical account of the formation of the current society. It draws upon a multiplicity of disciplines (political economy, sociology, anthropology, cultural theory, philosophy, and so on) and combines theoretical construction with empirical research, as well as uniting micro- with macrotheory. Since capitalism continues to be a major constitutive force in many contemporary societies, the Marxian theory and critique of capitalism continues to be a crucial element of a critical theory of society.

Yet since Marx failed to provide an adequate theory of the state, bureaucracy, nationalism, the public sphere, society, the psyche, gender, race and culture, a reconstructed critical social theory must draw on other traditions as well. Likewise, since the Marxian theories of revolution have so far failed to produce an adequate version of democratic socialism, the theory of political transformation also needs to be revised and updated. Critical theory is by nature historical and must revise its theories and practices in the light of historical transformations. It is also methodologically self-reflexive, normative, and willing to explicate and defend its theoretical and political commitments.

Postmodern renunciations of systemic social theory, by contrast, its apotheosis of fragments, its dull nihilism, and its sense of apathy and inertia are all theoretically and politically disabling and should be severely criticized and overcome. Indeed, most postmodern theories can make little sense of the dramatic events of the era, while its claims concerning the end of history, society, the masses, and so on are laughable in the face of the resurgence of historical drama and upheaval. Indeed, it is ironic that during this period of exciting historical and political development certain postmodern theorists are prohibiting precisely the sort of theory needed to make sense of current historical events. It is also ironic that in this era of worldwide struggles for democracy postmodern intellectuals are trying to dissolve the key concepts of the democratic revolution. Rather, it is precisely now, as Marshall Berman has noted, that radical democracy should be defended, secured, and expanded.[5]

Perhaps, indeed, the era of the postmodern frenzy in theory and culture is over. Perhaps postmodern theory was a fad and epiphenomenon of the 1980s, an expression of the failure of nerve and alienation of intellectuals in the face of the dashed utopian political hopes of the 1960s, their potential obsolescence in the new media and technological society, and their despair or cynical accommodation in the 1980s. The 1980s was an unparalleled era of corruption, cynicism, conservativism, superficiality, and societal regression and one could argue that postmodern theory expressed these trends, even when, upon occasion, maintaining a critical posture. From this vantage point, the postmodern frenzy was a mere ripple on the tides of history, a seduction for intellectuals which offered tempting new sources of cultural capital and which induced a desperate attempt for intellectuals to retain significance while becoming increasingly marginalized in the computer and techno-capitalist society.

As Zygmunt Bauman has noted (1987), the modern intellectual as a legislator of knowledge and cultural values has become superfluous with the rationalization of the modern state. To this must be added the erosion of the boundary between high and low culture, which previously secured the intellectual a privileged place in the interpretation of canonical texts. The result is a crisis in the role of the intellectual, and intellectuals in the humanities threatened with obsolescence have attempted to postulate a new postmodern era and discourse to legitimate their continuing relevance in technocratic societies where the sciences are increasingly displacing the humanities. Decentred in relation to technicists, the postmodern intellectual is an 'interpreter' whose cultural authority is safely confined within the academy. While the subversion of intellectual elitism can be seen as a positive development, postmodern discourse has provided the opportunity for some intellectuals to position themselves as new avant-gardes to garner new sources of cultural capital, or to theorize 'just for the fun of it'. Here postmodernism becomes just another specialized discourse that promotes what Edward Said (1983) calls 'the cult of expertise and professionalism'.

To be sure, aspects of the postmodern theory and critique will remain relevant for the current decade and coming century, but some aspects should be sharply criticized and rejected. As we enter a new historical terrain, it is clear that we need new critical theories to make sense of the current political conjuncture and new political theories and strategies as well. We need in addition an intensification of the radical cultural theory and critique that distinguished the best of postmodern theory. We must continue to develop supra-disciplinary theorizing, while developing new discourses, modes of writing, and forms of communication. Established theory and the academic division of labour hegemonic in the academies of both the East and West are thoroughly bankrupt and unable to deal with the new historical situation and problems.

Thus we would propose the need for new theoretical constellations and strategies to which postmodern theories could continue to contribute. It is certainly misguided, however, to talk glibly of a new synthesis between, say, critical theory and postmodern theory in the sense of a harmonious merger of positions. While we have noted interesting similarities between them, there are also significant differences which make such synthesis impossible. What is needed instead are new theoretical articulations which draw on both and other traditions of contemporary theory. Critical theory and postmodern theory need to be confronted and articulated in their disparities so that their very tensions and differences provoke new thinking and new theoretical and political practice. In some contexts, they can be articulated together, while in other contexts precisely their differences and oppositions could be fruitful.

In general, we believe that a combination of micro- and macrotheory and politics provides the best framework to explore contemporary society with a view to radical social transformation. The sort of microanalysis characteristic of some postmodern theory thus provides a corrective to the frequently over-generalizing and totalizing perspectives of critical theory. On the other hand, we have argued that postmodern theory lacks the dialectical and critical social theory necessary to conceptualize the complex and often contradictory features of contemporary societies. Likewise, a combination of micro- and macropolitics recommends itself in the light of contemporary events. The struggles in the Soviet Union and Eastern bloc countries initially took the form of micropolitics, with multiplicities of individuals and small groups standing up against the Stalinist dictatorships. As events unfolded, however, the microstruggles became macro, with groups and individuals coalescing in often spectacular mass demonstrations and actions. The cumulative force of hundreds of thousands of individuals in the streets forced out the Stalinist regimes, vindicating traditional modern theories of collective action and mass struggle as instruments of social change.

Thus it is a mistake simply to valorize micropolitics, otherness, and multiplicities *per se* as postmodern theorists are wont to do. In the current moment, for instance, new voices are breaking from the monolithic discourses of communist countries, and while some of them are calling for democracy or democratic socialism, other of these voices are ultra-nationalist, racist, and even fascist. One should not simply celebrate multiplicity or plurality *per se* since some of the multiplicities may be highly reactionary. Such laissez-faire politics is liberalism at its worst, renouncing a critical standpoint from which one can appraise competing political forces and voices.

Consequently, we believe that the critical social theory and radical politics of the future demand a combination of micro- and macrotheory and politics and that the postmodern prescription against macrotheory and politics is paralyzing and should be repudiated. Further, in light of the continued vitality and destructiveness of capitalism we would argue that analysis of contemporary conditions should take place in the context of investigations of the current configuration of 'techno-capitalism' (see Kellner 1989a). From this perspective, the current social order in the capitalist countries can be conceived as a synthesis of new technologies and capitalism that is characterized by new technical, social, and cultural forms combining with capitalist relations of production to create the social matrix of our times. Postmodern theory is often good at analyzing discourses, new technologies, and forms of culture, but weak in conceptualizing them in terms of broader developments in the socioeconomic system. Moving in this direction points to continuities with the social theories of the past (such as Marxism) and the need to revive, update, expand, and develop previous theories of capitalism in the light of contemporary conditions. Analyzing the new configurations of capitalism and technology would allow emphasis on the new role of information, media, consumerism, the implosion of aesthetics and commodification, and other themes stressed by postmodern theory, while situating these developments within a larger sociohistorical frame.

It is our view that postmodern theorists like Foucault, Baudrillard, and Lyotard, have made a serious theoretical and political mistake in severing their work from the Marxian critique of political economy and capitalism precisely at a point when the logic of capital accumulation has been playing an increasingly important role in structuring the new stage of society which can be conceptualized as a new economic and technical restructuring of capitalist society. Indeed, we would argue that Marxian categories are of central importance precisely in analyzing the phenomena focused on by postmodern social theory: the consumer society, the media, information, computers, and so on. Although theorists of both the postindustrial society and postmodern society posit the primacy of knowledge and information as new principles of social organization, it is arguably capitalism that is determining what sort of media, information, computers, and other technologies and commodities are being produced and distributed precisely according to its logic and interests. That is, in techno-capitalist societies, information, as Herbert Schiller and others have shown (1981 and 1984), is being more and more commodified, accessible only to those who can pay for it and who have access to it. Education itself is increasingly commodified as computers become more essential to the process of education, while more domains of knowledge and information are commodified and transmitted through computers (we're thinking both of computer learning programs which force consumers to buy programs to learn typing, maths, history, foreign languages, and so on, as well as modem-programs and data-base firms which provide access to an abundance of information, entertainment and networking via computer for those who can afford to pay its per minute information prices).

Interestingly, in a recent article, Lyotard himself has made this point, arguing: 'The major development of the last twenty years, expressed in the most vapid terms of political economy and historical periodization, has been the transformation of language into a productive commodity: phrases considered as messages to encode, decode, transmit, and order (by the bundle) to reproduce, conserve, and keep available (memories), to combine and conclude (calculations), and to oppose (games, conflicts, cybernetics); and the establishment of a unit of measure that is also a price unit, in other words, information. The effects of the penetration of capitalism into language are just beginning to be felt' (1986–7: p. 217).

Yet against Lyotard and others who reject macrotheory, systemic analysis, or grand historical narratives, we would argue that precisely now we need such comprehensive theories to attempt to capture the new totalizations being undertaken by capitalism in the realm of consumption, the media, information, and so on. From this perspective, one needs new critical theories to conceptualize, describe, and interpret macro social processes, just as one needs political theories able to articulate common or general interests that cut across divisions of sex, race, and class (Fraser and Nicholson 1988; Bronner 1990). Without such macrotheories that attempt to cognitively map the new forms of social development and the relationships between spheres like the economy, culture, education, and politics, we are condemned to live among the fragments without clear indications of what impact new technologies and social developments are having on the various domains of our social life. Cognitive mapping is therefore necessary to provide theoretical and political orientation as we move into a new, dangerous, and exciting social and political terrain. Mapping contemporary social, political, and cultural reality requires development of a strong macro social theory built firmly on historical and empirical analysis of the present age. While the postmodern mappings provide some help in orienting us to the new social conditions, ultimately they fail to provide adequate social and political theories for the challenges of the future. Consequently, while it would be a mistake to forget or ignore postmodern theory completely, it has so far failed to produce adequate perspectives on society, culture, and radical politics for the theoretical and political challenges now facing us.

Indeed, a Big Story is now going on; we are living through some dramatic changes that are putting into question previous social theories and policies. Yet an important part of the story is the transformation and restructuring of capitalism, the advent to a new stage of capitalism that is affecting, as developments in capitalism tend to do, the entirety of our life. Thus with Jameson we would prefer to read the dynamics of postmodern theory and culture as part of the continuing and fascinating drama of capital – capital in its transnational phase marked by new syntheses of capital and technology, a new internationalization of capital, new technologies, and modes of organization. Changing socioeconomic conditions require novel political responses and strategies. Theories of techno-capitalism would thus also require specification of a radical politics as both anti-capitalist and cognizant of new technologies, social movements, and political challenges. Such a new politics could thus be at once macro and micro, and concerned to provide links between existing radical movements and to demonstrate the links between the existing problems of the present age.

Finally, a critical theory of the present moment would provide an account of the profound ambiguity of our present age, rather than wallowing in fashionable postmodern pessimism, or regressing to technocratic or liberal optimism. For the present moment contains both utopian and dystopian aspects which open toward conflicting futures. *The information explosion* could work either to multiply and pluralize information, or to cancel all meaning in a meaningless noise; it could enhance literacy skills or deaden them; it could decentralize information so that all people have easy and equal access, or it could further the control and domination of ruling elites who monopolize information and computer technologies. Similarly, *computerization processes* could facilitate new learning skills or perpetuate class inequalities, promote militarist adventures, and increase population surveillance. Computers and robotics could eliminate harsh, physical labour, or produce new forms of slavery; the new technologies could produce a shortened working week and increase leisure time, or lead to massive unemployment. *New media technologies* could activate or stultify the mind, democratize and pluralize information and entertainment, or work for purposes of information control and homogenization; they could allow new voices to enter a reinvigorated public sphere or increase domination by corporate elites. And the Gulf war demonstrated that military technologies threaten the world with new forms of destruction and mass annihiliation.

Thus new modes of technology provide potentialities to enhance life as well as instruments to destroy it. Likewise new political struggles contain both threats and possibilities. The response to the Gulf war in the United States and elsewhere points to possibilities for a resurgence of militarist fascism, just as the new social movements point to new possibilities for democratization.

The turmoil in the communist world could bring an end to the Cold War, increase democratization, and inaugurate a new epoch of peace and prosperity, or it could produce new nationalist frenzies, social and economic instability, the total hegemony of capital, or an outbreak of new regional global wars. Thus, utopia and catastrophe are both part of the contemporary scene and if hope for a better future is to be rationally justified it must be grounded in a theory of both the possibilities and dangers of the present age which aims at development of a new set of global anti-capitalist political alliances and a reinvigorated democratic socialism.

Notes

1. What we are calling extreme and reconstructive themes in post-modern theory are found to different degrees in the various theorists that we have discussed. Baudrillard is an ideal type of an extreme postmodernist, rejecting modern theory completely. Theorists like Foucault and Lyotard combine extreme and reconstructive tendencies, while theorists like Jameson and Laclau and Mouffe are predominantly reconstructive. There is also some question as to whether it is even possible to escape from modern theory and modernity altogether, and it could be argued that there are many modern elements in even the most extreme postmodern theorists like Baudrillard and Kroker and Cook; yet their breaks are significant enough from modern theory and rhetoric of new positions and perspectives to earn the label 'extreme'.

2. We are using the term 'modern theory' as a general category which encompasses modern theoretical discourses ranging from philosophy, to social theory, to psychoanalysis. Following Antonio and Kellner 1991a, we are arguing that modern theory contains both critical and dogmatic themes and traditions, sometimes embedded in the same thinker or school. Our metatheoretical inquiry in this section is indebted to our

discussions with Robert Antonio, and although he does not share all of the positions advanced here our dialogue with him has helped us to sharpen our claims and vocabulary.

3. For an argument against 'the myth of the postmodernist break-through' see Graff (1973) who argues for continuities between postmodernism and modernism. He claims that 'postmodernism should be seen not as breaking with romantic and modernist assumptions but rather as a logical culmination of the premises of these earlier movements ... the revolutionary claims which have been made for the postmodernist new sensibility are overrated' (1973: p. 385). Callinicos (1990) develops a similar argument, claiming that modernism anticipated most of the allegedly new features of postmodernism. While this is true, we believe that it is often possible and useful to draw distinctions between modernist and postmodernist architecture, painting, literature, film, etc., though distinctions should be made within each field where such global categories are more or less salient.

4. Conversations with Habermas, Brighton, England, August 1988.

5. We cite here a talk by Berman at the Socialist Scholars Conference in New York during April 1990.

Bibliography

ADORNO, Theodor W. (1940) 'Husserl and the Problem of Idealism', *Journal of Philosophy*, vol. XXXI, no. I: pp. 5–18.

ADORNO, Theodor W. (1973) *Negative Dialectics*, London: Routledge.

ADORNO, Theodor W. (1977) 'The Actuality of Philosophy', *Telos*, no. 31: pp. 120–33.

ADORNO, Theodor W. (1983) *Against Epistemology*, London and Cambridge Mass.: Basil Blackwell and MIT Press.

ADORNO, Theodor W. (1984) 'The Idea of Natural History', *Telos*, no. 60: pp. 111–24.

ADORNO, Theodor W. (1989) *Kierkegaard: The Construction of the Aesthetic*, Minneapolis: University of Minnesota Press.

ANDERSON, Perry (1976) *Considerations on Western Marxism*, London: Verso.

ANDERSON, Perry (1984) *In the Tracks of Historical Materialism*, London: Verso.

ANTONIO, Robert and KELLNER, Douglas (1991a) 'Modernity and Critical Social Theory: The Limits of the Postmodern Critique', in David Dickens and Andrea Fontana (eds) *Postmodern Social Theory*, University of Chicago, in press.

ANTONIO, Robert and KELLNER, Douglas (1991b) 'Communication, Democratization, and Modernity: Critical Reflections on Habermas and Dewey', *Symbolic Interaction*, in press.

ANTONIO, Robert and KELLNER, Douglas (Forthcoming) *Discourses of Modernity*, London: Sage.

ARDAGH, John (1982) *France in the 1980s*, New York: Penguin.

BARRACLOUGH, Geoffrey (1964) *An Introduction to Contemporary History*, Baltimore: Penguin.

BARTHES, Roland (1962) *Mythologies*, New York: Hill & Wang.

BARTHES, Roland (1964) *Essais Critiques*, Paris: Edition du Seuil.

BARTHES, Roland (1968) *Elements of Semiology*, New York: Hill & Wang.

BARTHES, Roland (1983) *The Fashion System*, New York: Hill & Wang.

BARTHES, Roland (1974) *S/Z*, New York: Hill & Wang.

BATAILLE, Georges (1985) *Visions of Excess,* Minneapolis: University of Minnesota Press.

BATAILLE, Georges (1988) *The Accursed Share*, vol. 1, New York: Zone Books.

BATAILLE, Georges (1989) *Theory of Religion*, New York: Zone Books.
BAUDRILLARD, Jean (1968) *Le système des objets*, Paris: Denoel-Gonthier.
BAUDRILLARD, Jean (1970) *La société de consommation*, Paris: Gallimard.
BAUDRILLARD, Jean (1975) *The Mirror of Production*, St Louis: Telos Press.
BAUDRILLARD, Jean (1976) *L'échange symbolique et la mort*, Paris: Gallimard.
BAUDRILLARD, Jean (1981a) *For a Critique of the Political Economy of the Sign*, St Louis: Telos Press.
BAUDRILLARD, Jean (1981b) *Simulacres et simulation*, Paris: Galilée.
BAUDRILLARD, Jean (1983a) *Simulations*, New York: Semiotext(e).
BAUDRILLARD, Jean (1983b) *In the Shadow of the Silent Majorities*, New York: Semiotext(e).
BAUDRILLARD, Jean (1983c) *Les stratégies fatales*, Paris: Grasset, 1983.
BAUDRILLARD, Jean (1983d) 'The Ecstacy of Communication' in Foster (1983).
BAUDRILLARD, Jean (1984a) 'Game with Vestiges', *On the Beach*, 5 (Winter), pp. 19–25.
BAUDRILLARD, Jean (1984b) 'On Nihilism', *On the Beach*, 6 (Spring), pp. 38–9.
BAUDRILLARD, Jean (1984c) 'The Evil Demon of Images', Annandale, Australia: Power Institute.
BAUDRILLARD, Jean (1985) *La gauche divine*, Paris: Grasset.
BAUDRILLARD, Jean (1986a) Interview in *Französische Philosophen im Gespräch*, ed. Florian Rotzer, München: Klaus Baer Verlag, pp. 29–46.
BAUDRILLARD, Jean (1986b) *Subjekt und Objekt: Fractal*, Bern: Bentwli Verlag.
BAUDRILLARD, Jean (1987a) *Forget Foucault*, New York: Semiotext(e).
BAUDRILLARD, Jean (1987b) 'When Bataille Attacked the Metaphysical Principle of Economy', *Canadian Journal of Political and Social Theory*, vol. 11, no. 3, pp. 57–62.
BAUDRILLARD, Jean (1987c) 'Modernity', *Canadian Journal of Political and Social Theory*, vol. 11, no. 3, pp. 63–73.
BAUDRILLARD, Jean (1987d) *Cool Memories*, Paris: Galilée.
BAUDRILLARD, Jean (1988a) 'The Year 2000 Has Already Happened', in Arthur and Marilouise Kroker (eds), *Body Invaders: Panic Sex in America*, Montreal: The New World Perspectives, pp. 35–44.
BAUDRILLARD, Jean (1988b) in Mark Poster (ed.) *Jean Baudrillard: Selected Writings*, Cambridge and Stanford: Polity and Stanford University Press.
BAUDRILLARD, Jean (1988c) *The Ecstasy of Communication*, New York: Semiotext(e).
BAUDRILLARD, Jean (1988d) *America*, London: Verso.

BAUDRILLARD, Jean (1989a) 'Panic Crash!', in Arthur Kroker, Marilouise Kroker, and David Cook (eds) *Panic Encyclopedia*, New York and London: St Martin's Press and Macmillan, pp. 64–7.

BAUDRILLARD, Jean (1989b) 'The Anorexic Ruins', in Dietmar Kamper and Christoph Wulf (eds) *Looking Back on the End of the World*, New York: Semiotext(e), pp. 29–45.

BAUDRILLARD, Jean (1990a) *Seduction*, New York and London: St Martin's Press and Macmillan.

BAUDRILLARD, Jean (1990b) *La transparence du mal*, Paris: Galilée.

BAUDRILLARD, Jean (forthcoming) 'Transpolitics, Transsexuality, Transaesthetics', to appear in *Baudrillard in the Mountains*, New York and London: St Martin's (in press).

BAUMAN, Zygmunt (1987) *Legislators and Interpreters: On Modernity, Postmodernity and Intellectuals*, London: Cambridge University Press.

BELL, Daniel (1973) *The Coming of Post-Industrial Society*, New York: Basic Books.

BELL, Daniel (1976) *The Cultural Contradictions of Capitalism*, New York: Basic Books.

BENHABIB, Seyla (1984) 'Epistemologies of Postmodernism', *New German Critique*, 33 (Fall), pp. 103–27.

BENJAMIN, Walter (1969) *Illuminations*, New York: Schocken.

BENNINGTON, Geoffrey (1988) *Lyotard: Writing the Event*, New York: Columbia University Press.

BENOIST, Jean-Marie (1978) *The Structural Revolution*, London: Weidenfeld & Nicolson.

BERMAN, Marshall (1982) *All That is Solid Melts Into Air*, New York: Simon & Schuster.

BERNSTEIN, Richard (1985) *Philosophical Profiles: Essays in a Pragmatic Mode*, Cambridge: Polity Press.

BEST, Steven (1989a) 'Jameson, Totality, and the Post-Structuralist Critique', in Douglas Kellner (ed.) *Postmodernism/Jameson/Critique*, Washington: Maissoneuve Press, pp. 333–68.

BEST, Steven (1989b) 'The Commodification of Reality and the Reality of Commodification: Jean Baudrillard and Postmodernism', *Current Perspectives in Social Theory*, vol. 9, pp. 23–51.

BEST, Steven (1991a) 'Chaos and Entropy in Postmodern Science and Social Theory', *Science as Culture*, no. 11 in press.

BEST, Steven (1991b) 'Marx and Conflicting Models of History', *The Philosophical Forum*, vol. 22, no. 2, Winter, pp. 167–92.

BEST, Steven and KELLNER, Douglas (1987) '(Re)Watching Television: Notes Toward a Political Criticism', *Diacritics*, vol. 17, no. 2, pp. 97–113.

BLOCH, Ernst (1977) 'Nonsynchronism and Dialectics', *New German Critique*, 11, pp. 22–38.

BLOCH, Ernst *et al.* (1977) *Aesthetics and Politics*, London: Verso Books.

BOGARD, William (1986) 'Reply to Denzin: Postmodern Social Theory', *Sociological Theory*, vol. 4, Fall, pp. 206–11.

BOGUE, Ronald (1989) *Deleuze and Guattari*, London and New York: Routledge.

BOWLES, Samuel and GINTIS, Herbert (1986) *Democracy and Capitalism*, New York: Basic Books.

BRITTON, Andrew (1988) 'The Myth of Postmodernism: The Bourgeois Intelligentsia in the Age of Reagan', *CineAction!*, 15, Summer, pp. 3–17.

BRONNER, Stephen Eric (1990) *Socialism Unbound*, New York: Routledge.

BRONNER, Stephen Eric and KELLNER, Douglas MacKay (1989) *Critical Theory and Society. A Reader*, New York: Routledge.

BURGER, Peter (1984) *Theory of the Avant-Garde*, Minneapolis: University of Minnesota Press.

BUTLER, Judith (1987) *Subjects of Desire: Hegelian Reflections in Twentieth Century France*, New York: Columbia University Press.

CALINESCU, Matei (1987) *Five Faces of Modernity*, Durham: Duke University Press.

CALLINICOS, Alex (1985) 'Postmodernism, Post-Structuralism, Post-Marxism?', *Theory, Culture, and Society*, vol. 2, no. 3, pp. 85–102.

CALLINICOS, Alex (1990) *Against Postmodernism*, New York: St Martin's Press.

CARROLL, David (1987) *Para-Aesthetics*, New York: Methuen.

CHAMBERS, Iain (1986) 'Waiting on the End of the World?', *Journal of Communication Inquiry*, vol. 10, no. 2, pp. 99–103.

CLEAVER, Harry (1979) *Reading Capital Politically*, Austin: University of Texas Press.

CONNOR, Steven (1989) *Postmodern Culture*, Oxford and New York: Basil Blackwell.

COOPER, David (1971) *Death of the Family*, New York: Pantheon.

COWARD, Rosalind and ELLIS, John (1977) *Language and Materialism*, London: Routledge & Kegan Paul.

DARAKI, Maria (1986) 'Foucault's Journey to Greece', *Telos*, no. 67, pp. 87–110.

DAVIS, Mike (1985) 'Urban Renaissance and the Spirit of Postmodernism', *New Left Review*, no. 151, pp. 106–13.

DE BEAUVOIR, Simone (1953) *The Second Sex*, New York: Knopf.

DE LAURETIS, Teresa (1987) *Technologies of Gender*, Bloomington: University of Indiana Press.

DEBORD, Guy (1976) *The Society of the Spectacle*, Detroit: Black and Red.

DELEUZE, Gilles (1968) *Différence et répétition*, Paris: PUF.

DELEUZE, Gilles (1977a) 'Intellectuals and Power', in Foucault 1977, pp. 205–17.

DELEUZE, Giles (1977b) 'I Have Nothing to Admit', *Semiotext(e)*, vol. II, no. 3, pp. 111–35.

DELEUZE, Gilles (1983) *Nietzsche and Philosophy*, New York: Columbia University Press.

DELEUZE, Gilles (1986) *Foucault*, Minneapolis: University of Minnesota Press.

DELEUZE, Gilles (1989) *Logic of Sense*, New York: Columbia University Press.

DELEUZE, Gilles and GUATTARI, Félix (1983) *Anti-Oedipus*, Minneapolis: University of Minnesota Press.

DELEUZE, Gilles and GUATTARI, Félix (1986) *Kafka*, Minneapolis: University of Minnesota Press.

DELEUZE, Gilles and GUATTARI, Félix (1987) *A Thousand Plateaus*, Minneapolis: University of Minnesota Press.

DELEUZE, Gilles and PARNET, Claire (1987) *Dialogues*, New York: Columbia University Press.

DERRIDA, Jacques (1973) *Speech and Phenomena, and Other Essays on Husserl's Theory of Signs*, Evanston: Northwestern University Press. pp.

DERRIDA, Jacques (1976) *Of Grammatology*, Baltimore: Johns Hopkins University Press.

DERRIDA, Jacques (1981a) *Positions*, Chicago: University of Chicago Press.

DERRIDA, Jacques (1981b) *Margins of Philosophy*, Chicago: University of Chicago Press.

DESCOMBES, Vincent (1980) *Modern French Philosophy*, Cambridge: Cambridge University Press.

DEWS, Peter (1986a) (ed.) *Habermas: Autonomy and Solidarity*, London: Verso.

DEWS, Peter (1986b) 'Adorno, Post-Structuralism, and the Critique of Identity', *New Left Review*, no. 157, pp. 28–44.

DEWS, Peter (1987) *Logics of Disintegration*, London: Verso.

DIAMOND, Irene and QUINBY, Lee (1988) *Feminism and Foucault: Reflections on Resistance*, Boston: Northeastern University Press.

DICKENS, David and FONTANA, Andrea (eds) *Postmodernism and Social Inquiry*, University of Chicago Press, forthcoming.

DREYFUS, Hubert L. (1984) 'Beyond Hermeneutics: Interpretation in Late Heidegger and Recent Foucault', in Gary Shapiro and Alan Sica (eds) *Hermeneutics*, pp. 66–83.

DREYFUS, Hubert L. and RABINOW, Paul (1982) *Michel Foucault: Beyond Structuralism and Hermeneutics*, Chicago: University of Chicago Press.

DRUCKER, Peter F. (1957) *Landmarks of Tomorrow*, New York: Harper & Row.

DURING, Simon (1987) 'Postmodernism or Post-colonialism Today', *Textual Practice*, vol. 1, no. 1, pp. 32–47.

ETZIONI, Amitai (1968) *The Active Society*, New York: The Free Press.

FEATHERSTONE, Mike (1988) 'In Pursuit of the Postmodern', *Theory, Culture, and Society*, vol. 5, nos 2–3, pp. 195–216.

FEENBERG, Andrew (1990) *Critical Theory of Technology*, New York: Oxford University Press.

FERRE, Frederick (1976) *Shaping the Future: Resources for the Postmodern World*, New York: Harper & Row.

FERRY, Luc and RENAULT, Alain (1990) *French Philosophy of the Sixties: An Essay on Anti-humanism*, Amherst: University of Massachusetts Press.

FIEDLER, Leslie (1971) *The Collected Essays of Leslie Fiedler*, vol. II, New York: Stein and Day, pp. 379–400.

FIELDS, Beldon (1988) 'In Defense of Political Economy and Systemic Analysis: A Critique of Prevailing Theoretical Approaches to the New Social Movements', in Cary Nelson and Larry Grossberg (eds) *Marxism and the Interpretation of Culture*, Urbana and Chicago: University of Chicago Press, pp. 141–56.

FISKE, John and WATTS, Jon, (1986) 'An Articulating Culture', *Journal of Communication Inquiry*, vol. 10, no. 2, pp. 104–107.

FLAX, Jane (1990) *Thinking Fragments*, Berkeley: University of California Press.

FO, Dario (1986) 'A Short Interview with Dario Fo', *Social Text* no. 16, pp. 162–7.

FOSTER, Hal (1983) (ed.) *The Anti-Aesthetic: Essays on Postmodern Culture*, Port Townsend, Washington: Bay Press.

FOUCAULT, Michel (1972) *The Archaeology of Knowledge*, New York: Pantheon Books.

FOUCAULT, Michel (1973a) *Madness and Civilization*, New York: Vintage Books.

FOUCAULT, Michel (1973b) *The Order of Things*, New York: Vintage Books.

FOUCAULT, Michel (1974) 'Human Nature: Justice versus Power', in Fons Elders (ed.) *Reflexive Water: The Basic Concerns of Mankind*, London: Souvenir Press.

FOUCAULT, Michel (1975a) *The Birth of the Clinic*, New York: Vintage Books.

FOUCAULT, Michel (1975b) '*I, Pierre Rivière, having slaughtered my mother, my sister, and my brother*', New York: Random House.

FOUCAULT, Michel (1977) *Language, Counter-Memory, Practice*, Ithaca: Cornell University Press.

FOUCAULT, Michel (1979) *Discipline and Punish*, New York: Vintage Books.

FOUCAULT, Michel (1980a) *Power/Knowledge*, New York: Pantheon Books.

FOUCAULT, Michel (1980b) *The History of Sexuality*, New York: Vintage Books.

FOUCAULT, Michel (1980c) *Herculine Barbin, Being the Recently Discovered Memoirs of a Nineteenth Century French Hermaphrodite*, New York: Pantheon.

FOUCAULT, Michel (1981) 'Omnes et Singulatim', in S. M. McMurrin (ed.) *The Tanner Lectures on Human Values*, vol. 2, London: Cambridge University Press.

FOUCAULT, Michel (1982a) 'The Subject and Power', in Dreyfus and Rabinow op. cit., pp. 208–26.

FOUCAULT, Michel (1982b) 'On the Genealogy of Ethics', in Hubert L. Dreyfus and Paul Rabinow (eds) *Michel Foucault: Beyond Structuralism and Hermeneutics*, pp. 229–52.

FOUCAULT, Michel (1983) 'Preface' to *Anti-Oedipus*, op. cit.

FOUCAULT, Michel (1984) 'What is Enlightenment?' in Paul Rabinow (ed.) *The Foucault Reader*, New York: Pantheon.

FOUCAULT, Michel (1985) 'Final Interview', *Raritan*, no. 5, pp. 1–13.

FOUCAULT, Michel (1986) *The Use of Pleasure*, New York: Vintage Books.

FOUCAULT, Michel (1988a) *The Care of the Self*, New York: Vintage Books.

FOUCAULT, Michel (1988b) 'The Ethic of Care for the Self as a Practice of Freedom', in James Bernauer and David Rasmussen (eds) *The Final Foucault*, Cambridge, Mass.: MIT Press.

FOUCAULT, Michel (1988c) 'Technologies of the Self', in Luther M. Martin, Huck Gutman, and Patrick H. Hutton (eds) *Technologies of the Self*, Amherst: University of Massachusetts Press, pp. 16–49.

FOUCAULT, Michel (1988d) in Lawrence D. Kritzman (ed.) *Michel Foucault: Politics, Philosophy, Culture*, New York: Routledge.

FOUCAULT, Michel (1989) *Foucault Live*, New York: Semiotext(e).

FOUCAULT, Michel and SENNET, Richard (1982) 'Sexuality and Solitude', in D. Rieff (ed.) *Humanities in Review*, vol. 1, London: Cambridge University Press.

FRANK, Manfred (1989) *What is Neo-Structuralism?*, Minneapolis: University of Minnesota Press.

FRANKEL, Boris (1987) *The Post-Industrial Utopians*, Cambridge: Polity Press.

FRASER, Nancy (1989) *Unruly Practices*, Minneapolis: University of Minnesota Press.

FRASER, Nancy and NICHOLSON, Linda (1988) 'Social Criticism Without Philosophy: An Encounter Between Feminism and Postmodernism', *Theory, Culture and Society*, vol. 5, nos 2–3, pp. 373–94.

FRISBY, David (1986) *Fragments of Modernity*, Cambridge, Mass.: MIT Press.

FROMM, Erich (1941) *Escape from Freedom*, New York: Holt, Rinehart & Winston.

FUKUYAMA, Francis (1989) 'The End of History?', *The National Interest*, 16, pp. 3–18.

GANDAL, Keith (1986) 'Foucault: Intellectual Work and Politics', *Telos*, no. 67, pp. 111–20.

GERAS, Norman (1987) 'Post-Marxism?' *New Left Review*, no. 163, May/June, pp. 40–82.

GERAS, Norman (1988) 'Ex-Marxism Without Substance: Being a Real Reply to Laclau and Mouffe', in *New Left Review*, no. 169, pp. 34–61.

GRAFF, Gerald (1973) 'The Myth of the Postmodernist Breakthrough', *Tri-quarterly*, vol. 26, pp. 383–417.

GRIFFIN, David Ray (1988a) *The Re-enchantment of Science: Postmodern Proposals*, Albany: State University of New York.

GRIFFIN, David Ray (1988b) *Spirituality and Science: Postmodern Visions*, Albany: State University of New York.

GRUMLEY, John (1989) *History and Totality*, New York: Routledge.

GUATTARI, Félix (1979) 'A Liberation of Desire: An Interview with George Stambolian', in George Stambolian and Elaine Marks (eds) *Homosexualities and French Literature*, Ithaca: Cornell University Press, pp. 56–69.

GUATTARI, Félix (1981) 'The Molecular Revolution: A Talk with Felix Guattari', *Tabloid: A Review of Mass Culture and Everyday Life*, Winter, pp. 46–51.

GUATTARI, Félix (1984) *Molecular Revolution*, New York: Penguin.

GUATTARI, Félix (1986) 'The Postmodern Dead End', *Flash Art*, no. 128, May/June, pp. 40–1.

GUATTARI, Félix and NEGRI, Toni (1990), *Communists Like Us*, New York: Semiotext(e).

HABERMAS, Jürgen (1975) *Legitimation Crisis*, Boston: Beacon Press.

HABERMAS, Jürgen (1976) *Communication and the Evolution of Society*. Boston, Beacon Press.

HABERMAS, Jürgen (1981) 'Modernity versus Postmodernity', *New German Critique*, 22, pp. 3–14.

HABERMAS, Jürgen (1984 and 1987) *Theory of Communicative Action*, vols. 1 and 2, Boston: Beacon Press.

HABERMAS, Jürgen (1987a) *Lectures on The Philosophical Discourse of Modernity*, Cambridge, Mass.: MIT Press.

HABERMAS, Jürgen (1987b) 'Taking Aim at the Heart of the Present', in David Couzens Hoy (ed.) *Foucault: A Critical Reader*, pp. 103–8.

HABERMAS, Jürgen (1988) *Nachmetaphysisches Denken*, Frankfurt: Suhrkamp.

HABERMAS, Jürgen (1989a) *The Structural Transformation of the Public Sphere*, Cambridge, Mass.: MIT Press.

HABERMAS, Jürgen (1989b) *The New Conservativism*, Cambridge, Mass.: MIT Press.

HABERMAS, Jürgen (1990) 'Remarks on the Discussion', *Theory, Culture, and Society*, vol. 7, no. 4, pp. 127–32.

HALL, Stuart (1986) 'On Postmodernism and Articulation: An Interview', *Journal of Communication Inquiry*, vol. 10, no. 2, pp. 45–60.

HARLAND, Richard (1987) *Superstructuralism: The Philosophy of Structuralism and Post-Structuralism*, London and New York: Methuen.

HARMS, John and KELLNER, Douglas (1991) 'Toward a Critical Theory of Advertising', *Current Perspectives in Social Theory*, vol. 11 (in press).

HARVEY, David (1989) *The Coalition of Postmodernity*, London: Blackwell.

HASSAN, Ihab (1971) *The Dismemberment of Orpheus: Toward a Postmodern Literature*, Madison: University of Wisconsin Press.

HASSAN, Ihab (1979) *Right Promethean Fire*, Urbana: University of Illinois Press.

HASSAN, Ihab (1987) *The Postmodern Turn: Essays in Postmodern Theory and Culture*, Columbus.

HEBDIGE, Dick (1986) 'Postmodernism and "The Other Side" ', *Journal of Communication Inquiry*, vol. 10, no. 2, pp. 78–98.

HEBDIGE, Dick (1987) 'Hiding in the Light', *Art and Text*, vol. 26, pp. 64–79.

HEIDEGGER, Martin (1977) *The Question Concerning Technology*, New York: Harper & Row.

HIGGINS, Dick (1978) *A Dialectic of Centuries*, New York: Printed Editions.

HONNETH, Axel (1985) 'An Aversion Against the Universal', *Theory, Culture, and Society*, vol. 2, no. 3, pp. 147–57.

HONNETH, Axel (1986) *Kritik der Macht*, Frankfurt: Suhrkamp.

HORKHEIMER, Max and ADORNO, Theodor (1972) *Dialectic of Enlightenment*, New York: Seabury.

HOWE, Irving (1970) 'Mass Society and Postmodern Fiction', *Decline of the New*, New York: Horizon, pp. 190–207.

HOY, David (1986) 'Power, Repression, Progress: Foucault, Lukes and the Frankfurt School', in *Foucault: A Critical Reader*, op. cit., pp. 123–48.

HULLOT-KENTOR, Robert (1989) 'Back to Adorno', *Telos*, 81, pp. 5–29.

HUTCHEON, Linda (1989) *The Politics of Postmodernism*, London and New York: Routledge.

HUTCHEON, Linda (1990) *A Poetics of Postmodernism: History, Theory, Fiction*, New York and London: Routledge.

HUYSSEN, Andreas (1984) 'Mapping the Postmodern', *New German Critique*, 33, pp. 5–52.

JAMESON, Frederic (1971) *Marxism and Form*, Princeton: Princeton University Press.

JAMESON, Fredric (1972) *The Prison House of Language*, Princeton: Princeton University Press.

JAMESON, Fredric (1975) 'Notes Toward a Marxist Cultural Politics', *Minnesota Review*, no. 5, pp. 35–9.

JAMESON, Fredric (1979) 'Reification and Utopia in Mass Culture', *Social Text*, Winter, pp. 130–47.

JAMESON, Fredric (1981a) *The Political Unconscious*, New York: Cornell University Press.

JAMESON, Fredric (1981b) 'The Shining', in *Social Text*, no. 4, pp. 114–25.

JAMESON, Fredric (1982) 'On Diva', in *Social Text*, no. 6, pp. 114–19.

JAMESON, Fredric (1983) 'Postmodernism and Consumer Society', in Hal Foster (ed.) *The Anti-Aesthetic*, pp. 111–25.

JAMESON, Fredric (1984a) 'Postmodernism, or the Cultural Logic of Late Capitalism', in *New Left Review*, no. 146, pp. 53–93.

JAMESON, Fredric (1984b) 'Periodizing the 60s', in Sohnya Sayres, *et al.* (eds) *The 60s Without Apology*, Minneapolis: University of Minnesota Press.

JAMESON, Fredric (1984c) 'The Politics of Theory', *New German Critique*, no. 33, pp. 53–66.

JAMESON, Fredric (1984d) 'Foreword' to LYOTARD, Jean-François, *The Postmodern Condition*, op. cit.

JAMESON, Fredric (1986) 'Third-World Literature in the Era of Multi-national Capitalism', *Social Text*, no. 15, Fall, pp. 65–88.

JAMESON, Fredric (1988a) *'History and Class Consciousness* as an Unfinished Project, in *Rethinking Marxism*, vol. 1, no. 1, pp. 49–72.

JAMESON, Fredric (1988b) 'Cognitive Mapping', in Cary Nelson and Lawrence Grossberg (eds) *Marxism and the Interpretation of Culture*, Urbana, Chicago and Basingstoke: University of Illinois Press, pp. 347–60, and Macmillan.

JAMESON, Fredric (1989) 'Regarding Postmodernism' (interview with Anders Stephanson), in Kellner (ed.) (1989c).

JAY, Martin (1984) *Marxism and Totality*, Berkeley: University of California Press.

JAY, Martin (1989) 'Review of Habermas', *History and Theory*, vol. 28, no. 1, pp. 94–112.

JENCKS, Charles (1977) *The Language of Post-modern Architecture*, New York: Pantheon.

KEARNEY, Richard (1988) *The Wake of Imagination*, Minneapolis: University of Minnesota Press.

KELLNER, Douglas (1980) 'Television, Images, Codes, and Messages', *Televisions*, vol. 7, no. 4, pp. 2–19.

KELLNER, Douglas (1983) 'Science and Method in Marx's *Capital'*, *Radical Science Journal*, no. 13, pp. 39–54.

KELLNER, Douglas (1984) *Herbert Marcuse and the Crisis of Marxism*, London and Berkeley: Macmillan and University of California Press.

KELLNER, Douglas (1987) 'Baudrillard, Semiurgy and Death', *Theory, Culture, and Society*, vol. 4, no. 1, pp. 125–46.

KELLNER, Douglas (1988) 'Postmodernism as Social Theory: Some Problems and Challenges', *Theory, Culture, and Society*, vol. 5, nos. 2–3, pp. 239–70.

KELLNER, Douglas (1989a) *Critical Theory, Marxism, and Modernity*, Cambridge and Baltimore: Polity Press and Johns Hopkins University Press.

KELLNER, Douglas (1989b) *Jean Baudrillard: From Marxism to Postmodernism and Beyond*, Cambridge: Polity Press.

KELLNER, Douglas (1989c) 'Jameson, Marxism, and Postmodernism', in Douglas Kellner (ed.) *Postmodernism/Jameson/Critique*, Washington, D.C.: Maisonneuve, pp. 1–42.

KELLNER, Douglas (1989d) 'Boundaries and Borderlines: Reflections on Baudrillard and Critical Theory', *Current Perspectives in Social Theory*, vol. 9, pp. 5–22.

KELLNER, Douglas (1990) *Television and the Crisis of Democracy*, Boulder: Westview Press.

KELLNER, Douglas (forthcoming) 'Film, Politics and Ideology: Toward a Multiperspectival Approach', *The Velvet Light Trap* (in press).

KELLNER, Douglas and RYAN, Michael (1988) *Camera Politica: The Politics and Ideologies of Contemporary Hollywood Film*, Bloomington: Indiana University Press.

KROKER, Arthur (1984) *Technology and the Canadian Mind*. Montreal: New World Perspectives.

KROKER, Arthur and COOK, David (1986) *The Postmodern Scene*, New York: St Martin's Press.

KROKER. Arthur, KROKER, Marilouise and COOK, David (1989) *Panic Encyclopaedia*, New York: St Martin's Press.

KROKER, Arthur, and LEVIN, Charles (1984) 'Baudrillard's Challenge', *Canadian Journal of Political and Social Theory*, vol. VIII, nos. 1–2 (Spring/Winter) pp. 5–16.

KURZWEIL, Edith (1980) *The Age of Structuralism*, New York: Columbia University Press.

LACAN, Jacques (1977) *Ecrits*, New York: Norton.

LACLAU, Ernesto (1988) 'Politics and the Limits of Modernity', in Andrew Ross (ed.) *Universal Abandon*, Minneapolis: University of Minnesota Press, pp. 63–82.

LACLAU, Ernesto and MOUFFE, Chantal (1985) *Hegemony and Socialist Strategy: Toward a Radical Democratic Politics*. London: Verso Books.

LACLAU, Ernesto and MOUFFE, Chantal (1987) 'Post-Marxism Without Apologies', *New Left Review*, no. 166, November/December, pp. 79–106.

LAING, R. D. (1967) *The Politics of Experience*, New York: Pantheon.

LASH, Scott (1988) 'Discourse or Figure? Toward a Postmodern Semiotics', *Theory, Culture, and Society*, vol. 5, nos. 2–3, pp. 311–36.

LEFEBVRE, Henri (1969) *The Explosion*, New York: Monthly Review Press.

LEFEBVRE, Henri (1971a) *Everyday Life in the Modern World*, New York: Harper & Row.

LEFEBVRE, Henri (1971b) *Au delà du structuralism*, Paris: Anthropos.

LEMERT, Charles (1990) 'General Social Theory, Irony, Postmodernism', in S. Seidman and D. Wagner, (eds) *Postmodernism and Social Theory*, New York: Basil Blackwell.

LEVIN, Harry (1966) 'What Was Modernism?', in *Refractions*, New York: Oxford University Press.

LITTLE, Daniel (1986) *The Scientific Marx*, Minneapolis: University of Minnesota Press.

LOVIBOND, Sabina (1989) 'Feminism and Postmodernism', *New Left Review*, no. 178, pp. 5–28.

LUKÁCS, Georg (1971; orig. 1923) *History and Class Consciousness*, Cambridge, Mass.: MIT Press.

LUKÁCS, Georg (1980; orig. 1954) *The Destruction of Reason*, London: Merlin Press.

LYOTARD, Jean-François (1954) *La phénoménologie*, Paris: Presses Universitaires de France.

LYOTARD, Jean-François (1971) *Discours, figure*, Paris: Klincksieck.

LYOTARD, Jean-François (1973) *Dérive à partir de Marx et Freud*, Paris: Union générale é'éditions.

LYOTARD, Jean-François (1974) *Economie libidinale*, Paris: Minuit.

LYOTARD, Jean-François (1975) 'For a Pseudo-Theory', *Yale French Studies*, vol. 52, pp. 115–27.

LYOTARD, Jean-François (1977) 'Energumen Capitalism', *Semiotext(e)*, vol. 2, no. 3, pp. 11–26.

LYOTARD, Jean-François (1978a) 'Notes on the Return of Capital', *Semiotext(e)*, vol. 3, no. 1, pp. 44–53.

LYOTARD, Jean-François (1978b) 'On the Strength of the Weak', *Semiotext(e)*, vol. 3, no. 2, pp. 204–14.

LYOTARD, Jean-François (1980) 'Preface', *Des dispositifs pulsionnels* (second edition), Paris: Christian Bourgois.

LYOTARD, Jean-François (1983) 'Presentations', in A. Montefiore (ed.) *Philosophy in France Today*, Cambridge: Cambridge University Press, pp. 116–35.

LYOTARD, Jean-François (1984a) *The Postmodern Condition*, Minneapolis: University of Minnesota Press.

LYOTARD, Jean-François (1984b) *Driftworks*, New York: Semiotext(e).

LYOTARD, Jean-François (1984c) 'Interview', *Diacritics*, vol. 14, no. 3, pp. 16–21.

LYOTARD, Jean-François (1984d) 'The Unconscious, History and Phrases: Notes on *The Political Unconscious*, *New Orleans Review*, Spring, pp. 73–9.

LYOTARD, Jean-François (1986) *Le postmodern expliqué aux enfants*, Paris: Galilée.

LYOTARD, Jean-François (1986–87) 'Rules and Paradoxes and Svelte Paradox', *Cultural Critique*, vol. 5, pp. 209–19.

LYOTARD, Jean-François (1988a) 'An Interview', *Theory, Culture, and Society*, vol. 5, nos. 2–3, pp. 277–310.

LYOTARD, Jean-François (1988b) *Perigrinations*, New York: Columbia University Press.

LYOTARD, Jean-François (1988c) *The Differend*, Minneapolis: University of Minnesota Press.

LYOTARD, Jean-François (1989) *The Lyotard Reader* (ed.) Andrew Benjamin, London and Cambridge, Mass: Basil Blackwell.

LYOTARD, Jean-François and THÉBAUD, Jean-Loup (1985) *Just Gaming*, Minneapolis: University of Minnesota Press.

McCARTHY, Thomas (1978) *The Critical Theory of Jürgen Habermas*, Cambridge, Mass.: MIT Press.

McCARTHY, Thomas (1989) 'The Politics of the Ineffable: Derrida's Deconstructionism', *The Philosophical Forum*, vol. xxi, nos. 1–2, pp. 146–68.

McLUHAN, Marshall (1964) *Understanding Media*, New York: Signet.

McROBBIE, Angela (1986) 'Postmodernism and Popular Culture', *Journal of Communication Inquiry*, vol. 10, no. 2, pp. 108–16.

MacDONELL, Diane (1986) *Theories of Discourse*, Oxford: Basil Blackwell.

MANDEL, Ernest (1975) *Late Capitalism*, London: New Left Books.

MARCUSE, Herbert (1964) *One-Dimensional Man*, Boston: Beacon Press.

MARCUSE, Herbert (1972) *Counterrevolution and Revolt*, Boston: Beacon Press.

MARCUSE, Herbert (1980) 'Protosocialism and Late Capitalism: Toward a Theoretical Synthesis Based on Bahro's Analysis', in Ulf Wolter (ed.) *Rudolph Bahro: Critical Responses*, White Plains, N.Y.: M. E. Sharpe, pp. 24–48.

MARX, Karl (1973) *Grundrisse*, New York: Vintage Books.

MARX, Karl and ENGELS, Friedrich (1975–87) *Collected Works*, New York: International Publishers.

MARX, Karl and ENGELS, Friedrich (1978) in Robert Tucker (ed.) *The Marx–Engels Reader*, New York: Norton.

MEGILL, Allan (1985) *Prophets of Extremity*, Berkeley: University of California Press.

MERQUIOR, J. G. (1985) *Foucault*, Berkeley: University of California Press.

MERQUIOR, J. G. (1986) 'Spider and Bee', *Postmodernism*, London: ICA Documents 4 and 5, pp. 16–18.

MILLS, C. Wright (1959) *The Sociological Imagination*, New York: Oxford University Press.

MORSS, Susan Buck (1977) *The Origin of Negative Dialectics*, New York: The Free Press.

MOUFFE, Chantal (1984) 'Towards a Theoretical Interpretation of "New Social Movements"', in Sakari Hanninen and Leena Paldan (eds) *Rethinking Marx*, New York and Bagnolet: International General/ IMMRC, pp. 139–43.

MOUFFE, Chantal (1988) 'Radical Democracy: Modern or Postmodern?' in Andrew Ross (ed.) *Universal Abandon*, pp. 46–62.

MOUZELIS, Nicos (1988) 'Marxism or Post-Marxism?' in *New Left Review*, no. 167, January/February, pp. 107–23.

NEGRI, Antonio (1984) *Marx Beyond Marx*, South Hadley Mass.: Bergin & Garvey.

NICHOLSON, Linda (1990) (ed.) *Feminism/Postmodernism*, New York: Routledge.

NIETZSCHE, Friedrich (1967) *The Will to Power*, New York: Random House.

O'BRIEN, Patricia (1982) *The Promise of Punishment: Prisons in Nineteenth Century France*, Princeton: Princeton University Press.

OFFE, Claus (1988) 'Technology and One-Dimensionality', in Robert Pippin *et al.* (eds) *Marcuse, Critical Theory, and the Promise of Utopia*, South Hadley, Mass.: Bergin & Garvey.

PATTON, Paul (1984) 'Conceptual Politics and the War Machine in *Mille Plateaux*', *SubStance* nos 44–5, pp. 63–80.

PECHEUX, Michel (1982) *Language, Semantics, and Ideology*, New York and London: St Martin's Press and Macmillan.

POLAN, Dana (1986) 'Translator's Introduction' to *Kafka*, Deleuze and Guattari (1986).

POSTER, Mark (1975) *Existential Marxism in Postwar France*, Princeton: Princeton University Press.

POSTER, Mark (1990) *Mode of Information*, Cambridge: Polity Press.

POULANTZAS, Nicos (1978) *State, Power, Socialism*, London: New Left Books.

PRIGOGINE, Ilya and STENGERS, Isabelle (1984) *Order Out of Chaos: Man's New Dialogue with Nature*, New York: Bantam.

RAJCHMAN, John (1985) *Michel Foucault: The Freedom of Philosophy*, New York: Columbia University Press.

RAJCHMAN, John (1988) 'Habermas' Complaint', *New German Critique*, no. 45, pp. 163–91.

RASMUSSEN, David (1990) *Reading Habermas,* London: Blackwell.

READER, Keith (1987) *Intellectuals and the Left in France*, London: Macmillan.

RICOEUR, Paul (1984) *Time and Narrative*, vol. 1, Chicago: University of Chicago Press.

RODERICK, Rick (1986) *Habermas and the Foundations of Critical Theory*, London and New York: Macmillan and St Martin's Press.

RORTY, Richard (1979) *Philosophy and the Mirror of Nature*, Princeton: Princeton University Press.

RORTY, Richard (1984) 'Habermas and Lyotard on Post-Modernity', *Praxis International*, vol. 4, no. 1, pp. 32–44.

RORTY, Richard (1989) *Contingency, Irony, and Solidarity*, Cambridge: Cambridge University Press.

ROSENBERG, Bernard and WHITE, David (1957) *Mass Culture*, Glencoe, Il: The Free Press.

ROWBOTHAM, Sheila (1972) *Women, Resistance and Revolution*, New York: Vintage Books.

RYAN, Michael (1982) *Marxism and Deconstruction*, Baltimore: Johns Hopkins University Press.

RYAN, Michael (1988) 'Postmodern Politics', *Theory, Culture, and Society*, vol. 5, nos. 2–3, pp. 559–76.

RYAN, Michael (1989) *Culture and Politics*, London and Baltimore: Macmillan and Johns Hopkins University Press.

SAID, Edward (1983) 'Opponents, Audiences, Constituencies and Community', in Foster, *The Anti-Aesthetic*, op. cit., pp. 135–59.

SARGENT, Lydia (1981) (ed.) *Women and Revolution*, Boston: South End Press.

SARTRE, Jean-Paul (1956) *Being and Nothingness*, New York: Philosophical Library.

SARTRE, Jean-Paul (1976) *Critique of Dialectical Reason*, Atlantic Highlands, N.J.: Humanities Press.

SAUSSURE, Ferdinand de (1966) *Course in General Linguistics*, New York: McGraw-Hill.

SCHILLER, Herbert (1981) *Who Knows: Information in the Age of the Fortune 500*, Norwood, N.J.: Ablex.

SCHILLER, Herbert (1984) *Information and the Crisis Economy*, Norwood, N.J.: Ablex.

SEEM, Mark (1975) 'To Oedipalize or Not To Oedipalize, That is the Question', *SubStance*, nos. 11–12, 1975, pp. 166–9.

SHERIDAN, Alan (1980) *Foucault: The Will to Truth*. New York: Tavistock Publications.

SMART, Barry (1985) *Michel Foucault*, New York: Tavistock.

SMITH, Huston (1982) *Beyond the Post-Modern Mind*, New York: Crossroad.

SOMERVELL, D. C. (1947) (ed.) *A Study of History*, New York: Oxford University Press.

SONTAG, Susan (1966) *Against Interpretation*, New York: Deli.

SPIVAK, Gayatri (1989) *In Other Worlds*, New York: Methuen.

STEINER, George (1971) *In Bluebeard's Castle*, New Haven: Yale University Press.

STIVALE, Charles (1984) 'The Machine at the Heart of Desire: Félix Guattari's *Molecular Revolution*', *Works and Days*, no. 4, Fall, pp. 63–85.

TAYLOR, Brandon (1988) *Modernism, Postmodernism, Realism*, Hampshire: Winchester School of Art Press.

TAYLOR, Charles (1986) 'Foucault on Freedom and Truth', in Paul Rabinow (ed.) *Foucault: A Critical Reader*, op. cit., pp. 69–102.

THOM, Rene (1975) *Structural Stability and Morphogenesis*, Massachusetts: Benjamin/Cummings.

TOULMIN, Stephen (1990) *Cosmopolis*, New York: The Free Press.

TOYNBEE, Arnold (1963a) *A Study of History*, vol. VIII, New York: Oxford University Press.

TOYNBEE, Arnold (1963b) *A Study of History*, vol. IX, New York: Oxford University Press.

TRACHTENBERG, Stanley (1985) (ed.) *The Postmodern Moment: A Handbook of Contemporary Innovation in the Arts*, Westport and London: Greenwood Press.

ULMER, Gregory L. (1983) 'The Object of Post-Criticism', in Foster *The Anti-Aesthetic*, op. cit., pp. 83–110.

VATTIMO, Gianni (1985) *The End of Modernity*, Oxford and Baltimore: Polity and Johns Hopkins University Press.

WALZER, Michael (1986) 'The Politics of Michel Foucault', in Paul Rabinow (ed.) *The Foucault Reader*, op. cit., pp. 51–68.

WELLMER, Albrecht (1985) 'On the Dialectic of Modernism and Postmodernism', *Praxis International*, vol. 4, no. 4, pp. 337–62.

WELSCH, Wolfgang (1988) *Unsere postmoderne Moderne*, Weinheim: VCH.

WILLIAMS, Raymond (1977) *Marxism and Literature*, New York: Oxford.

WINNER, Langdon (1977) *Autonomous Technology*, Cambridge, Mass.: MIT Press.

WOLIN, Richard (1986) 'Foucault's Aesthetic Decisionism', *Telos*, no. 67, pp. 71–86.

WOLIN, Richard (1987) 'Critical Theory and the Dialectic of Rationalism', *New German Critique*, vol. 41, pp. 23–52.

WOOD, Ellen Meiksins (1986) *The Retreat From Class*, London: Verso.

Index